Diplomacy

How do adversaries communicate? How do diplomatic encounters shape international orders and determine whether states go to war? Diplomacy, from alliance politics to nuclear brinkmanship, almost always operates through a few forms of signaling: choosing the scope of demands on another state, risking a breach in relations, encouraging a protégé, staking one's reputation, or making a diplomatic approach all convey specific sorts of information. Through rich history and analyses of diplomatic network data from the Confidential Print of the British Empire, Trager demonstrates the lasting effects diplomatic encounters have on international affairs. The Concert of Europe, the perceptions of existential threat that formed before the World Wars, the reduction in Cold War tensions known as détente, and the institutional structure of the current world order were all products of inferences about intentions drawn from the statements of individuals represented as the will of states. *Diplomacy* explains how closed-door conversations create stable orders and violent wars.

Robert F. Trager is Associate Professor of Political Science at the University of California, Los Angeles. He has also taught at Yale and Oxford Universities, held an Olin Fellowship at Harvard University, and worked in investment banking in New York. His published work has appeared in such journals as the *American Political Science Review*, the *American Journal of Political Science*, the *Journal of Politics*, *International Organization*, *International Security*, and *Security Studies*.

Diplomacy

Communication and the Origins of International Order

ROBERT F. TRAGER

University of California, Los Angeles

CAMBRIDGE UNIVERSITY PRESS

CAMBRIDGE
UNIVERSITY PRESS

University Printing House, Cambridge CB2 8BS, United Kingdom

One Liberty Plaza, 20th Floor, New York, NY 10006, USA

477 Williamstown Road, Port Melbourne, VIC 3207, Australia

314-321, 3rd Floor, Plot 3, Splendor Forum, Jasola District Centre, New Delhi – 110025, India

79 Anson Road, #06–04/06, Singapore 079906

Cambridge University Press is part of the University of Cambridge.

It furthers the University's mission by disseminating knowledge in the pursuit of education, learning, and research at the highest international levels of excellence.

www.cambridge.org
Information on this title: www.cambridge.org/9781107049161
DOI: 10.1017/9781107278776

First published 2017

Printed in the United Kingdom by Clays, St. Ives plc

A catalogue record for this publication is available from the British Library.

Library of Congress Cataloging-in-Publication Data
Names: Trager, Robert F., author.
Title: Diplomacy : communication and the origins of international order /
Robert F. Trager.
Description: Cambridge, United Kingdom ; New York, NY : Cambridge University
Press, 2017. | Includes bibliographical references and index.
Identifiers: LCCN 2017018417 | ISBN 9781107049161 (hardback)
Subjects: LCSH: Diplomatic negotiations in international disputes. |
Communication in international relations. | World politics–20th century.
Classification: LCC JZ6045 .T73 2017 | DDC 327.2–dc23
LC record available at https://lccn.loc.gov/2017018417

ISBN 978-1-107-04916-1 Hardback
ISBN 978-1-107-62712-3 Paperback

For My Father

Contents

List of Figures   *page* viii

List of Tables   x

Preface   xi

1   Can Adversaries Communicate?   1

2   How Perceptions of Intentions Form   22

PART I THEORY

3   The Scope of Demands   47

4   The Risk of a Breach   71

5   Balancing Allies and Adversaries   103

6   Diplomatic Approaches   128

PART II EMPIRICAL ANALYSIS

7   The Fruit of 1912 Diplomacy   151

8   How Germany Weighed British Resolve in 1938–1939   174

9   Statistical Analysis of Diplomatic Communication   192

10   Creating International Orders   212

APPENDICES

A   Proofs for Chapters 3–6   229

B   The Inference Dataset   259

C   Demands, Offers, and Assurances Dataset   261

D   German Inferences Prior to World War II   263

References   269

Index   284

Figures

1.1	Diplomatic Representation from 1817 to 2005	6
2.1	Sources of British Inferences from 1855 to 1914	25
2.2	Inferences are Similar in and out of Crises	28
2.3	How Private Diplomacy Works	38
3.1	The Signaling Game	55
3.2	An Example of Signaler Utilities	56
3.3	Player Strategies in a Signaling Equilibrium	60
3.4	Signaling Equilibrium Dynamics	62
3.5	The Probability of War	63
3.6	How Private Diplomacy Works	69
4.1	Stages of the Game	80
4.2	Formal Game Structure	82
4.3	Player Utilities Satisfying Model Assumptions	83
4.4	Equilibrium Signaling Properties	92
4.5	Effectiveness of the Signal and Likelihood of Surprise	93
4.6	The Probability of War	96
4.7	How Private Diplomacy Works	99
5.1	Player Strategies in a Signaling Equilibrium	114
5.2	Equilibrium Signaling Properties	118
5.3	The Probability of War	120
5.4	How Private Diplomacy Works	125
6.1	Game Sequence	134
6.2	The Probability of War	139
6.3	How Private Diplomacy Works	145
9.1	Diplomatic Demands and Offers, 1900 to 1914	194
9.2	Diplomatic Demand Network	194
9.3	Diplomatic Offer Network	195
9.4	Conclusions Drawn from Threats and Offers	196

9.5   Private Threats and Relative Capabilities   201

9.6   Private Threats and Alliance Ties   203

9.7   Effect of Diplomatic Approaches on Perceptions of
Aggression   206

9.8   Public Versus Private Threats   208

9.9   British Inferences About German Aggression   210

Tables

7.1	Summary of Diplomatic Signaling Hypotheses	149
7.2	Russian Diplomacy in 1912	156
7.3	German Diplomacy in 1912	159
8.1	British Diplomatic Signals Related to Czechoslovakia	177
8.2	British Diplomatic Signals Related to Poland	182
9.1	Are Concessions Expected to Follow Concessions?	198
9.2	Determinants of Perceptions of Aggression	200
9.3	Interest Alignment and the Impact of Private Diplomacy	204

Preface

The aim of this book is to show how a few inferential logics explain most of what diplomats and leaders learn from their conversations. In ever denser networks of diplomatic exchange, across diverse contexts in the international system, time and again, fundamentally similar dynamics recur. The conclusions that state representatives reach shape decisions for war and how they understand the international order of the day.

The earliest elements of the argument evolved out of thinking about the trepidation with which diplomats and state leaders make demands. Often, their principal concern is not that their threats will not be believed, but what will happen when they are. This is common to alliance politics and nuclear brinkmanship, to attempts to deter and attempts to compel. It is important because the reasons some demands are not made, and others are not made lightly, are also the reasons they are meaningful at all. The fact that a leader does not hold back, in spite of reasons to do so, shows just how important an issue is.

"Obviously," US President John F. Kennedy told his advisors during the Cuban Missile Crisis, "you can't sort of announce that in four days from now you're going to take [the missiles] out."[1] Why–what prevented this threat of attack in four days from being made? Was it that the threat might not be credible? No. Such a threat could not be made lightly because of the escalatory dynamic that could result when the Soviets took the threat seriously, because "they may announce within three days that they're going to have [nuclear] warheads on them." Kennedy worried about what the Soviets would do in response precisely because they *would* find the threat credible. This was a form of brinkmanship,

---

[1] May and Zelikow (2002, p. 44).

but it could be carried on through private meetings and telegraph messages, and the danger was not of an accidental slide into conflict, but of what the sides would do intentionally in response to new information from their adversaries.

At a far removed time and place and in a different international context, German Chancellor Otto von Bismarck was loath to make even the subtlest diplomatic threat to Russia, even over an issue he considered essential to German security. Was his concern that his signal would not be believed or would be misinterpreted? Once again, his worry was instead how the Russians would react to the real information that the German stance would convey. Perhaps Russia would alter its benevolent attitude toward Germany. Perhaps she would ally with Germany's enemies, what Bismarck called his "nightmare of coalitions."[2]

The dawning appreciation that seemingly different fears about the consequences of credible threats would lead to essentially similar dynamics was the genesis of the project. Eventually, this led to what became the fourth chapter in this volume, which analyzes how the willingness of a leader to make a demand in spite of the diversity of dangers that result allows these closed door threats to convey information. The other theoretical chapters emerged similarly, from an identification of historical patterns and an engagement with theories of signaling.

This book could not exist in anything like its current form without the work of a great many scholars. These include the international relations theorists James Fearon, Robert Jervis, and Thomas Schelling. Their ideas are threaded through the whole of this book. I am grateful to have encountered their lively, provocative, and deeply insightful work. For comments, advice, and especially encouragement, I am profoundly grateful to two intellectual counselors, Bob Jervis and Helen Milner. My colleagues at UCLA have also given me invaluable advice on many occasions. I wish to thank, in particular, Michael Chwe, Jim DeNardo, Debbie Larson, Jeff Lewis, Barry O'Neill, Tom Schwartz, Art Stein, and Marc Trachtenberg. Marc read and commented on the entire manuscript and suggested the British *Confidential Print* as a good source of data on diplomatic inferences. James Alt, Stephen Ansolabehere, Jeremy Cato, Maria Fanis, Jim Fearon, Erik Gartzke, Matthew Gottfried, Arman Grigorian, Mike Horowitz, Andy Kydd, Dov Levin, Jack Levy, John Londregan, James Morrow, Chad Nelson, Bob Pape, Kris Ramsay, Sebastian Rosato, Anne Sartori, Branislav Slantchev, James Snyder, and Dessie Zagorcheva all read and commented on work that became portions of the manuscript. I also wish to thank the two superb anonymous reviewers of the book

[2] Rupp (1941, p. 230).

manuscript, and the many anonymous reviewers of the articles that became portions of Chapters 3 through 6. These reviewers dramatically influenced the direction and presentation of the work. This project is the product of our community of scholars.

The book also involved a large-scale data collection effort that began when, unasked, one student offered to put her extraordinary talents towards the dataset's creation. Christina Brown helped to build and then to manage the large team of researchers we assembled in those early days. In the final years of the project, Marko Perko III took over the task of leading the team of researchers. Without his insights and dedication, the full dataset might never have been finished. The superb students who worked on the project, at different times between 2007 and 2014, are: Adam Boche, Christina Brown, Jae Ellescas, Sabiha Khan, Elizabeth Lopez, Gisue Mehdi, Meena Menon, Henry Murry, Danielle Ohlemacher, Leah Osborne, Laura Patch, Sean Patel, Marko Perko III, Bridgette Pighin, Nathan Piller, Rachel Sandoval, Tania Shakoori, Arsenios Skaperdas, Suzy Smith, Greg Swartz, Paul Wallot, and Golnaz Zandieh. I am indebted to these many contributors for their generous, dedicated, and sometimes inspired work; they do not share blame for any faults in what we produced.

A number of institutions and individuals contributed to this project in other ways. Oriel College in Oxford and Bob and Judith Terry in Cambridge, MA provided room, and sometimes board, as well as conducive writing environments. Several institutions provided research support: the University of California, Los Angeles, the Burkle Center for International Relations, Columbia, Harvard and Oxford Universities, the Institute for Social and Economic Research and Policy, the Eisenhower Institute, the Olin Institute at Harvard University, and, at Columbia University, the Public Policy Consortium and the Center for Conflict Resolution.

Finally, I wish to thank my father and mother, who took me into the world by land, sea, and air; my wife Joslyn, for love and support, and for helping me to conceive and build; and my other family and friends. They all buoy, bolster, and cheer, and therefore have advanced this work on too many occasions to list.

I

Can Adversaries Communicate?

The relationship between Austria and Russia was without hint of conflict in the first half of the nineteenth century. Austrians wept with joy when Russia offered military assistance against the Hungarians, and the Austrian Emperor traveled to Warsaw, where he knelt on one knee to kiss the Tsar's hand. The two powers signed an agreement to conduct their foreign policies "only together and in a perfect spirit of solidarity," and the Tsar told foreign diplomats, "when I speak of Russia, I speak of Austria as well." Yet, in the latter half of the nineteenth century, the two empires were in constant tension, and often directly at odds. Russia offered aid and support against Austrian interests, first to Sardinia and Prussia, enabling those states to form Italy and Germany, and later to Serbia and other Balkan powers, leading to the World War.[1] This dramatic shift in Russian policy towards Austria happened suddenly in the 1850s and did not result from changes in national capabilities or material interests; what brought it about?

Another important shift in European politics occurred during the Great Eastern Crisis in 1876. Germany and Russia had previously had the closest of relations, while Germany and Austria had fought a war a decade before. Yet, during the Great Eastern Crisis, a rift formed between Germany and Russia, while Germany and Austria–Hungary drew closer together. The German statesman, Otto von Bismarck, was convinced that the words his ambassador to Russia had uttered to the Tsar had brought about this "new situation" in Europe.[2] Soon after, Germany signed the alliance with Austria that lasted until both Empires were destroyed fighting side by side in the cataclysm of the First World War. What did produce this new situation and how did it then convince Germany and

[1] Deak (2001, p. 289), Puryear (1931, pp. 20–21, 228), Trager (2012).
[2] Bismarck (1915, p. 286).

Austria to bind themselves in a rare, permanent alliance despite having recently fought each other in a war?

The twentieth century contains many examples of similar shifts in leaders' beliefs and policies with lasting consequences. At the turn of the century, for instance, Russo-Austrian relations were merely conflictual, but by 1914, the Austrian emperor had come to believe that Russian policy aimed at "the destruction of my empire."[3] Austrian statesmen, who had previously rated Germany an unreliable ally, came to believe instead during the July Crisis that Germany could be relied upon in an existential struggle.[4] In the latter half of the century, during the early Cold War, the German Chancellor Konrad Adenauer decided to build nuclear weapons with the expectation that this would ultimately be tolerated by his American and French allies. Not long after the Cuban Missile Crisis, however, Germany reversed course, deciding that it had to accept nonnuclear status because it came to believe that the United States would tolerate nothing else. This acceptance of nonnuclear status, and the American guarantee that it would remain in effect, was the essential final element of the settlement and associated reduction of Cold War tensions known as détente, which pulled the world back from the brink of nuclear disaster. In fundamental respects, this settlement is with us today, and Germany still has no nuclear weapons of her own.[5] These shifts in beliefs and policies were of great consequence; what were their causes?

The answers to all of these questions are the same: diplomatic encounters that occurred behind closed doors, away from public view. Some of these encounters occurred during military crises in which there was a danger of war, while others occurred outside of them. Some reactions were caused by demands, and others by acquiesences. The effects produced were often felt over the long term and had profound influences on history's subsequent course. But for such consequences to follow from diplomatic statements, something had to be learned from them, and it is often difficult to understand why diplomats and leaders should trust what each other say.

Consider the meeting of US President Kennedy and Soviet Premier Khrushchev in Vienna in June of 1961. Khrushchev threatened to sign a peace treaty with East Germany in December, thereby ending the right of the US to station occupying troops in West Berlin. A failure by the

---

[3] Die Österreichisch-Ungarischen Dokumente zum Kriegsausbruch (ÖUDK), Franz Josef to Wilhelm, July 2, 1914 .

[4] ÖUDK, Erster Teil, 58, Ministerrat für gemeinsame Angelegenheiten, July 7, 1914.

[5] Trachtenberg (1999, Chapter 9).

US to remove its troops would be taken as a challenge, he implied, and "the USSR will have no choice other than to accept the challenge; it must respond and it will respond. The calamities of a war will be shared equally." The decision to sign a peace treaty with East Germany, Khrushchev stated, was "firm and irrevocable."[6] Both leaders knew that they were talking about a potential nuclear war, a war whose effects, as Kennedy described them during the meeting, "would go from generation to generation."[7] Was Khrushchev to be believed? Given his incentive to overstate Soviet resolve in order to get his way, was his threat of escalation credible? How can leaders draw conclusions about their adversaries' intentions from mere statements? To answer these questions is to understand much about how international crises are resolved or lead to conflict and how international orders are created.

COMMUNICATING INTENTION

Social life involves cooperation within groups and competition between them. Yet, human group allegiances shift. Partners may become adversaries and one-time adversaries may make common cause and become partners. Appraising the intentions of potential adversaries and partners, therefore, is fundamental to advancement and, sometimes, to survival. For leaders in international politics, the stakes are particularly high. Sound appraisals of other leaders' intentions can lead to policies that avoid wars, while misapprehensions can lead to societal decline. When a false impression can have such dire consequences, how do leaders come to understand each other's intentions?

Because states are potential adversaries, communicating intentions is difficult. Many statements by diplomats and leaders cannot be taken at face value. Diplomats, who might divulge their state's plans in conversation, often have incentives to misrepresent the intentions of their state's leaders. In conversation, simply saying one thing, when one intends another, appears to carry little cost.[8]

Leaders that intend aggression against another state, for instance, have incentive to pretend that they do not, so that their adversary does not have time to prepare for conflict. François de Callières, the famous French student of diplomacy, argued along these lines in 1716 that a threat should be made just before the blow so that the threatened leader would "not have the time and pretext to guard himself against it by entering

---

[6] *Foreign Relations of the United States, 1961–1963*, Volume V, p. 230.
[7] *Foreign Relations of the United States, 1961–1963*, Volume V, p. 228.
[8] Fearon (1995).

into alliances with other princes."[9] The diplomatic statements of a leader following this advice would certainly be misleading, if not strictly dishonest, until a threat was finally made just before the sword fell. For similar strategic reasons, Japan, when it planned to attack the United States at Pearl Harbor, and Israel, when it planned to attack Iraq at Osirak, gave no warning at all.

Leaders willing to make concessions to avoid conflict also have incentives to hide their intentions from adversaries. Though a leader is willing to concede the issues of the day, she would surely rather not. For this reason, diplomats sometimes overstate their state's resolve to resist making a concession. During the Cuban Missile Crisis, for instance, the Kennedy administration signaled that it would accept a secret deal – removal of the Soviet missiles from Cuba in return for removal of the Jupiter missiles from Turkey[10] – but not a public agreement to the same effect. The truth, however, was that the Kennedy administration had decided to accept just such a public trade, under the auspices of the United Nations, if the Soviets declined the US offer of a secret deal.[11] Should Khrushchev have drawn an inference about US resolve from these diplomatic communications that occurred away from public view or should these exchanges have been ignored? Whatever the answer, the stakes could not have been higher. Today, Iran and North Korea maintain they would respond to United States attacks on their nuclear facilities with attacks on the United States. Should these threats be believed?

A state that has poor relations with another state, or intends an aggressive policy against that state, can also have an incentive to hide this fact from third parties. One reason is that a conflict is a drain on a state's resources and makes the state vulnerable to opposing coalitions. Thus, the prospect of a conflict will reduce a state's negotiating leverage with third parties whose allegiance could be swayed by one side or the other. States with known enemies often find they are less able to press their interests in negotiations with unaligned states. This is particularly visible at the start of conflicts, when poor relations can no longer be concealed, with the result that states commonly offer concessions to unaligned states to secure their allegiance or neutrality.

On occasion, leaders even have incentives to hide their intentions from their own allies. Suppose a leader is willing to support an ally in a war against a third state. If the ally were assured of support, it might provoke the third state and thereby precipitate a war. Even when a leader is willing

---

[9] de Callières (1983, p. 149).
[10] The US also offered a pledge not to invade Cuba.
[11] Fursenko and Naftali (1999).

to bring her nation into a war in necessity, she may well also prefer to avoid having to do so. For this reason, countries sometimes mistrust the attempts of their own allies to restrain their behavior and gamble that their allies will follow them into conflicts. In the middle of the nineteenth century, the Ottoman Empire correctly made this calculation in precipitating the Crimean War after the other Powers had agreed on a settlement. At the start of the twentieth century, Austria–Hungary made the same calculation in the July Crisis that developed into the World War.

Yet, in spite of the numerous reasons to mistrust the statements of adversaries and sometimes even of allies, for millennia, almost certainly longer than recorded history, diplomats and leaders have drawn inferences from conversations about each other's intentions. They have discussed, codified and reacted, and their reactions have been influenced by the content, form and context of messages from adversaries and friends. The Amarna Letters contain a record of the diplomatic correspondence between Egyptian Pharoahs and the other "Great Kings" of the fourteenth century BCE. Other writings from the ancient world contain records of treaties, such as the one concluded by the Egyptian and Hittite Empires around 1259 BCE. In the heroic period in ancient Greece, Odysseus was praised for diplomatic skill and words that "fell fast like snowflakes in winter."[12] Hundreds of years later, in 412 BCE, the Spartans conceded to recognize Persian sovereignty over the Greeks of Asia Minor. The concession must have signaled information about Spartan intentions because Persia supported Sparta against Athens thereafter, resulting in decisive Athenian defeat in less than a decade.[13] Similar evidence of important diplomatic exchanges is found in the records of many other ancient cultures including the Chinese, Indian, and Mayan.

An astounding volume of diplomatic exchange continues today. In 1817, there were fewer than 200 diplomatic missions in foreign countries, while today there are over 8,000.[14] The increasing density of diplomatic representation over the past 200 years can be seen in Figure 1.1. Whereas in the past it could take months for an ambassador to reach a host country, a Secretary of State, Foreign Minister, Prime Minister or President can now often reach a counterpart by telephone in moments. High-level officials regularly visit each other directly. In negotiating the removal of Soviet nuclear missiles from Ukraine following the disintegration of the Soviet Union, for instance, US President Clinton

[12] Adcock and Mosley (1975, p. 10).
[13] Thucydides (1989, Book 8: 18, 37, 58), Xenophon (1907, Book 2, Chapter 2).
[14] Bayer (2006).

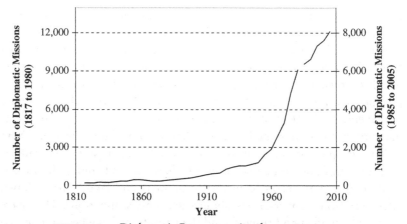

FIGURE 1.1 Diplomatic Representation from 1817 to 2005
Source: Correlates of War Diplomatic Exchange Data Set, Version 2006.1 by Resat Bayer. Note that the data up to 1980 is not comparable to the data after 1980 because the former counts multiple entries for single diplomatic representatives accredited to multiple countries, whereas the latter does not.

made stops first in Brussels, then in Prague, where he met with Central European leaders, and then in Kiev, before signing the finished agreement with Russian President Yeltsin and Ukrainian President Kravchuk in Moscow.[15] With so much industry devoted to diplomatic activity, it is not surprising that histories of modern times, even those that do not set out to analyze diplomatic events, sometimes point to diplomatic exchanges as key moments when perceptions were formed that determined important foreign policy decisions.

The presence of diplomatic activity throughout history and its ever-expanding nature today suggest that diplomacy plays a fundamental role in relations between states, and this leaves us with an old puzzle: how do adversaries communicate when they have so many reasons to deceive? The answer shows us how many of the expectations that are the basis of foreign policy decisions and constitute international orders form in the international system. It helps us to understand the processes through which actors demarcate spheres of influence, agree on settlements, and decide which dangers are the most pressing or which potential allies are reliable. Arguments for war or peace often hinge on what has been learned in diplomatic exchanges. Investigating this question means appreciating how diplomats and leaders develop beliefs about what their allies and adversaries plan to do through evaluating the *balances of conflicting incentives* of their foreign counterparts.

[15] For an exciting and amusing account of these negotiations, see Talbott (2003, pp. 110–115).

A fundamental thesis of this book is that, in spite of a variety of reasons to misrepresent their intentions, very often, conversations between representatives of adversarial states allow the sides to draw inferences about each other's plans. When diplomacy is conducted away from public view, as most of it is, this occurs through five principal mechanisms. The existence of diplomatic channels can increase or decrease the likelihood of conflict, depending on a complex, interacting set of factors. Often, communication is possible because one set of factors gives state representatives incentives to mislead in one fashion, such as by overstating their willingness to fight over an issue, but another set of factors provides incentives to mislead in an opposed manner, such as by understating their resolve to engage in conflict. This book derives the conditions under which balances of incentives occur that allow adversaries to communicate. Evidence for this theory of communication is drawn from a variety of cases and from analysis of large datasets drawn from decades of British diplomatic correspondence contained in the archive known as the *Confidential Print*.

Forming judgments from the diplomacy of potential adversaries is no simple task. Nevertheless, the empirical analysis of later chapters demonstrates beyond doubt that such conclusions are frequently drawn. Thus, as Niccolò Machiavelli wrote to an inexperienced diplomat, sent by Florence as ambassador to the court of Charles V, King of Spain and Holy Roman Emperor, "It is very difficult to penetrate the secret of such conclusions, and it is therefore necessary to depend upon one's judgment and conjectures. But to find out all the intrigues, and to conjecture the issue correctly, that is indeed difficult, for you have nothing to depend upon except surmises aided by your own judgment."[16] Through reason and conjecture, in conversations and negotiations, impressions are formed that constitute actor expectations about the intentions of others.

These conversations have immediate impacts on policies, within international crises and outside of them, but they also have longer-term effects on the international order of the day. This is because social orders consist of expectations about when and how actors will engage in cooperation or conflict. Such expectations become "settled" over time as they are shown to be substantially consistent with actors' true natures and intentions. Once settled, or to the extent that they are, they constitute an international order.[17] Settled expectations often identify the sets of states

---

[16] Berridge (2004, p. 42).

[17] The idea that an international order is constituted by settled expectations is associated with Bull (1977), but he defined order more specifically in relation to the processes that further particular primary purposes of the society of states. Among these purposes are the preservation of the society of states, the preservation of the independence of

that will balance against sets of other states, and the rules by which even the powerful have committed to live. In Ikenberry's (2008) terms, they define whether the order is hegemonic, constitutional, or based upon a balance of power. They indicate the conditions under which the powerful will comply with international law and exercise other forms of restraint, and the extent to which they will impose restraint on others.

Diplomatic conversations shape these expectations, which they settle and unsettle. In the short term, diplomacy often serves the cause of peace by allowing actors to reveal what they are willing to fight for, thereby enabling them to avoid the necessity of doing so. But diplomatic representations can also provoke, embolden, and alarm. Over the longer term, diplomatic exchange plays a leading role in constructing the international order, and different orders imply different frequencies and intensities of conflict. Thus, in shaping actor expectations, diplomacy is not universally on the side of greater order and peace.

PERCEPTIONS OF INTENTIONS AND
THE INTERNATIONAL SYSTEM

The question of how states draw inferences about each other's plans from a variety of sources, including diplomatic exchange, is central to the study of international politics because the issue of war or peace is often thought to depend on these perceptions of intent. When Kennedy met Khrushchev in Vienna, for instance, both men inferred that the other was likely to conduct a more aggressive foreign policy than each had believed previously, and both altered their own policies as a result. Immediately following the meeting, Khrushchev "approved most of a KGB plan to create 'a situation in various areas of the world that would favor the dispersion of attention and resources by the United States and their satellites, and would tie them down during the settlement of a German peace treaty and West Berlin'," and shortly thereafter Kennedy told the Joint Chiefs to plan for the possibility of a nuclear first strike against the Soviet Union.[18] What inferences did these men draw from their conversations that led them to take these drastic actions? More generally, how

individual states, and the limitation of violence. The definition given above is closely related to the one offered in Ikenberry (2008, p. 23), but with less emphasis on "explicit principles, rules, and institutions" and also less emphasis on "mutual" or intersubjective understandings. Settled expectations usually are shared, but to define them in that way introduces the question unnecessarily of how widely they must be shared. For discussions of other definitions of international order, see Hurrell (2007), Gilpin (1983), Reus-Smit (1997), and Fabbrini and Marchetti (2016, Chapter 1).

[18] See Fursenko and Naftali (1999, p. 138) and Lieber and Press (2006, p. 36).

do leaders draw such inferences and what sorts of factors play the largest roles in shaping leader perceptions of the international environment and of the intentions of other leaders?

Such questions have been a focus of scholarly inquiry. Thucydides addressed related questions in the fifth century BC, Morgenthau (1948) discussed these issues in the mid-twentieth century, Jervis (1970, 1976) later wrote two seminal works on the topic, and this field of inquiry remains active today. Some scholars argue that state reputations play a key role in other leaders' evaluations of state intentions (e.g., Schelling 1966, 1980; Jervis 1976; Sartori 2005), while other scholars argue the opposite (e.g., Press 2005, Mercer 1996). Fearon (1995) argues on rationalist grounds that diplomatic statements made behind closed doors are unlikely to affect other leaders' beliefs about intentions, and many studies have accepted this view, but Sartori (2005), Guisinger and Smith (2002), Kurizaki (2007), Trager (2010, 2011, 2012, 2013), Hall (2011), Yarhi-Milo (2013), and others argue to the contrary. Kydd (2005) argues that "trust," which itself is influenced greatly by state decisions to arm, is a central determinant of perceptions of intentions. He further argues that a state's perception of other states' perceptions of itself will determine what inferences about likely future behavior and intentions the first state draws from the actions of the other states. A state that knows it is perceived to have revisionist designs may realize that security measures taken by other states are taken out of fear rather aggressive intent. Slantchev (2005, 2010) models the inferences that states draw from military mobilizations. Fearon (1994a) and Tarar and Leventoğlu (2009) model the impact of public threats on adversaries' perceptions of state resolve. These works are a sampling from large literatures that address related topics.

The answers to many questions of great policy and scholarly importance hinge on how states draw inferences. Should wars be fought in the name of maintaining a reputation for resolve to defend a set of interests, as was, for instance, the Vietnam War? Certainly, they should only if state leaders draw inferences about what states will do in the future by looking to the past to evaluate each other's reputations. Do the closed-door conversations of diplomats constitute an essential element of the processes that determine the course of events in the international system? Again, they do only if leaders look to those conversations in understanding how states will act and in formulating courses of action themselves. Do decisions to build particular sorts of arms impact another state's evaluation of how hostile the arming state is? When a state arms, will other states conclude it is more aggressive generally or only more potentially hostile to a small set of states with which it has known conflicts? In short, we cannot understand the forces that shape events in the international system without understanding how states develop perceptions of each other's intentions. Answers to these and many similar questions are central to understanding international political processes.

THE STUDY OF DIPLOMACY

In contrast to the scholarly focus on how perceptions of intentions form generally, the specific attention devoted to the role of diplomatic exchange in these processes has been meager. Considering the volume of diplomatic activity that continues the world over, if diplomacy influences the course of events at all, the subject has been vastly understudied, particularly recently. In fact, the relative absence of scholarship focused on diplomatic processes is evident across diverse approaches to understanding international politics.

Within history departments, the turn away from traditional diplomatic history has been pronounced. One point of agreement among divergent twentieth century historiographic movements (the Annales School, Marxist history, the histoire sérielle, and others) has been to reject elite focused histories. The great currents of history, these scholars argued, are economic and social. From this perspective, traditional diplomatic history, with its careful reconstructing of specific actions and motivations of elite diplomats, appeared superficial and even immoral. Efforts to understand international events in terms of the logic of the international system nearly ceased in history faculties.[19]

Later, diplomatic history was superseded by "international history," which encompasses the study of diplomatic events but emphasizes the need to do so only while also placing these events in broader social and economic contexts. While this may appear reasonable and important, the constraint of time means that historians are less able to carefully reconstruct and analyze the complicated strategic calculations in which diplomats regularly engage. It has also proven nearly impossible to bring such depth of analysis to all societies that are involved, in some way, in many diplomatic episodes.[20]

One exception to the rule among historians proves its general validity. In his foundational study of the Crimean War, Paul Schroeder nearly

---

[19] For an insightful and humorous review of the Annales School alongside other historiographic schools, see Forster (1978).

[20] Happily, there are histories that do focus on the diplomatic calculus, including Trachtenberg (1999), Gaddis (2006), Elliott (2002), Parker (2000), Schroeder (1996), and Gavin (2004).

apologizes for writing a more traditional diplomatic history. He agrees that "diplomatic history should always be viewed and written as part of general political history, or as part of socio-economic or intellectual or even psychological history," if the goal is to "analyze foreign policy in terms of [the] determinants of decisions." But this is not the most important goal, Schroeder argues: "It is less important to know why statesmen took certain actions than to know what reactions and results these actions produced in the international arena, and why under the prevailing system they led to these results and not others."[21] We could not understand why actions produce certain reactions, however, without understanding the determinants of reaction decisions. Reactions happen later, but are otherwise similar to actions. Schroeder's solution pushes the problem of understanding the determinants of decisions one step into the future, but does not avoid it, and his own work beautifully investigates the sources of actor decisions. Thus, the attempt to understand the connections between the brute facts of international affairs seems to force scholars into analyzing the determinants of elite decisions. Usually, this involves understanding what actors wanted (sometimes, as with psychological history, perhaps better than the actors understood it themselves), what they believed, and what strategies they adopted to get what they truly wanted. With significant but few exceptions, historians have not focused on such analyses of diplomatic encounters in recent decades.

Within the field of political science, several important strands of international relations scholarship have also seemed to imply that diplomatic exchanges that occur away from public view have at most a marginal influence on events. A substantial portion of the field of international relations is composed of scholars who would identify themselves as "realists." Many of these scholars believe that state behavior can be understood as a direct response to the distribution of capabilities among states in the international system, leaving little room for diplomatic processes to influence important international events.[22] For instance, John Mearsheimer argues that the central movements of the system of states and even the actions of individual states can be understood in this way. He describes his theory as "a powerful flashlight in a dark room: even though it cannot illuminate every nook and cranny, most of the time it is an excellent tool for navigating through the darkness." On his own account, however, the drastically differing levels of security competition in the early and late periods of the Cold War are relegated to the dark unexplained corners of the room. One might wonder whether these

---

[21] Schroeder (1972, pp. xiii–xiv).
[22] See, for instance, Posen (1984) and Mearsheimer (2001).

features of the period were not better viewed as the focal point for the eye above the mantle. These differing levels of security competition, on which the very existence of the earth as we know it seemed to depend, were rooted in part in particular diplomatic episodes, such as the meeting between Kennedy and Khrushchev described above.

For neorealists like Kenneth Waltz, the distribution of resources in an anarchic system is seen as a structure that shapes and shoves, but does not determine foreign policy choices.[23] Waltz therefore explicitly leaves open the possibility that other factors, such as diplomatic processes, also systematically influence foreign policy choices.[24] While some scholars in the neorealist tradition have examined the influence of domestic politics, however, few have theorized diplomatic exchange as an important independent influence on world events.[25]

The dominant trend among scholars of conflict processes has been to argue that diplomatic signals made away from public view are costless, and therefore cannot convey information in adversarial contexts. According to this argument, if private diplomatic signals of resolve were effective, states would make threats to adversaries whether or not these states intended to follow through on them. As a result, statements made in private that carry no cost convey no information. Statements made in front of domestic audiences, by contrast, are thought to convey information through the "audience cost" that the domestic public imposes on leaders who make commitments on which they fail to follow through. Given the chance, for instance in a democracy, the public will then be more likely to throw the leader from office.[26]

As a result, many of these scholars have focused primarily on public threats and costly escalations such as the building of arms and the mobilization of military might.[27] This has contributed to the belief that other "costless" forms of communication, often identified with diplomatic correspondence that occurs out of view of domestic publics, do not convey information and therefore do not affect the course of events.[28]

---

[23] The clearest statement of this point is Waltz (2003, p. 53).

[24] As Levy (2003, p. 132) points out, Waltz (1979) was not entirely consistent on this point.

[25] Scholars in the neorealist tradition who have focused on domestic politics include Schweller (1994, 2006) and Kaufman (1992).

[26] Fearon (1994a), Tomz (2007), Trager and Vavreck (2011), Horowitz and Levendusky (2012), Weeks (2008), Weiss (2013), and Kertzer and Brutger (2015).

[27] See, for instance, Kydd (1997, 2005), Morrow (1989), Powell (1990), Fearon (1995, 1997), Schultz (2001), Slantchev (2005, 2010a), Smith (1998b), and Ramsay (2004).

[28] Note that, as Sartori (2005, p. 58) points out, while "audience costs" have been modeled as costly signals, this is probably best thought of as a modeling shorthand (when voters are not modeled explicitly) for what is really a costless process. See also Smith (1998b) and Ramsay (2004).

There are important exceptions to this characterization of the literature, however, and recent scholarship has shown a renewed interest in the mechanisms of private diplomacy. Sartori (2002, 2005) has demonstrated that private diplomatic communications can be made credible by the desire of states to maintain a bargaining reputation, which makes them reticent to send misleading signals for fear of being caught in a bluff.[29] Guisinger and Smith (2002) combine two strains of literature to show that, in the presence of a reputational mechanism along the lines of Sartori's, democratic selection of leaders results in an endogenous additional disincentive against bluffing. Kurizaki (2007) shows that if a publicly threatened state will lose face by backing down, then it is sometimes optimal for states to make private threats. Such threats do not increase the probability the threatened state assigns to the threatener following through, but neither do these private threats cause that probability to go to zero either.[30] Kydd (2003) presents a cheap talk model of third-party mediation.[31] Trager (2010, 2011) show how costless threats can convey information when the target of a threat has an opportunity to prepare for conflict or when negotiations involve multiple issue dimensions. Among these mechanisms for private information transmission, the staking of bargaining reputations has received the most attention. Some scholars argue that the benefits of maintaining a reputation for following through causes other states to take threats more seriously,[32] while others argue that reputations have no effect on state inferences,[33] and still others argue that the effects of reputations are indeterminate and that reputations can attach to many qualities of states beyond their levels of resolve.[34]

Earlier work describes several other mechanisms of private diplomacy.[35] Schelling (1966, 1980) argues that threats sometimes risk an

---

[29] Schelling (1966, 1980), Jervis (1970, pp. 78–83) and others have also argued in favor of a reputational signaling mechanism in private diplomacy.

[30] See also Fearon (1997, p. 84) and Yarhi-Milo (2013*b*) .

[31] Ramsay (2004) describes a cheap-talk model of public diplomacy.

[32] See, for instance, Sartori (2005) and Schelling (1966, pp. 51–55).

[33] Press (2005), Mercer (1996).

[34] Jervis (1997, pp. 255–258,266–271), Dafoe, Renshon, and Huth (2014).

[35] Jervis (1970), for instance, proposes three additional mechanisms through which private threats could convey information. First, if leaders are reticent to lie for moral reasons, credibility may attach to their statements. Second, if a country has a stake in the current functioning of the international system, a reticence to lie may derive from a desire to ensure that states do not too often deceive each other, since a baseline of honest communication may be required to maintain the overall systemic equilibrium. Third, lies may result in unwanted "changes in the international environment." Sometimes, if a statement is believed, other actors may act in such a way that the actor making the statement has an additional incentive to follow through on the statement. For instance, if one state

undesired event that neither side directly controls, which causes threats to convey information. The essence of this form of negotiation, which Schelling called brinkmanship, can be seen by analogy to two climbers roped together on the edge of a cliff. Neither can threaten to throw the other off the mountain because both would then perish, as with one of the superpowers launching a nuclear strike during the cold war, and thus no such threat would be credible. But if one moves closer to the edge of the cliff, both *may* slip. By demonstrating a willingness to risk slipping, they convey information about their resolve in the issue being negotiated.[36] Schelling's analysis focuses on how engaging in limited forms of conflict can constitute an implicit threat because it demonstrates a willingness to risk even more costly conflict. Private diplomatic threats may have a similar effect, however, in that they delay resolution of the issue and create a crisis atmosphere in which conflict may be more likely. Schelling's work bears important similarities to the analysis in Chapter 4. There, however, the emphasis will be on the intentional action of actors rather than the partly exogenous danger of sliding off a cliff, and on the implications of including the option to prepare in models of the conflict processes.[37]

Like their formal colleagues, quantitative scholars have focused on public threats.[38] The reason for this is compelling: there is no large-N dataset that covers threats or other diplomatic events that did not take place in the public view. In fact, scholars have not yet collected data to distinguish the sorts of inferences that are made infrequently or by less consequential actors in world politics from those inferences that constitute daily life in the international system. Thus, many excellent studies demonstrate either how state leaders drew inferences in a few particular cases, or how leaders *could* draw inferences based on theoretical models. For this reason, there is no consensus on the main drivers of inference

professes hostility towards another, the reaction of the second state may make it in the first state's interest to take hostile actions it had not originally planned on taking. In the model below, there will also be cases where the reaction of the threatened state provides incentive for the threatener to follow through on the threat.

[36] Powell (1988) formalizes this idea in the context of inadvertent war.

[37] Barry O'Neill (1999) and Robert Jervis (1970, 1976) have discussed how symbols acquire meaning in international politics and how inferences from them are drawn. O'Neill also developed related models of the dynamics of competition over honor symbols and analyzed the role of insults in bargaining. On these topics, see Jervis (1976, pp. 58–113) and Jervis (1978). Schelling (1966) also addressed the ways in which the framing of a dispute in conversation could signal resolve. For instance, by convincing an adversary that a state's leaders think the adversary is violating the *status quo* in their relations, a state might also convince the adversary of the state's determination to resist whatever the adversary is doing.

[38] This literature is vast. For a sample, see Huth, Gelpi, and Bennett (1993), Braumoeller (2003), Bueno De Mesquita and Lalman (1988), and Severson and Starr (1990).

and thus of behavior. A primary objective of this book is to bring the results of a systematic data collection effort to bear on these questions.

Even constructivist scholars have devoted relatively little attention to understanding diplomatic processes. These scholars are passionately interested in intersubjective understandings and the role of these understandings in influencing state behavior, but this field of inquiry has nevertheless focused on norms, which are usually seen as changing only over the long term. A normative structure, Wendt (1999, p. 339) argues, "by definition, is self fulfilling. It's no wonder why they last." Wendt's insight is that normative structures would not exist if they were not reproduced and reified by social processes. But this does not answer the question of whether there are not some intersubjective understandings or ideational structures that change more quickly as a result of brief diplomatic encounters, and still constrain behavior.[39]

Another strand of constructivist literature investigates the preconditions for different forms of diplomacy. Der Derian (1987) finds these in a particular *raison d'état* culture and the existence of a balance of power. Risse (2000) and Mitzen (2005) find these in the Habermasian concept of a common "life world." This provides the source for arguments that transcend self-interest, allowing for both persuasion and socialization. On Mitzen's (2005, p. 411) account, even disingenuous diplomatic justifications of actions can have an important socializing effect, which Elster calls the "civilizing force of hypocrisy" (Mitzen 2005, p. 411). Krebs and Jackson (2007) see less possibility for actors to persuade each other, but also view the shared elements of culture as determining what is acceptable in argument and therefore allowing for a sort of argumentative fencing that influences outcomes.[40] Other scholars examine the particular sorts of justifications that can be offered in changing cultural contexts (e.g., Goddard 2015, Stein 2000, Hurd 2015, Sending 2015b). All of these scholars focus on how cultural context *constrains* actors, rather than on whether actors can communicate and under what conditions they can *learn* about each other's intentions from diplomatic encounters.[41]

---

39 Alongside other scholars, such as Finnemore and Sikkink (1998) and Checkel (2001), Wendt does argue that international norms can be changed through action, and gives an account of stages norms pass through as their influence deepens, although the mechanism linking actions to normative structure outcomes is not fully elucidated (Wendt 1999, pp. 343–366). For examples of other constructivist work in this vein, see Katzenstein (1996) and Davis Cross (2007).

40 On diplomatic culture and the ways it facilitates compromise and therefore peace, see Sharp (2009).

41 For scholarship on affective responses to diplomatic signals, see for example, Jervis (1976), O'Neill (1999), Trager (2012), Barnhart (2015), Hall (2011, 2015), and Mercer (2010). Holmes (2013) addresses the neurological processes that enable judgments of

In summary, then, with important exceptions, diplomacy has recently been little studied by scholars for a variety of reasons. On different theoretical grounds, most historians, realists, constructivists, and political scientists interested in conflict processes have all turned their attention elsewhere. This has had a mutually re-enforcing effect. If historians had produced convincing histories of the effects of diplomacy, theorizing among political scientists would likely have followed suit. If theory had placed private diplomacy at the center of events, more empirical work would have been undertaken. I shall show, however, that on examination, the theoretical and empirical grounds for the view that adversaries cannot learn about intention from private diplomatic encounters, and therefore that diplomacy has only a marginal effect on events in the international system, are unsound.

For their part, practitioners of diplomacy have continued to develop their own theories about how diplomacy functions.[42] Often they focus on the medium and specific context of diplomatic messages. Credibility is sometimes thought to depend, for instance, on having a signed letter from the head of state or, better, a cabinet or higher-level official on hand to deliver the most important messages in person.[43] This at least helps to convince a negotiating partner that the message represents the will of the highest authorities in the signaling state. These analyses of experienced practitioners have great value for all students of diplomacy. However, a practitioner's ability to understand the impact and functioning of diplomatic practices is restricted by the fact that she can fully understand only one side of a diplomatic encounter. Unlike diplomatic historians and students of politics, practitioners do not have access to the policy calculus of their negotiating partners. Thus, diplomats are often unsure whether their actions have influenced the thinking of interlocutors, much less decisively affected the course of events. The analyses below, by contrast, employ data drawn from thousands of internal accounts of how foreign diplomatic signals were interpreted.

THE FIVE MECHANISMS OF PRIVATE DIPLOMACY

Diplomacy is the art of furthering a set of international political interests through speech.[44] Among the most difficult of the diplomatic arts is the

---

credibility in face-to-face diplomacy. For scholarship that attempts to identify particular diplomatic styles, see, for instance, Rathbun, Kertzer, and Paradis (2015), Chiozza and Goemans (2011), Horowitz and Stam (2014), and Rathbun (2014).

[42] Classic studies include Nicolson (1963), Kissinger (1994), Nicolson (1954), and de Callières (1983).

[43] Interview with Ambassador William Rugh, former US Ambassador to the United Arab Emirates and Yemen, July 18, 2006.

[44] There are many other definitions of diplomacy, most of which focus on the representation of states by individuals. Satow (1922, p. 1), in his famous study of diplomatic

art of creating commitment – that is, creating a perception in the minds of interlocutors that a state is committed to certain courses of action in particular circumstances.[45] Offers of cooperation, threats, and assurances are all attempts to create commitments. Since international actors gain an advantage if others form certain beliefs about their commitments, simple, costless statements of intention cannot always be believed.[46]

Much information is exchanged in diplomatic discussions when neither side is attempting to convince the other of a commitment to a course of action. In fact, in such cases, information is easily exchanged. Such exchanges are frequent because, for hundreds of years, diplomats have been provided with information about their states' plans, not just in the area of the world where the diplomat is posted, but more broadly. The reason for this practice, according to Machiavelli, is that "he who wants another to tell him all he knows must in return tell the other some things that he knows, for the best means of obtaining information from others is to communicate some information to them. And therefore if a republic desires that her ambassador shall be honored, they cannot do a better thing than to keep him amply supplied with information; for the men who know that they can draw information from him will hasten to tell him all they know."[47]

Since it is relatively easy to understand that inferences are drawn from diplomatic communication when there is no strong incentive to create perceptions of commitment, this book focuses on understanding how information is conveyed between potential adversaries who often have a large stake in convincing each other that they have particular intentions. I also focus on diplomacy conducted by elites away from public view, known as *private diplomacy* in contrast to *public diplomacy*. The seminal article on public commitments is Fearon (1994a), which argues that leaders face domestic political costs when they back down after making a

---

practice, defines diplomacy as "the application of intelligence and tact to the conduct of official relations between the governments of independent states." For a discussion of other definitions, see Sharp (1999) and Sending (2015a, Chapter 1).

45 See Schelling (1966, Chapter 2) and Jervis (1970) for subtle discussions of this art.

46 Philosophers have engaged in lively discussion about what, exactly, an intention is. Loosely following Bratman (1999), with reference to either individuals or states, I will use "intention" to refer to a particular piece of an overall plan of action, either of an individual or of a state, as conceived of by the leaders of the state. To speak of state intentions is to construct the state as an agent in its own right, which it is not exactly, but the state apparatus does produce plans, and parts of those plans look very much like the intentions of individuals. Thus, the common practice of speaking of state intentions is a useful shorthand that I shall sometimes employ. For a related definition of an intention that is similar to the game-theoretic concept of a chosen strategy, see Jervis (1976, pp. 48–57).

47 Berridge (2004, p. 42).

public commitment and then analyzes the implications for bargaining in international crises.[48] In private diplomacy between adversaries, by contrast, this book shows that five mechanisms of inference recur frequently and explain the vast majority of conclusions that are drawn from diplomatic conversations. These mechanisms actually apply to both private and public signals, but I shall focus primarily on the former.

To say that these are the five mechanisms that recur with substantial frequency in state relations is not to say that other mechanisms are not important in individual cases. The social world of diplomats and leaders is complex and the views and understandings of individuals can be idiosyncratic. Unusual states of affairs come to pass. In fact, the data on diplomatic encounters analyzed below demonstrates with certainty that other logics will sometimes play important roles. Even in those cases, however, the following mechanisms are likely to be a part of the strategic calculations that result from diplomatic exchange and more commonly, they will comprise the major part.

Scope of Demands

When a state makes a large demand of another state, the demanding state often lowers its chances of achieving a somewhat less favorable settlement without having to fight for it. To see why, consider the results of a US insistence that Iran or North Korea give up its nuclear program completely. If those states are unwilling to do so, they will likely refuse to enter negotiations on that basis and the US will lose the opportunity to gain other concessions such as a reduction in the size and scale of these programs. Thus, when states make larger demands, they run a risk, and since states would not be willing to run this risk unless a large concession (rather than an intermediate compromise) were of sufficient value to them, these threats convey information. One result is that when one side believes the other is sufficiently unlikely to make a full concession, then demanding a full concession allows the other side to be certain that the demanding state will fight unless such a concession is offered.

Risking a Breach in Relations

Very often, when states negotiate over important security concerns, there is a danger that a threat, or some other action contrary to the interests of one's negotiating partner, will result in a breach in relations, not merely

---

[48] Experimental evidence for these "audience costs" is discussed in Tomz (2007), Trager and Vavreck (2011), Horowitz and Levendusky (2012), and Kertzer and Brutger (2015).

with respect to the issue at hand, but also with respect to other aspects of the relationship. Diplomats understand this well and are therefore nearly universally preoccupied with the connections between a particular settlement of opposed interests on one set of issues and settlements on other sets of issues. The result, which may be surprising at first, but is clear once the logic is examined, is that states can send "costless" signals about their intentions. Information is conveyed by threats because states understand the dangers of altering other states' perceptions of their intentions, and yet choose to threaten anyway when they are sufficiently resolved. This implies that if foreign policy choices are responsive to perceptions of other states' intentions at all, then explicit threats from one state to another, whether in public or private, can convey information.

Signaling intention in this way is not always possible, however, and sometimes is not even desirable. On the one hand, if an adversary is too likely to refuse a demand and to make preparations for war, then states are better served to hide any aggressive intentions, decline to issue demands, and when the time comes, attack with little or no warning. On the other hand, however, if an adversary is thought too likely to comply with a demand, signaling is impossible because there will be too much incentive to make a threat, even if the threatening state is not willing to follow through with any punishment in the event the demand is refused. Thus, informative diplomacy occurs when these incentives to understate and overstate seriousness of purpose are in balance.

Encouragement of a protégé

Commitments made by a defender to a protégé may embolden the protégé in its relations with other states. As a result, the protégé may take actions that make a conflict more likely, in which case the defender will be forced to intervene to support the protégé if the defender is indeed willing to do so. As long as the defender and protégé's interests are sufficiently aligned, therefore, the defender would not wish to offer support to the protégé unless the defender were sufficiently resolved to follow through. The result is that the defender's statements of support can convey information to the defender and protégé's adversaries. In fact, adversaries need not even observe the defender's statements. They can infer whether or not the defender offered its support in private from the public bargaining behavior of the protégé.

Diplomatic Approaches in a Systemic Context

A diplomatic approach seeking improved relations implies a willingness to make concessions to achieve them. As a result, the state to which the approach is made will often conclude that the other state *needs* better relations. Several further conclusions will then be drawn. First, and most obviously, observers will understand that the approaching state is indeed willing to make the offered concessions. Second, the state to which the approach is made will – under conditions discussed in Chapter 6 – be reassured that the other state does not intend hostile actions against it. Third, depending on the circumstance, the conclusion will be drawn that the approaching state is either hostile towards or fearful of a particular third state. Fourth, the inference will sometimes be drawn that the approaching state wishes to create distance in the relationship of the approached state and some third state.

Maintaining a Bargaining Reputation

The most written-about mechanism of diplomatic communication derives from the efforts of diplomats to maintain a reputation for honesty. Since diplomats and leaders interact repeatedly over time, sending a signal that is demonstrated to have been false may mean that the signaler is not believed in the future. As Sartori (2005) explains in the clearest terms, when diplomats are not believed honest, their states will more often have to fight to get their way. As a result, there is a drawback to losing one's reputation for sending honest signals. Many scholars of diplomatic conduct, over the centuries, have recommended a truthful approach to negotiation for this reason. Cardinal Richelieu, for instance, believed that a "good reputation is so important to a great prince that no possible gain could compensate for its loss, which would be the result if he failed to hold to his pledged word."[49] Another practitioner and scholar of diplomacy, Harold Nicolson, believed that at one time, "a corporate estimate of character," was maintained by professional diplomats on a "Stock Market of diplomatic reputation."[50] He too believed this gave diplomats a powerful incentive to make honest representations and saw this as a basis for the inferences that could be drawn from them.

In spite of a substantial literature that argues to the contrary,[51] there is much evidence, presented in the next chapter, that diplomats often think in this way in sending and interpreting signals. Nevertheless, because

---

[49] du Plessis (1961, p. 101).

[50] Nicolson (1963, p. 40). He also believed that the age of professional diplomacy had passed and that, therefore, "this expert estimation of character will also pass." François de Callières was another of those scholars who believed diplomats should never say anything that is strictly untrue. See de Callières (1983). This contrasts with the view of Louis XI of France who is meant to have told his ambassadors, "If they lie to you, lie still more to them."

[51] See, for instance, Press (2005) and Mercer (1996).

these issues have been addressed elsewhere,[52] and because some of the questions raised are complex enough to merit a separate book, the theoretical chapters below focus on the first four of these five signaling mechanisms. Those four mechanisms account for a very large portion of the inferences leaders and diplomats draw from diplomatic signals. Subsequent chapters develop formals models to analyze each of these four mechanisms and then validate implications of the models statistically and through case analyses.

PLAN OF THE BOOK

The next chapter describes how states form inferences about each other's plans in general. It shows that there are many important sources of state inferences – including relative military capabilities, domestic politics, public sentiment, economic constraints, leadership changes, and other factors – but that, among all these, inferences drawn from diplomatic exchanges play a particularly significant role. The third through sixth chapters then analyze the four mechanisms of diplomatic communication described above. The seventh chapter begins the empirical analysis of the hypotheses developed in Chapters 3 through 6 by evaluating what the powers learned from German and Russian diplomacy in 1912. The chapter then describes how the inferences drawn then, and in related episodes prior to the Great War, formed the fundamental bases of the Austrian argument for war. Once these conclusions had been drawn and German support offered, the question of when and how to begin the war was, in the words of the Austro-Hungarian Minister-President, largely "a question of details."[53] Chapter 8 shows how German elites weighed British resolve to fight before the Second World War. The ninth chapter analyzes the signaling hypotheses statistically using a dataset of almost a thousand demands, offers, and assurances made by European great powers to other European great powers from 1900 to 1914, as well as data on all inferences made by European powers over the same time period. Chapter 10 discusses general implications of the findings for the creation of international orders.

---

[52] See, for instance, Sartori (2005), Jervis (1970), Schelling (1980), Weisiger and Yarhi-Milo (2015) and works cited in Dafoe, Renshon, and Huth (2014).

[53] ÖUDK, Erster Teil, 58, Ministerrat für gemeinsame Angelegenheiten, July 7, 1914.

2

How Perceptions of Intentions Form

The material and ideational structure of the state system does not limit states to a single reasonable course of action in all instances, and possibly not in any instances.[1] In order to set their own strategies in world affairs, therefore, states attempt to figure out the plans and intentions of other states. As we have seen, the question of war or peace is often thought to hinge on how these perceptions form.

This chapter provides a systematic overview of these processes by analyzing data from the *Confidential Print* of the British Empire between 1855 and July of 1914. This provides a baseline against which the role of diplomacy in shaping perceptions can be evaluated. The data show the frequencies of inferences from different sources and allow for comparisons of how different types of inferences are drawn in different international political contexts. Analysis of this data provides the first overarching view of how state leaders' perceptions are formed. In spite of the recognized importance of the topic, no study has systematically examined how inferences are drawn from a variety of sources across a wide range of foreign policy contexts. With the data analyzed in this chapter, we can distinguish, for the first time, the sorts of inferences that are made infrequently or by less consequential actors in world politics from those inferences that constitute daily life in the international system. We can see

---

[1] There is a scholarly consensus on this point, despite appearances. For instance, as has been mentioned, John Mearsheimer points out that such important features of the system as the differing levels of rivalry in the early and late periods of the Cold War do not appear to have a structural realist explanation (Mearsheimer 2001, pp. 8–12). On this aspect of the Cold War, see also Jervis (2001) and Kydd (2005). Waltz' theories about the systemic effects of polarity and the need for balances, eventually, to form also explicitly assume that states make choices that are not determined by material structure. One pillar of the argument for increased conflict as the number of system poles increases, for instance, is that alliance behavior becomes more uncertain (Waltz 1979, p. 163). At the other end of the materialist–ideationalist spectrum, constructivist scholars have emphasized the role of agency (Checkel 1998, Ruggie 1998, Adler and Barnett 1998, and Hopf 1998).

not just how states could draw inferences, but how leaders and diplomats actually develop perceptions of the likely future behavior of other actors. I examine how state leaders are reassured that another state is not aggressive, how leaders draw inferences about the use of force, and whether inferences in crises are drawn from different sources than inferences outside of crises. The data provide a picture of how the intersubjective space of state perceptions of intention is constructed.[2]

The *Confidential Print* is a record of documents circulated by the British Foreign Office to the cabinet, officials of the Foreign Office, and the King and Queen. The British Foreign Office had principal responsibility for the formulation of British foreign policy since 1782, and from the 1850s, nearly every important Foreign Office document was included.[3] The documents represent Foreign Office analyses, reports from ambassadors, commentary by other British government officials, and even private correspondence, but all of these documents were deemed important enough to circulate to this important audience. The dataset created from the *Confidential Print* covers *every security-related inference* about the future behavior of other European great powers (Austria, France, Germany, and Russia) made by members of the British Foreign Office and their internal, British government correspondents. An inference was defined as an estimate, prediction or expressed belief about the future behavior or intentions of a European great power other than Britain drawn by a member of the British government.[4]

The sixty years covered by the data included many varied international contexts, from the aftermath of the Crimean War through the unifications of Italy and Germany, the Franco-Prussian War, Bismarck's alliance system, the Scramble for Africa, the Balkan conflicts of the early twentieth century, the Anglo-German naval race and the buildup to the First World War. After major wars during the period, several important international conferences – such as the Peace of Paris and the Congress of Berlin – drew borders and adjudicated postwar settlements. The period also saw the rise of anarchist, panslavist, communist, and democratic movements as well as the continued press of nationalisms. European

---

[2] See also Yarhi-Milo (2014).
[3] Note that the Colonial Office and India Office and their successor departments had primary responsibility for colonial policy until 1968 when these departments were merged with the Foreign Office to form the Foreign and Commonwealth Office. See Cecil (2011).
[4] Inferences were categorized as "security-related" if they concerned relative power, decisions about the use of force, or influence or control over territory. Inferences about economic matters were also included when these were presented as affecting security concerns. If the same inference – in terms of the grounds for the inference and the predicted result – was drawn in multiple documents or by multiple British officials, only one inference was coded in the dataset.

powers participated in 145 international crises and thousands of negotiations over economic and political affairs. All of this produced almost
3,000 British inferences in the documentary record about the intentions
of other European powers. On average, this represents about one inference about the future behavior or intentions of another power per week.
The data represent the judgments of hundreds of individuals. Researchers
examined over 136,000 pages of diplomatic documents in the creation of
this data. Appendix B contains a more detailed description of the dataset.

   Most of the inferences made in the documents, about ninety percent, reference a specific cause or reason for the conclusion drawn. To
understand the sorts of reasons for inferences that were regularly given,
consider the memorandum written by a military attaché in 1887. He
wrote that France was increasing her forces on the German frontier
and also that he believed Germany had ordered arms from America in
response. This caused him to infer that "we are moving slowly towards
a period, the gravity of which cannot and must not be underrated." In
other words, he thought war between Germany and France had become
more likely.[5] This inference is coded as being caused by the military
state of affairs because the inference was based on changes in the military situation between Germany and France. Another example of how
inference causes were evaluated comes from an inference drawn in 1910
in a memorandum by British Foreign Secretary Sir Edward Grey. He
considered the merits of a "general political understanding" between
England and Germany, which Germany had sought. He argued against
the idea because "the duration of such an agreement would be strenu-
ously employed by Germany to consolidate her supremacy in Europe,
while England would remain as a spectator with her hands tied." In
effect, Grey believed an agreement with Germany would make Germany
more aggressive on the continent since Britain would then be expected
not to intervene.[6] The cause of this inference is coded as an alliance
matter since it was the change in alliance relations that was predicted
to alter German actions. Note that this is a case of an inference being
drawn about what would happen (increased German aggression) if something else were to happen (an alliance between England and Germany)
that had not yet occurred. Such cases are coded as "counterfactual inferences" and are included in the dataset. A third example of the inference
cause coding comes from the same memorandum. Grey went on to argue
that Germany would be aggressive towards England once Germany had
consolidated power on the continent. The cause of this inference was

[5] Stevenson (1990, part 1, series F, v. 18, p. 314).
[6] Stevenson (1990, part 1, series F, v. 21, p. 41).

coded as a military matter because it was the consolidation of power (i.e., a change in relative power) that lead to the prediction of German aggressiveness towards England. The coding rules for the wide variety of inference cause categories are relatively straightforward.[7]

Using the most general level of these inference cause categories, Figure 2.1 shows how the British drew conclusions about the intentions of the other European powers over this 60-year period. About 13 percent of all inferences, nearly 400, are derived from military factors such as relative power calculations, the building of weapons, the mobilization of troops and the seizure of territory. Such conclusions are very important in understanding the calculations on which foreign policy decisions are based, but, as the chart makes clear, are by no means the only or even the primary path by which British foreign policy elites reached conclusions.

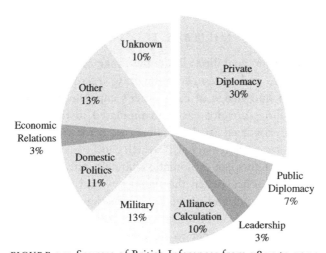

FIGURE 2.1 Sources of British Inferences from 1855 to 1914

Note: Data comprise security-related inferences in internal, British Government documents in the *Confidential Print* between 1855 and 1914, categorized by the cause or ground for the inference.

---

[7] In the creation of the data, an inference was defined in the broadest terms so as not to miss any sources of actors' perceptions of what the future holds. This implied coding inferences about expected *behavior* as well as about actor *characteristics*, such as beliefs and dispositions. In effect, no distinction was drawn between an inference and a prediction. The cause or ground of the inference was also conceived broadly as an insufficient but necessary part of a condition that was itself unnecessary but sufficient for the drawing of the inference (Mackie 1965). Thus, when an inference is coded as caused by an alliance change or military factor, for instance, this is because the author of the document pointed to that factor as a reason for the inference, but other aspects of the context are necessary for there to be sufficient grounds for the inference to be drawn. It is useful to bear this in mind in interpreting the data since inferences that are assigned a particular cause always rest on a broader set of implicit conditions.

Economic factors, by themselves, account for a surprisingly small percentage of security-related inferences over the period (3 percent), but this is not to say that economic factors are not important drivers of conflicts. Close examinations of the domestic political situations in other great powers accounts for a substantial 11 percent of inferences. About half of all inferences, the right half of Figure 2.1, relate to diplomatic signals. Private diplomacy accounts for almost a third of total inferences and statements made in public account for another 7 percent. Alliance calculations and the reputations of individual leaders, usually derived from the leaders' statements, account for another 13 percent of inferences. These percentages provide us with a first glimpse at an overview of how perceptions of intentions are formed in the international system. I now delve more deeply into what can be learned from each of these broad categories of inferences.

MILITARY FACTORS

The distribution of capabilities limits the range of the possible in international politics, and states certainly draw inferences, explicitly and implicitly, from knowledge of each other's capabilities. This is in part because capabilities are not easily manipulated in the short term. As Jervis (1970) recognized, such "indices" sometimes provide a firmer ground for inference than "signals," which can be manipulated. Signals, such as those sent through diplomatic channels, only provide a ground for rationalist inferences when the signaler would not wish to mislead even though she could, and as we have seen, signalers often appear to have incentives to mislead in international politics. Indices that cannot be easily manipulated in order to convey a certain impression, such as the size of military and armaments programs, are therefore perceived to be surer indicators of what a state can or will do.

Many scholars of international politics have also argued that foreign policy actions and outcomes in the international system are not merely influenced, but very often are driven by the distribution of capabilities.[8] Some scholars argue further that most diplomats and leaders implicitly or explicitly recognize the material drivers of international politics, and therefore that leaders' perceptions of actor intentions are also driven largely by the military balance. One example of this view is Press (2005), who explicitly applies an offensive realist perspective to theorizing how states understand each other's intentions. Another example is Slantchev (2010a, Chapter 4), who argues that military mobilization decisions are

---

[8] Mearsheimer (2001), Morgenthau (1948), Waltz (1979).

much more important indicators of leader intentions than other forms of signaling in crises.

The data presented here provide conclusive evidence that power, changes in power, and other shifts in material factors provide the ground for inferences, but no evidence that these factors are more salient than a host of other indicators of leader intentions. Inferences from military factors play a significant, but by no means dominant, role in the drawing of inferences. This is evident from Figure 2.1 as well as when the data are examined in other ways.

To get a fuller appreciation for the role of military factors in forming perceptions of intentions, it is useful to distinguish now between the cause of an inference and the type of inference or *conclusion* drawn. As we have seen, the cause of an inference may be an economic factor, such as whether a state received a loan or not, or it may be a military factor, such as whether or not a state mobilized troops, or the cause may be classified according to a variety of other categories. These categories refer to the state of affairs that produced the inference. The type of inference or conclusion, by contrast, refers to what the inference is about. The data categorizes the conclusions of inferences according to the type of prediction that was made about the future behavior or intentions of a state. One conclusion might be that a state will be more aggressive towards another state. Another conclusion might be that a state has less influence in the affairs of another state. Both conclusions could have as their causes either a military factor, an economic factor, a statement by a foreign diplomat, or some other aspect of the situation. As an example, consider the inference drawn by Sir George Buchanan, British ambassador in Russia, on January 1, 1913 in a letter to Grey. Buchanan argued that the recent reorganization of the Russian army would make France a more cooperative ally to Russia since France would now be more confident in Russian military capacity.[9] The inference cause was coded as a military matter. The conclusion was coded as "State [France] more likely to cooperate [with Russia]."

We can now ask whether military factors are much more important causes of particular sorts of conclusions. The answer, on the whole, is no. For instance, military factors account for approximately the same fraction of all inferences and of inferences about the likely use of military force. As the left-hand side bar in Figure 2.2 shows, when we consider conclusions related to the future use of military force, the percentages of inferences derived from military factors and from private diplomacy are each slightly greater than their shares of all security-related conclusions.

---

[9] Bourne and Watt (1983, part 1, series A, v. 6, p. 360).

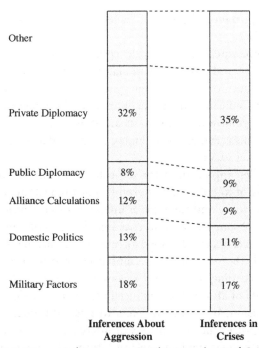

FIGURE 2.2 Inferences are Similar in and out of Crises

Note: Data comprise security-related inferences in internal, British Government documents in the *Confidential Print* between 1855 and 1914, categorized by the cause or ground for the inference, whether the inferences were about aggression and whether they occurred during international crises.

Similarly, military factors account for about the same fraction of inferences leading to conclusions related to alliance relationships, whether a country will offer a concession or not, or whether a country was likely to reciprocate cooperation. In forming all of these sorts of judgments, diplomats and leaders examine military factors, but they are by no means the first or last words on the subject.

The right-hand side bar in Figure 2.2 restricts attention to inferences drawn during military crises. It shows the percentages of the different categories of inference causes for those inferences that were drawn during a crisis. One might expect that military factors would play the most significant role here, but in fact, this is not the case.[10] Of the almost 900 inferences Britain made about states involved in crises, military factors account for about 17 percent. In understanding each other's intentions,

---

[10] Inferences were categorized as relating to a crisis if the state sending a signal or the state to which the signal was sent was involved in a crisis, according to the Militarized Interstate Dispute Dataset, in the month in which the event occurred which triggered the inference.

therefore, in crises and outside of them, states look to many more indicators than the balance of power and the interests that derive from it.[11]

A closer look within the broad category of inferences resulting from military factors is instructive. The British drew 38 percent of these inferences directly from an analysis of the balance of power at a particular point in time and another 15 percent from changes in the levels of arms production of other powers. Eighteen percent of inferences were related to mobilization decisions, 7 percent to military victories, and 13 percent to territorial transfers without military conflict.[12]

There are reasons this analysis of the frequency of sources of inference both understates and overstates the importance of military factors as a source of inferences. In one sense, the importance of military factors is understated because many inferences that could be drawn from the balance of forces are so clear that they need not be stated explicitly in internal government discussions. For instance, it is unlikely, today, that a small power will attack the United States. In fact, it is so unlikely that if we were to examine a record of US internal policy deliberation, we would see no such inference made explicitly in documents. In such cases, little uncertainty exists about whether the United States will be attacked. Therefore, this analysis of the relative frequency of different sorts of inferences really refers to instances when the material and ideational structure of the system leaves some scope to agency and thus creates uncertainty about the actions of international actors. Documentary evidence of a specific inference is more likely in cases where some member of the original, intended audience for the document might not have been sure of the inference. Of course, these are precisely the cases where understanding intentions is difficult and therefore requires analysis.

Within the set of cases where uncertainty exists about actor intentions, these simple percentages of the sources or causes of inferences may also overstate the importance of military factors. This is because when an action was anticipated in response to a change in the military situation, the military change was always coded as the cause unless some other cause of the inference was specifically mentioned. Thus, if a conquest by one power was thought to require a military response by another, military factors would be coded as the cause of the inference even though it is equally possible that the need to maintain reputation or honor are the real reasons that a military response is believed to be likely. The result is

---

[11] For a partly contrasting view, see Press (2005).

[12] Redeployments of forces accounted for another 4 percent of military derived inferences and alliances were sometimes discussed in terms of the increased capabilities that one side could marshal.

that a large number of inferences are listed as resulting from a military change when in fact the military change is probably only part of the ground for the inference.

As an example, consider the instance when a British official noted that France would be hostile to Germany after the latter took Alsace and Lorraine. This was coded as an inference based on the taking of territory even though French national honor and many other factors were involved. Similarly, the prediction that Germany would go to war if Russia attacked Austria in July 1914 was coded as resulting from a (yet to be realized) military change even though alliance politics likely played an important role in this judgement. These other grounds for inferences were only coded when they were explicitly mentioned in the document. In fact, in the majority of cases coded as resulting from a change in the military situation, an overall assessment suggests that a variety of other factors were essential to the drawing of the inference.[13]

There are many questions that these frequencies of the sources of inference do not answer, but they begin to give us an overall appreciation of how judgments of intention are formed. They do not tell us how important individual inferences were to decision makers as they weighed signals and indices from various sources. But they do show us the range of those sources and how often the makers of foreign policy thought that one aspect of situations or another clarified uncertainties. These frequencies demonstrate with all clarity that military factors play a role only alongside many other factors in shaping judgments of intention.

DOMESTIC POLITICS

There is a large literature on how the domestic political situation in one state will influence that state's foreign policy and what other states will believe about that state's policy. The autocratic or democratic nature of domestic institutions, the positioning of competing political parties, and the private interests of leaders are all thought to have substantial influence on the question of war or peace.[14] The inference dataset shows

---

[13] The dataset also covers episodes when countries actually went to war. In these, since conflict is taken for granted, military assessments naturally play large roles in the forming of judgments about what actors are most likely to do.

[14] Studies of how domestic politics influences foreign policy include Schultz (2001), Bueno de Mesquita et al. (1999), Smith (1998b), Milner (1997), Mansfield, Milner and Rosendorff (2002), Mo (1995), Lake (1992), Zaller (1992), Snyder (1991), Trager and Vavreck (2011), Allison (1971/1999), and Brown et al. (1996).

that states are indeed acutely concerned with the internal affairs of other states.

The aspect of the domestic affairs of other states that most preoccupied the British, however, is surprising. Inferences about public sentiment, which was often cited as a factor pushing for or against conflict, were particularly common, accounting for about two-thirds of inferences drawn from domestic politics. Interestingly, public sentiment was about three times as likely to be listed as a factor pushing a state towards increased aggression as it was to be suggested as a factor restraining a state from conflict. The remaining third of inferences drawn from domestic politics relate largely to judgments about the effects of party positioning and internal leadership struggles on a state's foreign policy. These most common types of domestic political inferences relate equally to the autocratic powers of the time (Austria, Germany, Russia, and France before 1877) and the one democracy in Europe other than Britain (France after 1877).[15] British statesmen took special notice, however, of the declarations of legislatures, as discussed below in the context of public diplomacy.

Overall, domestic political considerations, but particularly the sentiments of foreign publics in questions of whether a state would fight, had a significant influence on British perceptions of the intentions of all other powers during the entire period of study. Thus, British foreign affairs experts did not view public opinion as merely a function of elite manipulations; they assigned it causal force in influencing foreign policy outcomes in its own right.[16] Certainly, the British also understood that elite actions would sway popular opinion. In fact, they often discussed domestic political developments in foreign powers in the context of the sorts of public positions elites would need to take in order to prepare publics for chosen courses of action. It was frequently this need to prepare the public in specific ways that made domestic political maneuvering a signal of foreign policy intent.

ECONOMIC RELATIONS

According to Figure 2.1, economic factors might appear to play a small role in international affairs. This is, however, not the case, but the figure does show that a relatively small number of inferences were drawn

---

[15] On the similarity of domestic political signals drawn from democracies and autocracies, see Weeks (2008).

[16] For a contrasting view of the origins of popular opinion, see Zaller (1992) and Berinsky (2009), and for an analysis that reconciles elite and popular influences on foreign policy decision making, see Saunders (2015).

based only or primarily on economic factors. While many conflicts over the period centered on economic issues, economics was rarely enough, by itself, to cause an inference to be drawn. British diplomats generally drew inferences that other countries would contest particular economic resources, for instance, only after diplomats from those countries stated that that was their country's intention. Such cases were coded as private or public diplomacy. Economics also determines the long-run military potential of nations, but such inferences were categorized as based on evaluations of military rather than economic affairs. Thus, the data indicate that relatively few inferences were drawn from economic factors directly, not that economic factors are not an essential driver of the world system.

On the other hand, the data do contain 87 inferences based directly on economic matters. One diplomat concluded in 1905, for instance, that Russia would be able to continue the war with Japan as a result of the loans Russia had received from other powers.[17] Another diplomat concluded in 1909 that relations between Britain and Russia would improve as a result of the newly formed Russo-British Chamber of Commerce based in St. Petersburg.[18] Economic concessions were often seen as a sign of a desire for better relations, as when British diplomats inferred from Austria–Hungary's financial compensation of Turkey for Bosnia and Herzegovina in 1908 that Austria–Hungary wished to improve its relations with Turkey.[19] Sometimes, diplomats concluded that commercial production in one country that was sold to another was a sign of increasingly close relations between the two, as when the Italians sold shoes to the French military in 1871.[20] Finally, as one would expect, economic investments by a power in a region were seen as a sign of growing commitment to the region. In 1898, for instance, British diplomats saw Russian investments in the Persian Gulf and development of a railway system in Mesopotamia in this light and were concerned.[21] Such judgments based on economic factors were generally made only in the context

---

[17] Bourne and Watt (1983, part I, series A, v. 3, pp. 82, 105–106).

[18] Bourne and Watt (1983, part I, series A, v. 5, pp. 254–255). Austria–Hungary's tariff on British goods in 1876 was seen as a sign that Austria–Hungary might establish more distant relations with Britain. See Bourne and Watt (1987, part I, series F, v. 33, p. 158).

[19] Bourne and Watt (1987, part I, series F, v. 34, p. 273).

[20] Bourne and Watt (1983, part I, series F, v. 23, p. 451).

[21] Gillard (1990, part I, series B, v. 13, p. 191). Other examples include German investments in China in 1903 (Bourne and Watt 1995, part I, series E, v. 8, p. 29), further Russian investment in Persia in 1913 (Gillard 1990, part I, series B, v. 14, p. 353), and Russia's decision to limit the scope of the proposed railway in 1914, which the British greeted with relief (Gillard 1990, part I, series B, v. 14, p. 418) .

of a range of other considerations; they were often seen as corroborating evidence rather than as firm bases for judgments in themselves.

DIPLOMACY AND ALLIANCE CALCULATIONS

Inferences drawn from diplomacy – public and private, in speech and in writing – make up about half of all inferences over the 60-year time period. As Figure 2.2 shows, diplomacy of one variety or another accounts for an even higher percentage of inferences about whether states are more or less likely to use military force. Similarly, in crises, diplomacy accounts for more than half of all inferences drawn. Private diplomacy alone accounts for 35 percent of inferences about intentions in crises.

There are hundreds of important examples of diplomatic exchanges that shaped, in fundamental ways, how actors understood the international orders of their times. In the late nineteenth century, for instance, a great many conclusions were drawn by the British as a result of conversations with the Prussian Foreign Minister and later first German Chancellor Otto von Bismarck. When he told the British in private in 1867 that he preferred "to leave Belgium as it was, but that he would not interfere to prevent its annexation to France," the British concluded that this was an accurate representation of Prussian preferences and intentions.[22] A few weeks later, a separate conversation with Bismarck led to the conclusion that "Prussia, if supported by Southern Germany, would accept the war [with France], though [she was] anxious to avoid it if she could do so with honour." This judgment was proved prescient and precisely correct in the dispute surrounding the Spanish succession that led to the Franco-Prussian war three years later. At this same time in 1867, shortly after the war between Prussia and Austria–Hungary, conversations with Bismarck led the British to conclude that Prussia would likely conclude an alliance with Austria–Hungary.[23] Surprising as this judgment was following a war between those powers, it too was proven correct twelve years later when Bismarck signed the Alliance with Austria–Hungary that lasted until the Great War ended both empires.

Diplomatic exchanges sometimes settle questions, but more commonly, they influenced beliefs while leaving some questions open. For instance, in 1883 , when French representatives "spoke deliberately and more than once of the annexation of that country [Tonquin, in Vietnam]," the British concluded that France might indeed proceed with an annexation, something they had thought less likely before the French

---

[22] Krieger (1989, part 1 , series F, v. 9, p. 198).
[23] Krieger (1989, part 1, series F, v. 9, p. 202).

statements made to British Viscount Lyons in private. Although the British increased their estimate of the likelihood, however, they also expressed uncertainty about whether it would really come to pass.[24] In 1912, the British concluded from conversations with Russian officials that Russia was more likely to back down in the Balkan crisis because Russia was "anxious to avoid being dragged into a European war." [25]

Diplomacy is a particularly important source of reassurance. Of the nearly 400 instances where the British concluded that another European power was less likely to use force than the British had previously believed and where a ground for the inference could be determined,[26] nearly 70 percent are the direct result of some form of diplomacy and 46 percent are the result of private diplomacy in particular. Military factors accounted for about 9 percent of such inferences, public sentiment for 7 percent and other factors for substantially less than those.

An alliance relationship or even an informal understanding, which was categorized separately from private diplomacy but is closely related, was often cited as a reason for why countries would refrain from aggression or choose to cooperate. Thus, the British reasoned that an alliance with Russia would imply that Russia would only act defensively in Central Asia.[27] Similarly, in 1911, a tripartite agreement between England, France, and Italy was expected to result in cooperation that would secure each country's interests in the Mediterranean.[28]

The formation of an alliance between two powers was also often referenced as the cause of increased tension between one of those powers and another power. It was taken for granted, for instance, that a British alliance with Germany in the early twentieth century would sour relations between Britain and France, meaning that France would cease cooperating with Britain and would search for tighter alliance ties elsewhere.[29] And this was so for good reason, since it was also often expected that a state forming an alliance would be more hostile to states outside of the alliance. For instance, on several occasions, the argument was made that Germany would be more aggressive towards Russia and France once Germany had allied itself to England.[30]

---

[24] Krieger (1989, part 1, series F, v. 10, p. 194).

[25] Gooch and Temperley (1979, v. 9, part 2, p. 217).

[26] The source of the inference could not be determined in about 10 percent of cases.

[27] Gillard (1990, part 1, series B, v. 13, p. 86).

[28] Gooch and Temperley (1979, v. 9, part 1, pp. 315–316, 396–397, 428–429).

[29] Bourne and Watt (1990, part 1, series F, v. 20, pp. 85, 161). Agreements between Britain, France and Spain were also seen as a reason Germany searched for other states with whcih to ally in 1907. Bourne and Watt (1989, part 1, series F, v. 12, p. 256).

[30] Gooch and Temperley (1979, v. 6, p. 275).

But would the alliance of two powers lead other powers to be more or less aggressive towards the alliance members? The spiral model of international politics suggests the former, and the deterrence model the latter.[31] Consistent with both models, both expectations are found. On the one hand, Germany was expected to be less likely to attack France following a formal British alliance between France and Britain.[32] On the other, the British ambassador to France thought that an alliance between Russia, Japan, England, and France in the Far East would lead to increased German aggression in the region.[33] The expectation that an alliance would deter rather than provoke was the more common, however.[34]

These complexities of alliance politics in systems of states are a subject in their own right. Below, I shall focus on the closed door diplomacy of forging alliances rather than on the implications of public alliances as social facts once the alliance is formed. There is significant overlap between these areas of inquiry, however. As a result, the discussion of diplomatic approaches in Chapter 6 relates closely to the effects of alliances once agreements have been signed.

Of the inferences drawn from public diplomacy, a substantial percentage might be explained by a form of "audience" or "reputational" costs – states not wanting to renege on a public commitment out of fear either of the domestic political consequences or for their bargaining reputations. In some cases, the documentary evidence makes it clear beyond doubt that one of these mechanisms is at work. One British diplomat drew the following conclusion about the Austrian declaration of war in 1914: "There is ... no step which [Britain] could usefully take to stop war ... " since the "Austro-Hungarian Government [was] now fully committed by the declaration of war."[35] Had Austria–Hungary declined to prosecute the war, the author implies, there would have been domestic and international costs and the prospect of those costs convinced him that the Austrians meant what they said.

On the whole, however, the documentary material provides relatively little evidence of how inferences are drawn from public diplomacy. In more than half of the cases where some inference was drawn, the logic on which the inference is based is not addressed. In about 20 percent

---

[31] Jervis (1976, pp. 58–113), Levy (1988), Kydd (2005), Braumoeller (2008).
[32] Gooch and Temperley (1979, v. 3, p. 170), Bourne and Watt (1989, part 1, series F, v. 12, p. 176).
[33] Bourne and Watt (1989, part 1, series F, v. 12, p. 367).
[34] For statistical analysis of this question, see Leeds et al. (2002).
[35] *British Sessional Papers*, 1914, v. CI, p. 60.

of cases, the fact that a statement was made by a particularly influential leader was noted. In another 13 percent of cases, inferences were drawn from the actions of legislatures, and in 5 percent of cases from statements made in the foreign press. One particular mechanism is, however, discussed with relative frequency: leaders were sometimes seen to be preparing their publics to have a negative or positive view of another country in preparation for military action or some other shift in foreign policy. Reasoning of this sort is found in 9 percent of the cases of public diplomacy inferences where a basis for the inference was explicitly stated.

Many of the private diplomacy inferences were made in contexts in which the signaler had no particular interest in convincing the receiver of the signal of anything at all. Such statements made outside of negotiations account for 14 percent of inferences made from private diplomacy and one can assume that diplomats learned much else from their encounters with each other that was not thought worthy of mention in official correspondence. An example of what could be learned from fellow diplomats outside of the context of negotiatinos comes from January of 1914, when the German ambassador told the British that Austria had given Serbia the task of maintaining order in Albania. Since the Germans and British were not negotiating with each other in this context, the Germans had no reason to deceive and the British had no reason for skepticism.[36] Similarly, just prior to the Franco-Prussian war, a Russian diplomat told the British that Russia would remain neutral in the war and the British concluded that this was so. Russia had relatively little to gain from deceiving the British and was not bargaining with the British over any particular issue.[37] When the Austrians then told the British that if Austria did abandon neutrality, it would be in favor of Germany and not France, this too was believed.[38] These examples show that such statements outside of bargaining contexts can convey significant information that informs leaders' understandings of the dynamics of the international system of their times.

A substantial number of private diplomacy inferences could plausibly be described as deriving from the perceived desire of signalers to maintain reputations for honesty,[39] and in almost 4 percent of private diplomacy inferences, documentary evidence suggests beyond doubt that some sort of calculations based on the reputation of the signaler are at work. From this latter group, about half are related to a reputation for honesty and about half are related to prestige or to reputations for resolve. Diplomats

---

[36] Gooch and Temperley (1979, v. 10, pt. 1, p. 90).
[37] Bourne and Watt (1991, part I, series F, v. 31, p. 215).
[38] Bourne and Watt (1991, part I, series F, v. 31, p. 270).
[39] Sartori (2005).

and leaders drew conclusions such as that representatives of a state would be demanding in the future because they had been demanding in the past, and that a sovereign's dignity would or would not permit a concession if an adversary also made a concession. Jervis (1997) argues that states that make concessions or are caught in a bluff may be more aggressive in the future in order to reestablish their bargaining reputations. This "deterrence paradox" was rarely seen, however. In only a few instances, British diplomats concluded that because concessions had been made in the past, they would *not* be made in the future. Also rarely seen was the conclusion that because a state had misled other actors that the state was *not* willing to fight when it was, the state was believed generally more aggressive.

One example of an inference resulting from a belief in a sovereign's desire to maintain a reputation for honesty occurred during the prologue to the Second Italian War of Independence in which France colluded with Sardinia to strip Austria of its Italian provinces. Shortly before the French were revealed to have aggressive designs against Austria, the British ambassador to France, Lord Cowley, who had at times maintained to his own government that the French had no such intentions, asked the French Emperor for a guarantee. Cowley had staked his reputation on his report that the French had pacific intentions, he told the emperor, and he as much as asked the Emperor to stake his own reputation as well. The emperor's impassioned answer that Cowley was indeed "dans le vrai" convinced Cowley that he was – even though he wasn't.[40]

A particularly telling inference along these lines comes from the "Great Game" played by Britain and Russia in Asia. In 1873, Russia had committed not to acquire the Uzbek city of Khiva, but was thought likely to conquer it as result of military operations in the area. The British concluded – naturally, one might say – that Russia would raze the entire city to the ground, if it should fall into Russian hands, so that Russia could not be said to have violated its commitment.[41] In the fact, Russia did take the city, but allowed it to remain independent and unburned. On the whole, states seem to perceive each other to be especially concerned with their reputations for keeping promises, perhaps more so than their reputations for following through on threats.[42]

---

[40] British Parliament (1859, v. XXXII, pp. 191–192). Cowley's views vacillated to some degree. See British Parliament (1859, v. XXXII, p. 119).

[41] Bourne and Watt (1985, part I, series B, v. 11, p. 129).

[42] Levy et al. (2015) show experimentally, however, that Americans today punish leaders more for backing down from a threat than for breaking a promise to stay out of a conflict.

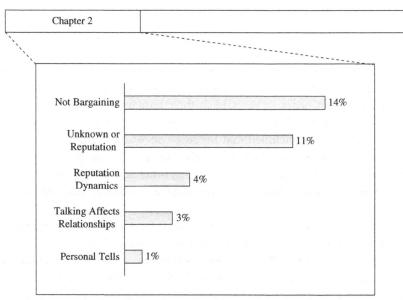

FIGURE 2.3 How Private Diplomacy Works

Note: The proportions shown are of the mechanisms by which private-diplomacy, security-related inferences were drawn in internal, British Government documents in the *Confidential Print* between 1855 and 1914. The bar at the top represents the total number of mechanism codings in the inference dataset; the area in the Chapter 2 portion represents the fraction of these mechanisms addressed in the chapter

Figure 2.3 shows the proportion of private diplomacy inferences that are most naturally explained by statements being made outside of a negotiating context or by states' perceived desires to maintain a reputation for keeping commitments. Note that the bar at the top of the figure represents the entire set of private diplomacy inferences and the left-hand portion shows the fraction discussed in this chapter. Fully 14 percent of private diplomacy inferences were drawn from statements made when neither side was attempting to win a better deal for its side. In 11 percent of cases, no explanation or ground for the inference was offered. Some of these may be inferences based on reputation since it may be that diplomats might have believed that no further explanation was required in such cases. The figure also indicates that British statesmen drew a substantial number of inferences from the bare fact that two countries were known to be engaged in diplomatic talks. In most of these cases, the British speculated that talks would produce an agreement that would draw the countries closer together, but in a few instances the British believed it more likely that the talks would produce a breach in relations. Together, the mechanisms shown in the figure and the inferences made without any discussion of the ground for the inference account for about a third of all inferences drawn from private diplomacy over the period. Chapters 3 through 6 are about the other mechanisms of inference from private diplomatic communications that diplomats and leaders use to develop understandings of the plans and intentions of other actors. Each of these chapters contains a figure similar to Figure 2.3 that illustrates the set of inferences that the model of the chapter appears to explain.

OTHER SOURCES OF INFERENCES – MADE AND UNMADE

A variety of inference types occur less frequently, but with some regularity. The British concluded on occasion that because a state had stood firm or backed down in the past concerning a particular question that the state would do the same again in the future.[43] For instance, in Eyre Crowe's famous memorandum of New Year's Day, 1907, the author argued that Germany's past actions demonstrated that "in no other country is there a conviction so deeply rooted in the very body and soul of all classes of the population that the ... realization of national ideals rest absolutely on the readiness of every citizen in the last resort to stake himself and his State on their assertion and vindication." Crowe concluded, based on a review of past actions, that Germany was more aggressive than other nations.[44] Similarly, when the British saw France proceeding in Morocco as France had done in Tunis, the British concluded in 1884 that France would seek to make Morocco a protectorate of France.[45] Overall, about 3 percent of inferences resulted explicitly from a belief that a state would take the same actions in the future as it had in the past.

The personal characteristics of individual leaders were another relatively frequent ground for inferences (almost 100 or 3 percent of all inferences). In 1870, for example, it was assumed that a Prussian ruler on the throne of Spain would be sympathetic to Prussia,[46] and in 1904, it was believed that Franz Ferdinand would be more aggressive towards Italy upon assuming power in Austria.[47] These inferences are closely related to diplomatic signals because, very often, the inferences were

---

[43] This contrasts somewhat with the argument in Press (2005), although some instances cited here represent the British drawing the conclusion that another power would behave in a certain way on *exactly* the same questions, rather than on questions that are merely similar in kind.

[44] Gooch and Temperley (1979, v. 3, p. 405).

[45] Krieger (1989, part 1, series F, v. 10, p. 253).

[46] Bourne and Watt (1991, part I, series F, v. 31, pp. 8, 37).

[47] Bourne and Watt (1987, part 1, series F, v. 33, p. 402).

made when a new leader took power and therefore must have been derived more from what the leader had said, in public and in private, rather than from anything else the leader had done before his or her decisions had the force of state behind them.

In addition to considering what inferences diplomats and leaders draw, it is interesting to consider what inferences are not made as often as one might expect. Most surprisingly, there is little evidence that normative arguments made by diplomats or the giving of reasons for actions serve as important grounds for inferences. This is surprising because it is equally clear that "argumentative battle" comprises a great part of what diplomats do.[48] And yet, diplomats almost never explicitly draw inferences from the quality of the argument offered in support of a position.[49] They will note that a demand, for instance, has been made, but only very rarely discuss whether the reasons offered for the demand are such that the demand is made in earnest. There is thus very little evidence that the variation in the ways that diplomats frame disputes influences the conclusions their counterparts consciously draw even though a great deal of diplomatic activity is devoted to framing.[50]

There are probably several reasons we do not find documentary evidence for such inferences. The first is that the giving of reasons for actions is a constant feature of international politics, and thus if it were not done effectively, significant conclusions would be drawn. But since this task is always performed, usually by competent state representatives, the fact that some reason can be offered does not surprise and little is made of it. Put differently, diplomats are expected to give justificatory reasons for the actions of the states they represent, diplomats do give such reasons, and justificatory reasons can be offered for most of the courses of

---

[48] See, for instance, Stein (2000), Goddard (2009), Krebs and Jackson (2007), and Mitzen (2006, 2005). The phrase "argumentative battle" comes from a British diplomat describing the willingness of a French diplomat to give reasons for the French annexation of Savoy in 1860 (Krieger 1989, part 1, series F, v. 9, p. 119).

[49] On some occasions, we see concern for the precedent that will be set by protesting or not protesting the justificatory reasons offered by another state. A clear example comes from Lord Russell's concern about the French justification for annexing the Savoy in 1860: " ...the reference to the Treaty of 1814 is disquieting. For other cessions, on other frontiers of France, were made in 1815; and the plea now put forth of the severity of the Treaty of 1815, if admitted, might be used in support of other arrangements which might be proposed, and which might alarm susceptibilities." Krieger (1989, part 1, series F, v. 9 p. 128).

[50] Note that the view expressed here is consistent with Hurd's (2015, pp. 49–50) observation that "the argumentation that makes up diplomacy does not move toward consensus ...diplomacy anticipates contestation over who is or is not complying with the law." On framing in international negotiation, see Schelling (1966, pp. 35–91).

action *that states actually entertain.* The fact that no justification could be offered for certain actions may be the reason those actions are not taken. Even Adolf Hitler was careful to offer justifications for aggressive acts based on the need to protect ethnic minorities.[51] These statements were taken quite seriously as public justifications, but only the German claims themselves, and not the justificatory arguments for making them, were discussed as indicators of German intentions. Thus, if a nation's diplomats *did not* offer a justification for their state's actions, this would likely arouse alarm in other states and result in a variety of conclusions being drawn. But since justifications are offered, as expected, such inferences are not drawn.[52]

A second reason we find little documentary evidence for this class of inferences is that much is simply taken for granted in the writing of memoranda and letters. Consider the British inference in 1903 that other powers would intervene if Turkey were to commit atrocities in the Balkans.[53] This is coded as an inference about what would happen as a result of military action, but it is likely that a moral consensus about appropriate actions for states also played a substantial role in the British conclusion. Because this is not stated explicitly by the author of the document, however, it is not reflected in the dataset. Thus, permissive causes of inferences are probably often excluded from the data. Rules of right conduct may fall into this category; essential to understanding behavior but assumed in discourse. Yet a third factor may be that moral consensuses shape foreign policy, but they are largely constructed at the domestic level rather than through state interaction.[54] This is consistent with the numerous inferences about international intentions that derived from observations about the sentiments of foreign publics and other internal political matters.

The framing of disputes is also likely to influence diplomats and leaders in ways of which they are not consciously aware. Psychological research has shown that holding a hot cup of coffee leads study participants to evaluate others as being warmer and less selfish.[55] The presence of a briefcase as opposed to a backpack in a room caused participants in

---

[51] Goddard (2015).

[52] For a discussion of this point in the context of Russia's decision not to contest the expansion of Prussian influence in 1860s and 70s, see Trager (2012, p. 261).

[53] British Parliament (1902, v. CX, p. 649).

[54] Fanis (2011). For a contrasting view, see Wendt (1999). On the whole, norms are very little discussed as a cause of inferences, but this again often appears to be because the rules of interaction are taken for granted rather than because they were not thought to influence behavior.

[55] Williams and Bargh (2008).

another study to negotiate harder.[56] Viewing a random number prior to agreeing on a price serves as an unconscious anchor in the mind, affecting the outcome of the negotiation. The impact of such factors on decisions is large, and often still holds if participants are aware of their own potential biases.[57] It is certainly the case that such factors influence leaders and diplomats without their knowledge, and therefore, important influences on perceptions will not be catalogued in the documentary record. This is a significant area for continuing research.

Taking such observations into account, one might wonder whether the reasons given in documents actually correspond to the true grounds of inferences made. It may be that the authors of the documents do not fully know their own minds. Or these authors may be expressing an opinion for a political reason rather than because it accurately reflects their thinking on the subject at hand. Relatedly, Holmes (2013) shows that face-to-face interaction allows for communication through physiological signals that are hard to fake and are immediately interpretable, but explicit inferences from such signals are almost never found in the documentary record. Although it is possible that unstated reasons are the true grounds for inference, the perceptions of individuals only result in government actions when these individuals carry the day in arguments among decision makers. Analyzing what decision makers say to each other, therefore, may be most essential for understanding the origins of policies. Nevertheless, for scholars of international affairs, understanding not just what factors affect the judgments of particular individuals, but what factors affect individual evaluations in ways that also influence state policies, remains an important area for research.[58]

FREQUENCY VERSUS DECISIVENESS

These considerations allow us to form an impression of the pathways through which states make calculations about each other's plans. When a class of inferences is commonly made, discussed, written down, and passed around among the makers of foreign policy, it is likely that the effect of such considerations on deliberation is substantial.[59] One might wonder, however, whether some categories occur more frequently while

---

[56] Kay et al. (2004).

[57] For an extraordinary overview of the psychology literature in these areas, see Kahneman (2011). The canonical work on the impact of such biases on international negotiations is Jervis (1976).

[58] Hall and Yarhi-Milo (2012), Wong (2016).

[59] Psychological research on the effects of frequency of experience on mental calculations also suggest that oft made arguments will have an impact even among those who

other types of inferences are more decisive when they do occur. In order to examine this possibility, inferences drawn between 1900 and 1914 were coded by degree of certainty. For instance, when a British diplomat concluded that another country would take a particular action, the inference was coded as having a higher certainty level than when the diplomat concluded that another country "might" or was "likely" to take an action.[60]

All categories of inferences resulted in a range of certainty levels. Inferences related to military factors stood out as occasioning the highest levels of certainty. A random sample of 106 military-related inferences between 1900 and 1914 indicates that 75 percent were at the "near certain" level. Among private diplomacy inferences, the percentage of near-certain inferences was lower, at only 60 percent. While inferences from private diplomacy tend to be less certain, however, there are nevertheless more near-certain inferences related to private diplomacy than related to military matters. Thus, while the more infrequent inferences from military matters have a more significant effect when they do occur, inferences drawn from diplomatic exchanges appear to have the greater overall effect on leader perceptions. In Chapter 9, I return to questions related to the certainty level following public versus private diplomatic statements.

WHAT WE KNOW SO FAR

This basic analysis of British inferences over 60 years tells us a great deal. It provides an overview of the sources of perceptions of intention in the international system. It demonstrates the variety of factors that influence calculations and provides reason to doubt the veracity of some arguments that particular sources of perception dominate others. The international environment is not constructed by calculations of power and material interest alone. Diplomatic processes of communication and interpretation inform every aspect of state expectations about the international system.

Overall, the documentary record provides support for many different theories of signaling and inference. When states are engaged in armed conflict, military factors are the primary sources of inferences about each other's behavior and intentions, but this is not so at other times. Popular opinion about foreign affairs is an important indicator of what states will do. Economic factors are not. Though many disputes revolve

---

disagree with the thrust of the argument. See Kahneman (2011), but cf. Yarhi-Milo (2013a).

[60] The coding rules for these variables are described in Appendices B and C.

around conflicts of economic interests, these factors are not seen as determining behavior in themselves. Foreign policy analysts use other measures to infer whether a particular economic interest will be defended or conceded.

A great many inferences are drawn from diplomatic exchanges, both those that occur in public fora and those conducted in private. Diplomacy conducted behind closed doors is the source of more inferences, and more near-certain inferences, than any other category of inferences cause. Diplomats and leaders learn alike from the statements of allies and adversaries. Thus, the incentives to mislead in international affairs do not preclude states from learning from private conversations.

Several specific sorts of inferences from private diplomacy have been discussed in this chapter. These cover about a quarter of all inference drawn from private diplomatic encounters. In an additional tenth of private diplomacy inference cases, the author of the document gives no indication of the reason the inference was drawn. That leaves about two-thirds of the inferences from private diplomacy to be explained. We know that they occurred, but we have not yet developed theories to explain how or why. The next four chapters describe four mechanisms that together offer convincing explanations for the majority of these unexplained diplomatic inferences. The conclusion of each of these chapters takes stock of the set of inferences from the dataset that are closely related to the signaling mechanism described in the chapter.

PART I

THEORY

3

The Scope of Demands

When the kingdom of Piedmont-Sardinia dreamt of forming Italy in 1859, it set about forging a secret alliance with France, inspiring insurrections in Austria's Italian provinces, and conducting military maneuvers close to the Austrian border. The Austrians mobilized in response and war appeared likely. A compromise proposal was floated by the Powers according to which the Austrians would pull their troops back from the boarder in return for Piedmontese demobilization. In private diplomatic communications, the Austrians rejected this compromise, insisting the Piedmontese demobilize first. In cases such as this, costless communication is difficult, and is often thought to be impossible. All parties knew what the Austrians wanted; what they did not know initially was whether Austria was willing to fight rather than accept a compromise. Why should words uttered in private convince anyone? Austria had incentive to make the more substantial demand even if it were not willing to fight over the matter. But nevertheless, observers did learn from the Austrian refusal. The British ambassador to Austria even concluded that he had "not the smallest hope that the Austrian Government will agree to any such [compromise]."[1] How did observers reach this conclusion?

The ambassador may have drawn this inference because he believed that Austria, having made the threat, would not have wanted to be caught in a bluff, but this could be said of every threat and diplomats sometimes believe that threats lack credibility. Although a range of factors certainly affected the ambassador's conclusion, he likely made the following simple inference: in demanding more, Austria had given up the opportunity to achieve a compromise solution that Austria believed Piedmont was much more likely to have conceded without fighting; therefore, Austria is resolved to fight for the more substantial demand. Through this

---

[1] *British Parliamentary Papers*, 1859, v. XXXII, 213.

mechanism, the scope of state demands commonly conveys information about resolve to adversaries in international politics.

Despite literature in international relations that argues the contrary, such simple inferences are often quite rational in diplomatic relations. This chapter analyzes a model similar to Fearon (1995) in order to demonstrate that higher demands can increase perceptions of a state's resolve to fight for more favorable outcomes when two conditions hold. First, when negotiations produce a peaceful outcome, both sides must share in the bargaining surplus from avoiding war. This tends to occur when goods are only partially divisible or when settling on a negotiated solution is the outcome of a bargaining process in which both sides take part, rather than a take-it-or-leave-it offer from one side. Second, higher demands must be less likely to be accepted even when the associated threat is credible. This condition can hold when compromise may prove impossible even when the sides know that the alternative is war.[2] Many approaches to modeling international negotiation produce dynamics that satisfy these conditions in equilibrium; one such model is analyzed below.

These two signaling conditions imply that less resolved signalers do not necessarily have incentive to imitate the signals sent by more resolved signalers. The first signaling condition ensures that a compromise has value to types that prefer the compromise to war. Since a credible, high demand will not necessarily be accepted according to the second condition, the two conditions imply that equilibria exist in which less resolved types must weigh an intuitive tradeoff: demanding more holds the possibility of receiving a larger concession from an adversary, but also implies a lower probability of receiving somewhat less without having to fight for it. Thus, when states do make large demands, they run a risk, and since states would not be willing to run this risk unless a large concession (rather than an intermediate compromise) were sufficiently important, these threats convey information.

These dynamics allow us to understand when offers of compromise will be made even though they signal a measure of weakness by increasing an adversary's perception that the compromising state would be willing to make an even greater concession.[3] This occurs only when an adversary

---

[2] Note that, as in the Fearon model, the options available to the sides must be more than simply making or not making a particular demand. If the target of a threat has only this binary choice, there can be no question of the *scope* of the demand. The result is that signaling will not be possible in contexts like the one analyzed here.

[3] Slantchev (2010b) and Trager (2010) show why states would sometimes feign weakness in order to catch an adversary unprepared, but not why states might allow an adversary to infer that the signaling state is weaker than it is even when the adversary cannot make substantial preparations for conflict.

is believed unlikely to accede to maximalist demands. In such cases, states that are unwilling to fight if they are offered no concession and those states that would choose not to fight if they are offered just a moderate concession both send the same signal of willingness of to compromise. Only states that are willing to fight unless they receive a large concession send that signal. The less resolved states accept the appearance of weakness because they understand that making a maximalist demand runs a substantial risk of receiving no concession at all whereas making a moderate demand implies a higher likelihood of a moderate concession. This is why states are sometimes willing to make offers that signal a form of weakness. If, on the other hand, an adversary is believed likely to make a maximalist concession, offers of compromise either will not be made, or if they are, they will not lead to the inference that the conceding state is more likely to be willing to make further concessions. The reason is that, in this context, states that are unwilling to fight if they are offered no concession nevertheless make maximalist demands; if offers of compromise are made at all, and they may not be, such offers will be made only by a state that is willing to fight unless it receives some measure of compromise. An adversary will be able to conclude following a moderate demand, therefore, that a moderate concession is required to avoid conflict.

INFERENCES BASED ON THE SCOPE OF THREATS

A debate continues over how and whether adversaries learn from diplomatic conversations that occur away from the public eye, and more generally, whether these encounters play an important role in constructing the international environment of states. Intuition suggests that adversaries will not take each other's statements at face value, but, in one model meant to represent international bargaining, Fearon (1995) showed additionally that the scope of costless demands would convey nothing whatsoever to an adversary. The analysis below illuminates the assumptions on which this conclusion rests and demonstrates a simple rationalist mechanism through which the scope of costless demands can convey information in many international contexts.

The models described and analyzed in this book follow in the tradition begun in the seminal paper by Crawford and Sobel (1982). They showed that actions that in themselves have no effect whatever on player utilities and options can nevertheless have substantial effect on the equilibria of game theoretic models. These "costless signals" affect equilibrium behavior by conveying information. These models have been thought to represent talking well, since speech often appears to have substantial effects on outcomes without directly affecting material contexts, or actor preferences and options. The effects that speech has on the course of events is usually the result of how other actors respond to it rather than a direct effect of the speech itself.

Most of the literature in economics and political science takes a different approach, modeling talk as costly in some fashion. By far the largest literature of this variety uses variants of alternating offer Rubinstein (1982) models. These articles have examined how player preferences over bargaining failure affect the results of bargaining, whether resolve can be signaled through delay in reaching agreements, the conditions under which bargaining outcomes will be efficient and other topics. In international relations scholarship, models that follow this approach include Powell (1988, 2002, 2004a, 2004b, 2006), Slantchev (2003), and Leventoglu and Tarar (2008). I do not follow this approach for several reasons. The most important is that these models are not designed to address questions related to when talking conveys information and effects the course of events as a result. On the contrary, these models assume that talking does so and therefore cannot pose the question.[4]

The question of how the scope of demands might convey information, the central question addressed in this chapter, has, however, been examined in this literature. One answer is that higher demands can convey resolve because such demands signal a willingness to accept *delay* in reaching a negotiated solution or even risk reaching a solution at all.[5] Because this literature assumes that demands inherently affect actor payoffs and the choices available to actors later on, it has not addressed the conditions under which higher demands convey information in this fashion. Below, I describe such conditions. I also give conditions under

---

[4] Relatedly, these models often assume a discount factor shrinks the benefits to be negotiated over in each round of negotiations. Thus, a bargaining tactic such as making a high demand has a direct cost resulting from the delay in reaching an agreement. In international politics, diplomats and leaders are sometimes keenly concerned to avoid delay, but this is a result of actions they believe other actors may take, not because the rewards of concluding an agreement are shrinking. Even though scholars often study the case where the discount factor has almost no effect (in the limit as the discount factor goes to one), the presence of the discount factor nevertheless drives the results of the model. This is particularly clear when the players are allowed to have different discount factors: even though the discount factors are arbitrarily close to one, a higher discount factor still produces substantial gains in the bargaining outcome. While discount factors have been interpreted in terms of the degree of player "patience," there is no evidence that degree of patience is a frequent, principal driver of international political outcomes.

[5] These models are reviewed in Ausubel, Cramton and Deneckere (2002). Note that studies have linked the scope of demands during wartime to the strength or resolve of the demanding side. Examples include Wittman (1979) and Reiter (2009). In these cases, costs may be incurred for each moment of delay, and so it may be reasonable to model such communication as a process that is inherently costly.

which higher demands may, in special circumstances, actually decrease adversaries' estimates of resolve. The approach employed in this chapter does not rely on a discount factor to generate a cost to making a risky offer that is unlikely to be accepted. As such, the costless signaling models are able to explain how the scope of demands can conveys information even when there is no direct cost to sending a misleading signal. Following the costless signaling tradition, the models presented in this chapter assist in understanding when relations are too adversarial to allow for communication and when, despite appearances, they are not.[6]

The models that bear the most similarity to the models described in this chapter are Farrell and Gibbons (1989), Ramsay (2011), Sartori (2005), Kurizaki (2007), and Trager (2011). Unlike the first two, the approach used here does not rely on multiple equilibria in the game without costless signals to demonstrate that costless signals can affect equilibrium behavior. The models in this chapter also employ a standard crisis bargaining framework often used to analyze credibility in international relations rather than a double auction framework from the economics literature. Unlike Sartori (2005) and Kurizaki (2007), the models below allow costless demands to have scope rather than allowing only a choice to threaten or not. In all of these works, signaling occurs through different mechanisms from those analyzed here.[7] Finally, unlike Trager (2011), the model below applies to cases where the players have opposite preferences over peaceful settlement outcomes on a single issue dimension. For instance, both may prefer to annex as much territory in dispute near their borders as possible. The amounts of territory demanded are questions of degree. In such cases, the model described below appears to be a good representation of international negotiation. If players may have strong or weak preferences over multiple issue dimensions, the model described in Trager (2011) may be more appropriate, although the mechanisms that allow for signaling are similar to those described here.[8]

---

[6] Understanding when relations are truly zero sum turns out to be far more difficult than it appears at first glance. See Axelrod (1970).

[7] Note that a number of models that allow states to choose the scope of a demand are not intended to analyze whether the scope conveys information. In fact, in these models, the state to which the demand is made has complete information about the preferences of the demanding state. Examples include Powell (2004a) and Filson and Werner (2008).

[8] Even in negotiations in which separate issues appear to be involved, the model presented below is appropriate as long as the preference ranking of each side over the possible peaceful outcomes is common knowledge and the two states' rankings are precisely reversed.

A striking example of the signaling context analyzed below comes from the negotiations prior to the first Gulf War. In February of 1991, the US promised to begin a ground offensive unless Iraq withdrew from Kuwait City in two days and from Kuwait in seven. The US demand consisted of two essential parts: the requirement to leave Kuwait and the specific timetable for withdrawal. Iraq had already offered to leave Kuwait in 21 days and Kuwait City in four. The importance of the second US demand for a shorter timetable was that Iraq would not be able to unwind its positions and leave with its equipment in the shorter time frame. By this point in the conflict, a key US goal was to degrade the ability of the Iraqi army to threaten its neighbors. The Iraqi regime accepted the first US demand, but not the accelerated timetable.[9] The US–Iraqi negotiations, conducted through Soviet mediation, concerned questions of degree: Iraq could not agree to the timetable, but refuse to leave Kuwait. Iraq was largely convinced by this stage that the US would fight to restore Kuwaiti independence, but Iraqi leaders and analysts did not know whether the US would go to war rather than accept the Iraqi timetable for withdrawal.[10] On February 23, the US bluntly informed the Soviets in a private exchange that the US would not accept the Iraqi timetable. The Soviets promptly communicated to the Iraqis that the US would invade unless Iraq agreed to a more accelerated timetable for withdrawal.[11]

Costless statements in such contexts can convey information. Signaling is likely to be particularly effective when the signaling state is believed likely to be resolved to fight at least for a partial concession from the second state, and the second state is believed sufficiently likely to be resolved to fight rather than make a full concession to the signaling state. The claim is not, however, that in such cases states are likely to reach a compromise, which would be unsurprising. It is rather the quite different claim that in this context, attempts at communication will change the threatened states beliefs about the threatening states intentions. In fact, in such cases, when the threatening state demands a full concession, the threatened state will know for sure that the threat is credible even though it did not believe the threatening state would fight for sure for a full concession before the threat was made.

To understand the intuition for the signaling dynamics described below, consider what the Iraqi government could have learned from the

---

[9] Even after the war began, when the Iraqi regime announced it was abandoning Kuwait, President Bush said US forces would continue to attack Iraqi soldiers who did not lay down their arms. See Pape (1996, 216–219).

[10] Woods (2008, Chapter 8).

[11] *The New York Times*, The Eve of War: Four Days of Diplomacy, January 19, 2011.

scope of the US demand. First, note that Iraq was itself very unlikely to comply with a demand that involved such a significant degrading of its military capability. Second, with the US insisting on the accelerated timetable, the Iraqi government would be hesitant to unilaterally remove its troops from Kuwait at the slower timetable because Iraqi forces leaving their chosen and prepared positions would have been the more vulnerable to US attack. Thus, by insisting on the greater Iraqi concession of the accelerated timetable, the US ensured that no partial Iraqi concession would be forthcoming. Suppose, by contrast, that the US government insisted only on the slower Iraqi withdrawal. This, the Iraqis were clearly much more likely to do. From the point of view of the US government, it only made sense to insist on the accelerated timetable if the accelerated timetable were of sufficient importance to US policy makers. Put in this way, it is obvious that Iraqi decision makers could conclude from US statements that US resolve not to make a concession was high. In diplomatic crises, similar dynamics to these recur. Of course, governments are always confronted with a range of signals and indices; this is but one.

A BARGAINING MODEL WITH A DISCRETE SET OF COMPROMISE OUTCOMES

In order to relate the discussion closely to previous literature on these topics, the model I shall describe is similar to the well-known model of cheap talk communication in Fearon (1995), except in these three respects:(1) states have a discrete set of compromise solutions available, (2) both sides are uncertain about the other's resolve, and (3) states are uncertain about each others utilities over compromise outcomes rather than over each other's costs of war.[12] These modifications in the model often better fit the facts of international politics. For one, negotiations often center on a few discrete options, and this is sometimes because only a discrete set of options are practical. (I consider an extension to a divisible issue space in Appendix A.) For another, no statesman could claim to have certain knowledge of how adversaries weigh proposed compromise solutions against one another and this is precisely what diplomats often strive to communicate.[13]

---

[12] O'Neill (2001) argues against thinking about the "issue space" negotiated over as a space in which one could define a sensible measure of distance between the possible outcomes. I take the standard approach here for simplicity and, again, to relate the results to previous scholarship.

[13] With additional restrictions on the type utility functions, this model is equivalent to one in which uncertainty is modeled as being over the costs of war. The choice to

As in Fearon (1995), the game described here has two players, a "Signaler" and a "Target" indexed by $i \in I \equiv \{s, t\}$, and four stages. In the first stage, Nature draws utility functions $u_i^z(x)$ for each player i over outcomes in the bargaining space $X \equiv [0, 1]$ (with generic element x) according to the independent, commonly known, discrete distribution functions $h_i(u_i^z)$. For each player, there are three possible utility functions, so $h_i(u_i^z)$ has support $\{u_i^l, u_i^m, u_i^h\}$. The superscripts l, m, and h will be used in several places in the model and can be interpreted as "low," "medium," and "high." In reference to the utility functions, the superscripts indicate the level of resolve of the player in a sense described below. The players have directly opposed preferences over the set of compromise outcomes so that, for all z, $u_s^z(x)$ is strictly increasing in x, while $u_t^z(x)$ is strictly decreasing in x. Player utility functions are the private information of each player.

In the second stage, the Signaler has the opportunity to send a message $y \in M$ to the Target from a large but finite set of messages. Assume that $m, h \in M$ s.t. $m \neq h$. After the message is sent, the Target chooses one of three settlement outcomes $\{x_l, x_m, x_h\}$, where $0 < x_l < x_m < x_h < 1$.[14] In the final stage, the Signaler chooses $r \in R \equiv \{0, 1\}$, where $r = 1$ indicates a decision to initiate a war and $r = 0$ indicates peace, and then the game ends. If war occurs, the Signaler wins with probability p, the Target wins with probability $1 - p$, and the victorious player attains its most preferred outcome in X, 1 for the Signaler and 0 for the Target. Players have commonly known costs of fighting c_i. $\mu(u_s^z \mid y)$ represents the Target's updated beliefs about the Signaler's type u_s^z given signal y in a particular perfect Bayesian equilibrium. The game is represented in Figure 3.1. To highlight the elements of the game most clearly, only one of the branches at the Signaler's messaging node and the Target's response nodes are shown. The superscripts on player utility functions at peaceful outcomes and the initial move by Nature are also suppressed.

In order to relate this model closely to other models in the literature, I shall assume that uncertainty about preferences relates only to player preferences over the compromise outcomes rather than to the extreme

---

model uncertainty as being over player utilities for compromise outcomes was made largely for clarity of exposition. On this point, see the discussion of the Fearon model in Appendix A.

[14] The assumption that the Target cannot choose the extremes of the bargaining space, which would guarantee war for sure by the assumptions made below, simplifies the cases to consider in the analysis. This assumption does not have substantively important implications, however, and in particular, allowing the Target to choose an extreme outcome does not eliminate costless signaling equilibria in the model.

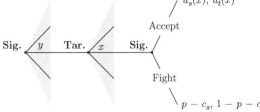

FIGURE 3.1 The Signaling Game

outcomes. Thus, we can set $u_s^z(0) = u_t^z(1) = 0$ and $u_s^z(1) = u_t^z(0) = 1$ for all z. This implies that expected utilities for war are $w_s = p - c_s$ for the Signaler and $w_t = 1 - p - c_t$ for the Target.

I also make several assumptions about player preferences. First, players prefer war to their least preferred outcome in X (formally, $w_i > 0\ \forall i$) and prefer at least one of the three possible negotiated outcomes in the interior of X to war (formally, $u_s^z(x_h) > w_s$ and $u_t^z(x_l) > w_t\ \forall z$). Second, each player is uncertain whether the other will or will not fight if offered anything but its most preferred compromise outcome. In other words, both sides are uncertain whether the other would be willing to fight rather than accept any but its most preferred of the three compromise solutions. Formally, for the Signaler, this implies $u_s^l(x_l) > w_s$, $u_s^m(x_m) > w_s > u_s^m(x_l)$ and $w_s > u_s^h(x_m)$. For the Target, this implies $u_t^l(x_h) > w_t$, $u_t^m(x_m) > w_t > u_t^m(x_h)$ and $w_t > u_t^h(x_m)$. Figure 3.2 is an example of Signaler-type utility functions that satisfy these assumptions.

This sort of uncertainty implies the possibility that there may be no negotiated solution that both sides prefer to war *ex ante*. This implication is controversial because it is often supposed that preferences should be modeled with weakly risk averse utility functions, which imply that a mutually preferred negotiated solution must exist when the good in contention is divisible. I nevertheless assume the sort of uncertainty described above because it represents what we see in cases. When Britain and Germany negotiated over Czechoslovakia before the Second World War, for instance, neither side knew whether the other would accept a negotiated solution in which Germany annexed only the Sudetenland. In fact, the essence of compromises is often an agreement that neither side knew the other would accept at the start of negotiations. Compromise frequently involves both sides giving up something that each had claimed to be unwilling to give up. To model this sort of uncertainty in the conventional way requires assuming that there are types that will agree to such compromises and types that will not. This directly implies, however, that

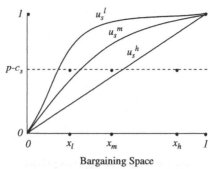

Bargaining Space

FIGURE 3.2 An Example of Signaler Utilities

there is a possibility that a negotiated solution may not exist to which both sides are willing to agree. Why this sort of uncertainty exists, and how it should be reconciled with traditional modeling approaches are difficult questions. That such uncertainties exist and should be accounted for in models of international politics is certain, and justifies the structure of uncertainty assumed here.[15]

The first proposition gives sufficient conditions for an equilibrium to exist in which the Target's beliefs are affected by the Signaler's cheap talk message. So long as both sides are sufficiently unlikely to be the least resolved type (the type unwilling to fight even if it is offered its least preferred of the three settlement outcomes), an equilibrium exists in which the least resolved and middle resolved Signalers claim they will fight unless the Target offers at least x_m and only the most resolved Signalers claim to be willing to fight unless they are offered the maximal concession x_h. Thus, when the Signaler says it will fight unless it is offered a maximal concession, the Target knows for sure that this is true. When the Signaler admits that it will settle for x_m, the Target knows that the Signaler would accept x_m, but is unsure whether the Signaler would also accept x_l. In fact, upon hearing the demand for x_m, the Target revises upwards its belief that the Signaler would not go to war if it were offered only x_l.

---

[15] A variety of circumstances can justify violations of global weak risk aversion of leader preferences. A leader might believe that an outcome at least as good as x_m is necessary for the viability of the state or for the leader to remain in power, for instance. The leader therefore draws no strong distinctions between lesser outcomes, leading to a violation of risk aversion around x_m. Or, some units of a good such as territory may be inherently more valuable than others. Similarly, Powell (2006) points out that commitment problems result in incentives that look very much like issue indivisibilities that make compromise impossible. The uncertainty assumed in the model might therefore result from uncertainty over whether an adversary thinks about the negotiation in these terms. For the view that assumptions about risk preferences in international politics are incoherent, on which understanding the assumptions about uncertainty made in the model are perhaps less controversial, see O'Neill (2001). For a discussion of related issues, see Reiter (2009, Chapter 3) and Gottfried and Trager (2016).

The next section describes how the equilibrium works algebraically as an example of a costless signaling logic for more technical readers. The subsequent section discusses the dynamics of signaling.

Equilibrium Algebra

In this equilibrium, when the least resolved Target type, u_t^l, observes the Signaler claim to be the most resolved type ($y = h$), this Target type offers the maximalist concession x_h because the Target knows that any other offer results in war. Other Target types are not willing to accept such a poor outcome, however, and refuse to compromise at all. In response to the message h, the two more resolved Target types offer x_l, knowing that this will result in war. This implies that the expected utility of sending the strong signal, h, is $h_t(u_t^l)u_s^l(x_h) + [1 - h_t(u_t^l)]u_s^l(x_l)$ for the least resolved Signaler type, u_s^l, because that type is not willing to go to war under any circumstances. The expected utility of sending h for the Signaler type whose resolve is in the middle range, u_s^m, is $h_t(u_t^l)u_s^m(x_h) + [1 - h_t(u_t^l)]w_s$ because that type prefers to go to war rather than accept x_l.

How will the Target respond when it observes the signal m? The Target knows that the Signaler will accept x_m rather than fight, but the Target also understands that the Signaler may be willing to accept x_l as well. However, as long as the probability that the Signaler is the least resolved type, u_s^l, is not too high and as long as the Target is not the most resolved type, the Target will settle for x_m. If the Target is the most resolved type, it risks war by offering x_l. This implies that the expected utility of sending the signal m is $(h_t(u_t^l) + h_t(u_t^m))u_s^l(x_m) + [1 - h_t(u_t^l) - h_t(u_t^m)]u_s^l(x_l)$ for the least resolved Signaler type and $(h_t(u_t^l) + h_t(u_t^m))u_s^l(x_m) + [1 - h_t(u_t^l) - h_t(u_t^m)]w_s$ for the moderately resolved Signaler type.

In this context, would the less resolved Signaler types be willing to admit that they are not the most resolved type, as the equilibrium requires? They would if their expected utilities for sending the signal m are greater than their expected utilities for claiming to be the most resolved type by sending the signal h. The expected utilities just stated imply that the least resolved Signaler type prefers to send the signal m when

$$[h_t(u_t^l) + h_t(u_t^m)]u_s^l(x_m) + [1 - h_t(u_t^l) - h_t(u_t^m)]u_s^l(x_l)$$
$$\geq h_t(u_t^l)u_s^l(x_h) + [1 - h_t(u_t^l)]u_s^l(x_l).$$

Moderately resolved Signalers also prefer to send the signal m when

$$Eu_s(m \mid u_s^m) = [h_t(u_t^l) + h_t(u_t^m)]u_s^m(x_m) + [1 - h_t(u_t^l) - h_t(u_t^m)]w_s$$
$$\geq h_t(u_t^l)u_s^m(x_h) + [1 - h_t(u_t^l)]w_s.$$

Notice that both conditions are satisfied as long as the probability that the Target is the least resolved type, $h_t(u_t^l)$, is not too high. If it is, then the prospect of achieving the very favorable deal, x_h, is too tempting, causing the less resolved Signaler types to misrepresent their levels of resolve, and signaling equilibria of this form become impossible. Proposition 3.1 formally describes the properties of this equilibrium and gives the sufficient condition for its existence: the probability that the players are the least resolved types cannot be too high.[16]

Proposition 3.1: If $h_i(u_i^l)$ is sufficiently low for all i, a perfect Bayesian equilibrium exists in which the signals m and h are sent with positive probability and

$$(1) \qquad \mu(u_s^h \mid h) = 1 \ \& \ \mu(u_s^h \mid y) = 0 \ \forall y \neq h$$

$$(2) \qquad \mu(u_s^m \mid m) = \frac{h_s(u_s^m)}{h_s(u_s^l) + h_s(u_s^m)} < 1 \ \& \ 1 > \mu(u_s^l \mid m)$$

$$= \frac{h_s(u_s^l)}{h_s(u_s^l) + h_s(u_s^m)} > h_s(u_s^l)$$

$$(3) \qquad \mu(u_s^l \mid y) = 1 \ \forall y \neq m, h.$$

When the signaler is somewhat more convinced that the Target is the least resolved type, an equilibrium with informative signals but different properties from those described in Proposition 3.1 can also exist. This equilibrium requires that player utility functions take on odd forms that are not contemplated in the international relations literature, however, and I therefore do not focus these equilibrium dynamics. Proposition 3.2 further demonstrates that whenever the Target is believed sufficiently unlikely to make the maximalist concession x_h, any separating or semi-separating equilibrium will have the properties described in Proposition 3.1. This means that the model gives us a strong empirical expectation: when there is reason to believe that the states involved are each unlikely to accept their least preferred among the three settlement outcomes, signaling will have the properties described in Proposition 3.1.

Proposition 3.2: For $h_t(u_t^l)$ sufficiently low, any pure strategy equilibrium in which Signalers do not pool on a single message has the properties described in Proposition 3.1.

In cheap talk models of this sort, so long as the probability that the Signaler is the least resolved type is sufficiently low, the possibility of

---

[16] All proofs are contained in Appendix A.

communication never increases the probability of war and sometimes communication makes war less likely. This result is proved as Proposition 3.3. Note that this is in contrast to models of signaling based on reputation and other models in the literature.[17]

Proposition 3.3: For $h_s(u_s^l)$ sufficiently low, no pure strategy PBE of the game with the cheap talk stage has a higher probability of war than the same game without communication.

A principal effect of the partial issue indivisibility in this model is to ensure that the Target does not capture all the gains from agreeing on a negotiated solution that both prefer to war. Many bargaining contexts will result in outcomes in which the gains from agreement are shared between the parties, however. As long as the gains from agreement are shared among the players and uncertainty is the sort characterized above, costless signaling is not impossible. The dynamics are the same as those described here in essential respects. These matters are addressed further in Appendix A.

DISCUSSION

Communication is possible between adversaries because some Signaler types admit that they are not the most resolved of the possible Signaler types. These types are willing to reveal this information, in spite of the fact that they also have incentive to misrepresent themselves as more resolved than they are in order to achieve a more favorable bargain, because demanding more sometimes also entails a risk they are unwilling to run. The risk is that an increased demand will be resisted where a more moderate demand would not be, with the result that the parties will not agree on a negotiated solution and a Signaler who had misrepresented its preferences may even be forced to fight rather than accept the unilateral action by the Target or the no agreement outcome. The strategies of the players in a signaling equilibrium are represented in Figure 3.3.

Signaling relies on the fact that when the Target believes that no compromise is possible that will avoid conflict, it makes no compromise in its actions.[18] This is the risk of overstating one's resolve. Thus,

---

[17] Sartori (2005), Slantchev (2010*a*, 136–141).

[18] Note that the incentive not to make a concession that appears to have no chance of placating an adversary is particularly strong when the concession influences the states' prospects in a conflict. That is not modeled explicitly here for simplicity, but is a feature of many historical international negotiations.

	Demand a Middle Range Concession	Demand a Middle Range Concession	Demand a Full Concession
Signaler	Accept Whatever Is Offered	Accept If at Least a Middle Range Compromise Is Made; Fight Otherwise	Accept If a Full Concession Is Made; Fight Otherwise
Target	If a Middle Range or Full Concession Is Demanded, Make One Otherwise, Do Not Make a Concession	If a Middle Range Concession Is Demanded, Make One Otherwise, Do Not Make a Concession	Do Not Make a Concession
	Least Resolved	**Intermediate**	**Most Resolved**

FIGURE 3.3 Player Strategies in a Signaling Equilibrium

this form of signaling can only occur in contexts in which the scope of demands is an issue, that is, when more than two non-conflict outcomes are possible. If the only choice of the Signaler is to threaten or not threaten and the only choice of the Target is to back down or not, in the signaling context analyzed here, no communication of resolve will be possible because demanding more carries no risk of getting even less at the bargaining table and therefore the incentives to misrepresent imply that no semi-separating equilibria exist.

Unlike in many other models of diplomatic signaling, therefore, resolve is not conveyed through risking conflict.[19] When the most resolved Signaler types send a signal that other types are unwilling to send, the probability that war occurs decreases. This is because only the Signaler has the option to initiate conflict and when resolved

[19] See Slantchev (2010a, 136–141) for a discussion of other models in the literature on this point. In a general class of crisis bargaining games with one-sided incomplete information, Banks (1990) demonstrates that more resolved states will run an equal or greater risk of conflict compared to less resolved states. As Fearon (1995) illustrates, however, more resolved states will not always be able to incur such increased risks to signal resolve. Further, as Fey and Ramsay (2011) demonstrate, Banks' result does not extend to the two-sided incomplete information context.

Signalers send such a signal, they are more likely to get a better offer and therefore less likely to initiate a conflict. Further, for most parameterizations of the model that seem reasonable, the existence of signaling mechanisms of the type described here either does not increase the likelihood of conflict or actually causes the probability of war to decline.

To understand the signaling dynamics, first note that the Signaler cannot conjure credibility out of nothing. If the Target starts out largely convinced that the Signaler will not fight even if offered its worst outcome, private diplomatic signals will not convince the Target otherwise. To see why, consider the Target's dilemma when the Signaler demands a compromise. The Target knows the Signaler would accept the compromise outcome, but will wonder if the Signaler would accept its least preferred outcome without going to war. If the Target is too convinced that the Signaler is the least resolved type following the compromise demand, then the Target will offer the Signaler the worst settlement outcome, in which case Signalers will never make compromise demands and signaling will not occur. Signaling therefore requires that there is a high enough probability at the start of the interaction that the Signaler is a "Compromiser" – a type that would fight unless the Target concedes at least the compromise outcome. So long as this is sufficiently high, then the Target will not be too certain that the Signaler would accept its least preferred outcome following a compromise offer, and therefore at least some Target types will concede to a compromise demand. These dynamics are illustrated in the vertical axis in Figure 3.4.

Proposition 3.1 makes clear that signaling will be possible as long as both sides are sufficiently unlikely to be the least resolved types. But if those probabilities are not very low, other factors come in to play. For instance, as the horizontal axis in the Figure 3.4 illustrates, if the Target is initially believed very likely to be the most resolved type, signaling may again fail. Here, the reason is that demanding a compromise is too unlikely to produce one, so Signalers gamble on making the highest demands even when they would accept less. Even though those high demands are unlikely to be accepted, if they are, at least the payoff will be better than the compromise outcome. The figure also shows one way that power dynamics can influence signaling. Higher Signaler capabilities can make the Signaler more willing to bluff, potentially eliminating a signaling equilibrium. On the other hand, higher Target capabilities can make the Target more willing to risk making additional demands following a compromise proposal by the Signaler, once again eliminating the possibility of communication.

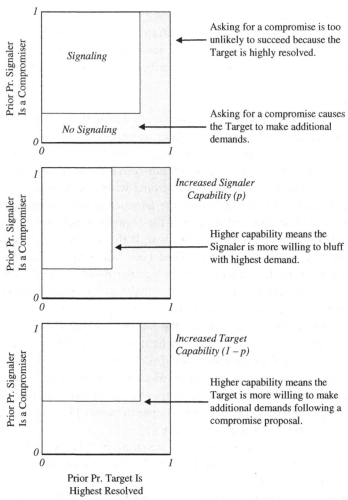

FIGURE 3.4 Signaling Equilibrium Dynamics

An example of the effect of communication on the probability of conflict is shown in Figure 3.5. On the left-hand side of the figure, communication strictly decreases the probability of war. As it becomes more likely that the Signaler is the most resolved type, the benefit of communication increases up to a point and then the probability of conflict in the equilibrium without communication falls discontinuously to be equal to the likelihood of conflict in the cheap talk equilibrium. The reason for this is that, as the Target becomes more convinced that the Signaler is the most resolved type, the Target becomes less willing to risk conflict even without a credible signal of resolve. On the right-hand side of the figure, as the Target becomes still more convinced that the Signaler is the most resolved type, the Target becomes less convinced that the

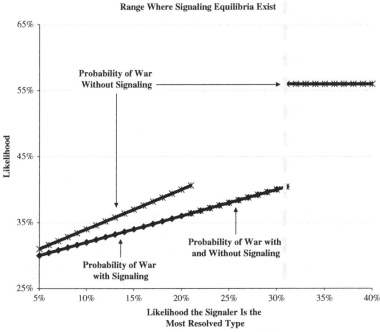

FIGURE 3.5 The Probability of War

Signaler's resolve is in a middle range. Therefore, the Target becomes less likely to be willing to offer a middle range compromise in response to a less than maximalist demand by the Signaler. The result is that the Signaler becomes unwilling to make less than maximalist demands, the communication equilibrium breaks down, and the probability of conflict increases dramatically.[20]

The primary reason these results are different from those presented in Fearon (1995) is the fact that in the Fearon model, the Target captures all of the benefit from avoiding war. The Target's disproportionate share of the benefits of peace results from (1) the take-it-or-leave-it aspect of the model and (2) the infinitely divisible issue space. This is because, in that model, when the Target of a threat knows the Signaler's type, its take-it-or-leave-it equilibrium offer leaves the Signaler indifferent between choosing war or peace. As a result, the Signaler has no incentive to reveal information: although peace may result, the nature of the peace is such that the Signaler finds war an equally compelling alternative. If either of these two assumptions is relaxed, the Target need not capture all of

---

[20] Parameter values for this simulation are $p = .5$, $c_i = .15$ $\forall i$, $x_1 = .25$, $x_2 = .5$, $x_3 = .75$, $u_s^1(x) = x^{\frac{1}{5}}$, $u_t^1(x) = (1-x)^{\frac{1}{5}}$, $u_s^2(x) = x^{\frac{9}{10}}$, $u_t^2(x) = (1-x)^{\frac{9}{10}}$, $u_s^3(x) = x^2$, $u_t^3(x) = (1-x)^2$, $h_s(u_s^1) = .3$, $h_s(u_s^2) = 1 - h_s(u_s^1) - h_s(u_s^3)$, $h_t(u_t^1) = .2$, $h_t(u_t^2) = .4$, $h_t(u_t^3) = .4$.

the gains from a negotiated solution, the Signaler can therefore have an incentive to reveal its type, and the scope of a costless demand can convey information to the Target.

While the take-it-or-leave-it model with an infinitely divisible issue space is interesting to study, it is likely that in most bargaining contexts, the players expect the benefits of peace to be spread more evenly between the players.[21] When states are highly resolved and willing to go to war over a particular set of issues, they still often have a strong preference for getting their way through the threat rather than the costly use of force. For this reason, resolved states are thought to have an incentive to reveal their types. In the Fearon model, by contrast, not only unresolved, but also resolved states have no incentive to reveal their types. If they do, they end up with their war payoff and if they are not able to, they still get their war payoff. Thus, what prevents costless signals from conveying information is *not merely that unresolved types have an incentive to misrepresent themselves as resolved* (that is true in the model analyzed here as well), but also that both resolved and unresolved types have no incentive to make their signals credible.

In many real world crises, a model in which even successful signalers receive no benefit from success does not appear to correspond actors' understandings of the situation. In the Cuban Missile Crisis, for instance, although the Kennedy administration was willing to initiate conflict with the Soviet Union through an air strike on Cuba, members of the administration were very glad to have forced the removal of the missiles without having to do so. That US policymakers were so relieved at the resolution of the crisis indicates that the Soviets were unable to capture all of the gains from peace in this case, as Targets are in the majority of instances of successful coercion.

One reason the gains from cooperation are shared in real world cases is that no continuously divisible issue space exists in many instances or, for complex reasons outside the scope of the questions considered here, in practice, actors do not consider the issue space divisible. Fearon (1995, 389–390) and Powell (2006) note that mechanisms, such as randomization devices or alternating possession of the good, exist to make the issue space divisible, and that therefore indivisibility is generally not by itself a rational explanation for war. They also emphasize, however, that for complex reasons, states often act as if issues are indivisible. This may result from the elite framing of what is at stake in the conflict,[22]

---

[21] The discussion here does not directly bear on, and does not constitute a critique of, the central theses of Fearon (1995) related to the nature of rationalist explanations for war.
[22] Goddard (2006).

from inherent features of the issues involved,[23] from the logic of commitment problems,[24] from the positions of other powers that limit the options of the two states,[25] or because the set of potential issues in contention in particular cases is not large enough.[26] Yet another reason issues may be indivisible in practice has to do with bargaining reputation. As Schelling has pointed out, the US would have a hard time offering to give up California and then establishing a credible commitment to give up no additional territory. It is the unavailability of other salient lines that leads to a sort of indivisibility of the initial grouping of territory.[27] Still another reason for indivisibility relates to what moral codes allow leaders to demand and offer each other. Hitler could demand the Sudetenland, and even that the West stand aside while he occupies Czechoslovakia in the name of protecting Germans in the Sudetenland, but he could not demand "three quarters of Czechoslovakia." At the Munich conference and in the diplomacy that preceded it, neither side considered such demands and offers.

Besides issue indivisibility, another reason Targets often are not expected to garner all gains from cooperation is that bargaining outcomes that are preferable to both sides often require actions taken by both sides. Each side may be willing to withdraw its troops from a border, but only if the other side also does so. Saddam Hussein may have been willing to withdraw his forces from Kuwait on a particular timetable, but only in return for a public guarantee of their safety from the United States. If neither side can achieve the preferred compromise outcomes unilaterally, we should expect that the sides negotiate and – if they reach agreement – that they share the bargaining surplus between them.

[23] Hassner (2003). Even territory is less easily divisible than it might appear. Often, given military technologies available at the time of a crisis, some groupings of territory are considered much more defensible, and thus much more valuable than others. A striking example is Hitler's calculation in 1941 that since war with the US was likely, control of the entire European landmass was essential to preserve German territorial gains. This made Hitler less willing to compromise on lesser territorial gains and resulted in the decision to attack Russia. On this points, see, for instance, Kershaw (2007, pp. 54–90). Fearon (1995, pp. 389–390) discusses the rise of nationalism in making territory less easily divisible.

[24] Powell (2006).

[25] Fearon (1995, pp. 389–390) mentions the practice of compensating a state for territorial acquisition of a rival state with territory somewhere else as a means of making the issue space convex. In many cases, however, this proved impossible because of the attitude of third powers. France's call for compensation in Belgium for Russian gains in the Ottoman territories prior to the Crimean War, for instance, was objectionable to Britain. See Puryear (1931, p. 272).

[26] The implications of "issue linkages" are discussed in Fearon (1995, pp. 389–390), Morrow (1992) and Trager (2011).

[27] Schelling (1966, Chapter 2).

Another important driver of the signaling dynamics of the model is the assumption that both sides are uncertain whether the other would or would not be willing to fight rather than accept some compromise solution. As a result, when the Target believes the Signaler is a type that would be unwilling to make a compromise that the Target would accept, the Target no longer has any interest in making concessions to the Signaler. This gives less resolved Signalers a disincentive to misrepresent themselves as more resolved than they are.

The assumption that both sides are uncertain whether the other would accept a compromise appears uncontroversial in that it faithfully represents the subjective states of international actors in crises. However, the implication of the assumption is that it is possible that no compromise exists that both sides prefer to conflict. Put in this way, the assumption appears more controversial, but we can think of this assumption as merely a simplification of a more complex strategic process that is not modeled explicitly. To see this, note that virtually all crisis bargaining models share the following property: for some combinations of player types, war occurs with certainty.[28] Whether this results from an explicitly modeled strategic context or directly from the preferences of actors is not important for the present inquiry. Thus, the assumption that player preferences can produce war could be justified by embedding many prominent crisis bargaining models from the literature in the game presented here. This would substantially complicate the analysis, as well as obscure the dynamics of the current framework, which is why the simpler approach is adopted here.

It is thus in a restricted set of cases that the logic of Fearon's take-it-or-leave-it model might be expected to operate: when the Target of a threat can unilaterally choose from a set of options that approximate a divisible issue space and when the signaler has few options short of conflict or acquiescence. In such cases, costless signals will not convey information. One might suspect, however, that such cases are relatively rare in international politics either because, in practice, inherent indivisibilities exist or because compromise outcomes preferable to conflict require the give and take agreement of both sides. Of course, signals may nevertheless convey little to adversaries for other reasons. A claim to be willing to fight for a large concession, for instance, will likely signal little to the adversary when all sides believe that the state making the claim believes that the adversary is likely to be willing make the large

---

[28] Examples include Fearon (1994a), Schultz (2001), Kurizaki (2007), Trager (2010) and many other models.

concession. Such threats may be effective even when they are not credible in themselves.[29]

The analysis here also demonstrates why states would make compromises even though doing so will often result in the perception that they would accept outcomes involving even greater concessions – thereby encouraging an adversary to demand these additional concessions. In the informative equilibrium characterized in Proposition 3.1, when the Target sees the Signaler send the signal that only the intermediate concession is important, the Target knows the Signaler is less likely to go war if the Target makes no concession at all to the Signaler. Nevertheless, the Signaler sometimes still prefers to send the signal that it would settle for the compromise position. The reason is that by demanding too much, that which the Target is relatively unlikely to give up, the Signaler risks getting nothing at all. By demanding only the compromise, the Signaler increases its chances of getting something. Proposition 3.2 demonstrates that this dynamic will be associated with any offer of compromise when the players are each believed, prior to the diplomatic signal, to be sufficiently unlikely to be willing to settle for their least preferred compromise outcome.

SIGNALING HYPOTHESES

The analysis of the model suggests the following hypotheses will hold when (a) adversaries are each believed sufficiently unlikely to settle for highly unfavorable outcomes and either (b1) the issue space exhibits indivisibilities or (b2) compromise outcomes are expected to result from the give and take agreement of both sides. Whether these conditions hold in individual cases is difficult to determine, and therefore it is particularly difficult to code for these factors in a standardized way across cases. Therefore, I state the following hypotheses without these conditions since they are likely to hold much of the time. *Hypotheses 3.1–3.3* follow directly from the discussion of the model. *Hypothesis 3.4* states that the higher the capabilities of the state making a concession relative to the state to which the concession is made, the more likely observers will conclude that the conceding state will not concede more. This follows loosely from Proposition 3.2, which implies that when the probability that a state is willing to accept an unfavorable compromise is low, then a concession to that state increases the probability that the conceding state would make further concessions. The rationale for *Hypotheses 3.4* is that

---

[29] See Fearon (2002) for a discussion of this point.

if a state is strong relative to another, it is less likely that the stronger state would accept the most unfavorable outcome. Many other hypotheses can be derived from the model; the four advanced here can be evaluated with available data.

Hypothesis 3.1: Private threats and offers will often cause observers to believe the state making the statement is more likely to be willing to carry out the threat or offer.

Hypothesis 3.2: Increases in the scope of demands will increase the certainty with which inferences from the threats are drawn.

Hypothesis 3.3: Offers of partial concession will increase the perception (though never to certainty) that an even greater concession would also be accepted.

Hypothesis 3.4: The higher the capabilities of the state making a concession relative to the state to which the concession is made, the more likely observers will conclude that the conceding state will not concede more.

THE EMPIRICAL RECORD

Specific tests of the signaling hypotheses are reserved for the empirical section of the book, but some initial observations about the empirical record can be made here. Figure 3.6 gives a picture of how the model of the scope of demands relates to inferences drawn in the British documents prior to First World War. Recall that the bar at the top of the figure indicates the fraction of all private diplomacy inferences explained by the mechanisms described in the chapter. Almost 5 percent of inferences from private diplomacy are grounded in the observation that a state's high demands risk that no agreement is reached and many of these explicitly conclude that this demonstrates the resolve of the demanding state. In 1908, for instance, the British noted that Austrian unwillingness to compromise on the issue of Austrian annexation of Bosnia and Herzegovina might prevent a more general agreement between the powers, and that this therefore indicated Austrian resolve on the issue.[30] Several times in the course on negotiations over the status of Morocco in 1906, the intractability of one or other of the powers was seen as risking an agreement and therefore as conveying information. In one instance,

---

[30] Gooch and Temperley (1979, v. 5, pp. 420–421).

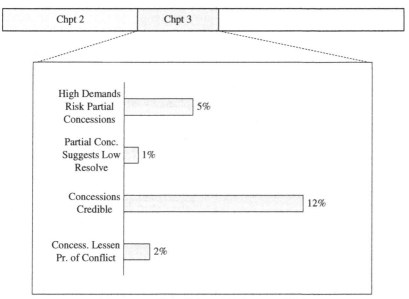

FIGURE 3.6 How Private Diplomacy Works
Note: The proportions shown are of the mechanisms by which private-diplomacy, security-related inferences were drawn in internal, British Government documents in the *Confidential Print* between 1855 and 1914. The bar at the top represents the total number of mechanism codings in the inference dataset; the area in the Chapter 3 portion represents the fraction of these mechanisms addressed in the chapter.

German insistence that France relinquish control of the Moroccan police force led the British to conclude that because Germany was unwilling to pursue negotiations for an intermediate compromise, Germany was more likely to be resolved to insist on the full concessions it was demanding.[31] Similarly, concessions were often made specifically in order to avoid the failure of negotiations. Thus, when the Germans did make concessions on the Moroccan police force, all sides understood that this was done in order to ensure that the conference for adjusting disputes would remain in session.[32]

German threats in Morocco and the conclusions that other powers drew from them also had longer-term influences on the international order. These were among the German actions that led the British to conclude that Germany was more aggressive than other nations. This conclusion, in turn, directly influenced the solidarity of other powers in relation to Germany. As Eyre Crowe put it, between Britain and France "there had emerged an element of common resistance to outside dictation

---

[31] Gooch and Temperley (1979, v. 3, part 2, p. 274).
[32] Gooch and Temperley (1979, v. 3, part 2, p. 288).

and aggression, a unity of special interests tending to develop into active co-operation against a third Power."[33]

Like other models, including those described in subsequent chapters, the mechanism of communication described here predicts that offers of concession will often be found credible. Indeed, 12 percent of inferences made by the British from private diplomacy are offers of concession that the British believed were sincere. The data also show a number of instances where concessions were taken to indicate that the conceding side would likely make further concessions to avoid conflict. The British understanding of Russian actions in the Balkans in the years before the First World War provides some striking examples. In 1912, for instance, the British concluded that Russia's tepid support for Serbia indicated that Russia was "anxious to avoid being dragged in to a European war" and might therefore make additional concessions.[34] The British drew a similar conclusion in 1913 when Russia urged the session of the fortress of Silistra from Bulgaria to Romania. The British view was that Russia urged this on its nominal ally, Bulgaria, because Russia wished to prevent a broader European war "almost at any price."[35]

CONCLUSION

Leaders can learn a great deal about the intentions of other leaders from the scope of the demands other leaders make. The magnitude of a demand conveys information because of the risks involved in larger demands. The demanding state may end up worse off than if it had negotiated for a compromise outcome that is more likely to be forthcoming. This conclusion is particularly certain when compromise outcomes require the give and take agreement of both sides or the issue space consists of discrete alternatives and when adversaries each believe the other relatively unlikely to accept the negotiated outcome that each most prefers. In such cases, compromises will be offered even though these compromises increase the perception that the compromiser would be willing to settle for even less than the compromise offered. This appears to be a commonly used and intuitive signaling mechanism in international politics.

---

[33] Gooch and Temperley (1979, v. 3, part 2, p. 403).
[34] Gooch and Temperley (1979, v. 9, part 2, p. 217).
[35] Gooch and Temperley (1979, v. 9, part 2, p. 508).

4

The Risk of a Breach

During the Great Eastern Crisis of 1876, Russia queried Germany what its position would be if Russia were to go to war with Austria–Hungary. Russia and Austria–Hungary were engaged in tense negotiations over the Russian desire to respond to Ottoman violence against Slavs. Germany did not wish to reply to Russia at all, but learned that the Tsar was asking about the German response nearly every day. So, Germany sent General von Schweinitz by train to a private audience with Tsar. Schweinitz communicated, as delicately as he possibly could, that Germany could not guarantee its neutrality in the event of war, and that "a lasting weakening of Austria would be contrary to [German] interests."[1] The German chancellor, Otto von Bismarck, thought that this created a "new situation" in European politics.[2] Germany had increased Russian expectations about Germany's willingness to go to war on behalf of Austria, and perhaps decreased Russia's appraisal of the extent to which Germany would support Russian aims generally.

According to most theories of communication between states, this should have been impossible. Germany communicated its position privately through diplomatic channels. Thus, German elites did not stake their reputation before a domestic audience, nor did their actions carry explicit costs, two commonly recognized mechanisms of communication.[3] Further, Germany's noncommittal statements can hardly

---

[1] Schweinitz (1927, p. 360). The Russians did not explicitly threaten Austria, but it was at this time that the saying, "the road to Constantinople leads through Vienna," (Rupp 1941, p. 232) gained popularity in Russian diplomatic and military circles and many Russians and Germans thought that the tense, ongoing Austro-Russian negotiations could lead to war. See Rupp (1941, p. 297), Ignatyev (1931, p. 391), Saburov (1929, p. 82), *Grosse Politik*, v. II, pp. 54–66, 74–79, Schweinitz (1927, p. 359).

[2] Bismarck (1915, p. 286).

[3] Fearon (1994a) and Kydd (1997).

be considered to have engaged its reputation before the Russian and interstate audiences such that anyone could have believed Germany significantly less willing to back down for fear of the repercussions of having been caught in a bluff. Theories of communication that rely on the staking of bargaining reputations, therefore, also fail to explain the case.[4] Yet, Bismarck's appraisal was correct: thereafter, Russia reckoned on German support for Austria–Hungary.[5] Why should the statements of ambassadors have such an impact?

This chapter describes a signaling mechanism that explains this case and many others. When a state is threatened, if it is not willing to concede the issue, and sometimes even if it is, it will often reorient its foreign policy. It may form new alliances, build weapons, initiate a first strike against the threatener, mobilize troops, or adopt policies to drain the resources of the menacing state. These actions have consequences for the threatening state whether or not that state decides to follow through on its threat. As a result, when there is a danger that a threatened state will take such actions, states only make threats when the issues involved are sufficiently important, or put differently, when they are sufficiently resolved to pursue their preferred outcome by force if necessary. The consequence of this is that statements of resolve convey information.

As we shall see, this strategic context can also result in wars that occur for an unexpected reason: states that are resolved to fight decide it is in their interest not to communicate their resolve even though they could, and even though doing so would prevent the war. That is, states decide to attack by surprise, not realizing that their goals could in fact be attained through diplomacy. This occurs when one state is highly resolved, believes that another is also, but believes that the other state does not believe that the first is highly resolved. In such cases, if the first state were to signal its resolve, there is a high probability the other state would prepare for conflict. In order to avoid this likelihood, the first state declines to convey its resolve to the other. Sometimes, however, the second state would have been willing to comply with the first state's demand in order to avoid war. Thus, in this situation, resolved states

---

[4] See, for instance, Sartori (2005). See Fearon (1995) for an analysis of the efficacy of costless diplomatic signals.

[5] As the German Ambassador wrote, "nothing was more natural" (Schweinitz 1927, pp. 350–351) than for the Tsar to expect a guarantee of German neutrality, and he remained openly disturbed by the German response for days (Rupp 1941, p. 204, Schweinitz 1927, pp. 360–364). According to the Russian diplomat Kartsov, the idea of declaring war on Austria "was abandoned" because, "Prince Bismarck forewarned that Austria was necessary for Germany for reasons of political balance of power and that Germany would therefore not permit delivering Austria a death-blow" (Rupp 1941, p. 297). See Trager (2007, Chapter 3).

mimic the behavior of unresolved states in order to catch the other side unprepared. This contrasts with other signaling models where it is generally unresolved states that would like to imitate the signals sent by resolved states.

This second point is similar to results derived from other recent models that have begun to expand the range of state options beyond those conceived of in traditional bargaining models. Ritter (2004, Chapter 2) argues that states sometimes make their alliances secret, in spite of the drawback from the point of view of deterrence, in order to prevent potential adversaries from taking counter measures. Slantchev (2010b) presents on ultimatum game in which rejected offers lead to conflicts in which each side must choose a level of effort in the fighting. Since the optimal effort of states depends on each side's perception of the strength of the other side, states sometimes have incentive to make offers in the pre-conflict stage that hide their true strength. The model below reveals a similar dynamic in the context of costless diplomatic encounters across a wide range of seemingly disparate contexts from alliance politics to nuclear brinkmanship.

The chapter has five sections. In the first, I describe strategic options available to threatened states that go well beyond the binary choice to comply or not in traditional models of coercion. The second section presents a model that allows states that are threatened to prepare for conflicts and to choose themselves to engage in conflict. When these preparations are effective, informative costless signaling occurs in plausible equilibria. This section discusses the conditions under which signaling can be effective, and under which wars occur that available but unused signals could prevent. The third section addresses implications of the analysis, the fourth describes empirical hypotheses derived from the model, and the fifth highlights some examples of these dynamics and discusses the empirical record.

THE STRATEGIC CONTEXT OF ANARCHY

In prominent models in the international relations literature, the strategic options of the target of a threat are limited: it can stand firm or concede. This conceptualization does not correspond to the options and incentives of states in the anarchic international context. If a state comes to believe it cannot achieve its key strategic aims through its current relationship with another state, it may choose to alter that relationship. In particular, rather than merely deciding whether or not to back down, threatened states must decide how to prepare for conflict if they believe a breach with a threatening state is imminent. In such cases, states often reorient their security policies in order to drain resources from the threatening state, and they also tend to form new alliances that are contrary to the threatening state's security interests. In addition, when the target of a threat believes future conflict more likely, it will sometimes choose to increase arms production, mobilize troops, or strike first. These decisions are often made before the threatening state chooses to back down or follow through on its threat and have consequences whether or not the states involved ultimately go to war.[6]

To illustrate the strategic choices available to Targets, recall from Chapter 1 the response of US President Kennedy and Soviet Premier Khrushchev to threats made by the other in their June 1961 meeting. Put simply, each threatened to escalate to war if the other did not accept a settlement of the Berlin question favorable to their side. Following the meeting, Khrushchev responded by adopting a new set of policies designed to drain the resources of the United States. On August 1, he approved a KGB plan to drain US resources around the world with the specific objective of ensuring that US attention and resources would not be sufficient to prevent a settlement in Germany favorable to the Soviet side.[7] For his part, hard as it is to imagine today, Kennedy began to take the idea of a nuclear first strike more seriously. He told the Joint Chiefs of Staff that "Berlin developments may confront us with a situation where we may desire to *take the initiative* in the escalation of conflict from the local to the general [nuclear] war level."[8] Thus, because both leaders were unwilling to back down, they considered or adopted policies to prepare for a conflict they thought might be imminent.

Alternatively, consider the Japanese strategic calculus in 1941. In November of that year, the United States demanded that Japan withdraw from China. This amounted to, "surrendering her position as a power in the Far East."[9] Japan was unwilling to accede to US demands, and, precisely because it found US threats credible, decided to take radical action to prepare for the coming conflict. In the hope of demonstrating its resolve to resist, and of engaging in only a limited war with the United

---

[6] Works that argue that states react to perceptions of intentions in ways described here include Walt (1987), Jervis (1976, Chapter 3), Schweller (1994), Schultz (2001), and Schelling (1966). One work that argues against state responsiveness to the intentions of other states is Mearsheimer (2001). Waltz (1979) does not argue against a causal role for perceptions of intentions. Rather, he argues only for a separate and independent effect of the distribution of capabilities. See Waltz (2003, p. 53).

[7] Fursenko and Naftali (1999, p. 138)

[8] Cited in Lieber and Press (2006, p. 36), italics added.

[9] Feis (1950, p. 327).

States, Japan opted to destroy the offensive capability of the US fleet at Pearl Harbor.[10]

The history of international relations is full of examples of states responding to diplomatic pressure with actions that go well beyond a simple refusal to comply with a demand. In fact, where important questions of security are concerned, simply declining to comply with demands is likely the exception rather than the rule. The Japanese response to US, British, and Dutch policy in 1941 is exceptional only in scale and decisiveness.

In response to Austrian threats during the Crimean War, Russia took actions it would not have taken otherwise. These included colluding with France and Sardinia to strip Austria of Northern Italy, tipping the balance in Germany in favor of Prussia, permitting the revolution in Hungary that resulted in the Austro-Hungarian Ausgleich (instead of assisting in suppressing the Hungarians as Russia had before the war), and declining to renew generous offers of Russo-Austrian cooperation in the Balkans leading to drastically increased security competition in the region between the two countries.[11] More speculatively, but with considerable reason, the historian Norman Rich argues that the Austrian threats during the Crimean War resulted in "a bitter hostility that was to culminate in war in 1914, the destruction of both imperial houses, and the liquidation of the Habsburg Empire."[12]

A particularly common response to dissatisfaction with another country's conduct of foreign policy and its perceived hostile intentions is the realigning of alliance commitments. In 1864, for instance, Napoleon III wished to use a European conference to revise the post-Napoleonic Wars settlement of 1815. When Britain, with which France was closely aligned, refused to support a conference, Napoleon was explicit: "So it seems we shall have no Congress. Well! I shall have to change my alliances." With that, the alignment between the two countries ended.[13]

The danger of a great power realignment resulting from a general breach in Russo-German relations is also the explanation for the information conveyed by Germany's statements in 1876 discussed above. Both sides understood that even a tacit threat from Germany might lead Russia to form an alliance with France, Germany's arch rival since the Franco-Prussian war six years before. The fact that Germany understood the

---

[10] See Russett (1967), and George (1991, p. 19).
[11] For a detailed comparison of Russian foreign policy before and after the Austrian threats, see Trager (2012).
[12] Rich (1965b, p. 123).
[13] Mosse (1958, p. 142).

danger, and yet chose to tacitly threaten anyway, meant that Germany had effectively communicated its resolve to defend Austria–Hungary.[14]

To fix ideas, and to see the relationship between preparation for conflict and communication, consider the following stylized examples of international contexts in which costless communication is possible. The model presented in the next section is designed to represent these situations in a stylized way. These narratives illustrate that signaling dynamics can be similar in seemingly diverse strategic contexts.

Example 1: External Balancing A conflict arises between two states, a Signaler and a Target, over a specific issue. In order to get its way, the Signaler would like to convey its willingness to go to war over the issue. The Signaler knows, however, that if the issue is particularly important to the Target, the latter may form an alliance with a third country in order to get its way or prepare for a possible conflict. The Target would prefer not to make the concessions to the third state required to get an agreement, and the new alliance is also likely to have a negative effect on the Signaler's security position, especially if the third country is already hostile to the Signaler. Threat-making therefore has both an advantage and a drawback. The advantage is the increased likelihood that the Target state will conceed the issue to the Signaler; the drawback is the possibility the Target will "balance" against the Signaler by forming a hostile alliance. As has been mentioned, this was the principal concern in German relations with Russia after the Franco-Prussian war. Signalers for whom the issue is not sufficiently important are unwilling to incur the risk of such a breach in relations by making a threat. When the Target state observes a threat, therefore, it learns the issue is relatively important to the threatening state.

Example 2: Internal Balancing As the name implies, this scenario is similar to the last, except that the principal strategic option of the Target (the threatening state's principal concern) is to transfer resources to its military sector in order, one day, to resist the demands of the threatening state. The timing of China's decision in the 1950s to devote enormous diplomatic and material resources to the pursuit of nuclear weapons, for instance, may have been partly a result of US threats in the First and Second Taiwan Strait Crises. Since arms production alters the future bargaining relationship between the nations, internal balancing will often constitute a significant long term drawback to threat-making.

Example 3: First Strike If a Signaler threatens a Target, the military and strategic context may be such that if the Target is unwilling to back down and believes the Deterring state is also sufficiently unlikely to back

---

[14] For an analysis of this case, see Trager (2007, Chapter 3). For a related argument on the follow-on effects of alliance realignments, see Healy and Stein (1973).

down, the Target's best option is to strike first. This was the situation for Japan in 1941. It was also a worry for US President Kennedy during the Cuban Missile Crisis. He recognized that a US threat to destroy the missiles in Cuba in four days could result in a Soviet threat to take action in three days, as well as further escalations that could result in nuclear war in that time frame.[15] In such military–strategic contexts, therefore, threat-making once again involves a trade-off similar to that in Examples 1 and 2. Threats increase the chance a state gets what it wants with respect to the issue at hand, but can also create a danger that the threatened side begins an unwanted military conflict. Once again, the willingness of the Signaler to incur such a risk can cause the threat to convey information to the Target.

Example 4: Too Costly Deterrence Faced with a threat, the Target might consider adopting policies that would deter the threatening state from attacking. Such activities, for instance mobilizing forces on a border, may be too costly to sustain for long. Rather than maintain a high level of preparation, therefore, the Target state might prefer to go to war. Powell (1993) analyzes a strategic context that leads to a similar dynamic. From the perspective of diplomatic signaling, if we think of the Target's decision as preceding the Signaler's decision to go to war or back down, the danger of such an outcome plays a similar role to the risk of a first strike in Example 3.

Example 5: Resource Drain Other reactions states may have to threats also have long-term consequences for the threatening state. A state may choose to drain the resources of another state in order to get its way on a particular issue, for instance, as the Soviet Union did following the 1961 Vienna meetings. As in Examples 1–4, the risk that a threatened state would adopt such a course provides a disincentive to less resolved states to signal their willingness to engage in conflict over such a contentious issue, making communication possible.

Example 6: Mobilization When a threatened state declines to back down and believes conflict likely, it may elect to mobilize its troops. With the cost of the mobilization paid, the choice to go to war looks more attractive to the mobilized state than it had previously.[16] Allowing for the possibility that the mobilized state may now choose to go to war, we once again have a tradeoff for states that consider threat-making, and this again results in the possibility of informative diplomatic signaling.

In each of these narratives, the decisions the Target of a threat takes when it means to resist the threatening state's demands have a negative impact on the Signaler's security. If the Target chooses either internal or

---

[15] May and Zelikow (2002, pp. 43–44).
[16] Slantchev (2005).

external balancing, the Signaler's utility will be negatively affected even if
it chooses not to go to war. This is true when the increased capabilities of
the Target increase the likelihood that the Target will decide to go to war
itself, and may also be true when the Target will not contemplate war
in the near term. In the context of Russo-German relations in 1876, Bismarck was explicit on this point. Even a tacit German threat to Russia, he
argued in one foreign policy circular, "could induce [the Tsar] to conclude
flawed resolutions and alliances that would be very disadvantageous for
both sides."[17] It is no mystery what combination Bismarck had in mind;
a Franco-Russian alliance would have had significant consequences for
Germany whether or not the Germans backed down in 1876.[18]

Internal and external balancing on the part of a Target negatively
affects the Signaler's security because it changes the balance of power
between them. If the two countries are involved in another crisis in the
future, the weaker relative position of the Signaler will usually mean that
it is less likely to get its way and more likely to fare badly if conflict
should actually break out. Thus, if future crises are of the sort described
here or, for example, in Fearon (1994a, 1997, 1998), Schultz (1998,
2001) or Slantchev (2005), the Signaler's expected future utility decreases
in the capabilities of its adversary.[19] While there may be some contexts
in which states are indifferent to the increasing capabilities of an adversary, they will more often view such developments with understandable
concern.

In the model described in the next section, we allow for the possibility
that the Target of a threat, having made costly preparations for war,
might choose to begin one. This results in a concrete risk to the coercing
state of appearing to menace the other state. Even if the coercing state
backs down, the other state may make preparations for war and choose
to fight one. More generally, however, we might think of the preparations
of the Target negatively affecting the coercing state's security because
of the effect of preparations on the balance of power, even when the
coercing state backs down and the sides are not in immediate conflict.

---

[17] *Grosse Politik*, v. II, p. 37.
[18] Note that Russia elected not to attack or explicitly threaten Austria–Hungary and that
Russia also did not pursue an alliance with France at this time. The Franco-Russian
alliance came about 15 years later, after much intervening history, including Russia's
declared frustration with German policy in the Congress of Berlin, the Austro-German
alliance of 1879 (directed partly, and only partly secretly, against Russia) and the
German failure to renew the Reinsurance Treaty with Russia in 1890.
[19] Kydd (2005) is a partial exception because increased relative capabilities of an adversary
may on occasion make it more trusting and thereby result in a net improvement of a
threatening state's expected utility.

A MODEL OF DIPLOMACY WHEN TARGETS HAVE OPTIONS

This section describes a formal model of diplomatic signaling that allows for the possibility that threatened states may decide to take actions that go beyond standing firm or backing down. As in the last chapter, there are two players, a Signaler or threatening state and a Target or threatened state. The players are indexed by $i \in I \equiv \{s, t\}$.

The model below is different from previous models in the international relations literature in two important respects. First, the Target can chose to prepare for conflict when it believes one is sufficiently likely, or reorient its foreign policy in other ways that adversely affect the interests of the threatening state. If the Signaler takes a threatening posture, and if the Target's costs of war are sufficiently low relative to the importance of the issue in question, the Target may be convinced to take these sorts of measures. Second, in addition to the Signaler having the option to attack the Target, the Target has the opportunity to attack the Signaler. Having prepared for war, the Target may opt for it even if the Signaler does not. Since the Target's actions may lead to an outcome that is even worse for unresolved Signalers than the peaceful outcome where the Target is undeterred, resolved Signalers have an incentive to make threats vis-à-vis a particular issue that less resolved states would be unwilling to make. As I show below, this dynamic causes threats to be meaningful even though no direct cost is associated with making them. One general implication of the model is therefore that if states respond at all to perceptions of other states' intentions in formulating foreign policy, then a verbal threat made by one state against another, whether in public or private, can convey information.

As before, there is a bargaining space $X \equiv [0, 1]$ such that the Signaler prefers outcomes closer to 1 and the Target outcomes closer to 0. The status quo at the beginning of the game is $s \in X$. Players have von Neumann–Morgenstern utility functions defined over outcomes in the bargaining space, $x \in X$, and whatever costs of fighting and preparation for conflict the players pay, c_i. Specifically:

$$u_s(x) = x - c_s$$

and

$$u_t(x) = 1 - x - c_t.$$

Thus, players have risk-neutral preferences over outcomes in the bargaining space. We assume this because it simplifies the exposition without substantively altering the key points of the analysis. The costs players pay in the game, c_s and c_t, will be defined as functions of other variables

	Signaler
1st Stage	Makes a costless threat or acquiesces
	Target
2nd Stage	Decides (1) whether to take the action in question and, (2) whether to prepare for conflict
	Signaler & Target
3rd Stage	Each decide whether or not to go to war

FIGURE 4.1 Stages of the Game

below to reflect the outcome of player actions during the game, so that, for instance, the players do not pay a cost of conflict when no war is fought. (They may still pay a cost of preparing for conflict, however.)

Figure 4.1 depicts the stages of the game. In the first, the Signaler can attempt to influence the Target by sending a costless signal $m \in M \equiv \{0, 1\}$. In the second stage, the Target has two decisions to make: whether to take the action in question or not (choosing $a_1 \in A_1 \equiv \{0, 1\}$), and whether to prepare for conflict (choosing $a_2 \in A_2 \equiv \{0, 1\}$). If the Target takes the action, setting $a_1 = 1$, it unilaterally moves the status quo to $s - \epsilon$, towards its ideal point, where $\epsilon \in (0, s]$. If the sides remain at peace, this will then be the bargaining outcome. Then, in the third stage, the Signaler and Target decide whether or not to go to war, where $r_i \in R_i \equiv \{0, 1\}$ and 1 represents conflict initiation. First, the Signaler chooses r_s. If $r_s = 1$, conflict occurs; if not, the Target chooses r_t. War occurs if either side opts to begin one; both sides must choose peace to obtain that outcome. We let r represent an indicator variable that equals 1 when the sides go to war and 0 otherwise. Thus, $r = 1$ if and only if $r_i = 1$ for some i.

If the sides should fight a war, the Signaler will win the war with common knowledge probability $p(a_2)$, and is then able to choose its ideal outcome in the bargaining range X. Similarly, if the Target should win the war, it may choose its ideal bargaining outcome. We assume that one of the two sides will win the war. When the Target prepares, the chances that it wins a war may increase: $1 - p(1) \geq 1 - p(0) \Leftrightarrow p(0) \geq p(1)$.

Costs of War and Preparation

We shall model the Target's costs of war and preparation as consisting of several components. If the sides go to war, the Target's war costs are $\eta_t \in [\underline{\eta_t}, \overline{\eta_t}] \equiv \Xi_t$ where $\underline{\eta_t} > 0$ and η_t is private information of the Target. If the Target chooses to prepare, it incurs some preparation costs,

$k_t \geq 0$, whether or not a war is fought, but reduces its costs of conflict by $\beta_t \in [0, \underline{\eta}_t)$. Thus, preparations imply an increase in sunk costs that the Target pays whether or not it goes to war and a decrease in the variable costs associated with the conflict itself. (We make no assumption about the net effect of preparations on the overall cost of conflict.) Thus,

$$c_t(a_2, r, \eta_t) = k_t a_2 + r(\eta_t - \beta_t a_2).$$

We take a similar approach to modeling the Signaler's costs, but we suppose the Signaler has already made any relevant preparations for conflict and do not model the Signaler's choice of preparations explicitly. For simplicity, we suppose the Target's preparations do not affect the Signaler's costs of conflict – only its probability of victory. Thus,

$$c_s(r, \eta_s) = r\eta_s$$

where $\eta_s \in [\underline{\eta}_s, \overline{\eta}_s] \equiv \Xi_s$, $\underline{\eta}_s > 0$ and η_s is private information of the Signaler. Both sources of private information are independently distributed according to the continuous, strictly increasing, common knowledge distribution functions Φ_{η_i}.

Thus, the Signaler's utility depends on the bargaining outcome, whether the players go to war, and the Signaler's type, while the Target's utility depends on those same factors and also on whether or not the Target chooses to prepare. Therefore, we shall write the players' utility functions as $u_s(x, r, \eta_s) : X \times R \times \Xi_s \to \mathbb{R}$ and $u_t(x, r, \eta_t, a_2) : X \times R \times \Xi_t \times A_2 \to \mathbb{R}$.[20] Substituting the cost functions into the player utility functions yields the following utilities for peace:

$$u_s(s, 0, \eta_s) = s - \epsilon a_1$$
$$u_t(s, 0, \eta_t, a_2) = 1 - s + \epsilon a_1 - k_t a_2.$$

Similarly, the players' expected utilities for war are:[21]

$$Eu_s(r = 1 \mid a_2, \eta_s) = p(a_2) - c_s(1, \eta_s) = p(a_2) - \eta_s$$
$$Eu_t(r = 1 \mid a_2, \eta_t) = 1 - p(a_2) - c_t(a_2, 1, \eta_t) = 1 - p(a_2) - \eta_t$$
$$+ \beta_t a_2 - k_t a_2.$$

[20] Note that although the Target's choice of preparation does not affect the Signaler's utility directly, it does affect the likelihood of outcomes (victory and defeat) over which the Signaler has different preferences.

[21] So long as player utility functions are bounded, we can derive these expected utilities without assuming risk neutrality over bargaining outcomes by setting $u_s(1, 0, \eta_s) = u_t(0, 0, \eta_t, 0) = 1$ and $u_s(0, 0, \eta_s) = u_t(1, 0, \eta_t, 0) = 0$ without loss of generality. Since the sides' war utilities do not depend on which side chooses war in the third stage, the order of player choices in this stage will have no substantive impact on the analysis.

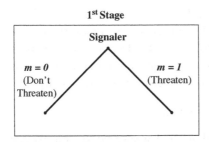
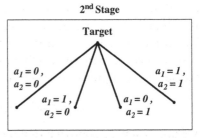

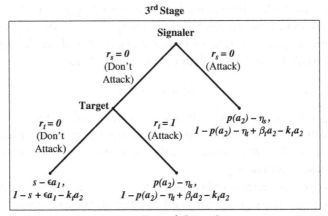

FIGURE 4.2 Formal Game Structure

The formal structure of the game is shown in Figure 4.2. Whichever choice the Signaler makes in the first stage, the Target has the four Stage 2 options shown in the figure. Whichever of these the Target opts for, the same Stage 3 structure shown follows. As the figure shows, the players' utilities over the Stage 3 terminal node outcomes depend on the Target's Stage 2 choice. The full game tree, therefore, has 24 terminal nodes (2 Signaler options in the first stage × 4 Target options in the second stage × 3 terminal nodes in each Stage 3 branch).

Additional Assumptions About Player Preferences

In order to make the signaling problem interesting, we shall make several assumptions about payoffs. First, we assume the Signaler prefers not to go to war when the Target complies with its wishes by not taking the action, and that there is a possibility the Signaler would be willing to fight if the Target does not prepare and takes the action in question and a possibility the Signaler would not be willing to fight in this case. This is equivalent to:

$$s > p(0) - c_s(1, \underline{\eta}_s) > s - \epsilon > p(0) - c_s(1, \overline{\eta}_s). \tag{1}$$

Second, we assume the Target prefers peace when it takes the action in question and does not prepare to its most preferred war outcome and that there is a possibility the Target would prefer a prepared war to accepting the initial status quo and a possibility the Target prefers the initial status quo to a prepared war. This is equivalent to:

$$1 - s + \epsilon > 1 - p(1) - c_t(1, 1, \underline{\eta}_t) > 1 - s > 1 - p(1) - c_t(1, 1, \overline{\eta}_t). \quad (2)$$

Similar to other models of coercion, these assumptions imply that the Signaler's most preferred outcome is when the Target complies with the Signaler's wishes by not taking the action in question (and also not attacking the Signaler). The Target's most preferred outcome is when it takes the action in question, does not prepare for conflict, and the Signaler does not attack. Players are willing to go to war when they consider the costs of war to be low relative to their evaluation of the issues at stake and their chances of victory.[22] An example of parameters satisfying these assumptions is shown in Figure 4.3. The figure also represents the model in terms similar to those used in Fearon (1995) and can be usefully compared to Figure 1 of that paper.

Effective Versus Ineffective Preparations

The preparations of the Target may or may not have an effect on the Target's costs of conflict and the players' probability of victory. We shall

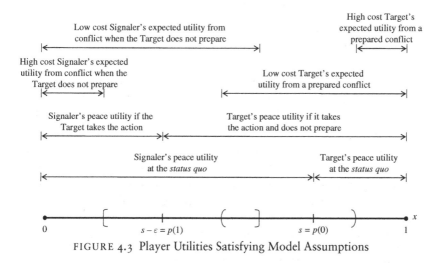

FIGURE 4.3 Player Utilities Satisfying Model Assumptions

[22] Here, players are uncertain about each other's costs of conflict. We might also consider a model in which players are uncertain about the importance of the issue in question to the other side. A model of this form, which generates similar results to those presented below, can be found in Trager (2007, Chapter 3).

say that preparations are *effective* if and only if $k_t > 0$, $p(0) > p(1)$ and $[(1 - p(1)) - (1 - p(0))] > k_t - \beta_t$. The last condition states that the Target prefers a prepared to an unprepared war, or in other words, that the overall increase in the Target's costs as a result of preparation (*if* preparing does involve a net increase in costs) must be outweighed by the benefit of the increased likelihood of victory. We shall say preparations are *ineffective* if $k_t = \beta_t = 0$ and $p(0) = p(1)$.[23] Note that in Figure 4.3, preparations are effective.

EQUILIBRIA WITH INEFFECTIVE PREPARATIONS

We can now ask whether, in such a strategic context, the Target can learn from the costless signals sent by the Signaler. Commonly, in cheap talk games, signalers can convey information that does not influence the course of events. If communicated information will not influence actions, it makes little difference to the receiver of the information whether or not she believes it to be true. In these equilibria, signals are *informative* but not *influential*. We shall focus on whether equilibria with influential signals can exist. In such equilibria there are signals that increase the probability that the Target both does not take the action in question ($a_1 = 0$) and does not attack the Signaler ($r_t = 0$). Let $q_t(m) = \Pr(a_1 = 0, r_t = 0 \mid m)$ be the probability the Target's strategy satisfies $a_1 = 0$, $r_t = 0$ given signal m induced by the players' strategies and beliefs in a particular equilibrium.

Definition An equilibrium is *influential* if there exist signals $m' \neq m''$ played with positive probability in the equilibrium such that $q_t(m') > q_t(m'')$.

If the Target's preparations do not affect its probability of victory or the players' costs of conflict, the Signaler's costless signals cannot convey information to the Target in a way that influences the Target's actions; no influential equilibrium exists. If preparations have no effect on player utilities over outcomes, then this model is very similar to others in the international relations literature. In such cases, the reason informative signaling is impossible is well understood: there is a benefit to being thought willing to fight and no drawback.[24]

---

[23] The effective/ineffective distinction does not exhaust all regions of the parameter space. We shall not analyze cases where preparations impact the probability of victory but are not costly or are costly but do not affect the chances of victory.

[24] The logic here is only slightly more complicated because, unlike in most models in the literature, the Target also decides whether or not to go to war later on. The proof of Proposition 4.1 must also demonstrate, therefore, that no influential equilibrium exists in which resolved, threatened Targets decline to take the action in question, thereby

Therefore, the Signaler always tries to send the signal that will most convince the Target of its resolve, but since that signal is sent in every case regardless of whether it corresponds to the truth of the matter, the Target learns nothing from it. Proposition 4.1 expresses this formally.

Proposition 4.1: If preparations are ineffective, no influential perfect Bayesian equilibrium exists (in pure strategies).

INFLUENTIAL EQUILIBRIA

When preparations have an effect, in some cases influential equilibria exist in the model. To understand how these equilibria function intuitively, suppose the Signaler makes a threat and the Target learns from this that the Signaler is more likely willing to go to war over the issue in question than the Target had previously thought. (We shall see that, in this equilibrium, this supposition is correct.) Realizing the Signaler is more likely to follow through, the Target is more likely to decide the issue is not worth risking a fight over and to back down. If the Target's costs of war are sufficiently low relative to the value it places on the issue, however, the Target may decide not to back down and to make costly preparations for war. The Target's decision may be a difficult one because on the one hand, preparations like forming alliances, building arms or striking first may provide additional security, but on the other hand, such actions carry their own additional costs. Since the Target's preparations affect its own calculations about the relative benefits of war and peace, having prepared, it may decide to attack the Signaler.

In the first stage, in deciding whether or not to threaten, the Signaler understands these dynamics. If the Signaler's costs of war are high relative to the value it places on the issue in question, then even though by threatening it stands a better chance of getting its way, it would not be willing to make a threat. This benefit to threatening does not outweigh the increased risk of a breach in relations with the Target and the attendant increased risk of a costly conflict. Thus, the Signaler would only be willing to threaten if it is relatively highly resolved. This, in turn, implies that our supposition that the Target learns from the threat is correct.[25]

---

committing themselves to fighting a war. If such a dynamic were possible, less resolved Signalers might decline to threaten, resulting in influential signaling. As the proof of Proposition 4.1 in the Appendix demonstrates, however, this cannot occur.

[25] As described, the logic may appear circular. But note that it is circular only in the way that the logic of any truly strategic Nash equilibrium (where players' optimal actions are dependent upon the actions of other players) must be circular.

A principal obstacle to influential cheap talk signals is the incentive that unresolved types have to mimic the signals sent by resolved types. In other models in the literature, unresolved types have every incentive to mimic because they can always back down and ensure themselves of an outcome they like just as well as the one in which they make no threat. In the model described here, however, there may be a danger that the Target will respond to a threat by preparing for war and, having done so, launch a strike of its own. When this is possible, low resolve types face a risk in misrepresenting their levels of resolve by mimicking the behavior of high resolve types.[26]

In order for this logic to operate, several conditions must be met. On the one hand, Signaler's cannot have so much to gain from threatening that even the least resolved Signalers would be willing to do it. If the Target is thought too likely to make concessions, for instance, the Signaler would always find it preferable to try its luck with a threat. Similarly, and as we saw above, if the preparations of the Target are not effective enough, there will be no disincentive to making threats all the time.

On the other hand, resolved Signalers must have enough to gain from threatening. If the Target is thought too likely to make preparations, if those preparations have a too large effect on the balance of power or if there is not a high enough likelihood that the Target will concede the issue, then the Signaler will prefer to mislead the Target about its true level of resolve. States willing to go to war will see it in their interest to convince Targets that they are not in order to catch the latter unprepared. This too can make informative signaling impossible.

Proposition 4.2 establishes one set of sufficient conditions for influential signaling. So long as preparations are minimally effective and both

---

[26] In the model, the Target can take an action that shifts the bargaining outcome in its favor by ϵ or not take that action. As a result, the Target sometimes prefers to go to war because the shift in the bargaining outcome is not sufficient to cause a fully prepared Target to prefer peace. If it were feasible for the Target to take an action unilaterally that moved the bargaining outcome sufficiently further towards the Target's ideal point following preparations for conflict, however, and if we allowed for this possibility in the model, then the Target would never choose war in equilibrium and influential signaling would be impossible. The assumption of a fixed action negotiated over by the states is probably reasonable in some cases and not in others. Even if we were to change the model to allow for an increase in ϵ following preparations, however, influential signaling would still be possible if we relaxed the assumption of risk neutrality over bargaining outcomes. More generally, for alternate bargaining protocols, influential signaling would be possible as long as Target types with higher expected values for war take actions that imply a strictly higher likelihood of conflict. This is an assumption or a result of nearly all crisis bargaining models. See Banks (1990) in particular, which demonstrates in a fairly general setting that the probability of war is at least weakly increasing in the expected conflict utility of an informed player.

sides are not too certain about the resolve or irresolve of the other side, an influential perfect Bayesian equilibrium exists when the sunk costs of preparation, k_t, are at least as great as the value of the issue in contention, ϵ. The significance of this last condition is that it ensures that when the Target finds war an unattractive option, it prefers to comply with the Signaler's demand rather than make preparations in order to deter an attack from the Signaler while declining to comply. If Targets preferred noncompliance with preparations to compliance and if the impact of Target preparations on the probability of victory were sufficient to prevent Signalers from ever attacking, then Signalers would have no incentive to signal resolve. They would have nothing to gain from doing so, and an influential equilibrium would not exist.

Proposition 4.2: When preparations are effective, for some set of beliefs Φ_{η_i}, an influential perfect Bayesian equilibrium exists if $k_t \geq \epsilon$.

As the discussion above makes clear, the sufficient conditions provided in Proposition 4.2 are not necessary for the existence of influential equilibria. In particular, if there is a sufficiently high likelihood that the Signaler would be willing to fight even against a prepared Target, influential equilibria exist in some cases when $k_t < \epsilon$. The reason is that the willingness of the Signaler to fight ensures that the Target might sometimes be unwilling to risk war and thus would prefer to comply with the demand rather than preparing and declining to comply. Thus, by demonstrating its resolve, the Signaler would have something to gain, enabling influential signaling.

To better understand how signaling operates in the model, we now consider a particular parameterization. Let us suppose that if the sides fight a war, there is a $p(0) = 50\%$ chance that each side wins when the Target has not made preparations. The status quo in the issue space, s, favors the Signaler at 0.6, but if the Target takes the action in question, it unilaterally shifts the status quo by $\epsilon = 0.2$ to 0.4. If the Target signs an alliance with a third country, mobilizes its troops and initiates a dramatic armaments program, the probability the Signaler is victorious in war decreases to $p(1) = 30\%$. The Signaler's costs of war range from small to quite large: η_s is uniformly distributed over $[0.15, 0.75]$. We shall suppose that the Target's costs of war are very high when it does not prepare, but similar although somewhat less than the Signaler's costs when the Target does prepare: $\beta_t = 0.585$, η_t is distributed uniformly over $[0.6, 0.85]$, and the Target's fixed costs of making preparations are $k_t = 0.2$. Thus, if the Target prepares, the additional costs it pays as a result of the conflict $(\eta_t - \beta_t)$ range from 0.015 to 0.265.

In such a world, there is an equilibrium in which the Signaler sends influential, costless signals of its resolve. Before the Target observes the Signaler's choice to threaten or not, it believes there is only a 14 percent chance the Signaler would be willing to fight over the issue. But the Target also knows that if it observes a threat, the Signaler is willing to take a risk on war. This is because the Target knows that the Signaler believes there is a 34 percent chance that the Target's war costs once it prepares $(\eta_t - \beta_t)$ are in the range $[0.015, 0.1)$. If the Target's costs of war are in this lower range, it prefers a prepared conflict to accepting the status quo. Its optimal response to a threat from the Signaler is to make maximal preparations for war. There are fixed costs of $k_t = 0.2$ associated with these preparations that the Target pays whether or not the countries go to war. Having paid this cost, the Target's expected utility from conflict is $1 - p(1) - k_t + \beta_t - \eta_t = 1 - 0.3 - 0.2 + 0.585 - \eta_t = 1.085 - \eta_t$. For low cost Targets (e.g., $\underline{\eta}_t = 0.6$), this is greater than its utility when conflict is avoided (even when it gets its way with respect to the issue in question), which is $1 - s + \epsilon - k_t = 0.4$. Thus, if the Target is threatened and if it is highly resolved (has relatively low costs of war), the Target will make preparations and go to war with the Signaler.

Optimal behavior by the Target therefore implies that threat-making by the Signaler entails a risk of conflict. For this reason, the Signaler would only be willing to make a threat when its privately known costs of conflict (η_s) are less than 0.42. Thus, the Signaler threatens only 46 percent of the time. Since the Signaler is willing to go to war against an undeterred and unprepared Target only when $\eta_s < 0.235$, the Target knows for sure when the Signaler declines to threaten that it will also decline to initiate conflict if the Target takes the action in question and does not prepare. On the other hand, if the Signaler does make a threat, the Target will believe there is a 31 percent chance that the Signaler would initiate conflict if the Target did not back down and did not prepare. This, in turn, causes the equilibrium to be influential: the probability the Target backs down is 0 percent when the Signaler declines to threaten, and 66 percent when the Signaler does.

The reason the equilibrium is influential is that the Target learns from the Signaler's costless statements. The Signaler's initial belief is that there is a 14 percent chance the Signaler would be willing to go to war over the issue. When Signaler threatens, that probability more than doubles to 31 percent. When the Signaler declines to threaten, that probability falls to 0 percent.

The difference from other deterrence models where the Signaler's statements could not convey information is the possibility that the Target will take an action that negatively affects the Signaler's utility whether or not the Signaler later opts for war itself. In deciding whether or not to threaten, therefore, the Signaler considers the trade-off described in the stylized examples of the previous section. If it declines to threaten, it reveals itself as a low type, ensuring that the Target will not concede the issue in question. Less resolved Signalers, those that have a high relative cost of conflict, are nevertheless willing to make this choice because of the risk of unwanted conflict that threat-making entails. On the other hand, the possibility the Target will back down without the need for conflict makes it worth it for resolved Signalers to apprise Targets of their intentions by making a threat.

NON-INFLUENTIAL EQUILIBRIA

Even when preparations are effective, influential equilibria may not exist. When Signalers risk too little by making threats, they will not be able to influence Targets. When they risk too much, they will not be willing to make threats at all. In either case, influential signaling is impossible.

Consider, for instance, Signalers that are known to have relatively low costs of conflict, when there is a low upper bound on Signaler cost types ($\overline{\eta}_s$). In such cases, Signalers risk relatively little by threatening. So long as there is a high enough likelihood that the Target has relatively high costs of war and therefore will be willing to back down, the Signaler will always prefer to make a threat. Thus, in such cases, signaling will be impossible for the traditional reason: low resolve types (high cost of war types) prefer to mimic high resolve (low cost) types.

Conversely, if the Target is thought very likely to be a relatively low cost type and thus likely to prefer war to complying with the Signaler's demand, signaling will again be impossible, but for a different reason. Instead of an incentive to misrepresent itself as resolved even when it isn't, the Signaler would have an incentive to misrepresent itself as unresolved even when it is. Rather than threaten in the hope the Target would improbably be willing to comply, resolved Signalers would prefer to pretend to be unresolved in hopes of catching the Target unprepared. If the incentive of resolved states to misrepresent themselves as unresolved is strong enough, influential signaling will again be impossible.

When resolved states have such incentives to mimic unresolved states, wars will occur that both sides would have preferred to avoid – and which could have been avoided if the Signaler had sent a different signal. We shall refer to these as "diplomatically avoidable wars." The intuition for why such wars occur is simple. Consider a Signaler willing to fight an unprepared Target unless the Target makes a concession. If the Signaler makes a threat, there is a chance the Target will give in, but there is also a chance the Target will make preparations, which means either that the Signaler will itself be deterred from attacking or that the Signaler will have to fight a prepared Target. Therefore, if the probability of Target resolve is too high, the Signaler will decide not to warn the Target about its intentions. The Israeli attack on the Osirak reactor in Iraq in 1981 illustrates these dynamics. If Israel had made a direct threat beforehand to bomb the reactor unless Iraq halted the reactor's construction, Iraq would most likely have mobilized its air defenses rather than comply. Israel would then have had to acquiesce to the Iraqi nuclear program or fight a prepared opponent, in which case Israel would have been better off hiding its intentions in order to catch the Iraqis unprepared.

Proposition 4.3 shows that in any material context, there always exist sets of beliefs of the two sides that imply that diplomatically avoidable wars occur. As the proof in the Appendix makes clear, such wars occur when the Signaler believes the Target very likely to be highly resolved, while the Target believes the Signaler relatively unlikely to be willing to fight. In such cases, the incentive of resolved Signaler's to mimic unresolved Signaler's completely eliminates the possibility of influential signaling. As we shall see below, however, surprise attacks and their correlate, diplomatically avoidable wars, also occur in some influential equilibria.

Definition A *diplomatically avoidable war* is an equilibrium outcome in which (1) the players go to war ($r = 1$), (2) the Signaler sends some signal m', and (3) the players' strategies imply that had the Signaler sent a signal $m'' \neq m'$, no war would have occurred ($r = 0$).

Proposition 4.3: When preparations are effective, for some set of beliefs Φ_{η_i}, a non-influential perfect Bayesian equilibrium exists in which diplomatically avoidable wars occur.

Another non-influential equilibrium also exists. Because all of the models in the book are cheap talk models, an uninformative, "babbling" equilibrium exists in all regions of the parameter spaces. In this equilibrium, the Target doesn't interpret the Signaler's signals as conveying information. Since all Signaler types are therefore indifferent between signals, the condition that each type is optimizing does not prevent them from sending signals that are uncorrelated with their costs of conflict. In such a case, the Target cannot use Bayes' rule to learn from the Signaler's signal.

When influential equilibria exist, empirical analysis of cases stands the best chance of judging whether the influential or babbling equilibrium most closely tracks international reality.[27] There are reasons to suppose the influential equilibrium is a more sensible social equilibrium, however. When the parameters of the model are such that an equilibrium exists in which all Signaler types willing to go to war would be willing to threaten, for instance, then all Signaler types that would be willing to go to war (when the Target does not prepare) would prefer to be in the informative rather than the uninformative equilibrium. If we therefore assume such types will attempt to communicate their resolve, then the uninformative equilibrium requires that the very least resolved types (those unwilling to threaten in the informative equilibrium) choose to imitate the behavior of the resolved types by threatening themselves. This, in turn, requires that we presume that these least resolved types attempt to send a signal that they would prefer not to have sent if the signal were believed. If this is unlikely, the informative equilibrium may be more reasonable than the uninformative one.[28]

Discussion of Equilibrium Dynamics

We can understand comparative statics in the model by considering the example of an influential equilibrium discussed above. The effect of the players' beliefs about each other's willingness to fight on signaling dynamics is shown in Figure 4.4. This figure and others below were generated through numerical simulations of the model. Recall that in our example, the players' costs of conflict are drawn from uniform distributions over $[\underline{\eta}_i, \overline{\eta}_i]$. We can model shifts in the players' beliefs about each other's resolve by shifts in $\overline{\eta}_s$ and $\overline{\eta}_t$. In Figure 4.4, $\overline{\eta}_s$ is on the vertical axis and $\overline{\eta}_t$ is on the horizontal axis. Thus, as we move rightward in the figure, the Signaler is less convinced of the Target's resolve, and as we move upward, the Target is less convinced of the Signaler's resolve (before a signal is sent).

When the Signaler is too much or too little convinced of the Target's resolve (very low or very high $\overline{\eta}_t$), or when the Target is too convinced of the Signaler's resolve (low $\overline{\eta}_s$), influential signaling is impossible. In the middle of the figure are the two ranges where influential signaling is

---

[27] It may be that process tracing of individual cases stands the best hope of evaluating whether influential or non-influential equilibria are better descriptions of state behavior. Documentary evidence will sometimes show very clearly, for instance, whether decision makers beliefs changed after a threat was made.

[28] For other arguments for the reasonableness of informative over uninformative equilibria, see Crawford and Sobel (1982, p. 1443) and Chen, Kartik and Sobel (2008).

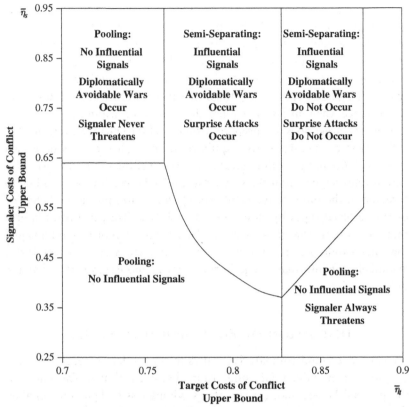

FIGURE 4.4 Equilibrium Signaling Properties

possible, but there are interesting differences in the dynamics of signaling and conflict between these two ranges. In both, the threats of the Signaler convince the Target that the Signaler is more likely willing to fight over the issue in question than the Target had previously thought. In the right most semi-separating equilibrium, however, the Target knows for sure when the Signaler declines to threaten that the Signaler will not fight over the issue. In the leftmost semi-separating equilibrium, this is not the case. There, the Signaler sometimes, but not always, misrepresents itself as *less resolved* than it actually is in order to catch the Target unprepared.

Figure 4.5 provides us with a closer look at the signaling properties when $\bar{\eta}_s$ is held fixed at 0.75, as in the example of the previous section. $\bar{\eta}_t$ is on the horizontal axis, as in Figure 4.4. Within the middle range where influential signaling is possible, the more convinced the Signaler is of the Target's resolve (the lower $\bar{\eta}_t$), the more informative is the Signaler's signal. When $\bar{\eta}_t$ increases, the probability the Target complies with the Signaler's demand increases, which causes the probability the Signaler

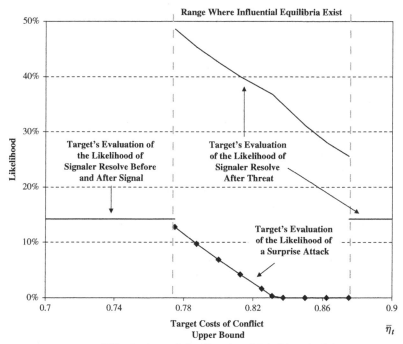

FIGURE 4.5 Effectiveness of the Signal and Likelihood of Surprise

is willing to threaten to increase as well, and the signaling value of a threat to decline. Thus, when $\bar{\eta}_t = 0.775$ a threat causes the Target's evaluation of the likelihood the Signaler would fight to jump from 14 percent to 49 percent. When $\bar{\eta}_t = 0.875$, by contrast, a threat causes the Target's evaluation of Signaler resolve to change only from 14 percent to 26 percent.

When $\bar{\eta}_t$ increases enough, the change in the Target's beliefs as a result of the Signaler's signal suddenly falls discontinuously to zero as signaling becomes impossible. This can be seen on the right-hand side of Figure 4.5. The reason is complex and relates to the interaction of a number of factors. As the Target comes to believe the Signaler is less likely to follow through on a threat (because the Target knows that the Signaler knows the Target is itself less likely to be willing to fight over the issue and thus the Signaler has less to lose from making a threat), Target types in the middle of the range of cost types have a new optimal strategy. Even if the Target did find the Signaler's signal to be somewhat informative, rather than low Target cost types preparing and then fighting and high Target cost types backing down, Target cost types in the middle of the η_t range would prefer to take the action in question without preparing at all. They find the chance that the Signaler is willing to fight to be too low to justify the expense of preparation, but neither are they deterred from taking the action in question. As a result of the change in the Target's strategy, the Signaler would have both less to fear from threatening and less to gain. The former effect dominates the latter, causing the Signaler to be even more willing to make threats, which in turn would cause even more Target types to prefer taking the action in question without preparation, and so on, with the result that influential signaling is impossible.

When the Signaler believes it is relatively likely that the Target will not back down over the issue, so that $\bar{\eta}_t$ is low, but still in the range where influential signaling possible, surprise attacks (i.e., attacks not preceded by a threat) occur in equilibrium. When the Signaler's costs of conflict are very low, it prefers not to threaten the Target at all in order to be able to attack the Target when the Target is unprepared. In such cases, as we saw in our analysis of non-influential equilibria and diplomatically avoidable wars, conflict can occur in equilibrium because the Signaler is unwilling to risk communicating its resolve. A signal exists that the Signaler could send that would result in compliance and avoid the need for either side to go to war, but because the Signaler does not know the Target would comply with a demand if the Target knew the threat were credible, the Signaler declines to send the signal.

In traditional crisis bargaining models, war can often occur because the Signaler does not have the means available to communicate its resolve.[29] As we saw above, in diplomatically avoidable wars, the Signaler has the ability to communicate but chooses instead to catch the Target unprepared.[30] Instead of the weak Signaler types mimicking the strong, in such cases, the strong pretend to be weak since they believe the Target is unlikely to back down even if it knew the Signaler were in earnest.

Unlike in the non-influential equilibrium of Proposition 4.3, however, in this example, diplomatically avoidable wars and influential signaling coexist in a single equilibrium. Signaler's adopt four different approaches, depending on their level of resolve. The very most resolved Signalers are unwilling to risk Target preparations and choose to use a surprise attack. They will attack an unprepared Target without first attempting to coerce through a threat. The next most resolved Signalers make threats which they will follow through on if the Target does not acquiesce. Signaler

---

[29] See in particular, Fearon (1995).

[30] Fearon (1995, pp. 395–396) also mentions this incentive to conceal information: "States can also have an incentive to conceal their capabilities or resolve if they are concerned that revelation would make them militarily (and hence politically) vulnerable or would reduce the chances for a successful first strike."

types that are slightly less resolved than these will make threats they would later be unwilling to prosecute and, finally, the least resolved Signaler types make no threat at all and later choose not to attack.

Because the likelihood of a surprise attack increases as $\bar{\eta}_t$ decreases, the lower $\bar{\eta}_t$, the less the Target can learn from the Signaler's decision to *decline* to threaten. When $\bar{\eta}_t = 0.775$, for instance, the Target's evaluation of Signaler resolve declines only slightly when the Signaler declines to threaten: from 14 percent to 13 percent. When $\bar{\eta}_t = 0.875$, the Target's evaluation of the likelihood of Signaler resolve falls from 14 percent to 0 percent. Thus, when there is a high probability the Target is highly resolved, the Target learns the most from a threat; but when there is a high probability the Target is unresolved, it learns the most when the Signaler declines to threaten.

As can be seen on the left-hand side of Figure 4.5, at the extreme, when the Signaler believes the Target very unlikely to back down in response to a threat, influential signaling is impossible because the incentive for a resolved Signaler to attempt to surprise the Target is too great. When the Signaler is highly resolved, it always prefers that the Target not knows this. Thus, in this region, the Signaler never threatens in the sense that low cost Signaler types have an incentive to imitate high cost types.[31] Once again, diplomatically avoidable wars can occur in equilibrium.

The existence of a communication mechanism lowers the probability of war in general. In the parameterization discussed here, when none exists, the probability of war is 14 percent for all values of $\bar{\eta}_t$ shown in Figure 4.6. The reason is that when the Signaler cannot affect the Target's beliefs, the Target's optimal strategy for all values of η_t is to take the action in question without preparing. Thus, war occurs if an only if the Signaler prefers to fight one, given that the Target has taken the action and not prepared.

When a communication mechanism exists, the probability of war is reduced over parameter ranges where influential signaling is possible, as Figure 4.6 illustrates. As we approach the left border of the range where influential equilibria exist from the right, the probability of war is arbitrarily close to the probability of war when no communication mechanism exists. This is so for two reasons. First, even though threats are very informative, as shown on the left-hand side of Figure 4.5, they are rarely used, as can be seen from the upward sloping line in Figure 4.6.

---

[31] In a cheap talk model, messages have no inherent meaning, so if there is an equilibrium in which all types coordinate on $m = 0$, there is also an equilibrium in which all types send $m = 1$. Nevertheless, we say that the Signaler "never threatens" in the left-hand range of Figures 4.4 and 4.5 because the resolved types have incentive to mimic the unresolved types.

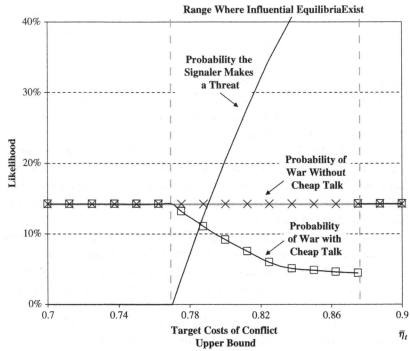

FIGURE 4.6 The Probability of War

When the Signaler is resolved, it often prefers the gamble of a surprise attack to gamble of diplomatic signaling. Second, when $\bar{\eta}_t$ is relatively low, there is a low probability the Target is willing to back down. As $\bar{\eta}_t$ increases so that the Target is more likely to be a high cost type, even though threats are less informative, they become more used, surprise attacks decline, and the Target is more likely to be willing to back down with result that the probability of conflict decreases. When $\bar{\eta}_t = 0.875$, for instance, the probability of war is 4 percent, less than a third of what it would be in the absence of a communication mechanism.

When $\bar{\eta}_t$ increases enough that signaling becomes impossible, however, the probability of war jumps discontinuously back from 4 percent to 14 percent for the reason given above. If we were to consider parameterizations where $\bar{\eta}_t$ were much higher, increases in $\bar{\eta}_t$ would again cause the probability of war to decline since Targets for whom war is extremely costly would either decline to take the action in question or make preparations such that the Signaler would itself be deterred from initiating a conflict. Thus, communication results in a non-monotonic relationship between the probability that the sides are willing to fight and the probability of war.

SIGNALING HYPOTHESES

The direct implications of the model, as well as its general logic, lead to several hypotheses. First, as with the Scope of Demand mechanism, we have the general prediction that diplomatic demands will often be informative, even if they are made in private. Second, threats are likely to be most informative when making them carries a potential consequence in terms of the reaction of the threatened state. Thus, the more powerful the threatened state is relative to the threatening state, the more information is conveyed by a threat and the more likely the threatened state is to draw the inference that the threatening state means what it says. This is stated as *Hypothesis 4.1*. Similarly, if relations between the two states are already extremely adversarial, then relations can't get much worse, which means there is less potential consequence to threat-making. This leads to *Hypothesis 4.2*.

Hypothesis 4.1: The higher the ratio of Target to Signaler capabilities, the larger the effect of a threat by the Signaler on observer beliefs.

Hypothesis 4.2: The closer are the relations of the states, the larger the effect of a threat by the Signaler on observer beliefs.

The logic of the model suggests that threats are more likely to cause a breach when the threatened consequence of noncompliance with demands has more negative consequences for the threatened state. If one state threatens another with action that is of little consequence, for instance, then the threatened state is hardly likely to make concessions to a third power in order to form an alliance directed against the threatening state. As Schelling (1966, Chapter 2) points out, however, a threat that is too costly to carry out will certainly not be credible, and the cost of execution and the severity of a threat are likely to be correlated. Thus, the severity of a threat will increase credibility, holding the costs of execution constant. *Hypothesis 4.3* captures this idea.

Hypothesis 4.3: The more severe the threat, the more credible, holding the costs of execution constant.

The model in Chapter 3 implies that concessions will be credible in the sense that observers will conclude that the conceding state will not go to war if the state of affairs proposed in the concession occurs. The model of this chapter makes clear, however, that there are sometimes incentives to hide hostile intentions through offers of concession. This occurs when the preparations for conflict that a Target state could make are particularly effective. This is the reasoning behind *Hypothesis 4.4*.

Hypothesis 4.4: Offers to allow an action, in public or in private, will convince observers that the offering state will not go to war if the action is taken, so long as the potential effect of the Target's preparations for conflict is not too great.

THE EMPIRICAL RECORD

The dynamics predicted by the model are present in many cases. In 3 percent of private diplomatic inferences from the Inference Dataset, the author of the document specifically argues that resolve can be inferred from a threat as a result of the negative consequences that could result from a potential breach in relations. In an additional 9 percent of cases, the British concluded that a threat risked hostile actions on the part of the threatened state.

Several examples of these dynamics can be seen in the relations between Britain and Russia in the early twentieth century. In 1906, for instance, because Russia had been willing to incur worsened relations with Britain to press its interests in the Near East, the British concluded that the Russians would not agree to any settlement of differences which did not address those concerns.[32] In 1910, the British drew a similar inference about German demands for influence in Persia. Though British statesmen still did not believe the Germans were entirely genuine in their statements, they certainly understood that the German willingness to risk relations with Britain demonstrated a measure of resolve.[33]

In the course of discussions, and in making offers and counter offers, diplomats often describe the political context in terms of the model's dynamics. They often say explicitly what their state will do if the other side is too demanding. Thus, the British understood that if they insisted on terms in relations with Germany in 1904, then the latter, in the words of Germany's Chancellor, Bernhard von Bülow, "would be compelled to lean towards Russia."[34] For their part, the Germans must also have understood that making such a statement might cause the British themselves to look for closer alignments with Germany's adversaries.

---

[32] Gooch and Temperley (1979, v. 4, p. 114).
[33] Gooch and Temperley (1979, v. 9, part 1, pp. 165–166).
[34] Bourne and Watt (1987, part I, series F, v. 19, p. 190).

To appreciate the ways that expressions of displeasure, insistence on terms and explicit threat-making affect negotiations in cases, it is instructive to study the concerns of decision makers contemplating such actions. Very often, decision makers worry not about the consequences for their reputations of being caught in a bluff, but about the result on their security positions *if their threats are believed*. In a multipolar context, Bismarck's tacit threat to Russia in 1876 during the Great Eastern Crisis conveyed information because all sides understood the danger that a frustrated Russia would form an alliance with France. In a bipolar context, Kennedy and Khrushchev's threats to each other over the status of Berlin in June of 1961 conveyed information because the two sides understood the danger that each would increase its efforts to harm the interests of the other side, exacerbating the security dilemma dynamic between the two countries.[35]

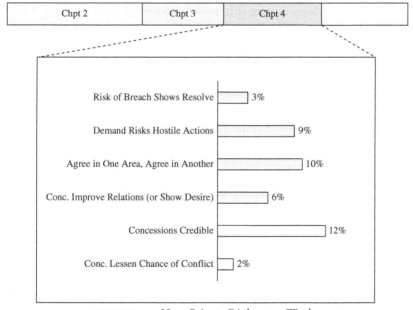

FIGURE 4.7 How Private Diplomacy Works

Note: The proportions shown are of the mechanisms by which private-diplomacy, security-related inferences were drawn in internal, British Government documents in the *Confidential Print* between 1855 and 1914. The bar at the top represents the total number of mechanism codings in the inference dataset; the area in the Chapter 4 portion represents the fraction of these mechanisms addressed only in this chapter. The white bars represent mechanisms that are relevant to the discussion in this chapter, but which were also discussed previously.

[35] See *Foreign Relations of the United States, 1961–1963* (1993), and Jervis (2001).

As we have seen, both episodes had longer term influences on international order. In Bismarck's view, the former created the "new situation" in Europe, which contributed the increased tension between Germany and Russia, the coming together of Germany and Austria, and the eventual formation of two alliance blocks. The latter deepened the Cold War rift, heightening the sides' expectations of the likelihood of conflict.

Also as the model predicts, in the period before the First World War, the British frequently concluded from offers of concession that the conceding state wished to establish better relations more generally, or that agreement in one area would lead to agreement in another. This accounts for fully 16 percent of inferences from private diplomacy. In 1859, for example, when the British took a neutral position in the conflict between Austria and France, the British expected that relations between Britain and Austria would improve and lead to increased cooperation between the two.[36] In 1906, during the First Moroccan Crisis, the British noted that Germany and France appeared to be coming to agreement on banking matters in Morocco and inferred that agreement in this area would enable a more general understanding.[37] In 1906–1907, the British noted German isolation on the continent and viewed German concessions to Russia as attempts to establish closer relations more generally.[38]

CONCLUSION

States often have incentives to adopt more adversarial policies against states they believe are more threatening to their interests. Policies states consider in such contexts include increasing arms production, forming hostile alliances, striking first, draining resources and joining the opposing side in conflicts. One implication is that costless signals of resolve sent by adversaries can convey information in a rationalist framework. A second implication of conceiving of the Target of a threat as having an array of responses is that conflict can occur because resolved states do not communicate their private information even when they could. States that are resolved to fight over a set of issues sometimes have incentive to imitate the behavior of unresolved states.

For the sake of clarity, the model presented in this chapter considered a particular crisis in isolation, but some state decisions have far reaching effects and this has implications for the dynamics described here. A key aspect of the model is the possibility that threat-making can result in outcomes that are worse, from the point of view of the threatening state,

---

[36] Bourne and Watt (1987, part 1, series F, v. 33, p. 8).

[37] Gooch and Temperley (1979, v. 3, part 2, p. 312).

[38] See, for instance, Bourne and Watt (1983, part 1, series A, v.3, p. 287) and Bourne and Watt (1983, part 1, series A, v. 4, p. 283).

than allowing the Target to take the action in question. In the model of a particular crisis, this results from the possibility that a Target might elect to prepare for war, and having prepared, to fight one. More generally, however, the reaction of a Target may have a negative effect on the Signaler's utility even if no war is fought or contemplated. If the Target builds arms or forms an alliance, its increased capabilities may tip the balance of power and result in diminished bargaining outcomes for the Signaler down the road. Thus, even in the event of a peaceful outcome in the current crisis, the Signaler will often find the Target's response to a threat unwelcome.

Similarly, the incentive of a threatened Target in this model to decline to make preparations when it declines to resist the Signaler in a particular crisis may not hold when decisions are made with a view to longer time horizons. If the Target learns from a threat that the Signaler defines its interests as more opposed to the Target's than the Target had previously thought, the Target may elect to form an alliance with a third state that would be detrimental to the interests of the Signaler, even when the Target has no plans to contest the particular issue of the moment. In these international contexts, the dynamics of signaling are likely to be similar to those in the model of an isolated international crisis; the same essential logics of costless diplomacy will apply.

Whether information can be conveyed in particular cases through this form of signaling depends on the context of beliefs and strategic options in which statements are made. For instance, there must be a significant *risk*, but not a near certainty, of a breach in relations. Put differently, there must be a possibility that a threatened state will react against the threatener, not merely by refusing to cooperate on the issue at hand, but with respect to other aspects of the relationship. Up to a point, the greater the likelihood of a breach, and the more serious its consequences for the signaling state, the greater the change in the Target's perceptions of the Signaler's intentions as a result of a threat. If the likelihood of a breach is too great or its consequences too severe, however, highly resolved Signalers may have incentive to deceive Targets by refraining from threatening behavior while planning to attack, thereby catching the Target unprepared. Since Targets are aware of Signalers' incentives, this dynamic can impair the ability of the Signaler to credibly signal peaceful intentions.

These considerations have several implications for the study of interstate coercion. First, increased power does not always increase the credibility of threats. Because, in some contexts, the increased efficacy of Target options will make states more reticent to threaten in the first place, such signals will carry more weight when they are actually used. Second, as in some models of public signaling and signaling based on reputation, beliefs are intersubjective. The statements and actions of other states are interpreted in light of what is believed about these states, and also what these states are known to believe about one's own state. If both sides understand that the Signaler believes the Target fairly likely to back down, for instance, statements by the Signaler will have little marginal effect on the Target's beliefs about the Signaler's intentions. Third, the dynamics of communication introduce unexpected non-monotonicities into the relationship between the factors that affect the likelihood that states are willing to fight over an issue and the probability of war. A decrease in the probability the Target of a threat is willing to fight can increase the probability of war because of the effect of the Target's perceived likely resolve on the possibility of communication. If the decrease in perceived Target resolve makes influential signaling impossible, as is sometimes the case, this increases the likelihood of war. This occurs not because of any actions the Signaler is emboldened to take, but because of the impact on states' ability to communicate. Fourth, sometimes resolved states have incentive to hide their resolve, which results in surprise attacks and wars that could have been avoided if states had just informed each other of the importance they attach to the issues of the day.

The 1876 and 1961 cases are examples of private diplomacy, but we should expect to find the same mechanisms operating alongside other mechanisms of communication in cases of public diplomacy as well. When US President George W. Bush said that Iran is part of an "axis of evil," for instance, this may constitute a tacit threat to take actions against the country's leadership.[39] If Iran were unwilling to comply with US demands, it might have adopted policies designed to drain US capabilities, for instance by frustrating US objectives in Iraq. By demonstrating its willingness to risk such a response, the President's statement may have conveyed information about US resolve to force changes in Iranian policy. A similar dynamic was at work when US Defense Secretary Robert Gates said that unless Russia acquiesces to Western demands in Georgia, "the US–Russian relationship could be adversely affected for years to come." If Russia does not comply with Western demands of this sort, and therefore believes the US more hostile to its interests, Russia will reorient its security posture in ways that have negative consequences for both sides. Though such statements must be interpreted in light of a multitude of factors, including subsequent interactions between the states, by increasing the risk of these negative outcomes, such statements convey intent.

---

[39] White House Press Release, January 29, 2002, "President Delivers State of the Union Address."

5

Balancing Allies and Adversaries

Commitments to fight alongside other states are constituent elements of international orders. The very existence of many states depends on these commitments. Belgium exists in part, for instance, because British security depended on keeping invasion-launching territory out of the hands of great powers. Taiwan, South Korea, and many other states in Europe and elsewhere have been protected by US commitments. A case can be made that the continued existence of most states has depended at some time or another on third party guarantees.

Making such commitments credible poses special challenges, however. It is easier for a state to convince another that it will fight if attacked than that it will fight in defense of a third state. When the costs of war were so high during the nuclearized Cold War, for instance, why should the Soviets have believed that the US would defend Western Europe, much less the isolated Berlin outpost? This difficulty of convincing adversaries has led states to send troops abroad whose role, in the event of combat, is largely to "die heroically, dramatically, and in a manner that guarantees that the action cannot stop there" (Schelling 1966, p. 47). Thus, the US stationed a few troops in Berlin during the Cold War, and maintains 28,500 soldiers in South Korea today. If these troops were attacked, surely the domestic reaction would push a US administration towards intervention.

Yet, in other cases, countries rely on private diplomatic commitments. When Germany committed to defend Austria–Hungary, and Russia Serbia, prior to the First World War, it was what diplomats said behind closed doors that counted with friendly and hostile governments. Today, the US maintains a partial commitment to defend Taiwan without basing any troops on the island. Upon what does the credibility such promises depend?

In negotiations involving three or more states, the signaling mechanisms analyzed in Chapters 3 and 4 are often available alongside others that have been described in bilateral contexts. If the interests of states in a coalition are closely aligned, the coalition can often be thought of as a single actor. When more than two states are involved, however, the possibilities for costless diplomatic signaling actually increase. This chapter analyzes a costless communication mechanism among three or more states that is an essential feature of many international negotiations: statements of a third party to a dispute on behalf of a "protégé" are credible because of the effect these statements can have on the protégé's conduct.

The signaling mechanism analyzed below relates to a central concern of the literature on alliance commitments, namely, the problem of "entrapment" (Jervis, Lebow and Stein 1985, Snyder 1997, Goldstein 2000, Zartman and Faure 2005). When a third party makes a commitment to a protégé, these commitments may embolden the protégé. When one state is emboldened by support from another state, the emboldened state may be more likely to take actions that risk conflict with its adversary, causing the third party to be more likely to be forced to intervene to support the protégé if the third party is indeed willing to do so. As a result, commitments to fight on behalf of other states can convey information to potential adversaries even when those commitments are made behind closed doors. In fact, states can sometimes infer from the bargaining behavior of an adversary whether a third party has committed to the defense of the adversary. These sorts of commitments only constitute entrapment when the third party would prefer to hold the protégé back from aggressive actions against the adversary, but the third party then finds it is unable to do so. When the third party knowingly undertakes a risk of conflict through emboldenment, however, this is a form of diplomatic signaling, and one that appears to be common in international politics.

Signals of this sort are likely to influence the calculations of adversaries when all sides understand that the protégé is in a bargaining relationship with an adversary and two other conditions hold. First, the emboldening effect of the third party's commitment on its protégé must increase the likelihood of conflict more than the deterrent effect of the commitment on the adversary state decreases the likelihood of conflict. This implies that the third party must be powerful enough, but also not too powerful. In fact, because it makes credible signaling impossible, an increase in the power of the third party can increase the likelihood of war. Second, the interests of the third party and protégé must be sufficiently aligned.[1]

---

[1] As discussed below, a number of factors determine whether the third party and Protégé's interests are aligned, including the probability the Protégé would win in a conflict without

One example of these dynamics that is of direct, current relevance is the three-way relationship between China, Taiwan, and the United States (O'Hanlon 2000; Benson and Niou 2005). Policymakers in Taiwan are very sensitive to the level of US commitment, and US policymakers are usually careful to affirm some commitment to defend Taiwan in the event of attack, and at the same time express support for the "one China" policy. If the US were to openly support full Taiwanese independence, it would increase the likelihood that Taiwan will take more concrete steps in that direction. These steps might well increase the likelihood that China would attack. Thus, as a result of making a firm commitment to independence, the US could well find itself forced to choose between the destruction of Taiwan and a military engagement with China. For this reason, if the US were to make such a commitment, even behind closed doors, Chinese officials would be right to revise upward their appraisal of the level of US commitment to defend the Island.

Another example from the diplomacy of the moment concerns the attempts by the United States and Israel to prevent Iran from acquiring a nuclear weapon. Support from the United States has an embolden-ing effect on Israel, perhaps making near term conflict more likely. As a result, US statements of support carry increased credibility. As in the Tai-wan case, all parties understand that in offering support, the US is taking the risk of being forced to fight with its ally or decline to do so, and this risk is entirely separate from any "audience costs" associated with back-ing down that public US commitments may incur. Such risks that arise in multistate contexts are equally felt when diplomacy is carried on behind closed doors, enabling diplomatic signaling.

DIPLOMATIC SIGNALING IN MULTISTATE CONTEXTS

Most scholarly analyses of signaling analyze bilateral contexts. While this is particularly true of formal scholarship, qualitative work, too, has most often examined episodes where one state threatens one other state or coalition of states (cf. Crawford 2003). When scholars have analyzed sig-naling in multistate contexts, they have often done so by applying lessons drawn from bilateral analysis (Fearon 1994*b*).

A substantial body of work examines "extended deterrence," when states commit to defend territories outside their own borders. Studies have analyzed the influence of many factors on deterrence success, includ-ing the local military balance (e.g., Huth and Russett 1984, Huth 1988*a*),

---

aid from the third party and the quality of the bargain the Protégé could strike without support.

states' actions in earlier crises (Huth 1988*b*, Huth 1988*a*), the scope of coercive demands (Werner 2000), and the geopolitical stakes in the region (Danilovic 2002), and some studies examine several of these factors in combination alongside others (Russett 1963). This chapter draws on this literature and the findings from the model analyzed below are often consistent with conclusions from this literature, but the analysis also suggests alternative ways of understanding the influence of some factors on deterrence outcomes. For instance, Huth and Russett (1984) and Danilovic (2002) argue that deterrence is successful when the "defender" has a strong interest in the survival and advancement of the protégé. The analysis below also finds that substantial alignment of the interests of the two is necessary for informative signaling. But this does not imply, as Danilovic suggests, that diplomatic signaling is inconsequential. Rather, uncertainty about whether a third party would join a potential conflict often remains even when interests appear aligned (Gartner and Siverson 1996, Smith 1996), and it is this uncertainty that costless, diplomatic signals can remove when the defender has a sufficient interest in the protégé. Similarly, the analysis provides a new perspective on the debate over the role of military power in successful coercion (Maoz 1983, Huth and Russett 1984, Karsten, Howell and Allen 1984, Lebow and Stein 1989, Fearon 1994*b*, Signorino and Tarar 2006). In the costless signaling model, while sufficient power is a necessary factor in coercion, too high a level of power makes signaling impossible and can thereby decrease the probability of coercive success.[2]

Scholars in this literature have recognized that extended deterrence is importantly different from bilateral coercion (Morgan 1983). It is commonly accepted, for instance, that extended deterrent threats are more difficult to make credible than threats to defend the homeland (Schelling 1966, Chapter 2). Nevertheless, researchers have not focused on whether the underlying signaling mechanisms involved mirror those of bilateral contests. For instance, one model that does examine three actors is Quackenbush (2006), which argues that when two states are in alliance and each would want to defend the other only if the other would defend it, then the more reliable of the alliance partners is the one that the third state is more likely to attack. This study and a few others examine dynamics among three players, but they do not analyze the effects of statements of commitment (Zagare and Kilgour 2003, Wagner 2004, Yuen 2009, Fang, Johnson and Leeds 2012).[3] Benson (2012) examines a three-player model with the possibility of emboldenment of a protégé,

[2] For related discussion, see Sechser (2010) and Snyder and Diesing (1977).
[3] Kilgour and Zagare (1994) examine extended deterrence through a two-player model.

but focuses on when a third party would make probabilistic, conditional or firm commitments and therefore assumes rather than demonstrates that the third party has such commitment options available. Perhaps the most similar model to the one analyzed below is the three-player costless signaling model investigated in Smith (1998*b*). This model shows how costless signals can influence beliefs, but, consistent with bilateral signaling models, does so through analysis of the reaction of a domestic constituency to public statements of commitment. The literature on intervention in the internal affairs of other states also considers dynamics among three actors, including when state signals can encourage and embolden a substate group, which is related to the analysis below. These works do not connect the emboldenment of the group to the credibility of signals, however (Cetinyan 2002, Kuperman 2008, Grigoryan 2010). No studies in the international politics literature of three or more actors examine the effect of costless statements of commitment that do not derive their credibility from the reactions of domestic constituencies to public actions.[4]

The literature on the credibility of alliance commitments is also closely related to the topic addressed here. Much of that literature has focused on factors that make allies more or less likely to fight together (e.g., Snyder 1997, Benson 2011), or examines empirically whether alliances influence adversary calculations (e.g., Huth and Russett 1984, Leeds 2003). Studies that explicitly investigate the mechanism through which alliance commitments influence adversary calculations have generally focused on the public aspect of alliance formation. When alliance commitments are modeled in a way that allows them to convey information, this is primarily a result of the domestic or international reputational costs that backing down from the public commitment would entail (Leeds 1999, Morrow 2000). Scholars have also considered the signaling effects of sunk costs involved in alliance formation (Morrow 1994, Smith 1995, Smith 1998*a*), and increased fighting ability through the harmonization of military planning (Morrow 1994, Smith 1998*a*), as well as the effects of regime type (Gaubatz 1996, Leeds 1999). Thus, these studies also view signaling in multistate contexts as essentially similar to bilateral signaling; the same mechanisms are thought to apply in the same ways.

This chapter examines a signaling mechanism that is available *only* in the multistate context, and one that does not depend on reputation or the sunk costs of alliance commitment. As in earlier chapters, information is communicated in equilibrium through costless signals. As such,

---

4 Walter (2002) and Clare and Danilovic (2010) discuss incentives to build reputation due to multiple strategic adversaries.

the model helps to explain inferences drawn from private diplomatic encounters and informal agreements (Trager 2013). The model is also intentionally very similar to other models of two players described in the literature. This makes it clear that the changed effects of costless communication are the specific consequence of the signaling possibilities that are created when more than two parties are involved.

The analysis here is consistent with a substantial theoretical literature that notes that increasing the number of players can increase the possibilities for communication, and thereby increase the set of equilibrium outcomes. Forges (1990), for instance, shows that with four or more players, any correlated equilibrium outcome of a game can also be an equilibrium outcome of the game with (unmediated) communication between the players. Since the set of correlated equilibria is often larger than the set of Nash equilibria, this shows that communication often increases the set of equilibrium outcomes. With fewer players, however, communication increases the set of equilibrium outcomes only in a more restricted set of games. This literature establishes the possible effects of communication without describing mechanisms that it is reasonable to expect would actually be used by diplomats and leaders, however.

This chapter, by contrast, develops a mechanism that is very simple and appears to track common considerations of decision makers in international politics. The analysis also shows that *even in the highly adversarial context* of international crisis bargaining, increasing the number of actors enables information to be communicated that otherwise could not be, which is surprising (Crawford and Sobel 1982). The availability of mechanisms for costlessly communicating resolve in turn affects expectations about the outcomes of crises.

A MODEL OF MULTI-PARTY NEGOTIATION

Consider a game in which a "Third Party" (d) sends a costless signal $m \in M$ to a "Protégé" (g) and a "Target" (t) where $0, 1 \in M$ and M is large but finite.[5] The set of players is $I \equiv \{d, g, t\}$ with generic element i. After the signal, a standard crisis bargaining game occurs that can be thought of as a much simplified version of the game in Powell (1996a,b). Following any message m, the Protégé makes a demand $x \in [0, 1]$ on the Target. If the Target accepts, the risk neutral payoffs are x for the Protégé and $1 - x$ for the Target. If the Target rejects the offer, the Protégé decides whether to fight or not. If the Protégé does not fight, the *status quo* is

---

[5] In some literatures, the Third Party is called the "Defender."

maintained, and payoffs for the Protégé and Target are $q \in [0, 1]$ and $1 - q$, respectively.

If the Protégé fights, the Third Party decides whether or not to join the conflict on the side of the Protégé. In a conflict, the Protégé wins with probability $p \in (0, 1)$ if the Third Party does not join in and probability $p^a > p$ if the Third Party does (where $p^a < 1$). The side that wins the conflict chooses its most preferred outcome in X, 1 for the Protégé and 0 for the Target. The Third Party and Protégé have the same preference orderings over outcomes in X, but possibly different costs of conflict. Thus, if the Third Party declines to join the conflict, expected utilities for the Protégé, Target, and Third Party are $p - c_g$, $1 - p - c_t$, and p, respectively. If the Third Party fights, expected utilities for the players are $p^a - c_g$, $1 - p^a - c_t$, and $p^a - c_d$.

Assume that the Protégé prefers the *status quo* to fighting alone and prefers fighting with the Third Party to the *status quo*. Formally, this means $p - c_g < q < p^a - c_g$. Assume that the Third Party and Target's costs of war are the private information of the player and can be either high or low. Formally, for $i = d, t$, $c_i = \underline{c_i}$ with probability h_i and $c_i = \bar{c_i}$ with probability $1 - h_i$ where $\underline{c_i} < \bar{c_i}$ and h_d and h_t are independent. The Third Party prefers to fight with the Protégé if and only if the Third Party has low costs of conflict, so $p^a - \bar{c_d} < p < p^a - \underline{c_d}$. Let $\mu_i(m)$ be player i's updated belief that $c_d = \underline{c_d}$ following message m.

In two-player contexts of this sort, no information can be conveyed by the Third Party's statements. In the three-player context, however, that is not so. I will show that a fully informative equilibrium can exist in which the two types of Third Party send different messages, so that, upon receiving the message, both the Protégé and Target know for certain whether the Third Party is willing to fight on behalf of the Protégé. In this equilibrium, the Third Party's statements change the Protégé's actions, and this influence on the Protégé's conduct changes the incentives of the Third Party and implies that the Third Party may have no reason to mislead the Target. In game theoretic terms, the equilibrium is fully separating: the Third Party sends a statement of support for the Protégé if and only if the Third Party is willing to fight on the side of the Protégé if necessary; the Protégé makes a high demand that risks conflict if and only if it is supported; the Target rejects an unsupported Protégé's demand if it is too high (which does not occur in equilibrium) or a supported Protégé's demand if the Target is a low cost type; and, on the equilibrium path, the Protégé fights if and only if it is supported and its high demand is rejected by the Target. For this sort of signaling to be possible at all, several formal conditions must hold. I will develop each of these conditions and the intuition behind them before stating sufficient conditions for the existence of such an equilibrium in a proposition.

First, note that in a signaling equilibrium of this sort, the Protégé and Target must be in a bargaining relationship, the Protégé's optimal behavior must be affected by its expectations about whether the Third Party will offer support in a conflict, and the optimal behavior of a Protégé that expects support must imply a greater probability of war than the optimal behavior of a Protégé that does not expect support. This implies that the Third Party cannot be so powerful that even a more resolute Target would prefer to give up the whole of the issues in dispute rather than wage a war against both the Protégé and Third Party. If the Third Party were so powerful, the Target would be completely deterred from contesting the issues, and the probability of conflict when the support of the Third Party is expected would be zero. This would give the Third Party too large an incentive to offer its support, even if it were not willing to really give it, and signaling would be impossible. Formally, since the expected value of war for the more resolute Target when the Third Party fights is $1 - p^a - \underline{c}_t$, signaling is only possible when $1 - p^a - \underline{c}_t > 0$ or $p^a + \underline{c}_t < 1$. Thus, while the Third Party must be strong enough that the Protégé would want to fight rather accept the *status quo* when the Protégé is assured of Third Party support ($p^a - c_g > q$ as assumed), this analysis shows that when the Third Party is too powerful (p^a too high), nothing the Third Party says will affect the beliefs of the other players about what the Third Party is actually willing to do.

For the expectation of support from the Third Party to generate a greater risk of conflict, the Protégé's demand must be large enough that there is a possibility the Target may reject the demand. If this is not so, for any demand that can be made in equilibrium, the probability of conflict is zero and so cannot be larger than in cases where the Protégé does not have an expectation of support. In equilibrium, when it expects support, the Protégé must make either a high demand ($p^a + \overline{c}_t$) or a low demand ($p^a + \underline{c}_t$). If the Protégé makes the low demand, the risk of conflict is zero if the players expect Third Party support in a conflict. Thus, in a signaling equilibrium, the Protégé must be willing to make the high demand, which it is when its expected utility of making that demand ($h_t(p^a - c_g) + (1 - h_t)(\min\{1, p^a + \overline{c}_t\})$) is greater than its expected utility for the lesser demand ($p^a + \underline{c}_t$). When the Target is willing to fight unless it receives at least some of the good in question so that $1 - p^a - \overline{c}_t > 0 \Leftrightarrow p^a + \overline{c}_t < 1$, the Protégé is willing to make the high demand when:

$$h_t \leq \frac{\overline{c}_t - \underline{c}_t}{\overline{c}_t + c_g}. \tag{3}$$

In other words, for signaling to occur, it cannot be too certain that the Target is a high resolve type because if it were, the Protégé would not be willing to make a high demand and an expectation of Third Party support would merely allow the Protégé to get more without incurring any increased risk of conflict. This, in turn, would make expressing support too tempting for the Third Party to resist, even when it would not be willing to follow through, and this makes signaling impossible.

For costless signaling to occur, the Third Party must of course be willing to reveal its type. If the Third Party reveals that it is not willing to support the Protégé, then no demand for an improvement in the *status quo* is credible. The Target will understand that the Protégé prefers the *status quo* to conflict and the Target will therefore reject any demand greater than q and the *status quo* will be the outcome of the game. The first condition for incentive compatibility in a separating equilibrium is therefore that the unresolved Third Party prefer to reveal its type, yielding a payoff of q, to pretending to be resolved, which yields an expected payoff of $h_t p + (1 - h_t)(p^a + \bar{c}_t)$ since, given that the Protégé makes a high demand, there is an h_t chance that the Target rejects the offer and a war is fought in which the Third Party does not join in and a $(1 - h_t)$ chance that the Protégé's high demand is accepted. Thus, the first incentive compatibility condition is satisfied when:

$$h_t \geq \frac{p^a + \bar{c}_t - q}{p^a + \bar{c}_t - p}. \tag{4}$$

Analysis of equation (4) immediately tells us that for signaling to occur, it must be the case that $p < q$. If this is not the case, then there is no drawback for the Third Party to pretend to be willing to offer support if it is not willing to do so. In effect, even if the Third Party isn't willing to join in the conflict, it still prefers that the Protégé and Target fight a war to maintaining the *status quo*. This is so because the Protégé's prospects in the war are sufficiently favorable relative to the current state of affairs. Thus, signaling requires that the Protégé be sufficiently weak. Equation (4) also indicates that there must be a sufficiently high likelihood that the Target is the more resolved type. If this probability is not sufficiently high, then unresolved Third Parties will again be too tempted to misrepresent their willingness to support their Protégé.

The final incentive compatibility condition for informative signaling is that a resolved Third Party prefer to reveal its type. If it does not do so, as we have seen, a high offer from the Protégé will not be accepted, the Protégé will not elect to fight, and the payoff to the Third Party will be q. When a resolved Third Party signals its willingness to fight on behalf of the Protégé, the Third Party's expected utility is $h_t(p^a - \underline{c}_d) + (1 - $

$h_t)(p^a + \bar{c}_t)$. Thus, resolved Third Parties are willing to reveal their type when:

$$h_t \leq \frac{p^a + \bar{c}_t - q}{\bar{c}_t + \underline{c}_d}. \tag{5}$$

For these conditions to be satisfied simultaneously, the parameters must be such that the right-hand side of equations (3) and (5) is greater than the right-hand side of equation (4). Proposition 5.1 gives sufficient conditions for this to be the case so that a range of values of h_t produce a separating equilibrium in which the costless signals of the Third Party convey its type. In the proposition, the condition that p is sufficiently low helps to ensure that less resolved Third Parties will not pretend to be resolved and thereby risk that their relatively weak Protégé finds itself in an unsupported conflict. Low $\underline{c}_d$ implies that a more resolved Third Party is willing to incur the risk of war that supporting the Protégé entails. The condition on the resolved Target's costs of war, $\underline{c}_t$, results from the influence these costs have on the quality of the bargain the Protégé can strike without risking war. The less the Target wants to go to war, the better the bargain for the Protégé. Thus, low $\underline{c}_t$ implies that the bargain the Protégé can negotiate without risking war may be poor enough that the Protégé decides instead to make an offer that risks conflict when the Protégé's costs of conflict, c_g, are also sufficiently low.[6]

Proposition 5.1: For $p, \underline{c}_d, \underline{c}_t, c_g$ sufficiently low, $p^a + \bar{c}_t < 1$ and h_t in a middle range, a separating perfect Bayesian equilibrium exists in which $\mu_i(0) = 0$ and $\mu_i(1) = 1 \forall i$.

When the conditions given in Proposition 5.1 are satisfied, the likelihood that the Target is highly resolved is neither too great nor too small. It is not so large that the Third Party would not be willing to risk war in offering to support the Protégé and the Protégé would not be willing to risk conflict in negotiations when it receives such an offer of support. Yet, the likelihood that the Target is highly resolved is not so small that the Third Party would always be willing to incur the risks of conflict that supporting the Protégé entails. When the actors' incentives are in balance in this way, signaling is possible.

To summarize, in the signaling equilibrium, the Protégé makes a high demand if and only if it receives support from the Third Party. The Target

---

[6] Note that since the Third Party's statements are costless, as in all such models, a babbling equilibrium exists in which none of the parties tries to communicate and thus none listens either. These equilibria, which do not appear to correspond to the understandings and intentions of diplomats and state leaders, are discussed in the previous chapter.

accedes to the Protégé's high demand if and only if the Target is not highly resolved. If the Protégé makes a low demand, the Target is certain to agree to that as well. If the Target does not accept the Protégé's demand and the Protégé has support from the Third Party, the Protégé will go to war. Thus, support from the Third Party improves the Protégé's bargaining position, but also increases the probability of war. Nevertheless, since only resolved Third Parties are willing to embroil their Protégés in a potential conflict, the Third Party's signal conveys information.

Several important extensions to the model are considered in Appendix A. These show that signaling of the form described above is still possible when separate private signals are sent to the Protégé and Target and when the Target may choose to attack the Protégé. It is also shown that even if the Target ignores the private signal from the Third Party, essentially similar equilibria exist in which (1) the Third Party's private signal to the Protégé allows the Protégé to infer the Third Party's type, and (2) the Target learns the Third Party's type from observing the Protégé's behavior. This last result is useful in interpreting cases.

DISCUSSION

The basic signaling mechanism formalized above is simple and the logic can be easily applied to cases. When a Third Party threatens to defend a Protégé against a Target state, the Third Party will affect the Protégé's behavior towards the Target. Often, the Protégé will adopt a more aggressive or defiant policy vis-à-vis the Target state as a result. These actions may, in turn, increase the likelihood that the Target and Protégé engage in military conflict. As a result, the Third Party's support makes it more likely that the Third Party will actually be faced with the choice of having to follow through on its commitments or risk the destruction of the Protégé. Thus, in Schelling's terms, the Third Party's threat leaves to chance the possibility that an emboldened Protégé will precipitate a conflict. The Third Party's support shows a willingness to take this chance, causing its statement to convey information to the other states.[7] The players' strategies are represented in Figure 5.1.

If, however, the Protégé has no opportunity to take actions that make conflict more likely or if the Third Party's statements – were they to be believed – would make conflict less likely, then the Third Party's messages would convey nothing to the other players. It is only the increased risk of conflict that sending a statement of commitment entails in equilibrium

---

[7] Note that in closely related models with a continuum of Third Party cost types, semi-separating equilibria exist in which signals convey information, but bluffing by Third Parties occurs in some cases.

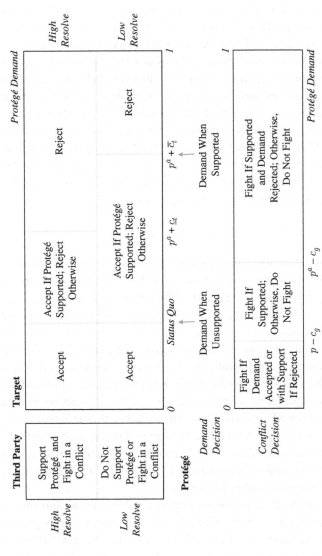

Figure 5.1 Player Strategies in a Signaling Equilibrium

that causes the statement to convey information about the Third Party's intentions. By incurring a greater risk of war, the Third Party is able to signal to the Target and thereby possibly gain a better negotiated outcome for the Protégé. Thus, entrapment is not just a cost associated with making a strong commitment to an ally. Emboldenment and even the possibility of later entrapment is rather what makes some commitments to allies credible at all.[8]

These considerations imply that this form of signaling is available in some international contexts, but not in all. Two general conditions must hold. First, through emboldenment of the Protégé, support from the Third Party must be expected to increase the likelihood of a disastrous conflict for an unsupported Protégé. Second, the Third Party and Protégé's interests must be sufficiently aligned. This second condition implies that the Third Party would not want to mislead the Protégé into fighting alone; the Third Party must prefer the status quo to a war that the Protégé fights alone.[9]

For the first of these conditions to hold, several subsidiary conditions must hold. The likelihood that the Target is highly resolved must be in a middle range. If the Target is too certain to be resolved, the Protégé would not make a high demand that risks conflict. If the Target is too certain to be of low resolve, the Third Party will be too tempted to support the Protégé even when the Third Party is not resolved to offer aid and the Protégé will be too tempted to make a high demand whether or not the Third Party offers support. Thus, signaling is impossible when Third Parties have an incentive to overstate their levels of resolve to come to the aid of their Protégés, as in many other models in the literature (Fearon 1995), and also when Third Parties have an incentive to understate their levels of resolve. The Third Party also cannot be too powerful; if it is, the Target will be deterred from risking conflict. Finally, the Protégé must prefer the *status quo* to fighting alone against the Target; otherwise, the Protégé's actions would not be contingent upon Third Party support.[10]

---

[8] Note that in the cheap talk model, messages do not change preferences. Unlike much of the literature relating to entrapment cited above, therefore, the model examines when preferences can be communicated, rather than how preferences can be changed such that a commitment is created. For further analysis of the relationship between emboldenment and entrapment, see the discussion of the related model in the Online Appendix to Trager (2015) and, for a partially contrasting perspective, Kim (2011).

[9] This is so in the model when $p < q$ because it is assumed that the Third Party and Protégé have the same preferences over the bargaining space. The condition that $p < q$ ensures that the Third Party would not want the Protégé to fight when the Third Party would not be willing to come to the Protégé's aid.

[10] The other specific conditions given in the propositions guarantee that the players are willing to take actions that risk conflict.

These considerations can be applied to cases of extended coercion. When Belgium is faced with invasion, for instance, Britain may well prefer that Belgium resist the invasion even without immediate British support because of the potential that an invasion of Britain could be launched from Belgian territory. In this context, therefore, the second general condition for signaling is violated: British and Belgian interests are not so aligned that Britain would be unwilling to risk the destruction of its Protégé when Britain is unwilling or unable to offer immediate support.[11] If British statements of commitment change adversary calculations, therefore, it is not as a result of the signaling logic described here. A key reason for this divergence in interests is the presumption that an invasion would result in the end of Belgium as a political entity. If, on the other hand, a neighboring country were only to threaten to invade a portion of Belgian territory, then Britain might reason that it would be in British interests that Belgium not resist the invasion in order to preserve the rest of Belgian territory – if Britain were in fact not willing to intervene. This dynamic more resembles the negotiations over Czechoslovakia in 1938. If Britain and France had committed to the defense of Czechoslovakia, the Czechs would have fought rather than give up any part of the Sudentenland. Since it was unclear whether the Czech negotiating stance would then have resulted in a conflict with Germany, British and French statements might have sent a strong signal to Germany about British and French resolve. In this instance, both general signaling conditions are satisfied: the British and French believed that support would increase the odds of conflict and British, French and Czech interests were sufficiently aligned such that the two Third Parties would not have wanted to commit to support they were not willing to provide.

When a Third Party, along with a Protégé, attempts to compel a Target to take a particular action that the Target may not be willing to take, known as "compellence" (Schelling 1966, pp. 70–71), the Third Party's statements may be quite likely to convey information to the Target. Making such a threat will change the Protégé's behavior towards the Target and, as Schelling (1966) argues, all sides will expect that the potentially humiliating demand that the Target's behavior also change may be resisted. Threats of coordinated action by allies to force behavioral modifications in a third state, therefore, where neither ally would wish to see the other left to face the third state alone and at least one ally is known to be keen to act, will often be credible (Benson 2012). Not all

---

[11] In the terms of the model, we can think of $q < p$ where q is the portion of territory with which Belgium is left following the invasion. Thus, Britain prefers that Belgium fight without support, but Belgium has the opposite preference.

compellent threats will convey information, however. The Target's calculus will not be affected, for instance, when the threat cannot engender a sufficient risk of conflict because the Target is expected to concede in response to a credible threat and the Protégé would not then have to engage in a conflict.

Similarly, some but not all deterrent threats will convey information through the mechanism described here. Suppose, as was the case with negotiations over Czechoslovakia in 1938 for instance, that the Target – Germany – is mobilizing to march to occupy a portion of the territory of the Protégé. We can think of the portion of territory that the Target intends to occupy as represented by $1 - q$ in the model. The Protégé may only be willing to resist the invasion if the Protégé expects support from the Third Party. In such cases, a statement of support from the Third Party may be able to convey information to the other two states about the Third Party's willingness to fight. In the absence of support from the Third Party, the Target will reject any offer from the Protégé in which the Target does not possess the disputed territory because the Target will understand that any threat of the Protégé's to fight is not credible. On the other hand, a Protégé that expects Third Party support will demand that the invasion cease. If the optimal demand of a Protégé that expects support implies a sizable risk of conflict, then the Third Party will only embolden the Protégé to risk conflict if the Third Party is willing to come to the Protégé's aid if conflict should result. This enables the Third Party to signal its resolve to fight or not to the other states. Since the Third Party's support provides the Protégé with a credible threat to resist an invasion, this support may deter the Target from invading. Note, however, that the Third Party's statements deter only because they *do not* reduce the likelihood of conflict. On the contrary, in order to deter an invasion, the Third Party must embolden the Protégé in such a way that war may result.

To see how these dynamics operate in the conflict model described above, consider a case where signaling is possible. This occurs in the middle of Figure 5.2, where the probability that the Target is highly resolved, h_t, is neither too small nor too large and the probability the Protégé wins a conflict with the Target without support from the Third Party, p, is not too high. Now, suppose that h_t increases.[12] If it increases enough, such that the Target is very likely to refuse the Protégé's demand, then the Third Party becomes unwilling to offer to support to the Protégé

---

[12] The following parameters produce the equilibrium shown in the Figure: $p^a = .75$, $\underline{c}_t = c_g = .01$, $\bar{c}_t = .25$, $\underline{c}_d = .2$, $\bar{c}_d = .9$, $h_d = .9$, $q = .7$. Note that while the Figure does not show the whole $(0, 1)$ interval for the parameters h_t and p, the illustrated signaling and non-signaling ranges naturally extend to this interval.

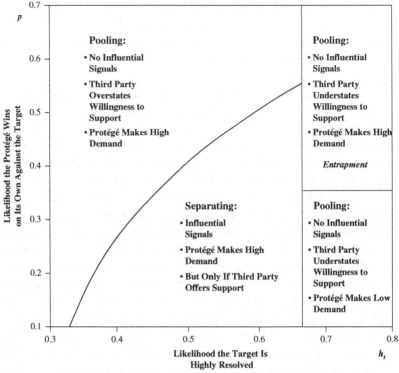

FIGURE 5.2 Equilibrium Signaling Properties

even when the Third Party would be willing to support the Protégé if a war were to result. Equation (5) does not hold; the interests of Third Party and Protégé are not sufficiently aligned. If the Protégé is sufficiently strong (so that p is sufficiently high), and is therefore willing to precipitate a conflict with the Target, this is a case of *entrapment*. Third Parties that are willing to fight would prefer not to have to, but the Protégé also understands this and will not pay the Third Party's signals any mind. The Protégé will press ahead without the Third Party's commitment of support because the Protégé understands that the lack of support does not mean that the Third Party will not come through when it is faced with the choice of whether or not to allow its Protégé to face the Target alone. The Third Party cannot restrain its own Protégé at the final moment.[13]

Signaling can also fail when h_t is too low. In fact, signaling must fail when h_t is sufficiently low because equation (4) cannot hold. The reason is that if it is too likely that the Target will accept a high demand by

---

[13] Note that for entrapment to be possible, the Protégé must have a sufficiently high expectation, h_d, that the Third Party will join in the conflict if a conflict were to begin.

a Protégé that is offered support, then the Third Party would always choose to offer support, even if it were not willing to really provide it. The Third Party has incentive to overstate its level of resolve because the Target is too likely to back down as a result. Although the interests of Third Party and Protégé are aligned, the Third Party's support does not sufficiently increase the likelihood of conflict. Thus, signaling requires sufficient uncertainty about what the Target will do. Without uncertainty *on both sides of a dispute*, signals cannot be meaningful. These dynamics are illustrated by the curved line between the Separating and Pooling regions in Figure 5.2.

Figure 5.2 further illustrates that increases in the strength of the Protégé relative to the Target, p, can also make signaling impossible. The reason is that, when the Protégé is strong, there is less risk to the Third Party in supporting the Protégé when the Third Party is unwilling to come to the Protégé's aid. If the Third Party's support emboldens the Protégé and the Protégé and Target end up at war as a result, the Third Party reasons, the Protégé still has a good chance of emerging victorious without assistance. This gives the Third Party a powerful incentive to claim to be willing to support the Protégé even when the Third Party isn't. When the Protégé is sufficiently weak, the Third Party has no such incentive. Then, emboldening and not supporting the Protégé incurs a real risk of disaster – the destruction of an unsupported Protégé.[14]

This form of signaling can both increase and decrease the probability of war, relative to the case where no communication is possible, depending on the values of the parameters. This can be seen in Figure 5.3, which shows how the probability of conflict is affected by the probability that the Target is highly resolved.[15] The figure illustrates a case where the probability that the Third Party will assist the Protégé is thought to be relatively high by all players at the start of the game. When the probability that the Target is highly resolved is low, but not so low that signaling is impossible, the existence of a signaling mechanism decreases the probability of war. In the absence of a signaling mechanism, believing that the Target is relatively unlikely to be highly resolved, the Protégé makes

---

[14] Note also that if there is a danger that the Target will attack a pacific Protégé in order to demand more than the status quo, signaling may also be impossible when p is too low. In the main model described above, for clarity of exposition of the dynamics of the model, a conflict is started if and only if the Protégé elects to begin one. If instead the Target chooses whether or not to begin a conflict, the dynamics are similar as long as the emboldenment of the Protégé outweighs the deterrent effect of the Third Party's statement on the Target so that the overall likelihood of conflict is increased. A model that formalizes this is available in the Online Appendix to Trager (2015).

[15] Numerical values used to generate Figure 5.3 are: $p^a = .85$, $\underline{c}_t = .01$, $c_g = .05$, $\bar{c}_t = .1$, $\underline{c}_d = .2$, $\bar{c}_d = .9$, $h_d = .9$, $q = .75$, $p = .4$.

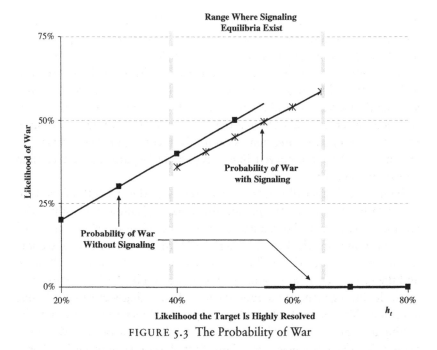

FIGURE 5.3 The Probability of War

a high demand on the Target and if the Target refuses, the Protégé then prefers war to the *status quo*. Thus, the probability of conflict is simply the probability that the Target is highly resolved. When costless signaling is possible in equilibrium, however, the probability of conflict is less. The reason is that the Protégé makes a very high demand only when it has the support of the Third Party. The probability of war when signaling is possible is simply the joint probability that the Third Party and Target are both highly resolved. In fact, this is the probability of conflict in the signaling equilibrium over the entire range where signals are possible.

On the right of the figure, we see the result when the Target is believed likely to be highly resolved. In the absence of communication, the Protégé would decide to make a low demand that the Target would be certain to accept and which both sides prefer to war. Thus, when the Target is believed sufficiently likely to be highly resolved, the probability of war is zero. When signaling is possible, this is dramatically lower than the probability of conflict in the communication equilibrium. It is also worth noting that in cases where the probability that the Third Party is willing to help the Protégé is not so high, different from the case illustrated in Figure 5.3, communication often substantially increases the probability of war because in the absence of a communication mechanism, the Protégé would not dare to challenge the Target. The effects of communication on conflict, therefore, are not straightforward. The existence of diplomatic channels raises or lowers the probability of conflict, depending on the context.

As a final observation about the model, note that even though there are many messages that the Third Party could send, there is no equilibrium in which the Third Party can credibly convince the other players that the Third Party will defend the Protégé if and only if the Protégé maintains the status quo and is attacked by the Target. The reason is that when a war is win or lose without the possibility of an intermediate outcome, Third Parties either prefer to support the Target in war or prefer to remain out of a conflict. Indeed, in such cases, how could a Third Party acquire a preference to support a Protégé only if the Protégé were attacked? If the Third Party's preferences derive from the objective, material outcome, then no Third Party could acquire such a contingent preference and therefore no such mixture of threats could be credible. Therefore, when a war will result in decisive victory or defeat, if contingent threats are ever to be credible in a rationalist model of politics, the Third Party must have a preference for being listened to, possibly because observers will take note of whether the Third Party was listened to and this will have implications for the future. Contingent signaling is generally impossible in models of a single crisis, considered in isolation, at least when wars, should they occur, will be decisive.[16]

SIGNALING HYPOTHESES

In general terms, the analysis of the model leads to the following three necessary conditions for the form of signaling described above. First, for the model to apply, the sides must have common knowledge that the Protégé will consider pressing its advantage against the Target if the Protégé is supported by the Third Party. I refer to this as emboldenment. For purposes of empirical testing, emboldenment shall be specifically defined as either pressing for a better deal in negotiations or taking actions that run a higher risk of conflict. Second, the expectation of the states must be that the increased stridency of the Protégé will increase the likelihood of conflict. This ensures that the Third Party and Protégé will not have too much to gain from overstating their levels of resolve. If the deterrent effect on the Target is so strong that the overall likelihood of conflict is reduced by the Third Party's commitment, then, while the commitment may still be credible, the Target's beliefs will not be altered by the fact of the commitment by virtue of the mechanism described here. Third,

[16] Contingent and probabilistic alliance commitments are examined, both theoretically and empirically, in Benson (2011) and Benson (2012).

the interests of the Third Party and Protégé must be sufficiently aligned. These considerations lead to the following three testable hypotheses.

Hypothesis 5.1: Diplomatic support will cause observers to infer that the supported state has been emboldened.

Hypothesis 5.2: Diplomatic support will sometimes cause observers to infer that the support has increased the odds of conflict.

Hypothesis 5.3: The more closely aligned the interests of Third Party and Protégé, the more likely are statements of support to cause observers to revise upward their belief that the Third Party will support the Protégé.

Note that the analysis of this chapter more precisely implies that *Hypothesis 5.1* will hold when support increases the likelihood of conflict and the interests of the Third Party and Protégé are aligned. The hypothesis is stated without these conditions because the first is difficult to evaluate empirically and because the signaling logics of earlier chapters can also imply the credibility of a threat to the Target and therefore emboldenment. Further, since support never discourages a Protégé, the hypothesis is true on average.

It is interesting to note that intuition might actually predict the opposite of *Hypothesis 5.3*. One might reason is that if the Third Party and Protégé are already closely aligned, the probability observers assign to the likelihood of material support may already be high. As a result, a statement of support might be less likely to cause a change in observer beliefs. The model predicts the opposite, however.

A variety of other complex, interacting factors discussed above will also influence what observers infer from support and its lack. These are difficult to formulate as hypotheses that could be convincingly tested with existing data. One corollary to *Hypothesis 5.1* can be stated, however. Observers can understand the Third Party's intentions equally well from the behavior of the Protégé as from the direct statements of the Third Party.[17]

Hypothesis 5.4: The more uncompromising a Protégé, the more likely are observers to conclude that the Protégé has received diplomatic support.

---

[17] This logic is complicated somewhat if we model uncertainty about the Protégé's resolve in addition to uncertainty about the Third Party's resolve, but even in that case, the Protégé's actions can still serve as a signal of the Third Party's intentions.

THE EMPIRICAL RECORD

In many empirical cases, the three conditions for informative signaling appear to hold. I shall discuss a couple cases in which the interests of the Third Party and its Protégé were closely aligned and understood as such by the states involved. To evaluate the model in general terms, I briefly examine whether (1) the Protégé was understood to be emboldened by support (or restrained by its absence), (2) the Third Party's support and the changed behavior of the Protégé were thought to increase the odds of conflict, (3) support or its absence affected the calculations of observers, and (4) these observers grounded their inferences – at least in part – in whether support would increase the risk of conflict.[18]

In the crisis that led to the Second Italian War of Independence in 1859, France declined to insist that Piedmont-Sardinia disarm in the ongoing crisis with Austria. This amounted to French support, as observers at the time understood. Later, when the French emperor told other powers that "if means were not found, and that immediately, for restoring Europe to its natural equilibrium, he must at once put the French army on a war footing," this too was understood as a threat to support Sardinia in a war with Austria.[19]

Austria was much stronger than an unsupported Sardinia, and all observers therefore understood that the aggressive Sardinian negotiating stance was the result of French support.[20] As the Austrians put it to the British, "We are not afraid of Sardinia ... but we consider Sardinia to be the advanced guard of France."[21] It was also generally appreciated that the Sardinian stance increased the likelihood of conflict because Austria would not accept being dictated to by an inferior power. In fact, war was seen as so likely that a conference of the powers was convened to try to avert it.

As the model predicts, the British and Austrians concluded that French support indicated that France was more likely to join Sardinia in a conflict. The British ambassador to France, Earl Cowley, who had hitherto taken the position that France would not support Sardinia, changed his

---

[18] Literature on extended deterrence analyzes when deterrent threats are likely to be coercive. Fearon (1994*b*) and Huth (1988*a*), for instance, examine 58 cases between 1885 and 1988 of extended "immediate" deterrence, where conflict appears likely prior to the threat. They find mixed evidence that the Target was more likely to back down in response to the threat. As we have seen, however, coercive success is not the same thing as convincing the adversary and the model above demonstrates that states will often be convinced when they are unwilling to be coerced.

[19] British Parliament (1859, v. XXXII, p. 119).

[20] For an overview of events, see Beales (1982).

[21] British Parliament (1859, v. XXXII, p. 212).

view. He wrote to the British Foreign Office that France would, "go to [Sardinian] assistance, if she is attacked by Austria ...[the French emperor] is jealous of the preponderance which Austria exercises over the Italian Peninsula. ...[and] to diminish it he is ready to accept war."[22] This inference was correct: France colluded with the aspirants for Italian unification to bring about the war that resulted in the Austrian loss of most of the northern Italian province of Lombardy.[23] In discussing events, observers did not explicitly ground their inferences in the increased risk of conflict that France incurred through its support of Sardinia, but their conclusions were consistent with this understanding.

In July, 1914, following the assassination of the Archduke, Germany communicated its support to Austria–Hungary in what has become known as the "blank check." This support emboldened Austria–Hungary to press aggressively for a permanent settlement with Serbia.[24] In discussing the scope and tone of the Austrian ultimatum, the British ambassador to Austria told the German ambassador, "Germany knew very well what she was about in backing up Austria–Hungary in this matter."[25]

Diplomats argued that honor and prestige would cause each side to choose war over any overly humiliating settlement. Thus, observes believed that emboldenment of allies increased the prospect of war and viewed Austria's aggressive ultimatum in this light.[26] And from this, among other factors, the British drew the inference that German diplomatic support was an indication of the likelihood of German military support. The British also recognized that because Germany and Austria perceived their interests to be aligned, and because Russia was unlikely to stand aside if Serbia were attacked, German support for Austria was particularly telling.[27] Along with a variety of other factors, this lead to a "consensus" that Germany would join Austria in a war. By contrast, in the instances when Germany sought to restrain Austria, the Austrians and other observers were led to question whether Germany would fight with Austria.[28] In the end, of course, Austria understood that Germany would have no choice but to back Austria and both went to war.

---

[22] British Parliament (1859, v. XXXII, pp. 119, 240).

[23] Cowley believed the emperor when he said that he had not colluded with Sardinia in advance, and in this, Cowley was mislead.

[24] For one authoritative accounts of these events, see Strahan (2005).

[25] Gooch and Temperley (1979, v. 11, 111). For the British view at the time, which was entirely consistent with the characterization given here, see *Great Britain and the European Crisis*, 1914, pp. 102–103.

[26] Gooch and Temperley (1979, v. 11, 166) and *British Sessional Papers*, 1914, v. CI, 28.

[27] Gooch and Temperley (1979, v. 11, 63, 266).

[28] Gooch and Temperley (1979, v. XI, 191, v. IX, part 2, 506).

A cursory appraisal of many other cases suggests that similar dynamics drove the perceptions of the states involved. British and French support for Ottoman Turkey prior to the Crimean War is an example. The genesis of the war was the Turkish refusal to maintain the *status quo* on issues related to rights of Orthodox Christians at the "Holy Places" in Palestine. The Ottomans certainly would not have pressed the issue without the encouragement of the British ambassador, Stratford Canning. All parties also understood that the British and French support, which led to the Ottoman refusal to compromise, had increased the likelihood of conflict. And certainly, British and French statements of resolve affected the assessments of observers, who found the threats credible.[29]

It also seems likely that the dynamics of the model are at work in relations between the United States and China over Taiwan. The United States wishes to maintain the status quo in the region and therefore

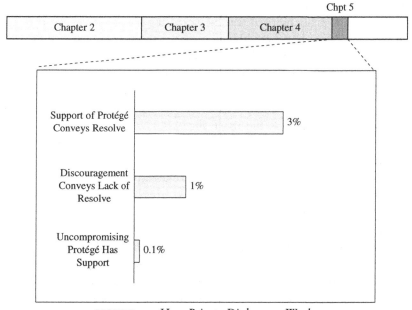

FIGURE 5.4 How Private Diplomacy Works

Note: The proportions shown are of the mechanisms by which private-diplomacy, security-related inferences were drawn in internal, British Government documents in the *Confidential Print* between 1855 and 1914. The bar at the top represents the total number of mechanism codings in the inference dataset; the area in the Chapter 5 portion represents the fraction of these mechanisms addressed in this chapter.

---

[29] For two excellent accounts of these negotiations, see Rich (1965*b*) and Schroeder (1972).

attempts to signal both that it is willing to defend Taiwan from China and that its Protégé should be restrained in its behavior towards China. The fact that some Taiwanese leaders are at times tempted to declare independence even with only partial US support probably increases the credibility of the US threat.

The encouragement of Protégés directly relates to a small number of British inferences in the *Confidential Print*, relative to the mechanisms discussed in previous chapters. Figure 5.4 shows the fractions of private diplomacy inferences accounted for by the dynamics of Third Parties and Protégés. While the percentages are small, the impact in individual cases was highly significant. In 1914, for instance, the Austrians were emboldened by Germany, the Serbs by Russia, and the Russians by France.

CONCLUSION

The benefits of signaling resolve to third parties come at cost, namely, increasing the probability of war by increasing the assertiveness of allies. Just because signals are credible does not make them worth sending. In fact, the higher the risk and more severe the drawbacks, the more likely the signal will be found credible.[30] The implication for policymaking is not that particular courses of action be taken, but to be aware of the tradeoffs. For observers and analysts, it is important to be aware that the policies that appear the most successful with the benefit of hindsight will often be the policies that entailed the greatest risks at the time.

The mechanism of diplomatic inference described in this chapter sheds light on signaling in a range of substantive areas that are often examined independently. The model illuminates new dynamics in extended deterrence when the interests of Third Party and Protégé are aligned and the Protégé and Target are negotiating over issues that could result in costly conflict. The same prediction applies to compellence cases, where the Third Party and Protégé may seek to coerce the Target together. Through these processes, states form the expectations about who will side with whom that inform calculations of interest. The effects of signals are thus likely to be felt past the resolution of particular diplomatic episodes or crises and to influence the construction of the international orders of the day.

---

[30] Similarly, in Fearon (1994a), audience cost dynamics imply that the weaker a state and the more likely its adversary is to stand firm, the more information a threat that precipitates a crisis conveys about the state's resolve.

The mechanism of diplomatic inference described here will never be the sole means by which diplomats and leaders draw conclusions about each other's intentions. In all of the cases described above, researchers have pointed to other factors that influenced the calculations of the parties involved. The model itself points to ways that other factors, such as the balance of power, influence signaling. Although other mechanisms are also operative in signaling among multiple powers, however, the evidence in documents from a broad range of cases suggests that the private signals of Third Parties to conflicts play consequential roles in significant and well-studied historical episodes.

6

Diplomatic Approaches

When Japan told Britain, at the end of the Russo-Japanese War, that Japan would not come to an adjustment of differences with Russia, British statesmen were genuinely reassured. They concluded that they could adopt a stronger negotiating position in talks on a cooperative arrangement with Japan.[1] Why did the British draw this conclusion from the Japanese signal and, more puzzlingly, if the British could have been expected to draw this conclusion, why did the Japanese send the signal?

Following the Crimean War, Russian attempts to cultivate close relations with France were a factor in convincing the British that Russia would not help Austria–Hungary in the Second Italian War of Independence. The Russian overtures to France were proof that Russian hostility was greater towards Austria, which had been Russia's ally before the war, than it was toward the powers against which Russia had actually fought in the war. Beyond convincing the British that Russia was resentful towards Austria, which European powers already had reason to understand,[2] Russian diplomacy helped to persuade the British that this resentment would have a significant impact on Russian policy.[3] No public alliance signing was required for these conclusions to be drawn. In fact, diplomats around Europe were able to read the implications of the private diplomatic encounters of which they, through their own networks, became aware. Similarly, in 1910 and 1911, when Germany offered Britain an expanded and exclusive sphere of influence in Persia, the British concluded that Germany wanted a "free hand" in dealing with France and Russia and other neutral powers.[4] Why did the British

---

[1] Gooch and Temperley (1979, v. 4, p. 40).
[2] Trager (2012).
[3] British Parliament (1859, v. XXXII, p. 9).
[4] Gooch and Temperley (1979, v. 6, pp. 456–460, 725; v. 7, p. 331).

conclude in these cases that Russia was more hostile to Austria and Germany more hostile towards France and Russia, than the British had believed previously?

This chapter demonstrates that a very simple mechanism allows for inferences of this sort in systems of states. Further, many inferences that may appear very different in kind are in fact similar and can be understood as the results of identical processes of reasoning by the actors involved. In particular, when one state proposes to form closer relations with another state, three conclusions are often drawn: (1) that the state wishes to establish closer relations, at least in the short term, and is willing to make concessions to achieve them, (2) that the state intends or expects some form of conflict with third-party states, and (3) that the state wishes to create distance between the state to which the offer is made and other states in the system. As the simple model described below illustrates, these conclusions are sensible inferences in the strategic context of international politics in some circumstances.

When a state admits that it has poor relations with a third state and may find itself in conflict with that state, the logic of inference is nearly identical. In general, the state to which the admission is made will infer that the statement is true and further that the state making the admission will make concessions in negotiations to the state with which it is communicating. The principle is simple: hostility in one relationship implies that a state cannot afford hostility in another and therefore that it will settle for a worse outcome in negotiations to maintain the health of the other relationship. The puzzle, then, is why states would ever freely admit to having poor relations with a third state. Often, the reason they do so is to renegotiate their relationships with other states in order to prepare for a possible conflict.

Thus, statements that may appear very different often convey the same content. A state may signal to another state that it wishes to establish relations on a "firm basis that is beneficial to both sides." Or it may say directly that "the conduct of a third state is unacceptable and we may become involved in a conflict with them in the near future as a result." In both instances, when the potential for conflict with the third state is known to exist, the conclusions of the state to which the signal is sent will be largely the same.

HOW DIPLOMATS THINK ABOUT DIPLOMATIC APPROACHES

As Chapter 4 demonstrates, diplomats understand that relations in one issue-area influence relations in other areas; threats may engender general hostility and concessions invite increased cooperation. As Eyre Crowe put the point in his famous memorandum, "The likelihood of other Powers actively taking sides in a quarrel which does not touch them directly may reasonably be expected, and, indeed, is shown by experience, very much to depend, quite apart from the merits of the dispute, on the general trend of relations existing between the several parties."[5] In anticipation of such calculations on the part of other states, diplomats and leaders often try to establish closer relations when the opportunity presents itself. I refer to the attempt by one state to initiate talks to improve and tighten relations with another state as a diplomatic approach. Such approaches are often deemed prudent because it is impossible to know what situations may arise in which allies will prove useful or even essential to survival.

For this reason in part, in the early years of the twentieth century, several British statesmen recommended tightened ties between Britain and France. In the words of Lord Landsdowne: "An all-round settlement with France upon the lines now suggested would, I believe, be enormously to our advantage. It would be worth while to sacrifice something in order to minimize the chances of future trouble with that country."[6] As Landsdowne also recognized, improved relations with France would require concession and sacrifice, and this is generally true when one state makes an approach to another with an offer of improved relations. Thus, the recommendation to shore up ties with a second state often comes when a state believes it may find itself in conflict with a third state, either because the third state is believed hostile to the first state's interests or because the first state is contemplating aggressive action against the third state itself. This was the case, for instance, when Germany sought an agreement with Russia before the Second World War. The German representative in Moscow offered "Neutrality [for Russia] and staying out of a European conflict and, if Moscow wished, a German–Russian understanding which, just as in former times, would work out in the interests of both countries."[7] Within a month of these offers, the Molotov–Ribbentrop Pact was signed, and the German invasion of Poland began a week after that.

The model of three states analyzed below demonstrates that as a result, offers of concession are both credible and suggest hostile intentions towards third parties. These dynamics arise out of a strategic context in which there is uncertainty over whether one state wishes to compromise

---

[5] Gooch and Temperley (1979, v. 3, p. 399).
[6] Quoted in Monger (1963, pp. 132–133).
[7] Schorske (1994, p. 507).

or fight with the other states. Equilibria exist in which the state can and will signal its private information to a potential ally – even though that state gains bargaining leverage as a result – under the following conditions. First, the *status quo* in relations between the Signaler and one of the other states (the Target) must sufficiently favor that state. Second, the stakes must be such that the players find the costs of conflict sufficiently low. Third, the state to which the signal is sent (the Potential Ally) must be sufficiently satisfied with the status quo in its own relations with the state with which the signaler may intend to engage in conflict.

If these conditions hold, then the state to which the signal is sent learns from the Signaler's statement whether or not the signaler intends to initiate a conflict with the Target. In some contexts, this will be understood as a military threat. In others, however, conflictual relations may be expected to take another form, including a trade dispute, a decision to build controversial weapons, or a foreign policy that takes less account of the Target's interests. From the diplomatic approach, the Potential Ally also learns from the Signaler how much it can demand of the bargaining space that these two states dispute with each other. Further, even though the initial signal is sent in private from the Signaler to the Potential Ally, the Target can infer from public aspects of their revised relations what the Signaler's message was and therefore whether or not the Signaler intends to have more conflictual relations the Target.

The logic of the model presented here is consistent with the findings (e.g., in Leeds 2003) that states are more aggressive when they have an alliance partner who has pledged to remain neutral or join in a conflict. But it is not just the audience costs that backing down from a public commitment entail, or even necessarily the dynamics of third parties and protégé's described in the previous chapter that influence the expectations of states in the system. For the parties directly involved in talks, it is rather the costless private signals they send to each other. For other states, it is the news that often travels to them about those talks and the public aspects of the deals that were struck. Thus, it is not only the signing of an alliance that gives excluded states cause for concern. Conclusions are drawn from the moment an approach is made. It is at that moment that the dynamics of the "alliance security dilemma" sometimes begin. The diplomatic approach of one state threatens the security of a third party, who then makes a diplomatic approach itself to another state, and so on. Since the number of potential alliance partners is small, competition can quickly become intense.[8] Schorske (1994) describes the diplomatic approaches of Britain, France, Germany and Russia before the Second

---

[8] Snyder (1984), Jervis (1978).

World War in precisely this way as a diplomatic game musical chairs. Germany decided to make further concessions to achieve an agreement with Russia on July 25, 1939 because Germany learned that day that France and Britain were sending military missions to Moscow.

So, the model demonstrates that public statements of commitment are not necessary to engender credible commitments or precipitate the dynamics of a security dilemma. The data on inferences, discussed further below, show that observers draw conclusions long before an alliance is signed, merely from the willingness to make the approach. Just talking about coordinating policies is enough, and states are keenly observant of the movements each other's political leaders and diplomatic representatives. Domestic audiences need not witness commitments and bargaining reputations need not be staked for commitments to be believed genuine. When a third state hears about a diplomatic approach of this sort, or witnesses the effects in tighter cooperation between two other states, the third state will often see these events as ominous indicators of hostile intent on the part of the state making the approach. Observers will even understand that private understandings have been reached simply by observing the overt results of agreements, and in such cases will draw the same conclusions as if they had been in the room to witness the negotiations.

A striking example of these dynamics comes from a critical moment during the early Cold War when Germany and France were in talks to cooperate more closely, particularly on nuclear matters, to the detriment of US interests. The US administration had learned in 1962 that the German government had "offered to bear some of the cost" of developing French nuclear capabilities.[9] The American administration, and President Kennedy in particular, understood this as directed at the United States. It was seen as a German attempt to set foreign policy independently of US counsels. Germany was also seeking to acquire a nuclear capability of its own over US protests and there was the real possibility of a Paris–Bonn axis that excluded the US from key European decisions. Thus, the German diplomatic approaches to France indicated the likelihood of more conflictual relations between Germany and the US. The US response was to threaten to remove its troops from Western Europe, which effectively ended this phase of Franco-German cooperation.[10]

Following the same logics, observers will understand that an approach to one state may be explicitly intended to sour relations between that state and a third state. When Bismarck authored German foreign policy,

---

[9] Trachtenberg (1999, p. 373).
[10] Trachtenberg (1999, pp. 374–376).

the British saw German approaches to Russia in this light. On this point, Eyre Crowe was explicit: "Maintenance of a state of tension and antagonism between third Powers had avowedly been one of the principal elements in Bismarck's political combinations."[11] Similarly, some years later, another British diplomat understood that the mere existence of talks between Russia and Germany would be of concern to France. As a result, he said, the French "are doubting Russia's commitment to the [Dual Alliance], and are unwilling to make sacrifices if the other states will not either."[12]

These dynamics mean that the analysis of signaling in this chapter can be viewed as a complement to the analysis in Chapter 4 of risking a breach in relations. That chapter examined, in part, what could be learned about State A's aggressive intentions toward State B from a threat by State A to State B that risked an alliance between State B and State C. This chapter examines what could be learned from a diplomatic approach by State B to State C about State B's aggressive intentions towards (or fear of) State A. In this sense, we might conceive of this chapter as analyzing what happens after the sorts of interactions described in Chapter 4 or as a closer look at the edges of the strategic calculus described above.

A MODEL OF DIPLOMATIC APPROACHES IN A SYSTEM OF STATES

To understand how states draw inferences from diplomatic overtures in a systemic context, consider the following simple game, represented in Figure 6.1. As in previous models, the Signaler sends a message to another state, that state then chooses a location in the bargaining space, and the Signaler then chooses whether or not to attack. Unlike in previous models, the Signaler also decides whether to attack a third state. If the Signaler elects to attack either of these two states, then the unattacked state chooses whether to join one side or the other or remain neutral.

We might think of the messages the Signaler sends to the first state along these lines: "We should like to make concessions to you to put our relationship on sounder footing." Or, alternatively: "Our relations with the third state are on a good footing. We do not foresee conflict on that front and therefore have no need to make concessions to you." The model allows us to understand what conclusions can be drawn from statements of this sort.

---

[11] Gooch and Temperley (1979, v. 3, p. 400).
[12] Bourne and Watt (1989, part 1, series F, v. 12, p. 250).

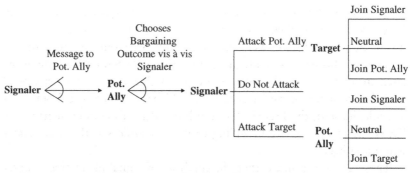

FIGURE 6.1 Game Sequence

Structure of the Game and Preferences

Formally, the game has three players, a "Signaler" (s), a "Potential Ally" (1), and a "Target" (2) indexed by $i, j \in I \equiv \{s, 1, 2\}$, and five stages. Each of the players is in a bargaining relationship with each of the other players over some set of goods. The set of goods in dispute between each pair of players does not overlap with the set of goods that either member of the pair disputes with the third player. We might think of these sets of goods as three territories, one between each pair of states. There are thus three bargaining spaces: $X^{s1} \equiv [0, 1]$ (with generic element x^{s1}) between the Signaler and the Potential Ally, $X^{s2} \equiv [0, 1]$ (with generic element x^{s2}) between the Signaler and the Target, and $X^{12} \equiv [0, 1]$ (with generic element x^{12}) between the Potential Ally and the Target. Each player has a utility function over each of the two sets of issues the player disputes with the other two players, and a player's overall utility for a peaceful outcome is the sum of these utilities. To state this formally, first let $x^{ji} = 1 - x^{ij}$. $u_{ij}^{z_{ij}}(x^{ij})$ is the utility of player i over the bargaining space it disputes with player j, given that player i is type z_{ij} with respect to the bargaining space that i disputes with j. These utility functions are strictly increasing $\forall i, j \in I$, which has the interpretation that each player prefers strictly more of the bargaining space. The utilities of the Potential Ally and the Target are commonly known, as is the utility of the Signaler over X^{s1}. Thus, let $z_{ij} = 1 \forall z_{ij} \neq z_{s2}$. In the first stage of the game, Nature draws the utility function of the Signaler over the bargaining space that the Signaler disputes with the Target, $u_{s2}^{z_{s2}}(\cdot)$. This utility function is the private information of the Signaler and is drawn from a commonly known, discrete distribution function $h_{s2}(u_{s2}^{z_{s2}})$, which is common knowledge. $h_{s2}(u_{s2}^{z_{s2}})$ has support $u_{s2}^1(\cdot)$ and $u_{s2}^2(\cdot)$. Again for simplicity, assume that the Signaler's utilities over the endpoints are known, so that $u_{s2}^1(0) = u_{s2}^2(0)$ and $u_{s2}^1(1) = u_{s2}^2(1)$.

In the second stage, the Signaler sends a cheap talk message, m_y, which is observed only by the Potential Ally. The messages are sent from a large but finite set of messages indexed by y. Then, in the third stage, the Potential Ally chooses a location in the bargaining space it disputes with the Signaler, $x^{s1} \in X^{s1}$. In the fourth stage of the game, the Signaler has three choices: it can attack one of the other two states or attack neither. If the signaler decides not to go to war, then the outcome of the game in the three bargaining spaces is the x^{s1} chosen by the Potential Ally in the third stage, and the status quo at the start of the game in the other bargaining spaces, $x_q^{12} \in X^{12}$ and $x_q^{s2} \in X^{s2}$. If the Signaler decides to attack one of the other states, then in the fifth and final stage of the game, the side which is not attacked has the opportunity to decide whether to fight on one side or the other or to remain neutral.

Assumptions About Coalition Wars

In order to model the military potential of the states if they fight each other alone or in a coalition with another state, we give each state a resource endowment r_i. In any war, each of the three states is on one side or on the other or remains neutral. For any war, let $D_A \subset I$ be the set of states on side A and $D_B \subset I \backslash D_A$ be the set of states on side B. The probability that side A wins the conflict is $\frac{\sum_{i \in D_A} r_i}{\sum_{i \in D_A \cup D_B} r_i}$. As in previous models, any states in a victorious coalition achieve their best outcomes in the bargaining ranges with states on the losing side, but states also pay a cost of fighting $c_i > 0$ whether their side wins or not.

We shall assume that if the Signaler is of the first type, u_{s2}^1, it prefers the status quo in its relations with State 2, x_q^{s2}, to a war against the Target alone, while u_{s2}^2 is such that the Signaler prefers a war only against the Target to the status quo. Partly for simplicity, we also assume that $u_{s1}(x^{s1})$ and $u_{1s}(x^{1s})$ are linear functions. Substantively, this implies that the Signaler and the Potential Ally are both sensitive to movements of the negotiated solution within their bargaining range at any point in that range.

Analysis of the Model

In this model, under certain conditions, an equilibrium exists in which the Signaler can convince the other states of its type and chooses to do so. When (1) the *status quo* in relations between the Signaler and the Target sufficiently favors the Target, (2) the costs of conflict are low, and (3) the *status quo* between the Potential Ally and the Target sufficiently favors the Potential Ally, an informative perfect Bayesian equilibrium exists. In this equilibrium, (1) the Potential Ally learns from the Signaler's offer whether or not the Signaler intends to attack State 2, (2) the Target negotiates for a better deal in the bargaining space it contests with the Signaler, and (3) the division of the bargaining space between the Signaler and the Potential Ally conveys to the Target whether the Signaler will attack the Target. This result is stated formally as Proposition 6.1 in the Appendix and informally below.

Proposition 6.1 (informal): When the costs of conflict to the Signaler and the Potential Ally are sufficiently low, the *status quo* in relations between the Signaler and Target sufficiently favors the Target, and the *status quo* in relations between the Potential Ally and the Target sufficiently favors the Potential Ally, a perfect Bayesian equilibrium exists in which,

(1) The Signaler's decision to approach the Potential Ally reveals whether or not it intends aggression against the Target, and
(2) The level of concessions that the Potential Ally insists on in its relations with the Signaler signals to observers whether or not the Signaler will attack the Target.

DISCUSSION

Statements that a country would like to establish better relations are often credible. For one thing, such statements often mean that the two countries would make concessions to each other that would be visible to others, and in particular, the country that approaches the other is signaling that it is willing to make concessions. Further, while the initial discussion is private, the potential outcomes of those discussions are not. Thus, moving closer to one state risks a breach with that state's adversaries who will come to believe that the states that make concessions to each other are more likely to be hostile to them in the future.

Another mechanism is also at work, however. When a state tells another state that it wants closer relations and is willing to sacrifice in order to achieve closer relations, the state that approaches the other gives up bargaining leverage; the other side knows that an agreement is viewed as important. Similarly, when the Signaler admits to the Potential Ally that the Signaler has poor relations with the Target, this decreases the bargaining leverage that the Signaler has in its negotiations with the Potential Ally. The Potential Ally will be encouraged to hold out for a better deal, which in turn means that the Signaler will not make such an admission lightly.

In the model, the Signaler will nevertheless admit when it has poor relations with or intends aggression against the Target. If doing so decreases the Signaler's bargaining leverage with the Potential Ally, why would the Signaler do it and why would the Potential Ally expect the Signaler to do so? If the Signaler did not make such an admission and did not come to terms on a basis favorable to the Potential Ally, then if the Signaler were to find itself in a conflict with the Target, the Potential Ally might join with the Target against the Signaler. Because two are stronger than one, the Signaler can have a powerful incentive to come to terms with the Potential Ally in advance.

Proposition 6.1 gives a set of sufficient conditions for signaling of this type to be possible. These clarify when the Signaler has an incentive to reveal its type and thereby receive a worse outcome in its negotiations with the Potential Ally. First, when the Potential Ally knows that the Signaler intends aggression against the Target, the Potential Ally must be able to get a sufficiently favorable arrangement from the Signaler such that the Potential Ally prefers to remain out of the conflict between the Signaler and the Target (or to join the conflict on the side of the Signaler). The assumptions of the model imply that this must be so since a negotiated solution always exists between the Signaler and the Potential Ally for any likelihood that one side or the other wins a war. Second, the Potential Ally's behavior towards the Signaler must be contingent upon the deal the Potential Ally gets from their negotiations. For instance, the Potential Ally could be expected to join with the Target in a war against the Signaler if the Signaler attacks the Target without first having come to an arrangement and made concessions to the Potential Ally. This in turn implies that the deal that the Potential Ally gets when it believes that the Signaler does not intend hostile actions against the Target cannot be too favorable to the Potential Ally. This is the reason for the condition in Proposition 6.1 that the Signaler's costs of conflict not be too high.[13] If they were, because of the take-it-or-leave-it nature of the bargaining following the signal, the Potential Ally would always make such high demands of the Signaler that there would never be a reason for the Potential Ally to go to war.[14] The condition given in Proposition 6.1 that

---

[13] This second condition that the Potential Ally's behavior be contingent on the deal it gets in negotiations with the Signaler also implies that the Potential Ally must care enough about the quality of the deal it gets. This is guaranteed by the assumption that the Potential Ally has risk neutral preferences over the bargaining space it disputes with the Signaler.

[14] Equilibria can also exist in which the Potential Ally would fight against the Signaler if the Signaler fought against the Target and did not first come to terms with the Potential Ally, but in which the Potential Ally would join with the Signaler against the Target if the Signaler first made concessions to the Potential Ally.

the *status quo* in the Potential Ally's relations with the Target be sufficiently favorable to the Potential Ally also ensures that the Potential
Ally's behavior will be contingent on the deal it strikes with the Signaler because such a *status quo* ensures that the Potential Ally would
not prefer to go to war against the Target or even remain neutral in all
contingencies. Third, if the Signaler is the type that is dissatisfied with the
status quo, then the Signaler must be sufficiently dissatisfied. Only when
the Signaler is sufficiently dissatisfied will it be willing to sacrifice negotiating leverage in its relations with the Potential Ally in order to settle
matters with the Target.

The model is much simpler than the real world in many respects. One
important respect is that states do not have preferences over the bargain
that the other two states strike with each other. For instance, one state
may not want to see its neighbor gain too much in territory. The model is
intentionally simplified so that the fundamental signaling dynamics can
be seen sharply. In developing a theory of war in the context of negotiations, however, it may be that such preferences should be taken into
account.

One might also ask, given the setup of the model, why states would
not wait to reveal their poor relations or intention to initiate an aggressive policy against another state until just before the conflict itself. The
answer is probably that bargaining in the world, as opposed to the take-
it-or-leave-it model, is such that negotiations result in outcomes in which
neither side receives all the benefits from agreement. Since such negotiations take time, states will pursue them in advance of when the having
of the agreement is critical to their security. It may also be beneficial to a
state, in the position of the Signaler in the model, to carry on negotiations
when there is uncertainty about whether the agreement will be essential
to the Signaler. Following the Signaler's message, such uncertainty does
not exist in the model, but we can very easily imagine complicating factors that would allow a measure of uncertainty to remain in similar real
world situations.

Another interesting implication of the model is that signaling may,
on some occasions, be impeded by a harmony of interests between the
Signaler and the Potential Ally. If the *status quo* in relations between
the Potential Ally and the Target is such that the Potential Ally would
choose to join the Signaler in an attack on the Target, for instance, then
the Signaler will be hesitant about disclosing to the Potential Ally that
the Signaler also considers its relations with the Target to be intolerable.
Doing so decreases the leverage that the Signaler has vis-à-vis the Potential Ally without actually securing any advantage since the Potential Ally
will join in a war on the Signaler's side in any case. This logic suggests

the following: potential allies will not be entirely open with each other about their aggressive intentions vis-à-vis third states. Rather, diplomatic approaches will take place between countries that are not on perfectly good terms with each other and when the approached country is on at least reasonable good terms with the country against which the country making the diplomatic approach may find itself in conflict.

Further insight into the dynamics of diplomatic approaches and the overall effect of this signaling mechanism on the probability of conflict can be gleaned from Figure 6.2. The horizontal axis is the utility of a dissatisfied Signaler type for the *status quo* in the bargaining range the Signaler disputes with the Target $(u_{s2}^2(x_q^{s2}))$. The dotted lines show the offers that the Potential Ally makes to the Signaler following the latter's message. On the left-hand side of the figure, when the Signaler reveals that it intends aggression against the Target, the Signaler's bargaining leverage is reduced and the Potential Ally proposes that a lower share of the bargaining space that these two players dispute go to the Signaler. The more dissatisfied the Signaler may be – the further left in the figure – the worse the Potential Ally's offer when the Signaler reveals its type. Moving to the right, as the Signaler becomes less potentially dissatisfied, the Potential Ally's offer improves almost up to the point where the Potential Ally makes the same offer no matter what message the Signaler sends. Before that point can be reached, however, signaling that influences the

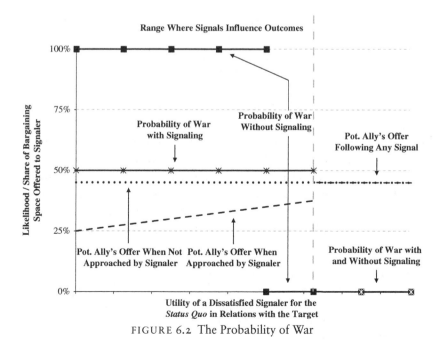

FIGURE 6.2 The Probability of War

course of events becomes impossible because, in this case, the best deal that the Potential Ally can get from the Signaler following the Signaler's admission that it plans to attack the Target is still not so good that the Potential Ally would remain neutral if the Signaler were to attack the Target. Rather, the Potential Ally would join with the Target against the Signaler. Given the expectation that the Potential Ally would join with the Target, the Signaler would choose not to attack the Target. Since the Signaler would choose not to attack the Target, it would be willing to attack the Potential Ally if the Potential Ally's offer were lower than the offer the Potential Ally would make following the Signaler's message that it did not intend to go to war against the Target. As a result, the Potential Ally reacts in the same way following any message the Signaler sends and signaling does not influence the course of events.[15]

This sort of diplomacy might be expected to increase the probability of conflict. If an aggressor can negotiate the neutrality of one state in order to attack another, the argument might run, the overall probability of conflict will increase. As the figure shows, however, this is not the case. The availability of this signaling mechanism can increase or decrease the probability of conflict, depending on the case.

On the left-hand side of the figure, surprisingly, conflict is certain in the absence of signaling. The reason is that, since the Signaler may be very dissatisfied with the *status quo* in its relations with the Target, the Potential Ally finds it optimal to make a low offer to the Signaler. There are then only two possibilities: either the Signaler is in fact dissatisfied with its relations with the Target or the Signaler is not. In the former case, the Signaler attacks the Target and in later case, because of the Potential Ally's high demand, the Signaler attacks the Potential Ally.

If signaling is possible, however, the Signaler can reveal its type. the Potential Ally makes the low offer only when the Signaler intends aggression against the Target. Following the Potential Ally's offer, the Signaler indeed attacks the Target. When the Signaler reveals that it does not intend aggression against the Target, however, the Potential Ally makes a high offer to the Signaler and the Signaler chooses not to attack either state. Thus, on the left-hand side of the figure, Signaling dramatically reduces the probability of conflict, from a certainty to whatever the

---

[15] Parameter values used in the simulation are: $r_i = 1 \forall i$, $c_s = c_1 = .05$, $c_2 = .5$, $h_{s2}(u^1_{s2}) = .5$, $u^1_{ij}(x^{ij}) = x^{ij} \ \forall ij \neq 12$, $u^1_{12}(x^{12}) = (x^{12})^{.001}$, $x^{12}_q = .5$, $x^{s2}_q = .5$, $u^2_{s2}(0) = -2$, $u^2_{s2}(1) = 2$, and $u^2_{s2}(x^{12}_q)$ from -0.25 to -0.075. Note that the dissatisfied Signaler's utility for the *status quo* is not such that the Signaler would choose to attack the Target whatever the strategies of the other players.

likelihood that the Signaler intends aggression against the Target is, or 50 percent in the figure.

In the middle range of Figure 6.2, communication dramatically increases the probability of conflict. The reason is that, here, in the absence of communication, the benefits to the Potential Ally of a low offer to the Target do not justify the risk of conflict. As a result, the Potential Ally makes a high offer to the Signaler. This means that the Signaler never finds it optimal to attack the Potential Ally. Further, because the Potential Ally has taken less of the bargaining space it disputes with the Signaler, the Signaler understands that if it were to attack the Target, the Potential Ally would join the conflict on the Target's side. Thus, even if the Signaler is the dissatisfied type, it is deterred from aggression and peace is the certain outcome. Note that, in this middle range of the figure, the probability of conflict when a communication mechanism exists is still 50 percent.

On the right-hand side of the figure, where the Signaler is less potentially dissatisfied with its relations with the Target, the probability of conflict is the same with and without communication. This is because, as we have seen, the Potential Ally chooses to make the same high offer to the Signaler following any message. As a result, once again, the probability of conflict is zero because satisfied types are unwilling to go to war with either state and dissatisfied Signalers are unwilling to go to war against the Target because of the knowledge that the Potential Ally will join the conflict on the opposing side.

SIGNALING HYPOTHESES

The model implies that inferences can be drawn from the Signaler's behavior under certain conditions. But what would the Signaler do when these conditions do not hold? Of the three requirements for signaling given in Proposition 6.1, consider the need for the *status quo* in relations between the Potential Ally and the Target to be sufficiently favorable to the Potential Ally. If it weren't, the Signaler would not need to offer concessions in a diplomatic approach to buy the Potential Ally's outright cooperation or neutrality. Thus, the signaler would be unlikely to make such an approach; the *status quo* in relations between the Signaler and Potential Ally would likely be sufficient for an aggressive Signaler's purposes. Similarly, with respect to the other two signaling requirements from the proposition, if the costs of conflict were not low enough or the *status quo* in relations between the Signaler and Target not such that the Signaler would contemplate conflict, the Signaler would have no need to initiate a diplomatic approach to the Potential Ally. Thus, it seems likely that Signalers would not attempt diplomatic approaches when they are ineffective and potentially detrimental to their interests. The implication is that the conditions for effectiveness hold in the minds of the policy makers at the time the approach is made, and the implication of that is that empirical hypotheses about the effects of those approaches can be stated without these conditions.

The model also contains the assumption that there is a significant chance that the signaler might intend to initiate more conflictual relations with a Target state. If, however, observers do not believe this to be the case, then these hypotheses also would not necessarily follow. I state the hypotheses without this condition because it is hard to evaluate empirically, and because the condition is likely to hold in most or even all cases. States are generally suspected of intending to initiate some policy that would be to the detriment of some party, leading to more conflictual relations between the two. Whether that policy is expected to involve military or some other form of confrontation depends on the context, in particular on the web of actors' prior beliefs before the approach is made. Since this context is once again difficult to evaluate empirically, and since the hypotheses will be evaluated at times and places where the powers were suspected intending violent aggression against each other, *Hypothesis 6.2* is stated in these terms.

Hypothesis 6.1: Diplomatic approaches will generally cause observers to believe the approaching state will do what it offers.

Hypothesis 6.2: Diplomatic approaches increase the odds that observers conclude that the approaching state intends aggression against a third state.

Hypothesis 6.3: Diplomatic approaches increase the odds that observers conclude that the approaching state wishes to sour relations between the approached state and a third state.

THE EMPIRICAL RECORD

As we have seen, when one state tells another that relations with a third state have deteriorated, this involves giving up bargaining leverage with the state to which one is signaling, and the signaler generally has little reason to lie and the signal will be believed. Thus, in 1902, when Austria–Hungary accused Italy of "not playing fair," other powers understood that relations between the two powers within the Triple Alliance had deteriorated. Austria had no incentive to pretend if it were not so.[16]

By the same token, attempts to cultivate closer relations are generally taken as a sign that a country is willing to make concessions in order to achieve closer relations as well as a sign of increased hostility toward a third country. Examples from the diplomatic record are numerous. The British concluded that Russian overtures to France after the Crimean War were an indication of Russian hostility to Austria.[17] In 1907, when Austria attempted to establish better relations with powers other than Britain, Britain concluded that Austria was less desirous of a cooperative policy with Britain than Britain had thought previously.[18] In that same year, French attempts at closer relations with Italy were seen as indicating a French desire to see weakened relations between Italy, on one side, and Austria and Germany, on the other.[19] When Britain negotiated closer relations with Japan, Russia believed Britain more hostile to Russian interests.[20] When England renewed close relations with France in 1912, the British concluded that Germany would view this as a sign of British intent not to establish closer relations with Germany.[21] When Russia and Turkey seemed to be establishing closer relations, Bulgaria saw this as an indication of a more hostile policy toward it on the part of these countries. As a result, Bulgaria turned to Austria for support.[22] In 1910, when Austria–Hungary sought better relations with Russia, Britain concluded that tensions must exist in the relationship between Austria–Hungary and Germany.[23]

In the early years of the twentieth century, German attempts to form closer relations with one power and then with another played a significant role in convincing Europe that Germany intended to overturn the status quo, through violence if necessary. In 1906, Eyre Crowe drew precisely this conclusion from attempts by Germany to improve relations with Britain.[24] In 1907, another diplomat drew the conclusion that German attempts to establish better relations with France indicated hostility to other countries and yet another diplomat concluded from German attempts to establish better relations with other countries that Germany intended a hostile policy specifically against France. These attempts by

[16] Krieger (1989, part 1, series F, v. 11, p. 295).
[17] British Parliament (1859, v. XXXII, p. 9).
[18] Gooch and Temperley (1979, v. 5, pp. 201–202).
[19] Bourne and Watt (1989, part 1, series F, v. 12, p. 180).
[20] Gooch and Temperley (1979, v. 4, pp. 206, 211, 212).
[21] Stevenson (1990, v. 21, p. 236).
[22] Gooch and Temperley (1979, v. 9, part 1, pp. 517–519).
[23] Bourne and Watt (1989, series F, v. 35, pp. 17–18).
[24] Gooch and Temperley (1979, v. 3, p. 359).

Germany to move closer to multiple powers suggested that Germany perhaps intended to bid for hegemony.[25]

In 1907 and 1908, German attempts to improve relations with Britain were seen as an attempt to weaken the Entente.[26] Again, in 1910 and 1911, when Germany offered Britain an expanded and exclusive sphere of influence in Persia, the British concluded that Germany wanted a "free hand" in dealing with France and Russia.[27] In 1911, the hostility to Britain that German overtures to Spain implied led Britain to consider a closer relationship with France.[28] Yet again, in 1912, German attempts to establish closer relations with France were seen as implying a more aggressive policy towards Britain.[29] German overtures to Russia in 1911 were seen as "the thin end of the wedge which was eventually to split up the Triple Entente."[30]

Thus, far from ending Germany's political encirclement, these frantic diplomatic overtures only deepened it. Even after they were rejected, the fact that they were made at all continued to influence the expectations of European powers. Thereby, these diplomatic approaches played a significant role in driving the alignment calculations that solidified the political order of the day.

Similar dynamics sometimes manifest themselves in subtler ways, including when states decline to offer concessions that were expected. In 1901, for instance, the British noted that Germany had given an interpretation, which favored Russia over Britain, to an agreement that Germany had signed with Britain. The British noted that this risked worsening German relations with Britain in order to ensure continued good relations with Russia. The British concluded that German policy made a priority of avoiding conflict with Russia and that the two countries would therefore not end up at war.[31]

CONCLUSION

In earlier chapters, we saw that states draw conclusions about the degree to which other powers define their security interests as in tension with states' own interests from whether those powers are willing to make

---

[25] Gooch and Temperley (1979, v. 12, p. 249; v. 8, p. 145), Krieger (1989, part I, series F, v. 13, p. 5) and Bourne and Watt (1989, part 1, series F, v. 12, p. 366; v. 20, p. 104).

[26] Gooch and Temperley (1979, v. 6, p. 190; v. 8, p. 145).

[27] Gooch and Temperley (1979, v. 6, pp. 456–460, 725 and v. 7, p. 331).

[28] Gooch and Temperley (1979, v. 7, p. 189).

[29] Krieger (1989, part I, series F, v. 13, p. 447).

[30] Stevenson (1990, part 1, series F, v. 21, p. 185).

[31] Gooch and Temperley (1979, v. 2, p. 75). A similar episode occurred in 1909; see Gooch and Temperley (1979, v. 6, p. 286).

concessions to improve relations. This chapter analyzes how such concessions are viewed in the context of a system of states. A simple mechanism implies that costless, private diplomatic approaches will often result in the inference that the state that offers concessions or asks for closer relations has conflictual relations or intends aggression against some other state. This simple mechanism nevertheless implies some complicated dynamics that may increase or decrease the probability of conflict relative to the case where no communication mechanism exists.

As Figure 6.3 illustrates, the models in Chapters 2 through 6 provide an understanding of 93 percent of the inference mechanisms in the dataset. This includes all categories of inferences that were drawn more than three times over the 60-year period covered in the data. Less frequently seen means of drawing inferences about intention may be important in particular cases, however. For instance, on one occasion, British statesmen inferred that Germany wished to prevent cooperation between Austria–Hungary and Russia because Germany intervened in

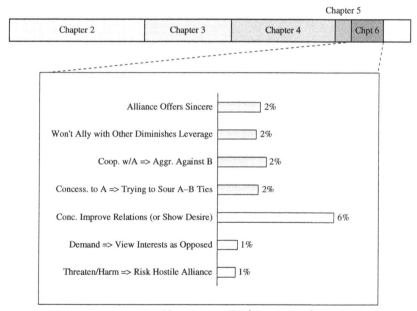

FIGURE 6.3 How Private Diplomacy Works

Note: The proportions shown are of the mechanisms by which private-diplomacy, security-related inferences were drawn in internal, British Government documents in the *Confidential Print* between 1855 and 1914. The bar at the top represents the total number of mechanism codings in the inference dataset; the area in the Chapter 6 portion represents the fraction of these mechanisms addressed only in this chapter. The white bars represent mechanisms that are relevant to the discussion in this chapter, but which were also discussed previously negotiations only when cooperation appeared imminent.[32] In a couple instances, the British argued that allowing an additional country to take part in negotiations would make it more difficult to reach an agreement. The rationale in these cases is transparent, but other inferences appear quite idiosyncratic. In 1905, for instance, the British concluded that the United States was in close communication with Germany, and might even side with that state in a conflict, because the US President asked about British views on the situation in Morocco.[33] It is little wonder that parsimonious models do not account for every notion of British statesmen. Rather, these chapters describe the ways of communicating diplomatically that constitute daily life in the international system.

---

[32] Bourne and Watt (1987, ser. F, v. 34, pt. 1, p. 303).
[33] Gooch and Temperley (1979, v. 3, p. 67).

PART II

EMPIRICAL ANALYSIS

This section of the book evaluates the signaling hypotheses developed in the earlier chapters, and relates diplomatic processes to the formation of international orders and to decisions for war and peace. I also evaluate an additional hypothesis. This is the Audience Cost Hypothesis, formulated in Fearon (1994*a*) and discussed in Chapter 1, which states that threats and offers are more credible when they are made in public. All of the hypotheses are summarized in Table 7.1.

Hypothesis 7.1: Public threats and offers will cause observers to believe the state making the statement is more likely to be willing to carry out the threat or offer than would have been the case if the statement had been made in private.

The hypotheses are evaluated both qualitatively and quantitatively when the nature of the hypothesis and the available data permit.

TABLE 7.1 *Summary of Diplomatic Signaling Hypotheses*

Hypothesis	Case Analysis	Statistical Analysis
3.1. Credibility of Private Threats	Yes	Yes
3.2. Increased Credibility of Increased Scope	Yes	–
3.3. Concessions Follow Concessions	Yes	–
3.4. High Capability Means Concessions Don't Follow Concessions	–	Yes
4.1. Target Capabilities Increase Pr. Change in Beliefs Following Threat	–	Yes
4.2. Closer Relations Increase Pr. of Change in Beliefs Following Threat	–	Yes
4.3. Increased Credibility of Increased Severity	–	–
4.4. Offers Are Credible When Preparations Are Not Too Effective	Yes	Yes
5.1. Diplomatic Support Emboldens	Yes	Yes
5.2. Diplomatic Support Sometimes Increases the Probability of Conflict	Yes	Yes
5.3. Close Alignment of Def. and Prot. Incr. Pr. of Chng. in Beliefs	–	Yes
5.4. Emboldenment Signals Diplomatic Support	Yes	–
6.1. Credibility of Diplomatic Approaches	Yes	Yes
6.2. Diplomatic Approaches Signal Aggression Against Third Parties	Yes	Yes
6.3. Diplomatic Approaches Signal Wish to Weaken Other Alliance Ties	Yes	Yes
7.1. Audience Cost Hypothesis: Publicity Increases Credibility	Yes	Yes

Nevertheless, some could only be evaluated through one approach or the other. For example, *Hypothesis 5.4*, which states that the degree of intransigence of a Protégé in bargaining signals the level of support of the Third Party, is evaluated through documentary evidence, but not through statistical analysis. The reason is that data on degree of intransigence is not available across a range of cases, and the coding of such data in a consistent way in varied contexts would be extremely difficult. By contrast, *Hypothesis 4.1*, which states that higher capabilities of a threatening state relative to a threatened state decrease the change in observer beliefs as a result of a threat, could not be tested through case analysis. Here, the reason is that there could be no expectation of documentary evidence of what conclusions would have been drawn, had relative capabilities been other than they were in a particular instance. Therefore, this hypothesis is evaluated only statistically.

The next two chapters examine diplomatic signaling before the World Wars. The analysis demonstrates how diplomatic encounters produce impressions that are long-lasting, and how these motivate later decisions for war. The third empirical chapter tests the hypotheses statistically and discusses how diplomatic signals are interpreted alongside other signals and indices.

7

The Fruit of 1912 Diplomacy

In precipitating a European war in 1914, the Austrian Emperor followed the advice of all of his most senior counselors save one. The Emperor knew his actions were likely to result in a titanic clash between at least four great powers of Europe. He knew he risked the very existence of his centuries-old empire. And yet, the decision was not directly forced upon him. The German Chancellor had written that "the German Emperor cannot take a position on the current issues between Austria–Hungary and [Serbia], as it is a matter not within his competence" but Germany would "faithfully stand by" Austria.[1] Later, the German emperor advocated an alternative to war, known as the "Halt in Belgrade" proposal; Britain advocated a similar solution. It was Austria that insisted on the course that it knew would bring on the war, and the result was the destruction of the state and the Habsburg dynasty. At the war's end, it was left to an American captain to tell an Austrian Archduke that he would never return to power in Hungary. Captain T. C. Gregory cabled home: "Archie on the carpet 7 P.M. went through the hoop at 7:05."[2] Why did the Austrians hazard their place in the world? What made them willing to bring on a modern, mechanized war, deaths in the tens of millions, a storm of steel?

The answers to these questions are found, in large part, in what the European powers learned from prewar diplomacy. Diplomacy played the major part in the formation of the actors' beliefs about each other's intentions and these intersubjective understandings formed the essential elements of the arguments for war. Diplomacy allowed the powers to understand that France would support Russia in a war against the Triple Alliance and eventually convinced Germany that England would

---

[1] Kautsky (1919, v. I, pp. 32–33, "Der Reichskanzler an den Botschafter in Wien," July 6, 1914).
[2] Andelman (2009, p. 33).

join Germany's adversaries. But roots of the conflict can be found further
back in European diplomacy.[3] The threats Austria made to Russia during the Crimean War in the middle of the nineteenth century, threats that
were never acted upon, engendered the enmity between Russia and Austria, and thereby played a significant role in the creation of the German
state as Russia shifted to favor Prussia over Austria.[4] In the late nineteenth and early twentieth centuries, the diplomacy of other powers often
left Austria relatively isolated, save for its close relationship with Germany after 1879. As a multiethnic empire in the age of nationalism, this
isolation made Austria–Hungary particularly vulnerable to both internal
and external threats, thereby contributing substantially to its grasp at a
desperate solution in 1914.[5]

Here, I show that what Austria learned from the diplomatic encounters in the years immediately before the war constituted the foundation
of the specific Austrian arguments for war in 1914. To facilitate evaluation of the signaling hypotheses in detail, I focus on Russian and German
diplomacy in 1912. I describe the predictions of the hypotheses in the
context of the events of the day and analyze whether these predictions are
born out in 1912. I then show how these inferences from 1912, alongside confirmatory evidence from other diplomatic encounters, provided
the essential grounds for the Austrian arguments in favor of war. This
requires an examination of the early days of the July Crisis, when Austria
made the decision for war. I do not examine, as so many other histories
do, how the other powers stumbled into war once Austria had set the
course.[6]

CRITERIA FOR EVALUATING HYPOTHESES AGAINST DOCUMENTARY EVIDENCE

The diplomatic episodes that preceded the world wars were moments of
profound impact on history's subsequent course. The Austro-Hungarian
decision for war in 1914 brought about the destruction of the Austro-
Hungarian and Russian empires, the rise of communism in Russia before
its emergence elsewhere, and the redrawing of many of the world's political boundaries. The decisions of the Nazi war machine in the late 1930s

---

[3] On the topic of early roots of the conflict, see in particular Albertini (1952–1957).
[4] Rich (1965a), Trager (2012).
[5] Schroeder (2004, Chapter 8).
[6] The evidence presented below argues against theses that deny agency to actors other than
  Germany (Fischer 1967, Röhl 2002), in favor of the thesis of shared responsibility for
  events (Renouvin 1925, Albertini 1952–1957, Schmitt 1988, Trachtenberg 1991, p. 50,
  Williamson 1991, Schroeder 1997, Ferguson 1999, Clark 2012, pp. 560–561).

were the prime moving force of that era. Had these decisions been different, it is likely that many aspects of today's world would be substantially altered as well. The enormous complexity of these moments before the world wars provide much fruitful material for analysis. If the simple (by comparison) models of Chapters 3 through 6 cannot contain the true complexity of signaling in international politics, this is where they are most likely to fail.

The focused analysis of the signaling hypotheses in this chapter covers Russian and German diplomacy in 1912 through the effective resolution of the Adriatic port crisis in early December. I do not consider the diplomatic conference of the powers in London that was only just beginning in late December and continued through the first half of the following year. The cases from this period were chosen for several reasons. For one, because of their influence on the coming of the Great War, they are of high historical interest. Yet, in spite of this fact, their relationship to the war has not been fully appreciated in the scholarly literature. The complexity of these cases also allows analysis of a wide range of signaling hypotheses. Finally, the choice to analyze the diplomacy before both World Wars in this chapter and the next is not accidental. These chapters demonstrate how very consequential private diplomatic encounters are and, since there have only been two World Wars, examining both of them will dampen suspicion that the cases have been "cherry picked" (Fearon and Laitin 2008).

To evaluate the signaling hypotheses, I first analyze the historical record to determine the predictions of the hypotheses in this particular series of episodes. I then evaluate these predictions against the documentary evidence to determine whether there is specific documentary evidence that the predicted inference was drawn and further that the reasoning used to justify the inference corresponds to the reasoning predicted by the model. In this sense, the standard for confirmation of a hypothesis is higher than for the quantitative analysis in Chapter 9. Here, confirmation requires not just that the predicted inference be drawn but that the reasoning behind it tracks the dynamics of the models.

The documentary record is only a partial record of the conversations and thoughts of foreign policy elites, however. Some inferences from behavior that actors drew will not have been recorded. Therefore, in Bayesian fashion, the documentary evidence of the predictions of the hypotheses is treated as increasing the likelihood that the theory is correct. Absence of documentary evidence is considered to reduce the likelihood that the theory is right but is not grounds for rejecting a hypothesis outright. Absence of documentary evidence predicted by a hypothesis tells particularly against the theory if documentary evidence of *other* sorts of inferences does exist, suggesting that considerations of these matters were conducted and recorded without the predicted inference being drawn.

SIGNALING HYPOTHESES PREDICTIONS IN 1912

The diplomacy of 1912 was conducted in the knowledge that a disagreement between Balkan powers could result in war. This had been demonstrated with all clarity by the crisis that followed from the Austro-Hungarian annexation of Bosnia and Herzegovina a few years before. Alliance relations and new technologies of violence meant that a "storm of steel" could cover Europe and even much of the rest of the world in the most destructive war in human history. Of these dangers, diplomats in 1912 were well aware.

Russian Diplomacy in 1912

The annexation of Bosnia and Herzegovina in 1908–1909 by Austria–Hungary precipitated a crisis atmosphere in Russia. In 1912, the Tsar still had strong feelings about the episode and he expressed them succinctly: "The annexation was the biggest dishonor for Russia; such a dishonor must not occur again."[7] The solution to the perceived past failure of Russian policy was understood to be moving closer to an ally, and debate centered on which to approach. It was in this context that, in late 1911 and the early months of 1912, Russia launched a major diplomatic initiative to bring two major Balkan powers, Serbia and Bulgaria, into an alliance with each other that would operate in close cooperation with Russia.[8] The Balkan powers committed to taking joint actions only in consultation with Russia, which they called the "guarantor" of the alliance, and to engage Russia as a mediator in any disputes between them. Serbia referred to this as the "principal condition" of the agreement,[9] and French Prime Minister Raymond Poincaré observed that this condition "appears in every line of the convention."[10] In order to achieve the alliance, Russia made concessions to the Balkan states on territorial and other questions. Whereas Russia had previously insisted that an

---

[7] Bogitchvich (1928, p. 246).

[8] Note that the urgency of the Balkan powers to come to agreement was related to the outbreak of the Italo-Turkish war, which provided opportunity for gains against the Ottoman Empire, but the Russian desire for the Balkan alliance predated the war. See Sontag (1966, pp. 116–125).

[9] Rossos (1981, p. 38).

[10] Clark (2012, p. 296).

alliance between Bulgaria and Serbia include Turkey, Russia dropped this demand and even allowed Serbia and Bulgaria to agree on their plans for the partition of European Turkey.[11] In Russian eyes, the most important clauses in the agreement were those that guaranteed a united defense, such as against an attack on one by Austria–Hungary. For Russia, the Balkan league was a weapon that could be turned either against Turkey or Austria as needs and opportunities arose.[12]

Within months of the creation of the alliance, the Balkan states contemplated war against Turkey. The Russian foreign minister, S. D. Sazonov, declined to give official Russian support, but many Russian elites offered encouragement and a promise of Russian aid in the event of Austrian involvement. In public and in private, Russian and Austrian representatives declared that they would accept no changes to the territorial *status quo* in the region. The Balkan states fought the First Balkan War in spite of these warnings, however, and decisive victories by their side forced rapid alterations in the diplomatic landscape. By early November, Russia expressed its view to the Powers, through private diplomatic channels, not only that the Balkan states should be allowed to keep territorial gains that they had already made, but that Serbia should be allowed a port on the Adriatic. Since Austria vehemently opposed this Serbian objective, Russia's proposal constituted a clear threat to support Serbia against powers that sought to block Serbia from the Adriatic. Sazonov then reversed course and informed Serbia that Russia would not support the drive for a port and he also represented Russia to other powers as restraining Serbia in this regard. Once again, however, other Russian elites, including the Russian ambassador to Serbia, continued to encourage Serbia in making the demand and promised Russian support.[13] With Serbia looking to Russia for support, Austria looked to Germany. By mid November, Sazonov had reversed himself again, telling other powers that if Austria and Germany did not acquiesce in the matter of the Serbian port, Russia might "prefer not to postpone the inevitable conflict." Then, at the end of November, Russia reversed herself a final time, declaring that it would not support the Serbian demand. When Serbia made its case for a port in *The Times of London*, Sazonov called it a "provocation" which "could only do damage to Serbia."[14] These principal events of Russian diplomacy in 1912 are represented in Table 7.2.

---

[11] Rossos (1981, pp. 40–42).

[12] Rossos (1981, pp. 9–59), Bogitchvich (1928, p. 232), Sontag (1966, p. 114), Helmreich (1969, Chapter 8).

[13] Helmreich (1969, Chapters 8, 11), Rossos (1981, pp. 95–106), Clark (2012, pp. 265–266), Bogitchvich (1928, pp. 245–254).

[14] Rossos (1981, p. 105).

TABLE 7.2 *Russian Diplomacy in 1912*

Date	Action	Description
January to April	Diplomatic Approaches	Russia oversees and furthers the alliance of Serbia and Bulgaria. Russia makes commitments to safeguard particular interests of each nation. Serbia and Bulgaria commit to cooperation with Russia and Russian mediation of disputes between themselves.
September	Support/ Decline to Support	Russian foreign minister Sazonov declines to support the Balkan states in a war against Turkey. Other Russian elites offer encouragement. Proposals for joint action by the powers come to naught.
Early October	Joint Declaration	Russia and Austria jointly declare that they will accept no changes to the *Status Quo* in the Balkans.
October	Limited Demand	Russia assures Austria that Russia would not support Serbian control of the Sanjak. But if Austria occupied the Sanjak, it "would be a breach of neutrality which would inevitably entail Russian intervention."
Late October and Early November	Demand	"Russia would regard any attempt made by another Power to take permanent possession of [Constantinople and surrounding areas] as a *casus belli*." Proposes that Balkan states be allowed to keep territory. In particular, Russia directly threatens that "Serbia must be given access to the Adriatic."
November 11	Support/ Decline to Support	Sazonov tells Serbia that Russia might withdraw support for Serbia and, around this time, represents Russia to other states as restraining Serbia. Hartwig and others continue to offer assurances of Russian support.
Mid November	Demand	Sazonov directly threatens that if Germany and Austria do not allow Serbia a port on the Adriatic, then Russia might "prefer not to postpone the inevitable conflict."
Late November	Concession	Russia will not support the Serbian bid for a port on the Adriatic.

According to *Hypothesis 6.1*, to the extent that they were aware of Russian actions, observers should have understood from the Russian diplomatic approach to the Balkan powers early in the year that Russia was indeed more likely to be willing to fulfill the promises it made in the course of these negotiations. Further, the Russian approach should have given Austria reason to revise upward its estimate of the likelihood that Russia had aggressive intentions towards Austria (*Hypothesis 6.2*), and should have convinced Austria of Russian intentions to drive a wedge between Austria and the Balkan powers (*Hypothesis 6.3*).

The lack of Russian support for the Balkan states in September, prior to the start of the first Balkan war, would not be expected to convey much information. In itself, Russia's stance was neither a threat, nor a concession, and since the Balkan states did not require Russian assistance, their interests were not tightly aligned and therefore, *Hypothesis 5.3* does not predict that observers would learn about Russian intentions from Serbian political posturing. Similarly, the joint threat issued by Russia and Austria in October would be expected to have had little influence. Neither was risking a significant breach in relations or a negotiated compromise that might otherwise have been reached. By making the demand jointly, they also ensured that neither risked much in the way of relative prestige if events turned out otherwise. Thus, the signaling hypotheses do not predict that states would have altered their beliefs in response to this joint demand.

The Russian statement later in October, that Austria must not occupy the Sanjak, but that Russia would not support Serbia doing so either, would have been difficult for Austria to interpret. Was it a limited demand, or did Russia in fact not wish for its protégé to take this step, even if it were allowed by Austria? It hardly constituted a change in Russian policy that Austria not take possession of the territory. One might argue for one interpretation of events or another, but again, there is no clear signaling hypothesis prediction.

Following the dramatic victories of the Balkan states, the European powers did not seriously consider attempting to reverse the territorial gains made because there was no practical way to do so that the powers were willing to contemplate. Russia's proposal in the fall that the Balkan states be allowed to keep territory was not so much a demand as a statement of what all the powers understood to be necessary. The most significant Russian demand of the period was Russia's vacillating support for the Serbian port. Since these Russian demands were made in the context of a compromise proposal to guarantee Serbia economic access to the Adriatic, *Hypothesis 3.1* predicts that the Russian demand that Serbia be given territory on the Adriatic should have influenced the calculations of the other powers.[15] Similarly, the Chapter 5 hypotheses predict

---

[15] The case does not allow a test of the increased credibility of increased scope of demands (*Hypothesis 3.2*) because the Russians essentially made only the one demand for a Serbian port during the crisis. There is also little opportunity to test the inference that further concessions would be tolerated following offers of concession (*Hypothesis 3.3*)

that Serbia would be emboldened by Russian support (*Hypothesis 5.1*), that support would be expected to increase the likelihood of conflict (*Hypothesis 5.2*), and that therefore an emboldened Serbian stance would be a signal of Russia's intentions (*Hypothesis 5.4*).

German Diplomacy in 1912

In the early years of the twentieth century, Germany made several diplomatic approaches to Britain. This pattern continued in the first months of 1912 when Germany expressed a willingness to meet a variety of British requests, including over the German naval building program, in return for an agreement in which each power "engages not to take part in any plans, combinations or warlike complications which are directed against the other."[16]

In the fall, as the First Balkan War approached, Germany attempted to restrain rather than support its ally, Austria. In September, the German Foreign Secretary Kiderlen-Wächter directed the German Chancellor, Bethman Hollweg, to communicate to Austria that Germany was "not bound to support [Austria] in her schemes in the East, let alone adventures...Some special case might easily arise in which we should be forced to separate ourselves from our ally."[17] This was consistent with German policy following its support of Austria in the latter stages of the annexation crisis. Back in 1910, Germany had told Russia directly that "Germany had never obligated herself to support Austro-Hungarian plans in the Balkans."[18] Following the Serbian and Bulgarian gains in the First Balkan War in October and November of 1912, a new series of questions was forced on the powers, the most consequential being whether Serbia would acquire the Adriatic port. In the early stages of the conflict, Germany discussed joint representations with other powers and was reticent to intervene at all. In early November, with matters coming to a head, Germany offered its ally Austria no reassuring support. The German Emperor declared to his ministers that he would "not march against Paris and Moscow for the sake of Albania and Durazzo."[19]

because Austria demanded only that Serbia not be given a port during the crisis and with the high danger of a European war, the parties focused exclusively on whether war could be avoided, which again implied an exclusive focus on the port question during the crisis itself.

[16] Gooch and Temperley (1979, v. 6, pp. 704–705).
[17] Dugdale (1930, p. 112).
[18] Helmreich (1969, p. 180).
[19] Dugdale (1930, p. 121).

TABLE 7.3 *German Diplomacy in 1912*

Date	Action	Description
February and March	Diplomatic Approach	Germany expresses a willingness to meet British demands, including over the naval buildup, in return for an agreement in which each "engages not to take part in any plans, combinations or warlike complications which are directed against the other."
October	Offer	Germany offers to "maintain a strict neutrality" in the conflict between the Balkan states and Turkey. Along with other powers, discussed joint representations and actions.
November	Decline to Support /Support	The German Kaiser declares that Germany would support Austria in a conflict with Russia and Serbia over a Serbian port; German ministers signal that Germany would not support an aggressive Austrian Balkan policy.
December 2	Support	Germany states publicly that it would "step resolutely to the side of our ally."

Austria pressed the matter by sending the heir to the Austrian throne, Franz Ferdinand, and the Austrian Army Chief of Staff, Blasius Schemua, to Berlin. They received assurances of support from the German Emperor and the Chief of the General Staff, but then immediately learned that Kiderlen had published an article in the *Norddeutsche Allgemeine Zeitung*, which seemed to imply a much reduced degree of German backing and effectively advocated a multilateral solution to the crisis. Kiderlen stated specifically that it was untrue that Austria would soon confront Serbia with an ultimatum. Rather, the Albanian and Adriatic questions would be settled "only in conjunction with the other Balkan issues." Instead of unequivocal backing for the Austrian opposition to a Serbian, Adriatic port, Kiderlen insisted that the powers "were agreed not to determine [their positions on] any questions in advance." This was intended to convey a lack of German support for vigorous Austrian actions in the crisis. It was, in Kiderlen's words, "a cold douche" for Viennese statesmen.[20]

[20] *Grosse Politik*, v. XXXIII, pp. 424–425, Helmreich (1969, pp. 244–245), Stevenson (1996, pp. 250–251), Clark (2012, pp. 289–290).

On December 2, Bethman Hollweg gave a stronger statement of support for Austria in a public speech in the Reichstag. In particular, he stated that if Austria–Hungary were "attacked by a third party, and thereby their existence is threatened, then we would, true to our alliance obligations, have to step resolutely to the side of our ally."[21] This strong but still qualified statement of support came, however, after the final Russian disavowal of support for the Serbian port. It came, in other words, after the crisis was effectively over. These principal events of German diplomacy in 1912 are represented in Table 7.3.

Hypothesis 6.1 predicts that the German approach to England early in the year would have been found credible and led the British to conclude that Germany would indeed be willing to make concessions in the context of an agreement. The approach would also have led observers to conclude that Germany was more likely to intend aggression against a third state (*Hypothesis 6.2*) and wished to provoke worsened relations between England and a third state (*Hypothesis 6.3*). The hypotheses from Chapters 3 through 5 predict that observers' beliefs would have closely tracked Germany's decisions to support or abandon its ally. Germany's reticence to fully support Austria in the early fall would be expected to make Austrian statesmen question whether Germany would indeed support Austrian policy by force of arms if necessary (*Hypothesis 4.4*). To the extent that Germany did make statements of support, these would embolden Austria (*Hypothesis 5.1*), possibly increase the likelihood of conflict (*Hypothesis 5.2*), and thereby influence expectations about whether Germany would fight with Austria in a war (*Hypothesis 5.4*). German statements that implied a lower level of support would have had the opposite effects. Finally, the Audience Cost Hypothesis predicts that the public nature of the December 2 statement would be referenced as a reason to believe that that statement was especially credible.

EVALUATION OF THE SIGNALING HYPOTHESES

Russian and German Diplomatic Approaches

Following the formation of the Balkan alliance, the powers quickly came to understand that it was the result of a Russian diplomatic approach to the Balkan states. In the course of negotiations, the Balkan states understood that the Russian approach was genuine and that Russia would accept terms that it had resisted in the past (*Hypothesis 6.1*).[22]

---

[21] Helmreich (1969, p. 245).
[22] Helmreich (1969, Chapters 2 and 8).

As expected, Russian actions were immediately perceived as aggressive towards Austria, as an attempt to worsen relations between Austria and the Balkan states (*Hypothesis 6.3*) and as indicating a Russian policy of confrontation for the future (*Hypothesis 6.2*). Just five days after the alliance between Serbia and Bulgaria was signed, the British noted that Russia's actions demonstrated "that the Russian Government have no intention to work hand in hand with the Austrian Government in Balkan affairs."[23] Poincaré also inferred that the purpose of the Russian actions was to move the Balkan states away from Austria, assuring Russia of "hegemony in the Balkans."[24] He further argued that the treaty "contains the seeds not only of a war against Turkey but of a war against Austria. ...It not only reveals the ulterior motives of the Serbs and the Bulgarians, but also gives reason to fear that their hopes are being encouraged by Russia."[25] When the German Kaiser was told that Sazonov had claimed that Russia had insisted that the Balkan alliance should have no aggressive tendencies, the Kaiser commented that "it was clear to Russia that [no one] would take this seriously."[26] For their parts, Russian statesmen also saw the Balkan league under Russian auspices as a way to counter Austro-Hungarian influence, and further understood that it would be seen as an indicator of Russia's aggressive intentions.[27]

The reaction of the British to the German diplomatic approach supports the same set of hypotheses. The British believed that Germany earnestly desired an agreement, but suspected the approach was motivated by Germany's aggressive intentions toward other states. Thus, the British Ambassador to Germany reasoned that "putting two and two together it looks very much as if they were trying to square us in good time."[28] This inference was not an isolated one. In each year, from 1906 through 1910, Germany made proposals to England to improve relations, and each time the British drew the conclusion that Germany was willing to negotiate an agreement, but only because of its aggressive intentions towards others. Several times, the British also concluded that

---

[23] Gooch and Temperley (1979, p. 601).

[24] Helmreich (1969, p. 147).

[25] Clark (2012, p. 296).

[26] *Grosse Politik*, v. XXXIII, no. 12256 .

[27] Sontag (1966, pp. 114, 122, 125). It was for these reasons that Russia attached such great importance, during negotiations, to keeping Russian participation a secret. In fact, the Russian ambassador to Belgrade was prevented from visiting Sofia for fear that this would arouse suspicion that alliance talks between Serbia and Bulgaria were in progress. See Sontag (1966, p. 125) and Rossos (1981, p. 32).

[28] Gooch and Temperley (1979, v. 6, p. 725).

Germany's interest in an agreement derived from a desire to weaken the
Entente between Britain and France.[29]

Credibility of Russian and German Demands

The Russian and German demands and offers were made in the context
of available compromise proposals, a Protégé that could be emboldened,
and to a degree these demands risked worsening relations between the
powers. The logics discussed in Chapters 3 through 5 therefore suggest that private communications of resolve would be informative. This
expectation is born out in the diplomatic documents.

As the analysis predicts, the degree to which Serbia was emboldened
to challenge Austria–Hungary was highly sensitive to Russian support.
The Russian ambassador to Serbia, N. G. Hartwig, encouraged the Serbs
to believe in full, unequivocal Russian support and this clearly influenced
Serbian calculations. In particular, Hartwig told the Serbs that Russia
would back a Serb demand to keep its wartime territorial gains, including
on the Adriatic.[30] When Sazonov's support for the port appeared to
wane, the Serbs were keen to understand the extent to which they could
count on Russia and, supporting the emboldenment hypothesis (5.1),
admitted to the British that "if they find themselves themselves entirely
unsupported ... they would certainly come to terms."[31] Also consistent
with the Chapter 5 model, when Sazonov represented himself to other
powers as attempting to restrain Serbia, observers concluded that even
though Russia "officially tells Serbia to keep quiet," Serbian boldness
implied that Russia "privately urges her to claim and to seize all the
territory which she possibly can."[32] Arthur Nicolson, the British Under
Secretary for Foreign Affairs, believed it would be "childish" for Serbia
to "imagine they can resist the advance of any Great Power, unless they
were assured of Russian support."[33] The British ambassador to Serbia
reported that "Hartwig manipulates the Serbians as he pleases and if he

---

[29] Gooch and Temperley (1979, v. 3, 359; v. 6, pp. 190, 286, 315, 456–460, 725), Bourne
and Watt (1989, Part 1, Series F, v. 12, p. 366).

[30] See Bogitchvich (1929, p. 304) and note that even though Sazonov denied to outsiders
that Hartwig could have made such representations, Sazonov at least eventually believed
that his ambassador was significantly exceeding his instructions. See also Bogitchvich
(1929, p. 319), Bogitchvich (1928, pp. 245–246, 254), Bogitchvich (1919, pp. 39–40),
Helmreich (1969, pp. 156–157, 161), and the Serbian and Russian sources cited in
Rossos (1981, pp. 79, 95–97, 100).

[31] Gooch and Temperley (1979, v. 9, part 2, pp. 123, 193), Helmreich (1969, Chapter 8),
Rossos (1981, Chapter 3).

[32] Gooch and Temperley (1979, v. 9, part 2, pp. 123, 194).

[33] Gooch and Temperley (1979, v. 9, part 1, p. 558).

wanted could induce them to come to some reasonable arrangement."[34] When Russia did, finally and categorically, deny Serbia support, Serbia immediately made the decision to back down and the crisis was soon over. For his encouragement of Serbia, Hartwig received a "more decisive than usual" admonition from St. Petersburg, counseled the Serbians to yield, and the Serbians did so.[35] Observers immediately noted a change in the Serbian negotiating strategy. The Serbian government accepted that it would not receive a port and instead focused on negotiations with Austria for a commercial outlet on the Adriatic because Serbian elites understood "that they could expect no material support from Russia."[36]

All parties understood that the "excessive" (in British eyes) Serbian demands and Russian support posed a danger to peace (*Hypothesis 5.3*). The danger was perceived to be acute enough that the other powers favored holding a conference to adjudicate matters.[37] The British were explicit in arguing that it was Russian support which emboldened Serbia and resulted in a danger to the peace. The British Ambassador to Vienna wrote to Nicolson: "If Russia goes one step too far in supporting Serbia ... I cannot see how war is to be avoided." The Ambassador believed it was "honor" that would cause the Austrian emperor "to draw his sword."[38] For their part, the Austrians concluded that "peace can only be obtained if the hope of the South Slavs for Russian support is definitely set aside."[39]

As the Chapter 3 through 5 models predict, observers concluded from Serbian actions that Russia was encouraging Serbia and both the British and the Serbians concluded from this encouragement that Russia was more likely to support Serbia diplomatically and even militarily.[40] Several prominent British diplomats concluded that Russia was more

---

[34] Helmreich (1969, p. 157). Grey's view was that "the primary cause of all that has happened is the secret alliance which Russia encouraged the four states to conclude ... by encouraging and promoting the close understanding between the four Balkan powers he was practically raising hopes and aspirations which they had some grounds for thinking Russia would enable them to realise" (Helmreich 1969, p. 147). Note also that there are many other examples of emboldenment from the period, for instance France's extraordinary encouragement of its Russian ally (Helmreich 1969, p. 148).

[35] Rossos (1981, p. 106), Helmreich (1969, pp. 218–219).

[36] Gooch and Temperley (1979, v. 9, pt. 2, p. 257).

[37] Gooch and Temperley (1979, v. 9, pt. 2, pp. 189, 194).

[38] Gooch and Temperley (1979, v. 9, part 2, p. 191). Edward Grey's view was similar. See Gooch and Temperley (1979, v. 9, part 1, p. 729). The Italians also saw Russian encouragement of Serbia as endangering the peace. See Gooch and Temperley (1979, v. 9, part 2, p. 195).

[39] Helmreich (1969, p. 238).

[40] Gooch and Temperley (1979, v. 9, part 2, pp. 156, 165).

likely to join Serbia in a war. Referring to the effects of private Russian support, one British diplomat wrote: "Serbia ... may, by persisting in a provocative attitude, become engaged in a war with Austria and Russia will then be inevitably drawn into it."[41] Thus, consistent with the model of informative signaling in Chapter 5, Russian statements of support were perceived as emboldening Serbia and Serbian emboldenment was perceived as increasing the likelihood of conflict. In such a context, observers would be right to conclude that Russian support, in public or in private, was an indicator of Russian resolve. Consistent with the Chapter 4 model, observers argued that demands influenced relationships, could have long-term effects, and therefore conveyed information. For instance, the Austrian foreign minister noted that Serbian demands for an Adriatic port "can be taken as a sure sign that Serbia does not hope to live in friendship with the monarchy for any length of time."[42]

Sazonov's vacillation was also noted, however, and when he proposed at the end of November that Serbia should only ask for a commercial outlet to the Adriatic in late November, the British were hopeful, but only cautiously so. "It is only to be hoped that ... this conciliatory attitude will last longer than the favorable period of about two weeks ago."[43] Thus, even when the intentions underlying signals were understood to be changeable, private threats and offers were seen as credible signals of intentions in the moment. Such signals did not always lead to certain conclusions, but they did influence adversary calculations.

Russia had a strong incentive to overstate its resolve in order to promote the bargaining leverage of its Protégé, Serbia. It is striking, therefore, that observers took Serbian actions to be such strong indicators of Russian support and private expressions of Russian support to be such strong indicators of Russian resolve. The British were not entirely convinced that Russia would go to war if it came to a conflict between Serbia and Austria, but the British certainly thought this more likely as a result of Russian statements of support for Serbia. One British diplomat argued, in fact, that the affair would result in "a good drubbing" for Serbia. In this respect, the lack of a direct public threat of Russian support may have diminished Russo-Serbian credibility. The private nature of Russian dealings through November, however, allows us to see the effects of the strategic context without the confounding effect of audience costs.

---

[41] Gooch and Temperley (1979, v. 9, part 2, p. 58).
[42] Helmreich (1969, pp. 206–207).
[43] Helmreich (1969, p. 218).

The diplomats that learned of the private, German diplomatic signals during the port crisis also drew the predicted conclusions. In the early stages of the crisis, the powers generally understood that Germany had not given its full backing to Austria. For their part, the Austrians were so worried that they sent both the Archduke and the army's Chief of Staff to Berlin to ascertain the German stance. The British noted German hesitation as well. According to the British Ambassador to Vienna: "There is no doubt ... Germany felt annoyed with Austria and showed some fear lest she should be dragged into international complications through Austria pursuing adventurous policy in the Balkans."[44] Indeed, German foreign policy elites had precisely this fear. The Kaiser believed that support for Austria could lead to "a European war and for us a battle for existence with three great powers."[45] The British thought that Germany's lack of support "put the drag on Vienna."[46] This led one British diplomat to conclude that Germany would likely "act only on the defensive against Russia," and not support Austria if her policy were viewed as aggressive.[47] Other diplomats concluded that Germany did not believe there was "a sufficient reason for war between Great Powers" and that Germany might not support Austria if a war resulted.[48]

The Austrian reaction to Kiderlen's "cold douche" in the *Norddeutsche Allgemeine Zeitung* was significant. Austrian diplomats discussed the matter with their German counterparts and clearly indicated that the article had been interpreted in the sense in which it had been intended. Observers described Austrian elites as "stunned"; the lack of diplomatic commitment from their closest ally influenced the Austrian calculation of the likelihood that Germany would offer material support.[49] The Austrians expressed their gratitude for the December 2, public statement of German support in the Reichstag after the crisis had passed, but they did not discuss the public nature of the statement as a particular source of its credibility and, as we shall see in the July Crisis, it was the reticence with which Germany offered its support that made the more lasting impression.[50] In fact, already on December 11, 1912,

---

44 Gooch and Temperley (1979, v. 9, part 2, p. 192).
45 Helmreich (1969, p. 239).
46 Gooch and Temperley (1979, v. 9, part 2, p. 192).
47 Gooch and Temperley (1979, v. 9, part 2, p. 197).
48 Gooch and Temperley (1979, v. 9, part 2, pp. 37, 49, 217, 222).
49 *Grosse Politik*, v. XXXIII, pp. 424–425.
50 Consistent with the *Hypotheses 5.1* and *5.2*, however, to the British, these public statements of support were seen as potentially emboldening Austria and increasing the danger of war. "If Austria adopted a menacing attitude," British Foreign Minister Grey observed, "this would be resented in Russia, and there might be war" (Gooch and Temperley 1979, v. 9, part 2, p. 257).

Austrian Prime Minister Berchtold noted explicitly that the German ministers had refused to support aggressive actions by Austria–Hungary.[51] Later, Berchtold noted that Austria had not pursued a more aggressive policy because the Austrians "took our line from the word of command emanating from Berlin."[52]

Thus, while observers drew many inferences from Russian and German domestic politics during the period, these generally related to public sentiments that predated the port crisis rather than to the effects of specific public statements. The British ambassador to Russia, for instance, believed that if Austria occupied Belgrade or the Sanjak, Russian public opinion would be a factor forcing Russia to take action.[53] The documentary record does not provide specific evidence that the public nature of some statements was associated with greater credibility.

SIGNALING AND THE ONSET OF THE GREAT WAR

Probably no events in modern human history have been so much turned over, in so many minds, as the events that precipitated the First World War. Among diplomats and politicians who wished to justify or accuse, and participants and bystanders who wished to know how seemingly reasonable leaders could have made decisions that lead to the catastrophe, the causes of the great war have been a consuming interest. And yet, this extreme focus of attention has not produced a consensus on the causal origins of the war or on which actors were the most to blame.

The reason for this lack of consensus is at least in part that, viewed in its details, the immense complexity of the event makes the particulars appear contingent. If the Archduke's motorcade had not turned down a wrong street, if it had not then stopped feet from the 19-year-old Gavrillo Princip, for instance, perhaps Franz Ferdinand would have continued to advocate for peace and federalism, and perhaps no war would have occurred, and the whole subsequent international history of the world would have been entirely different. Such extreme contingency appears to leave little place for social science.[54]

But a causal account of the war must also come to grips with the fact that a world war, or at least a European war, very nearly occurred several times in the years before 1914. Thus, there were likely permissive causes

---

[51] Stevenson (1996, p. 258).
[52] Albertini (1952–1957, p. 245).
[53] Gooch and Temperley (1979, v. 9, pt. 1, pp. 529–532, 730).
[54] Lebow (2010, Chapter 3).

and other factors – configurations of power, beliefs and attitudes among diplomats, nationalist ideologies – that mitigated for and against conflict during the period. Many of these factors were similar in the annexation crisis of 1908–1909, the negotiation over a Serbian port on the Adriatic in late 1912, and the winter crisis of 1913. Why did the events of 1914 produce war when other very similar European crises between the same actors did not? Why did Austria decide then to reject the opportunity offered it by the Powers to march unimpeded into the capital city of its rival and extract satisfaction for the death of the Archduke and opt instead to precipitate the World War?

Accounts of the causes of the great war have often focused on Germany – its large share of military power on the European continent,[55] and its aggressive intentions.[56] But it was Austria–Hungary that made the decision to go to war. In earlier crises, as in 1912, Germany had attempted to restrain Austria, and Germany did again in the July Crisis in 1914. Austria could not have precipitated a war against Russia and France without the expectation of German support, but Austria's actions were not forced on it by Germany.[57] Austria decided not to negotiate with Serbia, and despite appearances, was not bargaining when it delivered its ultimatum. Austrian statesmen did not have political goals that they wished to achieve through threat of war, as they had in the port crisis of 1912 and the other crises of the prewar years. On the contrary, Prime Minister Berchtold began a key meeting on July 7 by asking "if the moment had not come to make Serbia forever harmless through the use of force." The Austrian political triumphs in earlier crises had only raised Austrian prestige briefly, he argued, and were of little use.[58] Thus, by the time of the ultimatum, the Austrians had decided to go to war,

---

[55] Mearsheimer (2001).

[56] Fischer (1967).

[57] In an Imperial War Council in December of 1912, the German government did decide on some war preparations, but this was not a result of aggressive designs. Rather, the Germans were reacting to a private British communication that Britain would side against Austria if Austria attacked Serbia. The German view was that if war were inevitable, then sooner would be more advantageous, but the meeting was essentially motivated by fear given the British statement and the likelihood of war, and not by inherently aggressive intent, at least not on the part of several of the key decision makers. See the report of the meeting by Admiral Georg Alexander von Müller in Röhl (2002, pp. 175–176). For an alternative account of the development of German policy that sees in this meeting a smoking gun, see Fischer (1967) and Röhl (2008). Clark (2012, pp. 626–627) characterizes this as "a minority view."

[58] Die Österreichisch-Ungarischen Dokumente zum Kriegsausbruch (ÖUDK), Erster Teil, 58, Ministerrat für gemeinsame Angelegenheiten, July 7, 1914 and Berchtold to Szápáry, July 25, 1914, Österreichisch-ungarischen Rotbuch (ÖUR), n. 26, 3530.

and they understood that Russia and France and possibly Britain would likely fight against them.[59] Why did the Austrians do it?

The fundamental bases of the Austrian case for the necessity of war derived from two conclusions that Austria drew from private diplomatic encounters in the years before the war.[60] They were in fact the same conclusions that Austria had drawn in 1912, that were not forgotten in two years, but continued to inform Austria's understanding of other countries' intentions, and were reinforced by subsequent events. The documentary evidence from 1914 ties Austria's calculations in deciding on war directly to these previous events. This is evident in the internal Austrian memorandum outlining their evaluation of the international situation that Austria decided to send to Germany at the start of the crisis to build the case for an aggressive response to the assassination. The memo begins: "With the great shocks of the past two years, the conditions in the Balkans have so clarified themselves, that it is now possible to see ... what conclusions for the European and Balkan policies [of Germany and Austria] can be drawn."[61] The memorandum and the accompanying note from Franz Josef to Wilhelm arrived in Berlin on July 5. The following day, Germany issued its blank check to Austria.

The first essential conclusion the Austrians drew from recent events concerned the character of Russian intentions in the Balkans. Austria had come to believe that the goal of Russian foreign policy was, in the words of Franz Josef, "the weakening of the Triple Alliance and the destruction of my empire."[62] This inference rested on the diplomatic support that Russia had given to Serbia against Austrian interests, and on the Russian diplomatic approaches to Balkan states. These were the Russian tendencies that were so evident in 1912 and they continued in the following

---

[59] How much the powers reckoned on a wider war at different points in the crisis is debated, as are questions about which specific actions were thought to make war inevitable (Levy 1990, Trachtenberg 1990). But the likely expansion of the planned war beyond Austria and Serbia was assumed in Austrian discussions. See, for instance, ÖUDK, Erster Teil, 58, Ministerrat für gemeinsame Angelegenheiten, July 7, 1914 and Berchtold to Szápáry, July 25, 1914, Österreichisch-ungarischen Rotbuch (ÖUR), n. 26, 3530.

[60] Some important military and political figures, including the Austrian Chief of the General Staff, Minister-President, and Minister of War, had advocated war with Serbia for some time, but the general tide of opinion turned towards war only in the days following the assassination of the Archduke.

[61] ÖUDK, Denkschrift zum Handschreiben Kaiser und König Franz Josephs an Kaiser Wilhelm, July 2, 1914. The great historian of the war, Luigi Albertini, also held the view that "the chain of events which, in November 1918, brought the Empire of the Habsburgs to its doom began, not with the crime of Sarajevo, but with October 1912, and even with the crisis caused by the annexation of Bosnia-Herzegovina in 1908–1909" (Albertini 1952–1957, v. 1, p. 380).

[62] ÖUDK, Franz Josef to Wilhelm, July 2, 1914.

years. Thus, Berchtold, who had argued against war before the assassination, maintained that "we could not allow the possibility [of a World War] to deter us in our dealings with Serbia because ... [of] the charter that Russia had given Serbia, enabling continual, unpunished pressure on the Monarchy."[63]

The Russian diplomatic approaches to Balkan states were also at the center of the Austrian evaluation of the situation during the July Crisis. In fact, the Austrian arguments in favor of war, made both in internal discussions and in correspondence with Germany, focused on the alliance relations among Balkan states. The diplomatic approach that Russia made in 1912 to Serbia and Bulgaria was repeated with other Balkan nations in the following years. Bulgaria was courted again, and Romania was approached afresh. Russia signed an alliance with Montenegro which obligated Russia to provide a military subsidy of 600,000 rubles as well as military instructors, equipment and arms.[64] These approaches to Balkan states continued to be interpreted as a sign of Russia's aggressive designs. In his letter to Wilhelm, Franz Josef wrote that "the new Balkan alliance system ... could only be directed against my Empire."[65] According to the Austrian Foreign Ministry analysis, there "can be no doubt" about Russian intentions in building the new alliance system in the Balkans: "Since joint action against Turkey is no longer under consideration, the alliance of Balkan states can only be directed against Austria–Hungary ... and in the last analysis, [is formed] to enable an expansion of territorial borders from east to west."[66] In the critical ministerial meeting on July 7, the Austrian Foreign Minister opened the discussion by arguing that while Russia was likely to fight if military action were taken against Serbia, Russia had in any case a policy "whose goal was to bring together the Balkan states, including Romania, and then to engage them in a suitable moment against the Monarchy." He then stated that a permissive policy would only make the situation worse. Thus, "the logical conclusion that arises from what has been said would be to anticipate our enemies ... by timely settlement with Serbia" even though this was understood to mean war with Russia and therefore a European war.[67]

Russian diplomatic approaches to the Balkan powers and support of Serbia in Balkan crises allowed Austria to develop an understanding of

---

[63] Berchtold to Szápáry, July 25, 1914, ÖUR, n. 26, 3530.
[64] Sontag (1966, p. 109).
[65] ÖUDK, Franz Josef to Wilhelm, July 2, 1914.
[66] ÖUDK, Denkschrift zum Handschreiben Kaiser und K'onig Franz Josephs an Kaiser Wilhelm, July 2, 1914.
[67] ÖUDK, Erster Teil, 58, Ministerrat für gemeinsame Angelegenheiten, July 7, 1914.

Russian foreign policy intentions. Austria was not mistaken. In 1913, Sazonov specifically directed the Serbs against Austria. To complete its "historical path," he told the Serbian government, Serbia "must still undergo a terrible struggle ... Serbia's promised land lies in the territory of today's Austria–Hungary...."[68]

The second important inference that Austria drew from recent diplomatic encounters was that, while Germany had offered support following the assassination, its support could not be relied upon in the future. This fact was made plain in 1912, as we have seen, and the events of the following year reinforced this view among Austrian statesmen. In February 1913, in the midst of another Balkan crisis, Wilhelm wrote a letter to Franz Ferdinand "urging a de-escalation with Russia on the grounds that the matters at issue were not important enough to justify a continuation of the current armed stand-off." In October, after briefly seeming to support aggressive action against Serbia, Wilhelm suggested buying off the Serbian leadership instead.[69] It is no wonder, then, that in April of 1914, the influential Austro-Hungarian ambassador to Russia argued that the Monarchy could not count on German support in the future. On the contrary, German policy in recent years constituted a "sacrifice of Austria–Hungary's Balkan interests."[70] The intervening years had not assuaged, in the words of the Austrian Foreign Minister, "the ever-present doubts of the adequacy of the German Alliance" that were already present in 1912.[71]

When Germany did offer its unqualified support to Austria in July of 1914, therefore, this represented a significant window of opportunity for Austria.[72] Berchtold and the other leading Austrian statesmen referenced the importance of the private German communication of its support. The Austro-Hungarian Minister-President argued specifically that if the Monarchy were not to seize the current moment for action, then "through a policy of hesitation and weakness, we run the risk of not being so certain of the unqualified support of the German Empire at a later time." This, he said, was the second factor to be taken into account, in addition to "producing orderly conditions in Bosnia," that together implied that "how the conflict should begin is a question of details."[73] Thus, German attempts to restrain Austria in the past acted like a spur

---

[68] Clark (2012, pp. 349–350).

[69] Clark (2012, pp. 289–290).

[70] Clark (2012, p. 290).

[71] Helmreich (1969, p. 182).

[72] On windows of opportunity as explanations for war, see Lebow (1984).

[73] ÖUDK, Erster Teil, 58, Ministerrat für gemeinsame Angelegenheiten, July 7, 1914.

when Austria did receive German backing. This serves as an interesting cautionary tale for powers who wish to restrain their own allies.

To summarize, the Austrian decision to hazard a world war followed almost as a syllogism from these three premises: (1) Russia intended to support Serbia and would not respect Austrian interests in the Balkans, (2) the pressure that Serbia, supported by Russia, placed on the Monarchy threatened its territorial integrity and even its existence, and (3) German support could not be counted upon in general, but Germany would support Austria in July of 1914. The second premise was a matter for debate and rested on the multiethnic character of the Austro-Hungarian Empire and the desire among Austrian elites to hold on to the newly acquired provinces of Bosnia and Herzegovina. As Schroeder (2004, Chapter 8) notes, this was in part a product of the failure of other powers to understand the Austrian position and take measures to decrease its sense of isolation and desperation. The first and third premises followed directly from the private diplomatic encounters of the prewar years described above. The primary reasons earlier crises did not lead to war were that Austria had not yet definitively reached these conclusions and was not given unqualified German support. The reason 1914 was different was not merely that Russia had acquiesced to Austrian demands in the past because there was no acquiesence in the July Crisis that would have satisfied Austria short of the destruction of the Serbian army.[74]

The causal threads that produced the war were many and tangled and it is impossible to know what would have happened if the Archduke had not been assassinated (Lebow 2010, Chapter 3). The military balance and expectations about its evolution were considered by decision makers and influenced calculations. In the July 7 ministerial meeting, for instance, there was some debate about whether power was shifting for or against the Triple Alliance. While the three premises of the Austrian case appear to have been the most important immediate considerations

---

[74] It is sometimes argued that the Archduke's absence from decision making was a decisive change from earlier crises that lead to war. Clark (2012, pp. 394–395), for instance, makes this case forcefully. While this certainly could have been a factor, it is impossible to know how the Archduke would have evaluated the situation in July. He had previously resisted calls for war on most occasions, but he did argue for a military confrontation with Serbia in December of 1912 (Clark 2012, p. 291); he was not categorically against armed confrontation. In fact, his views often paralleled those of his childhood friend Berchtold, the Foreign Minister in 1914. In the July crisis, as we have seen, Berchtold became a strong advocate for war for the first time. It is also noteworthy that the Foreign Ministry analysis that was sent to Germany along with the note from Franz Josef (which together elicited Germany's blank check) was prepared before the Archduke's death. Thus, even the views of the Austrian doves had evolved substantially following the crises of the Balkan wars.

discussed in the context of deciding whether or not to wage war, military matters were also considered. The conversation on specific military matters actually took place after the participants had stated their arguments in favor of or against war. The details of the military discussions are not known, however, because they were not recorded out of concern for military secrecy.[75] The nature of the great power alliance politics of the day and the personal and cultural biases of actors also influenced events.

Thus, other accounts of the permissive and immediate causes of the war might illuminate further back the causal chains of the narrative given here. Alternative accounts may focus on psychological motivations, deeper historical roots, and systematic material influences on decision making. But even so, these causal strands operated through the evolving perceptions of intentions that were shaped by the diplomatic encounters of the day. [76]

CONCLUSION

The 1912 diplomacy of Russia and Germany allows for the evaluation of eight signaling hypotheses from Chapters 3 through 6. All are supported by documentary evidence. The inferences of observers about these states' intentions generally tracked the demands and concessions that were offered. The one exception was when Serbia made strident demands for a port even though Russia professed to be counseling restraint. Consistent with the Chapter 5 model of diplomatic signaling among three states, however, observers inferred that Russia must in fact be encouraging Serbia in private. Substantial evidence demonstrates in particular that in multistate contexts, diplomatic support emboldens and emboldenment is often expected to increase the likelihood of conflict. Diplomatic approaches also had the predicted effects. Offers of cooperation in this context were deemed credible, but also signaled either an expectation of conflict with a third state or a desire to weaken the alignment of the approached state with that third state.

These inferences about intentions were not forgotten two years later. On the contrary, they were at the heart of the Austrian case for war. Much scholarship on the July Crisis has misunderstood the lessons Austria drew

75 ÖUDK, Erster Teil, 58, Ministerrat für gemeinsame Angelegenheiten, July 7, 1914.
76 On the military balance as an explanation for actor choices, see Miller, Lynn-Jones and Van Evera (1991) and Mearsheimer (2001). On the influence of expectations about the future balance, see for instance, Copeland (2000, Chapters 3, 4). Holsti (1991, Chapter 7) discusses the influences of great power alliance politics in 1914, and Holsti (1965) and Jervis (1976, Chapters 4, 11) analyze the effects of the belief that one's own actions are determined by circumstance while other's actions are freely chosen.

from the past because scholars have often focused on the latter stages of the crisis, including the mobilization decisions and diplomatic maneuvers designed to locate blame for the coming war elsewhere. Yet, these Austrian inferences from recent, private diplomatic encounters are essential to understanding why Austria risked all. The history of these years illustrates how diplomatic exchanges construct expectations and thereby create international orders for years to come.

8

How Germany Weighed British Resolve in 1938–1939

The confluence of imperialist ideologies, power and opportunity produces extreme violence in the international system from time to time. In the aftermath, the question arises whether actions taken in time might have averted the disaster. Could carefully conceived diplomatic interventions have altered the paths of Napoleonic France or Imperial Japan? Many observers of international affairs have argued that well-calculated diplomacy can indeed influence world affairs to this degree. Russian statesmen believed, for instance, that Prussia's rise to power in Germany was postponed for more than a decade by the Tsar's personal intervention in 1850 in a dispute between Prussia and Austria. One leading Russian diplomat wrote at the time to his brother that it was "a result of the legitimate influence of our Emperor that Germany and Europe are at peace."[1] In the 1930s, later British Prime Minister Winston Churchill believed that the rise of Nazism would have been arrested if British policy towards Germany had not been "decided only to be undecided, resolved to be irresolute, adamant for drift, solid for fluidity, [and] all-powerful to be impotent."[2]

This chapter focuses on the British attempt to thwart German imperialism in 1938–1939. It examines British threats, offers and assurances and the German high command reactions. It considers what the British did, and what they might have done. Through a systematic analysis of documentary material, it evaluates the signaling hypotheses against the documentary record of determinants of German perceptions of British intentions, from the posturing over the Czechoslovakia question to the start of the Second World War.

[1] Mosse (1958, pp. 39–40).
[2] Winston Churchill, Speech to the House of Commons, November 12, 1936.

The series of cases embodied in German views of British intentions in 1938–1939 are well-suited to evaluating the signaling hypotheses for three principal reasons. First, the facts of the cases correspond closely to the setup of the formal models and, of particular note in this regard, the bargaining involved decisions about the scope of demands. In the crises over both Poland and Czechoslovakia, the sides negotiated over several recognized options to settle the disputes and the parties had opposite preference rankings over these possible outcomes. Prior to diplomatic signaling, both sides were also believed by the other to be relatively unlikely to be willing to make maximalist concessions. Thus, the basic facts of the case suggest informative costless signaling based on the Scope of Demand mechanism. Since this mechanism proved uniquely difficult to analyze using the statistical techniques employed in Chapter 9, it was important to choose cases that would permit evaluation of these Chapter 3 hypotheses. Second, these cases represent a prominent piece of history with which most international relations scholars will be familiar and against which the theories advanced here will naturally be evaluated. As was mentioned in the previous chapter, World War cases cannot be cherry picked since there are only two. Third, Press (2005) has argued that only a "current calculus" of power and interest substantially affected German evaluations of British intentions during the period.[3] In effect, the argument brings an Offensive Realist position of the sort most prominently represented by John Mearsheimer (2001) into the field of signaling dynamics: relative power explains foreign policy and perceptions of other states' foreign policies. Since the conditions in the case appear to be such that informative signaling about intentions should have been possible, Press's analysis directly challenges the theories of communication described here. If a reevaluation of the history of the time demonstrates that past diplomacy did indeed influence contemporary evaluations of the intentions of other states, therefore, this adds significantly to the plausibility of the theory.

While a gigantic literature examins the sources of German motivations, this is tangential to the current inquiry.[4] The goal here is to examine the sources of German perceptions of what Britain would do, rather than evaluate all of the varied sources of German motivations. This is accomplished largely through a systematic analysis of all

---

[3] One might therefore argue that this constitutes a "hard case" (Eckstein 1975).

[4] For a titanic and greatly lauded recent historical analysis of this question that focuses on economic factors, see Tooze (2006). For an interesting recent analysis by a political scientist that argues that the conflict itself was not caused by incomplete information while admitting that both sides had incomplete information and engaged in protracted negotiations, see Powell (2006, pp. 195–199).

inferences about the intentions of Britain in 1938–1939 made by a high-ranking German official in the comprehensive *Documents on German Foreign Policy, 1918–1945* series.[5] No such systematic investigation of this material has yet been conducted.

I begin by describing the record of British diplomacy during the period. As in the previous chapter, I evaluate this history with respect to the predictions of the signaling hypotheses. I then turn to evaluation of the hypotheses against the record of internal German government documents. Lastly, I discuss the role of diplomatic signals in the context of all signals and indices employed by Germany at the time.

BRITISH DIPLOMACY THROUGH THE INVASION OF CZECHOSLOVAKIA

Between March of 1938 and the signing of the Munich agreement in late September, Germany pressed for territorial concessions from Czechoslovakia and threatened invasion. The Chamberlain government, on a series of occasions, declined to support Czechoslovakia and agreed to partial concessions to German demands. Some of the most important of these episodes are listed in Table 8.1.[6]

Negotiations between Britain, Germany, France, Italy and Czechoslovakia involved whether Germany would invade Czechoslovakia and subjugate it entirely or settle for the transfer of the Sudetenland, as well as on the precise mechanism of the transfer (through outright cession or following a plebiscite) and on the timing of events. For our purposes, it is important to note that there was no discussion of dividing Czechoslovak territory aside from the Sudetenland. The reason for this, while not a primary object of this study, seems relatively clear: Hitler believed it to his advantage that a territorial acquisition have a moral justification, namely the treatment of the Sudeten Germans by the Czechoslovak state. This moral reason could justify invasion if Czechoslovakia were portrayed as intractable in negotiations or a transfer of Sudetenland territory, but such a reason could not justify a negotiated agreement to acquire, say, half of Czechoslovakia. The issue of exactly how the borders of the Sudetenland itself would be drawn also played a relatively minor role in the talks. Thus, abstracting from subsidiary issues, there were three settlement outcomes: Germany would not invade and not annex

---

[5] The complete list of inferences is available in Appendix D.

[6] A more detailed timeline of events can be found in Loewenheim (1965, pp. ix–xi).

TABLE 8.1 *British Diplomatic Signals Related to Czechoslovakia*

Date	Action	Description
March 24, 1938	Decline to support ally	Chamberlain, in speech to House of Commons, rejects a formal British guarantee to Czechoslovakia.
April 28–29	Decline to support ally	British and French agree to press Czechoslovakia to make concessions to Sudeten Germans.
June 2	Decline to threaten	Chamberlain's speech makes no specific commitments or threats.
September 15	Partial Concession	Chamberlain makes a concession: Britain will accept self-determination for Sudeten Germans.
September 18–21	Decline to support ally	British and French press Czechoslovakia to accept German demands. Czechoslovakia does.
September 26	Partial Concession	Sir Horace Wilson delivers Chamberlain's letter to Hitler. Chamberlain says publicly that German demands can be satisfied peacefully.
September 27	Decline to support ally	Britain demands further concession from Czechoslovakia to Germany.
September 28	Partial Concession	Britain and France make further concessions. Chamberlain assures Hitler that his demands will be met.
September 29–30		Munich Conference and Agreement.

the Sudetenland, Germany would be allowed to peacefully annex the Sudetenland, or Germany would invade Czechoslovakia.[7]

Two factors suggest that the parameters of 1938 are a particularly good fit to the logic of scope of demand signaling described in Chapter 3 (*Hypotheses 3.1–3.4*). First, the British clearly believed that Germany was relatively unlikely to be willing to settle for no territorial or other gain in the negotiations. Thus, as Proposition 3.2 demonstrates, signaling should accord with the dynamics described in Proposition 3.1 and in these signaling hypotheses. Second, since Germany eventually did invade Czechoslovakia, and Britain decided to acquiesce, we can infer

---

[7] As the parties, and particularly the Czechoslovaks, also understood, a qualitative distinction existed between having Germany on one side of the ring of defensive forts on the Czech borders in the Sudetenland and having the Germany army on the other side of those defensive fortifications.

that Britain was likely willing to settle for very little gain in the earlier negotiations that resulted in the transfer of the Sudetenland. Claiming to be willing to fight unless a partial compromise is offered, even when one is not willing to fight for a partial compromise, is exactly what Proposition 3.1 predicts.[8]

In this context, the signaling hypotheses lead to several clear predictions about the expected determinants of German perceptions of British resolve in 1938. *Hypothesis 3.2* predicts that these British concessions would cause German leaders to believe it more likely that Britain would accept even greater concessions than Britain had offered. *Hypothesis 4.4* predicts that Britain's offers of partial concession would cause Germany to be certain that Britain would not fight to prevent Germany from acquiring the Sudetenland since the British had little to gain in the short run, from a military standpoint, from deception. In particular, in the extended deterrence context, the expectation is that Germany would see Britain's decisions to decline to support forcefully the Czechoslovak position in negotiations as evidence that Britain would not be willing to fight to preserve Czechoslovak independence. *Hypothesis 5.1* predicts that Germany would view the level of British support as predictive of the degree of intransigence of the Czechs in negotiations. *Hypothesis 5.2* predicts that British support would be seen as increasing the chances of conflict. Finally, *Hypothesis 5.4* predicts that Germany would look to the firmness of the Czech negotiating posture as evidence of the commitment that Britain had made to Czechoslovakia and thus of British resolve in the crisis.

BRITISH DIPLOMACY OVER POLAND THROUGH THE START OF THE WAR

In 1939, a similar crisis developed in which Germany demanded territorial concessions from Poland. Germany had designs on the culturally predominantly German city of Danzig and the "Corridor" of Polish territory between the city and the German border. Britain's response to German posturing was a mixture of attempted deterrence and conciliation in the hopes of reaching a negotiated solution. Because the chronology of these threats and offers involves some complexity, I shall

---

[8] If the parameters were such that the dynamics described in Proposition 3.4 in Appendix A were expected to hold, we would expect that if the British were willing to settle for little, they would have protested a willingness to fight unless Germany conceded Britain's most preferred settlement outcome, namely, not invading Czechoslovakia and not annexing the Sudetenland. This, the British did not do.

give a brief account of them here before turning to the implications of the signaling hypotheses over the period.

Even before a German invasion appeared imminent, the statements of the foreign secretary, Lord Halifax, expressed a low level of British commitment to defend the territorial integrity of Poland. In May 1938, Halifax told the Germans that "Danzig and the Corridor [are] an absurdity." He continued approvingly to discuss the possibility that Danzig might hold an election in which, "the National Socialist Party polled a two-thirds majority, [allowing for a] constitutional amendment [which] would doubtless be approved by the League of Nations." In other words, Britain was willing to see Danzig become part Germany, at least in certain circumstances.[9]

In March 1939, Chamberlain declared publicly that Britain and France would defend Polish *independence*. British and German observers immediately noted, however, that *independence* is different from *integrity*. Would Britain defend Poland if Germany were to seize Danzig and the Corridor? The German Charge d'Affairs noted that the British Foreign Office made the following clarification of the Prime Minister's speech: the commitment to Poland would only be activated if "German action clearly threatens Polish independence (in the judgement of Britain)" and the British pledge, "operates only for the period up to the conclusion of the negotiations still in progress." In other words, British support for Poland was partial, and the reason was clear. Britain wished to see the two sides arrive at a peaceful solution to the dispute and would almost certainly have tolerated the cession of Danzig to Germany if only the Poles would have it.[10]

As in the earlier negotiations over Czechoslovakia and the Sudetenland, then, abstracting from subsidiary questions, there were only a few possible negotiated solutions that each side considered or believed that the other side did. These particular potential solutions also bore a striking similarity to those from the earlier case: either Germany would gain no Polish territory, or it would gain an area around Danzig and the Corridor, or Germany would attack and invade all of Poland. Exactly how much territory around Danzig was a relatively minor issue. Other options, such as the cession of a larger portion of Poland to Germany, were not considered. The reason is probably also the same as in the earlier case: standards of conduct required that territorial demands make an appeal to moral principle. Hitler could therefore demand the right to intervention and

[9] *Documents on German Foreign Policy*, Series D, v. V, pp. 48–49.
[10] *Documents on German Foreign Policy*, Series D, v. V, pp. 172–173. See also Watt (1989, pp. 185–187).

even to territory to protect the Germans in Danzig and elsewhere, but he could not demand half of Poland just for the sake of it.

In March and April, public speeches by Chamberlain continued in a similar vein, but a firmer message was conveyed in private by Halifax in early May. He wrote to Henderson, British ambassador to Germany: "It is clear from your reports that Herr von Ribbentrop and others who think like him still believe that His Majesty's Government are not prepared to implement their guarantee to Poland, or at all events do not regard the Danzig question as coming within the scope of the guarantee." Halifax then instructed Henderson to make the following representation: "If the German Government should demand the unconditional return of Danzig, . . . there is no doubt that both we and the French would come in . . . if Herr Hitler provoked a war over Danzig, it would result not only in the destruction of the Nazi regime, but also very probably in the final collapse of the Great-German Reich." In conveying the message, Henderson may have softened the language, but this telegram was copied to Rome in a way that was intended to allow it to be decoded by the Italians. The Italians did decode the telegram and promptly and urgently passed it on to the German Foreign Minister on May 14.[11]

The next shift in British diplomacy occurred in July and early August in a series of diplomatic conversations that remain controversial among historians to this day. According to reports from two separate German sources, who did not know each other well and among whom there is no evidence of collusion, Sir Horace Wilson made extraordinary offers to Germany during this period. Although Wilson has denied the charge and there is no record of these offers on the British side, the weight of the evidence suggests that the offers were made.[12] Whether Wilson actually said what was attributed to him is, for our purposes, less important than the fact that the Germans believed that these representations were made. And what was reported to Berlin was that "the Fuehrer had only to take a sheet of paper and jot down his points; the British

---

[11] *British Documents on Foreign Policy*, Series III, v. V, pp. 478, 517, 549; *Documents on German Foreign Policy*, Series D, v. VI, pp. 487–488

[12] One reason it is unlikely the offers were a fabrication is that the two Germans, Wohlthat and Dirksen, with whom Wilson spoke noted very similar terms, implying that Wohlthat and Dirksen would have had to collude if Wilson did not in fact make a similar offer to both. Since they did not know each other well, and since engaging in this sort of operation would have meant each trusting his life in the hands of the other, it is likely each reported the offers he understood to have been made. This point and others that lead to a similar conclusion are made in Shore (2002, pp. 87–99). Note also that Halifax's personal secretary and others believed that members of the British government, including Wilson, were working to undermine the British commitment to Poland. See Shore (2002, pp. 99–100).

government would be ready to discuss them." Wilson reportedly suggested that Germany and England agree on spheres of influence, which would, "make Britain's guarantees to Poland and Roumania superfluous, [because] as a result of such a declaration, Germany would not attack these States, and they could not therefore feel that their national existence was threatened by Germany." Also discussed, according to the German report, was how Britain could "rid herself of her commitments vis-á-vis Poland."[13] There is some question about whether Hitler actually heard of these offers, but it is likely that he did. Goering and State Secretary Weizsäcker were informed and Goering had three meetings with Hitler prior to the decision to invade.[14]

On August 22, Chamberlain publicly reaffirmed Britain's commitment to Poland in somewhat stronger terms, and on August 23, Henderson delivered Chamberlain's letter pleading for German–Polish negotiations and offering to support a solution in which Poland would make territorial concessions. On August 25, Britain and Poland signed an agreement for their mutual defense. A final round of diplomatic posturing followed from August 28 through September 1. This produced no agreement, as Hitler intended; by August 28, the decision for war on the 1st had been made. After a final poking about for an exit, Britain and France declared war on September 3. The timeline of British diplomacy is summarized in Table 8.2.

In light of this history, what do the signaling hypotheses predict about the evolution of German perceptions of British resolve in 1939? *Hypothesis 4.4* predicts British concessions would have caused Germany to be certain that Britain would not fight if Germany accepted the British offer. *Hypothesis 3.2* predicts that Halifax's statement in May conveying a hardened British position on the integrity of Poland should have had the effect of increasing German perceptions that Britain would fight to defend Polish integrity – until subsequent British offers of concession again weakened the commitment. By 1939, Britain clearly believed it

---

[13] See, for instance, Thorne (1968, p. 163).

[14] See Shore (2002, pp. 87–99) and Hill (1974, p. 158). Note that several other Britons also met with German government representatives during this period and also suggested negotiated solutions involving British concessions. Wilson's proposals were by far the most extensive. Shore (2002, pp. 92–93) uses Hitler's failure to mention the Wilson offers to Lord Kemsley, the owner of Allied Newspapers, to argue that Hitler did not know of the Wilson offers. The more likely explanation is that Hitler then, as later, wished to avoid negotiations in which he might be forced to make concessions as, in his view, he had at Munich. This explanation is also consistent with Hitler's decision, in the very same conversation with Kemsley, to decline explicitly to pursue the attempts by British Secretary of the Department of Overseas Trade, Robert Hudson, to find a negotiated solution.

TABLE 8.2 *British Diplomatic Signals Related to Poland*

Date	Action	Description
May 23, 1938	Concession	In private, Halifax declares Danzig and Corridor "an absurdity." Danzig could go to Germany through democratic self-determination.
March 31, 1939	Threat, partial concession	Chamberlain declares that Britain and France would defend Polish *independence*. Observers note lack of support for Polish *integrity*.
May	Threat	Halifax through Henderson makes unequivocal threat to support Poland. Speeches from Chamberlain similar to March continue.
July 18–21	Offers	Wilson to Wohlthat: "The Fuehrer had only to . . . jot down his points." Suggests non-interference in spheres of influence, and an agreement allowing Britain to "rid herself of her commitments vis-à-vis Poland."
August 3	Offers	Wilson makes similar offers to Dirksen, the German ambassador to Britain.
August 22	Threat	Britain reaffirms commitment to defend Poland.
August 23	Threat, partial concession	Henderson delivers Chamberlain's plea for German–Polish negotiations to Hitler.
August 25	Agreement/ Threat	Anglo-Polish agreement signed.
August 28– September 1	Threats, partial concessions	Final furious round of diplomacy; the German decision to effect a breach with Poland and march on September 1 has been made.
September 3	War declarations	Britain and France declare war.

highly unlikely that the Germany would agree to a settlement in which it did not annex some Polish territory. Thus, as in 1938, *Hypothesis 3.3* predicts that the implicit and explicit offers of concession made by the Chamberlain government to allow territory to be transferred from Poland to Germany – first in March of 1939 and then in July and August – can be expected to have increased the German perception that Britain would make even greater concessions, such as permitting the invasion and destruction of Poland. By similar logic, we should expect the concessions of 1938 over Czechoslovakia to have a continuing influence on German perceptions of what to expect in 1939. Further, the public nature of some of Chamberlain's statements of commitment to Poland should have generated a measure of audience costs, which would have been perceived by the other side as increasing the likelihood that Britain would defend Poland (*Hypothesis 7.1*).

According to *Hypothesis 5.1*, the diplomatic support that the Poles did receive in German eyes should have emboldened Poland, and yet the lack of *total* support should also have been seen as restraining Poland to a degree. This support, to the extent that it was forthcoming, is expected to increase the likelihood that the sides end up in conflict (*Hypothesis 5.2*). *Hypothesis 3.1* predicts that Germany should have observed the level of British support for Poland as a signal of British commitment. Similarly, according to *5.4*, the degree of confidence the Poles displayed in negotiations should also be a signal of the strength of the British commitment.[15]

EVALUATION OF THE SIGNALING HYPOTHESES

I now turn to evaluating the predictions of the signaling hypotheses against the evidence from internal German government documents. *Hypothesis 4.4* is the most easily dealt with as it is entirely supported by the facts; the Germans never have any doubt that the British will make the concessions they offer. It is also clear that German perceptions were affected by British concessions; the Germans were not certain that a concession would be forthcoming beforehand. Since these points are uncontroversial, I shall move on to the more surprising signaling hypotheses. I first examine the signaling hypotheses derived from the analysis of the Scope of Demands in Chapter 3. I then examine the evidence for the Chapter 5 hypotheses related to Support of a Protégé, and finally turn to the documentary support for the Audience Cost Hypothesis.

Hypotheses 3.1–3.3: Credibility and Scope of Demands

For expository reasons, I begin with the predictions of *Hypothesis 3.3* before turning to *Hypothesis 3.1* and *3.2*. On several occasions, we find

---

[15] I do not add hypotheses about the diplomatic approach that Britain arguably made to Germany during this time because Germany did not reckon at all on British aggression prior to the approach.

crystal clear documentary evidence for the *Hypothesis 3.3* prediction
that concessions will cause observers to believe that further concessions
are more likely to be forthcoming. In other instances, we see at least
circumstantial evidence of the expected result.

In the negotiations over Czechoslovakia, each time the British offered
a concession, the Germans had no doubt that the British offer was
credible and members of the German foreign policy establishment further concluded that these concessions indicated that further concessions
were likely to be forthcoming. By July of 1938, the German ambassador
to Great Britain had become "convinced that Chamberlain, the Prime
Minister, Lord Halifax, the Foreign Secretary, and a number of leading
members of the Cabinet earnestly desire to initiate a policy of appeasement with Germany." The reason the ambassador gives is Chamberlain's
"sense of practical politics," in other words Chamberlain's willingness
to find a practical compromise solution rather than insist on principle.[16] Two weeks later, again as *Hypothesis 3.3* predicts, the ambassador
argued that since the British cabinet had been the first since the First
World War to make significant concessions to Germany, it was likely
that Britain would make further concessions.[17] To be certain that these
inferences are not being "cherry-picked" from the mass of documentary evidence, which may also provide contrary evidence, the reader is
invited to consult Appendix D, which lists *every inference* about British
intentions made by a high-ranking German official during the period.

The history of British concessions in 1938 continued through 1939 to
have an effect on the German perception of the preferences of the individuals involved on the British side. Many in Germany became convinced
that Chamberlain and others were the sort of men who would make further concessions to avoid war. After Munich, the "official" view among
the German high command was that Britain and France would not have
attacked if Hitler had simply invaded Czechoslovakia.[18] Hitler's statement that "the men I got to know in Munich are not the kind that start
a new World War"[19] was far from an isolated example of his or other
German foreign policy elites reflecting on the meaning of the events of
1938. On another occasion, on August 22, 1939, for instance, Hitler
said, "there are no men of the necessary calibre to carry through, firmly

---

[16] *Documents on German Foreign Policy*, Series D, Vol. 2, p. 472.

[17] *Documents on German Foreign Policy*, Series D, v. 1, p. 1158.

[18] Hill (1974, p. 149). Weizsäcker also makes it clear here that this conclusion was drawn
     as a result of much discussion of historical "what - ifs," although Weizsäcker's own view
     is that such discussions cannot lead to definite conclusions.

[19] *Documents on German Foreign Policy*, Series D, v. VII, p. 554.

and heroically, the very difficult decisions which must be taken, especially on the English side." When he then goes on to discuss the English interests involved in intervention, his point is that men such as these will not make the difficult intervention decision without more at stake.[20] Hitler was far from the only member of the foreign policy elite to draw a similar conclusion. In January of 1939, the British ambassador looked over Britain's past actions and drew the following conclusion: "It can be assumed that, in accordance with the basic trend of Chamberlain's policy, [Britain] will accept a German expansionist policy in eastern Europe."[21]

After the British Foreign Office statement in March in which the British committed to defending Poland's existence but not its integrity, *Hypothesis 3.3* predicts that German observers should have believed Britain less likely to fight even for Poland's existence. There is no documentary evidence for this, but neither is there any record of other inferences being drawn around this time about whether Britain would defend Poland's existence. Thus, the evidence here does not support the hypothesis, but neither does it tell heavily against it.

The British offers of concessions in July and August, by contrast, clearly affected German calculations. As the German ambassador came to learn: "my report of my conversation with Wilson had been taken as a further sign of Britain's weakness."[22] The "picture of the situation" was that "Chamberlain and Halifax in particular wish to avoid bloodshed."[23] The German reaction to Chamberlain's attempts in late August to convey firmness that Britain would defend Polish independence but also willingness to compromise over Danzig and other issues was particularly telling. The summary of High Command opinion in German General Halder's notes reads as follows: "Chamberlain's letter conciliatory. Endeavor to find a *modus vivendi*. ... Concept of vital interests and integrity [of Poland] elastic. England to participate in definition

---

[20] *Documents on German Foreign Policy*, Series D, v. VII, pp. 557–558. Press (2005, p. 164) argues that the famous quote from Hitler's August 22 speech, "Our enemies are worms [or small fry]. I saw them at Munich," is taken out of context. Press further suggests that only one of the three accounts of the meeting contains a record of a statement along these lines. In fact, judging by the notes, Hitler devotes almost a quarter of the meeting to discussing the capacities of the leaders involved on all sides, and this is reflected in all accounts of the meeting. For instance, in one account of the meeting, Hitler's argument is summarized: "The other side presents a negative picture as far as authoritative persons are concerned. There is no outstanding personality in England and France. ... Our enemies have leaders who are below average. No masters, no men of action." (*Documents on German Foreign Policy*, Series D, v. VII, pp. 200–204.) Another set of notes from the August 22 meeting gives the quote in the text above.

[21] *Documents on German Foreign Policy*, Series D, v. IV, p. 367.

[22] Thorne (1968, 163).

[23] *Documents on German Foreign Policy*, Series D, v. VI, 556.

. . . General impression: England, 'soft', on the issue of a major war."[24]
Exactly as *Hypothesis 3.3* predicts, an offer of concession by Britain
strengthened the belief in Germany that Britain would make even greater
concessions to avoid war. On the whole, then, the documentary evidence
strongly supports *Hypothesis 3.3*.

Turning now to *Hypotheses 3.1* and *3.2*, we first ask whether Halifax's
private, unconditional threat to fight for Danzig had the expected effect
on German beliefs. *Hypothesis 3.1* predicts that the private threat, with
its increased scope, should have increased the credibility of the British
position in German eyes. As noted above, no direct documentary evidence related to German evaluations of any specific factors relating to the
likelihood that Britain would defend Poland exists between February and
June of 1939. After Halifax's threat over Danzig in early May, however,
while there is no direct evidence that this threat affected German calculations, we do see an otherwise unexplained shift in Hitler's thinking. After
Munich, Hitler and others believed that Chamberlain would "accept a
German expansionist policy in eastern Europe."[25] Shortly after Halifax's
blunt statement in May that Britain would fight over Danzig, Hitler's
view is different. These are excerpts from a summary of a speech given
to foreign policy elites on May 23: "Further success cannot be achieved
without bloodshed. We cannot expect a repetition of Czechia. There will
be war. . . . The Fuehrer doubts whether a peaceful settlement with England is possible. It is necessary to be prepared for a showdown. England
sees in our development the establishment of a hegemony which would
weaken England."[26] Halifax's increased demand that Poland's integrity
as well as its existence be respected is perhaps the only change in the
situation that can plausibly explain the shift in Hitler's thinking. The
public nature of Chamberlain's earlier commitments in March and April
to defend Poland's existence likely also played some role, but as we have
seen, these statements had been viewed with skepticism by members of
the German foreign policy establishment.

Further evidence for this interpretation is provided by the fact that
Hitler and others again changed their views on the likelihood that
Britain would intervene after additional private diplomatic communications from Britain later in the summer again weakened the British
commitment to Poland. Even though the public rhetoric remained essentially the same, Hitler and other German leaders concluded that Britain

---

[24] *Documents on German Foreign Policy*, Series D, v. VI, p. 568.

[25] *Documents on German Foreign Policy*, Series D, v. IV, p. 367.

[26] *Documents on German Foreign Policy*, Series D, v. VI, p. 576. The German Foreign
Ministry drew a similar conclusion in early July. *Documents on German Foreign Policy*,
Series D, v. VI, p. 576.

would not fight for the integrity of Poland. In fact, these leaders concluded, as we have seen, that Britain was unlikely to fight even for
Polish independence. Thus, the balance of the evidence supports *Hypothesis 3.2* in the one instance where Britain increased the scope of its
demand, and in all other instances, where the reduced scope of the
demand led Germany to understand that Britain would not fight for
more.

Hypotheses 5.1–5.4: Support and Restraint of a Protégé

All hypotheses related to extended coercion receive unequivocal support
in the documents. As *Hypothesis 5.1* predicts, all sides understood that
British support would embolden first the Czechs and then the Poles.
According to one memorandum, "The Czechs will only become reasonable if the British and, by their agency, the French, express their intention
of not sacrificing soldiers' lives for the stupidities of Czech policy. The
Czech press, including the Beneš press, was persuading the Czechs that
Britain would help in any contingency. It must plainly be stated that she
would not help."[27] The German understanding of the situation in negotiations over Poland was similar. Hitler argued that Poland would not
have resisted the transfer of Danzig without British support.[28]

For their part, the British saw things in much the same way. They
understood that supporting their protégés would embolden them and
thereby increase the likelihood of full-scale conflict. Support for Poland,
for example, would be a signal of British resolve to defend Poland in part
because British support was expected by all sides to embolden Poland in
negotiations over Danzig and the Corridor and, therefore, to make military conflict more likely. The evidence from British documents is explicit:
"We are not in a position to assess the deterrent effect of such a Pact
upon Germany, but an important military implication is that if such a
Pact were to encourage an intransigent attitude on the part of Poland
and Romania, it would thereby tend to precipitate a European war before
our forces are in a any way fully prepared for it, and such a war might be
started by aggression against Danzig alone."[29] A stronger documentary
confirmation of *Hypothesis 5.2* could hardly be expected.

Further, precisely because he worried that emboldening Poland might
lead to conflict, Halifax tried to restrain the Polish government. He wrote

---

[27] *Documents on German Foreign Policy*, Series D, v. 2, p. 546, Memorandum, August
10, 1938.
[28] Watt (1989, p. 317).
[29] Quoted in Alexandroff and Rosecrance (1977, 411).

to them in the heat of the crisis: "I should not expect the Polish Government to abandon all hope of negotiation unless they were convinced that it afforded no possibility of averting a threat to Polish independence ... if [they] wished to establish that there 'clearly' was such a threat, they would naturally desire to consult with His Majesty's Government and would therefore do so *before* taking any irrevocable action."[30] In fact, there is also substantial evidence that Britain was in fact willing to give up Danzig and the Corridor and perhaps even all of Poland under some circumstances.[31] Thus, as the analysis in Chapter 5 predicts, Germany looked closely at both British statements of support and the Polish negotiating position to draw largely correct inferences about the strength of British support for its Protégé.[32]

Hypothesis 5.4 is also supported. Germany saw the degree of intransigence of the Poles in negotiations as a direct indicator of the strength of the British commitment to Poland. On the one hand, Hitler believed Poland would not have protested the transfer of Danzig without a measure of British support. But on the other hand, the Germans (along with the British[34]) realized that Poland would have been even less willing to negotiate if British support had been stronger. In discussions in mid August, Hilter argued that Britain would not defend Poland because if Britain were truly supporting Poland, the latter would have been more "cocky."[35]

The Audience Cost Hypothesis

As *Hypothesis 7.1*, the Audience Cost Hypothesis, predicts, there is documentary evidence that the public nature of some British threats influenced German thinking. The public nature of British commitments and the role of the British public in holding the government to these commitments is specifically referenced in April of 1938 and July of 1939. In the latter instance, the German Foreign Ministry specifically argued that because of Britain's six month propaganda campaign for "no more appeasement," public pressure would prevent the government from backing down.[36] Similarly, the ambassador to Britain concluded that if Poland were to respond with force to German action, Britain would fight, not because she is "vitally interested in the fate of Danzig, but [because] she is vitally

---

[30] Quoted in Thorne (1968, pp. 159–160).
[31] See, for instance, Shore (2002, 87–100).
[32] Further supporting the model of extended coercion in Chapter 5, Hitler also specifically noted that Britain had declined to offer Poland financial assistance and reasoned that "This suggests that England does not really want to support Poland."[33]
[34] Watt (1989, p. 185).
[35] *Documents on German Foreign Policy*, Series D, v. VII, p. 555
[36] *Documents on German Foreign Policy*, Series D, v. II, pp. 2, 223, and v. VI, p. 874.

interested in proving that she honors her political promissory notes."[37] Additionally, the fact that Hitler delayed the invasion of Poland upon hearing of the public Anglo-Polish agreement of August 25 suggests that the formal and public nature of Britain's commitment affected Hitler's calculations.

WEIGHING THE BALANCE OF SIGNALS AND INDICES

A variety of other factors influenced German calculations of British intent in 1938–1939. In particular, the German High Command considered the implications of Britain's military options and the British interests at stake.[38] Because so many factors had influence, which ones were the most decisive is difficult to weigh. The different factors also interacted with each other. When British signals convinced members of the German leadership that Britain had significant resolve to fight, for instance, German calculations would naturally have turned to the question of whether Britain had the ability to affect the situation and, in particular, whether Britain had the capability to help Poland in the short term.

That diplomatic factors loomed large in German calculations throughout the period is suggested by just how closely German evaluations of British intent tracked the scope of British demands. The concessions offered at Munich and elsewhere had a long-lasting impact by convincing many in the German leadership that Britain would make further concessions to avoid war, including permitting the destruction of Poland. The first indication that this perception had shifted comes immediately following Halifax's commitment to defend not just Poland's existence, but its right to possess Danzig and the Corridor. A few weeks after Halifax's message, while Hitler still maintains hope that Britain will be convinced to release its commitment to Poland, he suggests that this is unlikely because Britain understands that Germany is making a bid for hegemony. After Britain again attempts to make concessions over Danzig and other aspects of the Polish situation in late July and August, Hitler and others argue (although not only for this reason) that Britain will let Poland

---

[37] *Documents on German Foreign Policy*, Series D, v. VII, p. 141.

[38] Press (2005). Interestingly, however, when Hitler considered the military balance in the Polish crisis, his argument was that the British and French had few options to prevent Poland from being overrun by German forces. The critical question of whether Britain and France would fight on afterwards was largely unaddressed in this context. Here, Hitler's thinking seems likely to have revolved around his judgement that British and French leaders were "not the kind that start a new World War," and this judgment, as we have seen, had to do with the signals these leaders sent and the actions they had taken in the past.

fall.[39] Thus, although the documentary evidence does not permit precise weights to be assigned to the different factors the German leadership considered in its calculations, diplomatic signaling played a substantial role.

Finally, further support for the Scope of Demand mechanism comes from the reason that Chamberlain, on a series of occasions, declined to make maximalist demands. In the Munich crisis, Chamberlain did not demand that Hitler leave all of Czechoslovakia inviolate because Chamberlain believed Hitler would not accept this solution and would instead invade all of Czechoslovakia. Similarly, in the crisis over Poland, Chamberlain was hesitant to demand that Germany receive no cession of territory from Poland because Chamberlain worried that Hitler would then invade all of Poland rather than negotiate. As we have seen, this lack of British resolve was not feigned. Chamberlain made these partial concessions in the hopes of achieving a compromise outcome, exactly as the model predicts.

CONCLUSION

This well-known series of episodes allows for the evaluation of eight signaling hypotheses, and there is substantial evidence in favor of each of them. Threats to support Czech and Polish protégés clearly affected German calculations and did so in the predicted fashion. All sides understood that such threats were emboldening and that this increased the odds of conflict since Germany was unlikely to settle for a particularly poor negotiated outcome. Concessions were credible, as expected, and also caused German officials to conclude that further concessions might be forthcoming. Threats made in private, though relatively few, increased German perceptions that Britain would fight if it received no concession. Increased scope appears to have been associated with increased credibility, although here the evidence is circumstantial. Finally, the public nature of some threats was also important. As the Audience Cost Hypothesis predicts, this was an additional factor that reinforced the credibility of British threats.

Thus, German foreign policy elites took many factors into account in forming judgments about what Britain would do. Signals are complex and sometimes conflicting in real world cases. All are weighed against the others and reasonable people can disagree on which way the balance leans. Press (2005) is correct that German beliefs were not driven in a simple fashion by what Britain had done in the past. German leaders did

[39] Hill (1974, p. 160).

not assume that because Britain had backed down before that it would do so again. The German leadership also, at all stages, looked carefully at the military options of its adversaries. But there is no evidence that German beliefs were driven primarily by calculations of military power and interests derived from it. On the contrary, the documentary evidence shows consideration of all the factors that the theoretical models demonstrated could be a basis for drawing inferences about an adversary's intentions.

9

Statistical Analysis of Diplomatic Communication

This chapter turns to the statistical analysis of communication. It examines the signaling hypotheses and a range of fundamental questions about international affairs. In the last two chapters, we saw that private encounters influence the calculations of state actors in some cases, but are these the exception or the rule? Do public statements regularly convince in a way that private encounters do not? How does the context of alliance relations and material power influence the credibility of demands? Do the judgments formed from diplomatic signals or material factors merely confirm inferences drawn from the other domain? In other words, is one set of factors a leading indicator of state intentions? These and other questions are addressed using first-of-its-kind data on the public and private statements of diplomats and state leaders. The analyses of this data bear out the predictions of the theoretical models, in some instances in provisional fashion, where the data are limited, and in other instances, where the data are plentiful, with substantial confidence.

DEMANDS, OFFERS AND ASSURANCES DATA

To examine the signaling hypotheses statistically, data were collected on all demands, offers and assurances of which the British were aware, made by European great powers to other European great powers between 1900 and 1914. Like the inference dataset described previously, these data were drawn from the *Confidential Print* of the British Empire. The data comprise 955 unique statements, 83 percent of which were made by diplomats and leaders away from view of their publics. Slightly more than half of these statements were offers or assurances and the rest were threats or demands. If the same demand or assurance was made by the same state and to the same state on multiple occasions, this was coded as a single observation. More detailed information on data collection procedures and coding rules for all of the variables discussed in this chapter can be found in Appendices B and C.[1]

In combination with the inference data, this data enable a more precise test of hypotheses than has been possible in previous studies. Not only has most scholarship focused on public signaling, it has also nearly exclusively examined the connection between statements and whether an adversary makes a concession. A finding that certain factors are associated with concessions is taken as evidence that those factors are associated with the credibility of threats. As the models of earlier chapters show clearly, however, this can produce misleading results because credibility and successful coercion do not go neatly together. In fact, just the opposite is the case. Diplomatic threats are often at their most convincing precisely when an adversary is unlikely to comply. Therefore, the analyses in this chapter examine the direct effect of statements on the inferences that actors draw.

As Figure 9.1 indicates, the data show that the early years of the century were relatively quiet diplomatically. Only a few demands and offers were made by the powers each year. That changed with the First Moroccan Crisis in 1905, the effects of which continued to reverberate in the thinking of European diplomats for years. From then through start of the World War, diplomatic activity continued at a rapid pace. Crisis negotiations, diplomatic approaches, inter-alliance discussions, joint public representations, and private conferences were all common.

As it struggled to break free of its perceived encirclement, Germany was the most diplomatically active country. It did not rely largely on threats, as the common scholarly wisdom maintains, but equally on offers. Britain was a particular target of German diplomatic approaches, as far as the British knew. This can be seen dramatically in Figures 9.2 and 9.3. The large arrows emanating from Germany to the countries surrounding it represent the high frequency of threats and offers to those states. Of the ten bilateral relationships, however, by far the most conflictual was between Russia and Austria–Hungary. More than a quarter of all demands were made by one upon the other. Members of alliances certainly negotiated among themselves, but not to the degree that adversaries did. Countries that were more closely aligned made relatively few demands and offers – again, so far as the British were aware.

---

[1] The data used for hypothesis testing in this chapter were not used as an aid to theory generation. Data from 1854–1899 from the Inference Dataset, which has already been discussed, were used as an aid in the formulation of the models and hypotheses described in earlier chapters. Inference data from 1900 to 1914 were put aside for hypothesis testing alongside the threats, offers and assurances data, which was also not examined prior to the hypothesis testing phase of the project.

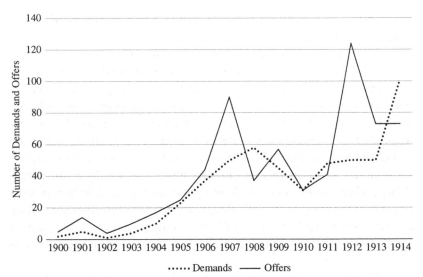

FIGURE 9.1 Diplomatic Demands and Offers, 1900 to 1914

Note: The data comprise security-related demands and offers made by European great powers other than Britain and recorded in the *Confidential Print* between 1900 and July 1914. Statements were included in the data when they proposed a change to the *status quo* or the maintenance of the *status quo*. They were classified as demands when the proposal was known to be against the preference of the state to which the statement was made and as offers otherwise.

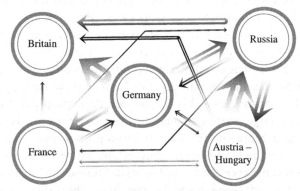

FIGURE 9.2 Diplomatic Demand Network

Note: The width of the arrows corresponds to the frequency of demands made over the period. The data comprise security-related demands made by European great powers other than Britain and recorded in the *Confidential Print* between 1900 and July 1914. Statements were included in the data when they proposed a change to the *status quo* or the maintenance of the *status quo*. They were classified as demands when the proposal was known to be against the preference of the state to which the statement was made.

Nevertheless, the divergent interests of Russia and Britain are apparent in the thick upper most arrow of Figure 9.2.

The data show unequivocally that diplomatic statements commonly affect the beliefs of officials of foreign powers. About three-quarters of

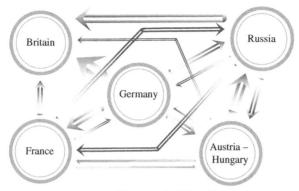

FIGURE 9.3 Diplomatic Offer Network

Note: The width of the arrows corresponds to the frequency of offers made over the period. The data comprise security-related offers made by European great powers other than Britain and recorded in the *Confidential Print* between 1900 and July 1914. Statements were included in the data when they proposed a change to the *status quo* or the maintenance of the *status quo*. They were classified as offers when the proposal was not known to be against the preference of the state to which the statement was made.

private threats and offers resulted in documentary evidence that a British observer believed the content of the statement more likely to be true after the statement was made than was believed beforehand. Statements were coded as having this effect when there was a direct documentary record of a changed belief or, more commonly, when diplomats or leaders suggested actions or changed planning for specific contingencies as a direct result of the statement.[2] Thus, beyond any doubt, private statements were regularly taken very seriously by foreign governments. While many conclusions were tentative, as we shall see below, there were substantial effects on the perceptions of observers.

This does not mean that statements were taken at face value. As the analysis in Chapter 6 suggests, for instance, following a diplomatic approach or offer of concessions, the British often concluded that the reason for the approach was that the approaching country had aggressive intentions toward a third state. A degree of duplicity was therefore suspected. Even in such cases, however, the offer of concessions was believed to be genuine. The British understood that the country making the approach would follow through on its offer and thus these cases and others of a similar nature count as part of the more than two thirds of private offers that increased British beliefs that the offering country would actually do what it had offered to do.

[2] The variable from the dataset used to calculate these figures is "Statement Believed." In the case of offers, indirect evidence that they influenced beliefs in the intended fashion includes a stated expectation or clear assumption that if a proposed agreement were accepted by the country to which the offer was made, the signaling country would be more likely to carry out or permit its offered concession.

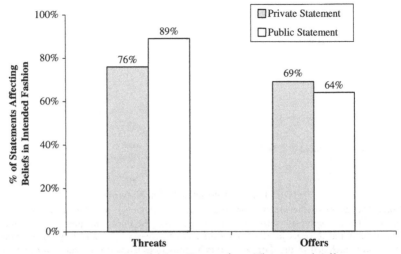

FIGURE 9.4 Conclusions Drawn from Threats and Offers

Note: Statements were coded as affecting beliefs in the intended fashion when there is a direct documentary record in the *Confidential Print* of a changed belief on the part of an internal British government actor or when an actor suggested actions or changed planning for specific contingencies as a direct result of the statement. The variable from the dataset used to calculate these figures is Statement Believed.

As Figure 9.4 shows, an even higher proportion of public threats than private threats resulted in positive inferences. Fully 89 percent of public threats affected the British calculations in the expected way. Supporting *Hypothesis 7.1*, this difference between the effects of private and public threats is significant at the .01 level.

I now turn to the evidence for the signaling hypotheses derived from the four signaling mechanisms described above. I then analyze differences between private and public threats and offers. The final section of the chapter discusses whether inferences drawn from diplomatic activity represent an independent source of information or merely follow, and closely track, changes in material factors and the inferences drawn from them.

SCOPE OF DEMANDS

States offer many compromises and concessions, and many inferences are drawn from these statements. Yet, the Scope of Demand mechanism proved the most difficult to analyze statistically. On the one hand, *Hypothesis 3.1*, that private threats and offers will often be found credible, is clearly supported by the simple fact that such large percentages of threats and offers affected the calculations of observers. On the other hand, however, *Hypothesis 3.2*, which states that increases in the scope of demands increase the credibility of threats, could not be evaluated.

This is because of the difficulty of assessing, in each instance of threat and offer, what demands and offers observers thought *might have been made* prior to the actual demand or offer that was made. Evidence for this hypothesis rests on the qualitative analysis of the previous chapter.

Hypothesis 3.3 states that offers of partial concession will increase the perception that an even greater concession would also be accepted. This hypothesis was also difficult to evaluate for a similar reason: it was impossible to systematically distinguish partial concessions from those that embodied the full scope of what adversaries deemed possible. It is noteworthy, however, that the data from 1900 to 1914 show relatively few instances where diplomats explicitly concluded, based on one concession, that a state would or would not concede more. Usually, it seems, when concessions are made, matters are resolved. States do not very often attempt to force further concessions at every hint of willingness on the part of the other side. As a result, they do not often speculate about what their adversaries would do if they were pressed further. One might take this as evidence against the hypothesis. I suspect, however, that it is rather that because states do not intend to negotiate for more in most cases, diplomats do not often speculate in written correspondence about what would happen if states did. These issues certainly merit further study and the reader must weigh the qualitative evidence presented above against the fact that such conclusions were infrequently recorded.

The small number of cases where such conclusions were drawn does allow for a provisional test of *Hypothesis 3.4*. This states that the higher the capabilities of a state that makes a concession, relative to the capabilities of the state to which to the concession is made, the more likely other states are to draw the inference that the conceding state will not concede more. Conversely, when the conceding state's relative capabilities are low, other states are more likely to conclude that the conceding state will make additional concessions to avoid war. In the data from 1900 to 1914, there are only 14 instances when one of these two conclusions was drawn following concessions made in private.

In spite of this small number of cases, a statistically significant pattern is evident, which is shown in Table 9.1.[3] The conclusion was drawn that a state would not concede more only in cases where the relative capabilities of the conceding state were greater than 1.25 times the capabilities of the state to which the concession was made. Similarly, the conclusion that a state would make further concessions to avoid conflict was drawn more frequently in cases where the conceder's relative capabilities

---

[3] Capabilities were measured using CINC scores, an aggregate measure of different sources of military capability, drawn from the Correlates of War database using the Eugene program (Bennett and Stam 2000).

TABLE 9.1 *Are Concessions Expected to Follow Concessions?*

Inference	Conceder Capabilities as % of Conceded to:		
	<75%	75% to 125%	>125%
Conceder Will Not Concede More	0	0	3
Conceder May or Will Concede More	4	5	2
	Pearson $\chi^2 = 7$	Pr. = 0.032	

Note: Capabilities were measured using the Composite Index of National Capability (CINC) scores, an aggregate measure of military capability based on total population, urban population, iron and steel production, energy consumption, military expenditure and military personnel. Data were drawn from the Correlates of War database, version 4.0.

were lower. According to a Pearson χ^2 test, this relationship between the inference drawn following a concession and the relative capabilities of the states was significant at conventional levels. Thus, the data provide some support for *Hypothesis 3.4*.

RISK OF A BREACH

Chapter 4 argued that costless signals are made meaningful by the fact that threatening behavior might result in a breach in relations. Since the costs and likelihood of the breach to the threatening state are increasing in the capabilities of the threatened state, threats by weaker states will have the greater effect on adversary beliefs, all else equal (*Hypothesis 4.1*). Further, a reorientation of the threatened state's foreign policy to the detriment of the threatening state will have greater impact on the threatening state the better were the two states' relations prior to the threat. Thus, the closer are the relations of the states, the more likely is a threat to alter beliefs about the intentions of the threatening state (*Hypothesis 4.2*).

The hypotheses identify factors that lead to a greater change in observer beliefs. Magnitudes of changes in beliefs are very difficult to measure, however. Therefore, I take the change in beliefs to be a latent variable and assume that the greater the change in beliefs, the more likely are observers to draw the relevant sort of inference. This motivates the use of a logit model to predict whether or not an inference was drawn.

The hypotheses were tested on a dataset of directed dyads of the five great powers of Europe prior to the First World War. To capture the dense nature of diplomatic signaling, an observation was a directed-dyad-day. The dependent variable in the regression analyses, *Aggressive Inference*, was coded 1 when the British drew an inference that State A was more likely to behave aggressively, in some contingency, towards State B and zero otherwise. If an aggressive inference specifically referenced some diplomatic or military action, the inference was coded as being drawn on the day of the action. In order to avoid the nearly impossible task of matching the precise content of a diplomatic statement with the precise content of an inference drawn, *Aggressive Inference* was coded 1 if an inference was drawn that State A was more likely to be aggressive against State B in some contingency. Since the data represent inferences drawn by the British about other powers, dyads with Britain in the position of State A were excluded from the analysis.

Several independent variables were coded to test the hypotheses. *Private Threat* was coded 1 when State A made a private threat to State B on that day, or when the British believed that such a threat by State A had been made to State B, and zero otherwise. If an identical threat was made on multiple occasions, only the first instance was included in the data. *Capability Share* was the share of dyad capabilities, measured by the CINC scores drawn from the Correlates of War database, possessed by State A. *S-Score* is a commonly used measure of alliance portfolio similarity between the members of the dyad.[4] This variable was used to represent the closeness of relations of members of the dyad. *Public Threat* was coded 1 when a threat was made in public on that day and zero otherwise.

Several commonly employed control variables in models of conflict were included in some models. *Joint Democracy* was coded 1 when both countries in the dyad were democratic and 0 otherwise. *Democracy* was coded 1 when State A was democratic and 0 otherwise. Country dummy variables were coded 1 when State A was a particular European power and 0 otherwise. Another variable included in some models, *Approach to Another*, is discussed in a subsequent section.

The models were estimated using a logit function and include the dyadic duration analysis terms described in Beck, Katz and Tucker (1998) and Carter and Signorino (2010). To test *Hypotheses 4.1* and *4.2*, a three-way interaction was estimated. In Model 1, shown in Table 9.2, the interacted variables were *Private Threat*, *Capabilities Share*, and *S-Score*. This allows for the effects of capabilities and alignment similarity on judgments about aggression to be contingent on whether or not a threat was made. The three-way interaction also implies, however, that the table

---

[4] Signorino and Ritter (1999).

TABLE 9.2 *Determinants of Perceptions of Aggression*

Variable	Model 1	Model 2	Model 3
Private Threat	4.3		6.9***
	(9.6)		(0.5)
Threat		0.1	
		(8.4)	
Capabilities Share	1.7	0.7	1.3
	(6.1)	(6.2)	(0.8)
S-Score	−3.9	−5.0	−3.1***
	(3.9)	(4.1)	(0.8)
(Pri.) Threat * Cap.	−17.5	−8.1	
	(18.8)	(16.2)	
(Pri.) Threat * S-Score	8.2	13.0	
	(11.6)	(10.0)	
S-Score * Cap.	−0.9	−0.5	
	(6.9)	(7.2)	
(Pri.) Thr. * S-Sc. * Cap.	14.8	3.8	
	(22.7)	(19.3)	
Public Threat	7.7***	1.0	7.6***
	(0.6)	(0.8)	(0.5)
Offer to Other	1.6***	1.6***	1.6***
	(0.3)	(0.3)	(0.3)
Controls			
Joint Democracy	−0.6**		−0.5
	(0.2)		(0.3)
Austria dummy			0.3
			(0.5)
Germany dummy			−0.2
			(0.3)
Russia dummy			−0.2
			(0.3)

***$p < .001$; **$p < .01$; *$p < .05$. Robust standard errors clustered by directed dyad. Estimates for time varying cubic polynomials suppressed.

of coefficients cannot be interpreted; we shall analyze marginal predicted probabilities instead. Robust standard errors were calculated accounting for clustering by directed dyad. This allows for the possibility that observations within directed dyads are not independent.

As one might guess, higher capabilities of an adversary increase the likelihood of concluding that the adversary's intentions are aggressive. In Model 1 from Table 9.2, when an adversary's capabilities increase from 40 percent of dyad capabilities to 60 percent, the probability of drawing an inference on a given day that the adversary is aggressive increases by 22 percent. This can be seen in the lower line shown in Figure 9.5, which is plotted against the right-hand axis.[5] All of the results presented here are robust across the model specifications shown in Table 9.2 that include the relevant independent variables.

Strongly supporting *Hypothesis 4.1*, when an adversary makes a specific threat, capabilities have the opposite effect, shown in the top, downward sloping line in Figure 9.5. In making a threat, a weaker adversary risks more and as a result conveys more. The result is that increases in the capabilities of the threatening state markedly decrease the likelihood that an inference is drawn from a private threat. An increase in adversary capabilities from 20 percent of dyad capabilities to 80 percent of dyad capabilities decreases the probability that an inference is drawn from 96 percent to 55 percent. This effect and the difference with and without a specific threat in the effects of capabilities on the probability

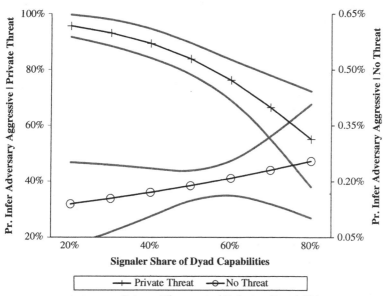

FIGURE 9.5 Private Threats and Relative Capabilities

Note: The figure illustrates predicted probabilities from Model 1 of Table 9.2. An aggressive inference was coded as occurring in a particular directed-dyad-day if an inference was drawn on that day by a British government actor in the *Confidential Print* that the first state in the directed dyad (the Signaler) was more likely to be aggressive against the second state in some contingency. Capabilities were measured using the Composite Index of National Capability (CINC) scores, an aggregate measure of military capability based on total population, urban population, iron and steel production, energy consumption, military expenditure and military personnel. Data were drawn from the Correlates of War database, version 4.0.

---

[5] Marginal effects in this chapter were calculated using the delta method, holding other variables at their medians.

of an inference that a state intends aggression are each highly statistically significant ($p < .001$).

Thus, while some of the threats of all the states produced no documented effect on the beliefs of the targets, this was more common when the more powerful threatened the less. During the Moroccan crisis in 1905, for instance, one German Ambassador claimed that "if the French Minister maintained his threat of military measures against the Sultan of Morocco, a German army would cross the French frontier." In spite of the drastic nature of the threat, it had no recorded influence on French or British beliefs about German intentions.[6] Consistent with the analysis in Chapter 4, more powerful states are more willing to threaten and thus their threats have less influence on observers. Conversely, when the relatively weak French made demands on Britain related to the Nigerian border in 1903, the British believed France would insist on these concessions.[7] This dispute was resolved in France's favor with the signing of the *Entente Cordial* in 1904.

Hypothesis 4.2 is also strongly supported. When no threat is made, a one standard deviation increase in the *S-Score* from its mean decreases the probability that an inference is drawn by 35 percent. This effect can be seen in the downward sloping line in Figure 9.6. When a threat is made, however, the situation is very different. The S-Scores between European powers over this time period range from 0.6 to 1. At the low end of alliance portfolio similarity, the model predicts a barely 40 percent chance of an inference following a threat. At the high end of portfolio similarity, a threat is nearly certain to result in a conclusion that the threatening state is in earnest. These effects of alliance portfolio similarity and the difference between the effects when a threat is made and when it is not are highly significant ($p < .001$). Thus, as the model predicts, the better the terms countries are on, the more likely is a threat to convey the information that the threatener means what it says.[8]

With documentary evidence that more than two-thirds of private offers influenced beliefs, the data provide on-average support for *Hypothesis 4.4*, which makes this prediction when the influence of preparations on the outcome of a conflict is not too great. Since the effectiveness of preparations is dependent upon so many factors, the full hypothesis statement could not be analyzed. This suggests several paths

---

[6] Gooch and Temperley (1979, v. 3, p. 95).

[7] Gooch and Temperley (1979, v. 2, p. 305).

[8] According to *Hypothesis 4.3*, the credibility of threat increases in the severity of the threat, controlling for the costs of execution. Severity and cost are highly correlated, however, and thus difficult to parse out one from the other.

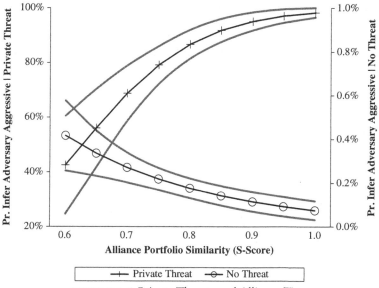

FIGURE 9.6 Private Threats and Alliance Ties

Note: The figure illustrates predicted probabilities from Model 1 of Table 9.2. An aggressive inference was coded as occurring in a particular directed-dyad-day if an inference was drawn on that day by a British government actor in the *Confidential Print* that the first state in the directed dyad (the Signaler) was more likely to be aggressive against the second state in some contingency. Alliance portfolio similarity was measured using S-Scores (Signorino and Ritter 1999).

for future research. In particular, a closer study is needed of how the type of offer influences its credibility. It is likely that *promising* to take action in the future and *allowing* an action to be taken immediately operate through different dynamics.

ENCOURAGEMENT OF A PROTÉGÉ

The dataset contains 36 explicit private threats or offers of support for a Protégé against some other state. In more than 94 percent of these instances (all but two), there is documentary evidence that observers believed support would embolden the Protégé. When states offer support, emboldenment is the near universal expectation. *Hypothesis 5.1*, which predicts exactly this, receives unequivocal support.

Although it proved impossible to analyze each case according to uniform standards to determine whether observers believed that this emboldenment would increase the odds of conflict, *Hypothesis 5.2*, which makes the relatively weak claim that diplomatic support will sometimes cause observers to infer that the support has increased the odds of conflict, was also consistent with the data. By any measure, it is clear that support was perceived to increase the odds of conflict in some

TABLE 9.3 *Interest Alignment and the Impact of Private Diplomacy*

	Defender/Protégé Interests Closely Aligned (High S-Score)	Defender/Protégé Interests Diverge (Low S-Score)
Private Support Affects Observer Beliefs	89% 17 cases	47% 8 cases
Private Support Does Not Affect Beliefs	11% 2 cases	53% 9 cases
	$N = 36$ Pearson $\chi^2 = 6$ Pr. $= 0.01$	

Note: Statements were coded as affecting beliefs in the intended fashion when there is a direct documentary record in the *Confidential Print* of a changed belief on the part of an internal British government actor or when an actor suggested actions or changed planning for specific contingencies as a direct result of the statement. Interest alignment was measured as alliance portfolio similarity using S-Scores (Signorino and Ritter 1999).

cases, including those described in detail above.[9] Thus, the data suggest that the strategic context analyzed in Chapter 6 and characterized in *Hypothesis 5.1* and *5.2* is an important feature of international political systems.

According to *Hypothesis 5.3*, the credibility of threats and offers of support should increase in the extent to which the Third Party and Protégé's interests are aligned. The hypothesis is not merely that states are more likely to come to the aid of those with which they share interests, but that statements are more likely to *change* observer assessments of the situation when interests are aligned. This is an important distinction because interest alignment could easily suggest that observers would believe support likely with or without specific statements of support. As before, we shall examine whether observers' beliefs were different before and after specific statements.

While 36 observations of a categorical dependent variable are not sufficient for multivariate regression analysis, the data nevertheless strongly support *Hypothesis 5.3*. Table 9.3 shows how credibility in such cases relates to interest alignment. Following common practice, the *S-Score*

[9] In this context, the study of Benson (2011) is also important, since it shows that alliances that are formed for purposes of compellence are much more likely to lead to conflict. It is also noteworthy that despite a debate about which alliances lead war to be more likely, there is a scholarly consensus that some types of alliances lead war to be more likely whereas other types lead it to be less likely. See, for instance, Gibler (2000), Gibler and Vasquez (1998), Colaresi and Thompson (2005), Leeds et al. (2002), Leeds (2003), Levy (1981), Maoz (2000), Morrow (1994), Siverson and Tennefoss (1984), and Smith (1996).

is again used to operationalize the harmony of interests between Third Party and protégé. When the S-Score is high (> .9), indicating that interests are closely aligned, almost 90 percent of private Third Party statements affect observer calculations. When the S-Score is low (< .9), less than 50 percent of threats result in documentary evidence of their influence on observers. This difference is significant at the .01 level.

Diplomatic Approaches

In Chapter 6, we saw that diplomatic approaches will often have a dual effect on the perceptions of other states. On the one hand, approaches will be credible in that they convince the approached state that the approaching state is sincerely willing to make concessions and to place the relations between the two on a more amicable basis (*Hypothesis 6.1*). On the other hand, when there is a reason to believe that the approaching state may find itself in conflict with a third state, the approach will signal more than that the approaching state wants closer ties. Since bids for closer ties often involve making concessions, the willingness to make concessions will also signal that the approaching state believes conflict with the third state to be relatively likely. Thus, the leadership of the approached state and other observers will be more likely to draw one of three conclusions: the approaching state intends aggression against the third state (*Hypothesis 6.2*); the approaching state believes that the third state intends aggression against it; or the approaching state wishes to weaken relations between the approached state and the third state (*Hypothesis 6.3*).

The data bear out these expectations. Statements were categorized as diplomatic approaches when one country approached another and offered a) a formal agreement to adjust differences or simply improved relations related to a specific set of issues, b) to relinquish a claim on a disputed good such as territory outside of a crisis, or c) to jointly oppose aggression by a third state. In about three-quarters of such cases, documentary evidence exists that the British believed the offers were sincere. As expected, supporting *Hypothesis 6.1*, countries do not make such proposals lightly. Ten percent of approaches led to the conclusion that the approaching state intended aggression against a third party[10] and in an additional 4 percent of cases, observers drew the conclusion that the approaching state wished to weaken ties between the approached state and a third state. These findings support *Hypotheses 6.2 and 6.3*,

---

[10] The percentage drops to 10 percent if the group c variety of diplomatic approach is excluded.

although it was far from every case in which such conclusions were drawn.

Returning to the regression analysis presented in Table 9.2, it is apparent that diplomatic approaches have a substantial impact on state perceptions of which countries intend aggression against which other countries. This is shown graphically in Figure 9.7. As we saw earlier, in the absence of a specific threat, the probability that states draw an inference that another state is aggressive appears to increase in capabilities. But an even more substantial impact derives from the diplomatic approach. This can be seen from the effect of the variable *Approach to Other*, which was coded 1 when State A satisfied one of the three conditions for initiating a diplomatic approach to a third state and o otherwise. Holding other variables at their means, the probability that an inference is drawn on a given day that one state intends aggression against another increases four fold when the first state makes a diplomatic approach to a third. For each offer or approach, the absolute increase in predicted probability that such a conclusion will be drawn is relatively small, but the data nevertheless support *Hypothesis 6.2*. A fruitful path for future research will be to further theorize which

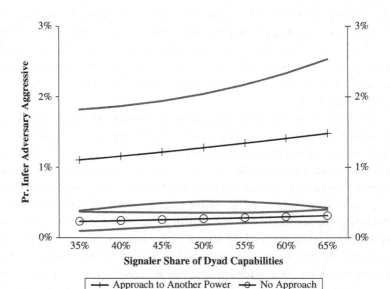

FIGURE 9.7 Effect of Diplomatic Approaches on Perceptions of Aggression
Note: The figure illustrates predicted probabilities from Model 1 of Table 9.2. Statements were categorized as diplomatic approaches when one country approached another and offered a) a formal agreement to adjust differences or simply improved relations related to a specific set of issues, b) to relinquish a claim on a disputed good such as territory outside of a crisis, or c) to jointly oppose aggression by a third state.

forms of approach, in which systemic contexts, lead to inferences of third party aggression. This is likely to depend on states' prior beliefs about the aggressive intentions of the approaching state, as in the Chapter 4 analysis. When states are already suspected of aggressive intent towards third parties, making a diplomatic approach will confirm these suspicions.

PRIVATE VERSUS PUBLIC THREATS AND OFFERS

Private and public threats and offers both often have substantial effects on observer beliefs. But are public threats and offers more likely to be believed? In the case of offers, the answer is no. As Figure 9.4 shows, a higher percentage of private offers than public offers lead to inferences. The difference is not statistically significant, however.

Model 2 from Table 9.2 was used to evaluate the Audience Cost Hypothesis that the public nature of a threat is an additional source of credibility, all else equal. This model is similar to Model 1, discussed above, except the variable *Threat* was used in the place of *Private Threat*. *Threat* was coded 1 when a public or private threat was made and zero otherwise. In this specification, the variable *Public Threat* captures the marginal effect of a statement's being made in public as opposed to in private.

The data support the Audience Cost Hypothesis. Holding all variables at their means, the model predicts an 84 percent chance that a private threat will lead to an inference about the aggressive intentions of the threatening state in some contingency. When the threat is made in public, the predicted probability of such an inference is 94 percent. This difference is statistically significant ($p = .05$).

I also find evidence that public threats lead to more certain inferences than private threats. To test this hypothesis, we coded the variable *Certainty* for the level of certainty associated with an inference by the author of the document. This was done by examining the specific words used in the drawing of the inference. Definitive statements such as "Austria will mobilize" were coded as "near certain." Inferences such as "France will *likely* concede more to Germany" were coded "moderately certain," while inferences such as "Germany *may* be trying to improve relations with Russia" were coded "uncertain." Further details of the coding procedure are in Appendix C. As Figure 9.8 illustrates, 68 percent of public threats lead to near certain inferences whereas only 48 percent of private threats do.[11] The Pearson Chi-squared test indicates that the relationship

---

[11] Because the *Certainty* variable could be coded in many cases, but not in all, the percentages shown in Figure 9.8 differ slightly from the percentages shown in Figure 9.4.

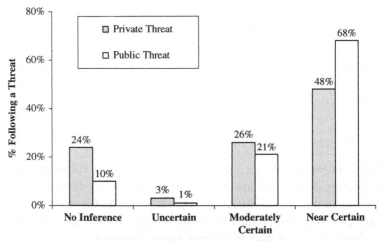

FIGURE 9.8 Public Versus Private Threats

Note: Definitive statements were coded "near certain" while words such as "likely" were coded were coded "moderately certain," and words such as "might," "may" and "possibly" were coded "uncertain" (Appendix C).

between the public nature of the threat and the certainty of the inference is significant at the .01 level.[12]

Overall Significance of Inferences Drawn from Diplomatic Activity

As a final set of observations, we return to the question of how diplomatic signals are interpreted in the context of the whole variety of other signals and indices. On the whole, inferences drawn from diplomatic exchanges and from military and other factors appear to lead to similar conclusions. This is to be expected since all are signals of the same underlying sets of intentions and preferences. Nevertheless, a focus on one set of determinants of perceptions of intentions would sometimes produce a false impression of the underlying causes of behavior in the international system.

British views of German intentions in the early years of the twentieth century provide a striking and historically significant example. In those years, it was a series of diplomatic exchanges, more than any preponderance of German power, that convinced the British to weigh the possibility of a conflict between Britain and Germany more heavily in their strategic thinking. In fact, in the first years of the century, while Britain certainly

[12] Statements of support by a Third Party for a Protégé constitute both a threat and an offer and are of particular interest. In the data from 1900 to 1914, *public* statements of support were few but highly credible. All caused inferences to be drawn and recorded in documents. As expected, nearly all of these occurred when the Third Party and protégé had very high degrees of interest similarity.

observed the German naval buildup closely, British diplomats rarely drew the conclusion that Germany intended aggression against Britain on the basis of the balance of power, shifts in power, or other military factors or actions. The buildup made Germany more powerful, and therefore more of a concern *if* it were to challenge Britain, but in the early years of the century, neither German power nor its military expenditure produced much documentary evidence of changes in British perceptions of German intentions.[13] It was rather the possibility that this new naval power could combine with the naval forces of France and Russia to challenge Britain, rather than the preponderance of German power, that was of particular concern to the British.[14]

In 1902, when asked to determine whether the German naval buildup was directed against Britain, the British ambassador to Germany first replied that it was not, but then, after a conversation with the Naval Attaché in Berlin, amended his view. This amendment, however, did not have noticeable effects on British policy.[15] Even some of those who argued that the German navy was "being carefully built up from the point of view of a war with us" also "[did] not believe that the German Emperor or Government are really unfriendly to this country."[16]

The factors that convinced many in Britain by 1907 that Germany might have aggressive designs against British interests were mostly diplomatic. Inferences drawn directly from military factors largely appear only after the shift in British thinking that was driven by diplomatic exchange. This lag of inferences based on military factors behind inferences based on diplomatic factors can be seen clearly in Figure 9.9. The figure shows a moving average of the number of inferences by the British about German aggression towards Britain in some contingency.

---

[13] In 1901, the view that largely carried the day was that "a naval war with France, or with France and Russia, is less improbable than any other naval war which we can foresee … France practically exclusively, and Russia largely, frames her naval policy with a view to war with us" (Lord Selborne speaking to the British Cabinet, quoted in Monger 1963, p. 11). Contrary to the view of Mearsheimer (2001), in the early years of the century, Germany was seen as an important counterweight to other powers on the continent rather than a force to be feared above all others and balanced against. Prime Minister Arthur Balfour argued that "It is a matter of supreme moment to us … that Germany should not be squeezed to death between the hammer of Russia and the anvil of France" (Monger 1963, p. 64).

[14] Monger (1963, pp. 94, 107).

[15] Monger (1963, p. 69).

[16] Monger (1963, pp. 82, 110). Britain's search for an accommodation with Russia began before the Russo-Japanese war and thus cannot have been caused by it (cf. Mearsheimer 2001, pp. 299–300). It was not Russia's weakness after the war that caused Britain to seek the agreement, but Russia's strength in the East beforehand. See Monger (1963, Chapter 6).

A variety of diplomatic signals influenced these changes in the British view. In 1900, statements by German diplomats convinced Britain that Germany would compete with Britain for influence in China and elsewhere.[17] Soon thereafter, Britain understood that German diplomacy implied that Germany wished to avoid a conflict with Russia even if that might mean antagonizing Britain.[18] In the beginning of 1904, as Britain moved closer first to France and then to Russia, the British understood from German diplomatic signals that the German reaction implied a more aggressive stance towards Britain. These moves towards the Triple Entente between Britain, France, and Russia antagonized Germany and this antagonism was first communicated through diplomatic channels,

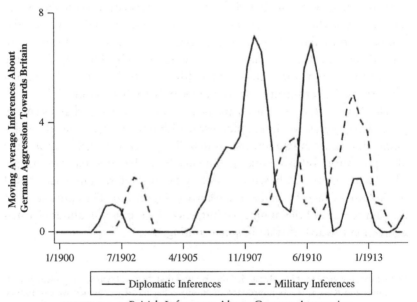

FIGURE 9.9 British Inferences About German Aggression

Note: Aggressive inferences are conclusions that a state is more likely to behave aggressively, in some contingency, towards another state. Military and diplomatic inference cause categories are shown. The series are smoothed to allow them to be more clearly distinguished.

[17] Gooch and Temperley (1979, v 2, p. 11).
[18] Gooch and Temperley (1979, v. 2, p. 75); Bourne and Watt (1987, part 1, series F, v. 19, pp. 189–191). The different implications of the military situation, which suggested that Russia was Britain's principal adversary, and the diplomatic signals, which suggested that Germany might be, led to a difference of opinion between the Committee of Imperial Defense (C.I.D.) and the Foreign Office. The C.I.D. thought the former and only the Foreign Office was significantly concerned about aggressive German designs. See Monger (1963, p. 99).

leading the British to a reevaluation of German intentions.[19] This view was summed up in the widely circulated Eyre Crowe New Year's Day memorandum of 1907: "Germany would, if she thought that such a coalition was being formed, ...not hesitate to take such steps as she thought proper to break up the coalition."[20]

Thus, the Triple Entente was not formed to balance German power. Rather, fears of German power, while present in mild form beforehand, coalesced and attained much greater force after the experience of the German reaction to the drawing together of the three Entente powers. It was at that point and in this context that British diplomats began discussing whether Germany might be striving after European hegemony. Each German attempt to create discord among the Entente powers, and each increase in German military and naval expenditure, was then seen in this light.[21]

This case and those discussed in previous chapters illustrate that the inferences drawn from diplomatic exchanges are not of marginal importance, and do not simply follow inferences about military matters. If anything, the opposite appears to be true in the data shown in Figure 9.9. Whether the framing of military matters systematically follows the impressions created first through diplomatic exchange is an interesting question for future analysis. The material presented here at least makes clear, however, that the reverse is not the case. While diplomatic and military judgements often reach similar conclusions, the inferences drawn from diplomatic affairs do not merely follow and confirm judgements based on military capabilities. Diplomatic exchange provides a partly independent source of information about the intentions of rival states.

---

[19] The British also noticed German attempts at a *rapprochement* with Russia and this also helped to sour relations. See Monger (1963, pp. 164–168). The diplomatic events of the First Moroccan Crisis in 1905 sparked the first serious British planning for the possibility of war with Germany in Europe with France the ally of Britain. See Monger (1963, p. 207).

[20] Gooch and Temperley (1979, v. 3, pp. 26, 208, 364, 400; v. 4, p. 253).

[21] See, for instance, Bourne and Watt (1989, part 1, series F, v. 12, p. 249) and Gooch and Temperley (1979, v. 3, p. 359).

Creating International Orders

According to the Austrian Secretary General of the Congress of Vienna, "England appeared at Vienna with all the glamour which she owed to her immense successes, to the eminent part which she had played in the Coalition, to her limitless influence, to a solid basis of prosperity and power such as no other country has acquired in our days – in fact to the respect and fear which she inspired and which affected her relations with all the other Governments. Profiting by this, England could have imposed her will upon Europe." Yet, England showed restraint and imposed restraint on other powers. Thereby, she helped to lay the foundation for a new political order, the peaceful transformation of European politics in the Concert of Europe.[1]

These orders are constituted by the settled expectations of the actors, but how do they form? Gradually and continuously, and the underlying realities and social processes on which they depend are constantly changing.[2] Just as there is uncertainty about the plans of others, there is uncertainty about the best plan for one's own state. Preferences and processes of socialization on which decisions depend are evolving with the courses of history. Thus, there is always more to learn about them.

Alongside material aspects of the system, domestic political dynamics and other factors, the basic processes of diplomacy articulated above play a large role in setting actor expectations. Agreements can serve as joint expressions of expectations, but diplomatic conversation results in much

---

[1] Nicolson (1946, p. 128), Schroeder (1996).

[2] Some expectations about when and how actors will cooperate or engage in conflict track underlying realities while others are more completely the products of social construction. For instance, the expectation that the public in a particular state will bear the costs of a certain conflict for a time tracks an underlying reality. The influence that a state has merely because other actors believe that the state has wide influence exists only in the realm of intersubjective understanding.

more than agreements. In peacetime as well as in international crises, processes of negotiation between state representatives inform about what states are willing to fight for and what issues they consider less important. The process of negotiating peace settlements after major wars, probably more than the documents these negotiations produce, form the mutual expectations that are the basis of many postwar orders.[3]

What is learned from the diplomacy of a moment can influence decisions for years to come. This occurred when Russia learned from Austrian threats at the time of the Crimean War that Austria would not play the part of the close ally as Russia had expected.[4] If the 23-year-old Emperor Franz Joseph had followed the advice of his famous elder states-man Prince Metternich to refrain from taking sides, the Austro-Russian rivalry that culminated in "the destruction of both imperial houses, and the liquidation of the Habsburg Empire" might never have begun.[5] During the Great Eastern Crisis in 1876 referred to above, if Russia had not asked Germany for neutrality in an Austro-Russian war, if Germany had not elected to decline, or if the Russian reaction to the German response had been more outwardly moderate, Germany would not have felt compelled to form its close, permanent alliance with Austria–Hungary. What Bismarck called the "new situation" in Europe would not have been created. Thus, if private diplomatic encounters had been conducted otherwise than they were, the whole nexus of factors that produced the First World War might never have come into being. What would have occurred instead is unknowable.

The negotiations at the end of major wars have particularly consequential and long-lasting effects.[6] In 1814, towards the end of the Napoleonic wars, British diplomats made clear that Britain would act in ways that recognized the interests of all. She did this at a time when she was at a height of power and prestige and thereby, she set expectations about how she would act in the future. But it was not merely the restraint that Britain showed and the concessions she made to the interests of other powers that transformed the order of the day. It was also the restraint she insisted upon from other powers through demands made upon them away from public view. When Prussia threatened to annex territory unilaterally, the British Foreign Secretary, Lord Castlereagh effectively threatened war and rallied a coalition of states to oppose Prussia. Castlereagh protested to Prussia against "this principle

---

[3] Trachtenberg (2008, 128), Trachtenberg (1999).
[4] For this argument in detail, see Trager (2012).
[5] Rich (1965*b*, p. 123).
[6] Ikenberry (2008).

... that it should be [acceptable] for one power to invade another, and by force compel a recognition which was founded upon no treaty."[7] He also formed a coalition of states to resist the full extent of Russian territorial designs and to bring her "to a more moderate and sound course of public conduct."[8] Having checked Prussian ambitions, he later defended Prussian interests against other powers. Thus, the restraint and moderation demonstrated by the powers in the formation of the Concert of Europe were in part imposed by the powerful. Many leaders at critical junctures before and since have not shown the same foresight.

At a conference of even greater scope following the First World War, state representatives drew many of the world's borders during closed-door negotiations. As had Castlereagh before him, US President Woodrow Wilson arrived at the peace conference as the man of the hour, the victorious leader of the most powerful state on earth, newly emerged on to the world stage. On this occasion, however, in spite of Wilson's deeply held moral convictions, the Powers did not achieve a moderate peace. In Wilson's own words, the Great Powers "parceled out the helpless parts of the world,"[9] and they imposed a punitive settlement on Germany that even to many contemporary observers sowed the seeds of another war. Where Castlereagh demanded and thereby imposed restraint on other victorious powers, Wilson merely counseled it. Wilson's diplomacy allowed the other powers to understand that the issue of paramount importance to the President was the creation of the League of Nations. Other policy objectives would be sacrificed in its pursuit, and the British and French exploited this knowledge. Had Wilson pursued a moderate peace with the same effectiveness as Castlereagh, the subsequent history of the world might again have been very different.

Closer to our own time, the new order that emerged with détente between the US and Soviet Union was also achieved through private diplomatic encounters. US President Kennedy demanded through private channels that Germany give up plans for a more independent policy. If Germany did not cooperate closely with the US, the Germans were warned, it would mean a likely reduction in US forces defending Europe and "the end of Berlin."[10] The threat to its ally allowed the US to make an offer to the Soviets: Germany would remain without nuclear weapons of her own. For his part, Soviet Premier Khrushchev reversed previous

---

7 Webster (1963, pp. 113–114).

8 Webster (1963, 104).

9 Wilson (2002, v. 2, p. 184).

10 Trachtenberg (1999, pp. 375–376).

policy in 1963 by conceding to the *status quo* in Berlin.[11] These diplomatic exchanges thus created a set of common expectations that the powers would not contest the *status quo* generally, thereby reducing Cold War tensions and the danger of nuclear war.

In all of these cases, fundamental aspects of international orders depended upon the decisions of groups of individuals represented as the will of a state. Castlereagh, Wilson, Kennedy and their advisors were not compelled by circumstance to make the sets of demands and offers they did. The material structure of the international system "shapes and shoves," but does not determine individual policy decisions.[12] Events like whether a particular war occurs are influenced by material structures, but in many cases if not in all, such structures leave much scope to human agency. Thus, capabilities alone do not determine outcomes, communication between states is not purely epiphenomenal on clashes of power and interest, and it is not the case, as even the diplomatic historian A. J. P. Taylor has written, that "wars make the decisions; diplomacy merely records them."[13] There is wide scope for human agency and diplomats in particular to shape the form clashing interests will take. Diplomatic conversations, even those between adversaries, are an integral part of the processes that construct perceptions of intention, constitute international orders, and determine the course of events in the international system.

DIPLOMATIC MECHANISMS

The central argument of this book is that the vast majority of the expectations that form through diplomatic encounters result from only a few signaling mechanisms. When relations are adversarial, when one side wants something from the other, there are incentives both to understate and to overstate one's resolve to bear costs in order to have one's way. When these conflicting incentives are in relative balance, informative signaling occurs. Evaluating this balance of incentives and understanding what the balance means for the sending and interpreting of diplomatic signals are an essential aspect of the art of diplomacy. In practice, this means estimating the relative magnitude of adversary preferences for one outcome versus another and weighing adversary beliefs about other states' preferences and beliefs. The interpretation of signals begins in this constellation of conjecture. With so many sources of uncertainty, it is

[11] Trachtenberg (1999, pp. 389, 398).
[12] Waltz (2003, p. 53).
[13] Taylor (1954, p. 246)

perhaps surprising that diplomatic encounters produce so many confident inferences. But they do.

These inferences result from careful scrutiny of other diplomats' statements and actions. Even the death of his long-time diplomatic adversary prompted Metternich to ask: "Now why do you suppose he did that?"[14] Such careful interpretation of signals and indeces from a variety of sources is evident in the documents of the British *Confidential Print* in the 60 years before the First World War. Most of these were drafted by senior statesmen whose judgments were informed by decades of experience observing and participating in international affairs. Knowing their letters and memoranda would be sent to cabinet ministers, colleagues around the world and to either Queen Victoria, King Edward VII, or King George V, these statesmen would have weighed their thoughts carefully as they put them down. Yet, they employed just a few inferential logics in reaching almost all of the conclusions drawn from private diplomacy in adversarial contexts across over 136,000 pages of diplomatic documents.

One means of understanding intention is through the Scope of Demands made. When the incentives to understate and overstate resolve are in relative balance, high demands convince by giving up the increased likelihood of a middle range compromise that results from a middle range demand. Middle range demands, in turn, convince by demonstrating a willingness to give up a most preferred outcome in order at least to achieve a middle range compromise. Interestingly, a middle range demand may convince even though it involves no risk. In such cases, it is the willingness to give up more for the greater certainty of somewhat less, but still more than nothing, that convinces an adversary of the importance a state attaches to a moderate concession.

States also convince when they risk a breach in relations. States react to other states that frustrate their designs by adopting policies that frustrate the designs of those other states. Such rivalries, once begun, can engender dynamics that perpetuate the rivalry, with the result that they endure for a long time. Thus, the willingness, possibly, to engender actions by another state, over the near and long term, that are contrary to the first state's interests conveys information. Observers will learn just how important the issues of the day are to countries that are willing to risk such consequences.

An implication of these dynamics is that restraint in extracting concessions from other powers has advantages beyond the resolution of a current dispute. When states do not make the most extreme demands on each other and take fewer costly measures to prepare for conflict, they

---

[14] Quoted in Schroeder (1972, p. xv).

all benefit substantially from the *status quo*. This actually enables forms of diplomatic signaling that reduce the likelihood of conflict. The reason is not merely that actors have more affinity for each other, but that they have more at stake when they make threats that are not expected to lead directly to war. This means states are both less likely to threaten and more convincing when they do. Both forces reduce the danger of conflict. A spheres of influence peace, such as the one eventually established in the Cold War, has these characteristics, and this may explain why conflict was so much reduced in the period of détente and during the Concert of Europe.

Today, the relations of the United States, China and Russia are often not characterized by restraint, relative to the set of issues the sides might reasonably contest, and the states have not settled into stable expectations about each other's intentions. The consequences should be appreciated. From the Russian point of view, NATO expansion up to Russia's borders pushes to the very limit of the tolerable. In such a context, Russia can be expected to resort to conflict, but Russian statements about its intentions in particular cases convey less information because there is less risk to Russia of consequences since it believes its interests are already disregarded. Russia has less stake in the *status quo*, leading to less effective signaling and a higher chance of conflicts that both sides would have preferred to avoid. Similarly, the US and China are actively contesting a wide range of issues. If relations were to worsen further, short of direct conflict, the scope of additional actions that the sides are likely to take is limited. Issues that the sides would contest if relations worsened are already contested. Once again, this hampers signaling such that the likelihood of conflict increases. In cases like these, states may fall back on signaling through the staking of bargaining reputations and dramatic public pronouncements, which often engage each other's honor, further increasing the chances of open hostilities.[15]

In multistate interactions, yet another signaling mechanism is available when two of the states have a sufficient harmony of interests. What a Third Party to a conflict communicates, in public or in private, will influence what its own protégé does. If the Third Party emboldens a protégé when the Third Party does not intend to give its support in necessity, it may hurt its own interests. Although the offer of support may improve the bargain the protégé can strike with the Target, often, it also increases the risk of conflict between protégé and Target by emboldening the protégé. This is yet another tradeoff for the Third Party to weigh and, in equilibrium, the Third Party's support may result in what is ultimately

---

[15] Gottfried and Trager (2016).

an unwanted conflict, which is known as entrapment. Thus, the possibility of entrapment and the effectiveness of signaling are not separable issues; sometimes the danger of an unwanted conflict is precisely what makes a statement of support credible.

A fourth mechanism by which leaders draw inferences relates to the decisions of leaders to initiate a Diplomatic Approach. When the representatives of one state approach the leaders in another state with a proposal for closer relations and a resolution of differences, the question the leaders of the approached state will ask is, why? A possible reason is simply that the leaders in the state making the approach wish to reduce the level of security competition between the two states. Making such an approach signals a willingness to make concessions, and so decisions to initiate and conduct such talks are not made lightly. The fact that a state's representatives express such a willingness to make concessions generally indicates that the state's leaders truly want to place relations on a better footing.

But observers will often draw a more sinister conclusion, namely, that the approaching state's leaders either intend aggression against another state or believe that the other state may attack them. In either case, this is useful information to the leaders of the approached state. They may decide, for instance, that the approach is really intended to sour their relations with a third state so that this third state becomes isolated and can then be bullied or attacked. As a result, aware of the conclusions that will be drawn by observers, the leaders of the approached state may even decide not to accept the concessions offered to them. Approached states frequently reason that convincing allies of the usefulness and credibility of present agreements and understandings requires a certain distance from potential mutual adversaries.

It is interesting that countries are often surprised by these dynamics. When France and Germany moved to establish closer ties during the Cold War, for instance, they were surely surprised by the ferocity of the US reaction. For their part, the Germans maintained that the treaty with France did not imply a less cooperative relationship with the US. This, the presidential advisor and former Secretary of State Dean Acheson told the German Ambassador, "was an insult to my intelligence." Other US officials, including US President Kennedy, had similar reactions.[16] The United States effectively told Germany, to borrow a phrase associated with the post-September 11 era, "you are either with us or against us." When Germany elected to moderate its intimacy with France, its dependence on the US facilitated the US guarantee of its nonnuclear

---

[16] Trachtenberg (1999, p. 375).

weapons status and thereby the establishment of détente between the super-powers.

A common theme in these costless signaling models is that credibility does not necessarily increase with power. It can, for instance because a Third Party state that is too weak will not embolden a Protégé to risk conflict and therefore will not send a credible signal of resolve itself. But states that are too powerful have more incentive to make demands and therefore their demands may signal less. The most powerful states have less to lose when an adversary forms a hostile alliance, or when the failure to negotiate a middle range compromise leads to war. The adversaries of their Protégés would back down from a credible threat. In such cases, the temptation of the over-powerful to make demands even when they are not willing to follow through is too high; costless diplomatic signaling is impossible. Thus, this partial disjuncture between power and credibility is not merely apparent; it is not limited to immediate crisis contexts where weaker powers only find themselves when they are highly resolved (Fearon 1994a). In costless diplomacy, the temptations of the powerful are real, inside and outside of crises, and they hinder informative signaling.

Another common theme is the inverse relationship between the effectiveness of signals at convincing adversaries and their effectiveness at coercing. Signals tend to be the most convincing when an adversary will not easily concede the issues of the day. When an adversary is not expected to contest a demand, there is no disincentive to bluffing. Such demands will often produce the desired effect, but not because they greatly influence adversary calculations. The dangers associated with an adversary's decision to resist coercion are often necessary for the signal to convince. Effective diplomacy is never without its risks.

THE FUTURE OF DIPLOMACY

The qualitative and quantitative evidence presented in these pages is drawn from over a century of history of the international system. Nevertheless, the question naturally arises: how specific are the findings to that time and place?

The presentation of the theory in game theoretic terms and the diversity of empirical evidence suggests universality. Indeed, if the assumptions and setup of the models reflect the state of affairs, so long as common media of communication exist, there is reason to expect the same dynamics to apply. Consistent with a generality to the findings, many ancient and modern cases appear fundamentally similar to the cases discussed above. Statements of diplomatic support, for instance, have been a central feature of international relations from the dawn of history to the present day. In some of the earliest known diplomatic exchanges from over 3,000 years ago, in correspondence between the Egyptian pharaohs and the other "Great Kings" of the region, there are what appear to be appeals for shows of support against rivals.[17] Today, some Taiwanese leaders appeal for US support against China. The US, for its part, is careful lest unequivocal support embolden Taiwan.

But there are aspects of the models which may appear to be less consistent with some international systemic environments. The models assume, for example, that states reckon on the possibility of conflict with one or more rivals. For most of human history, this has been a reasonable assumption, but it may be that among increasingly large sets of states in the modern world, armed conflict is increasingly unlikely. In Western Europe, where a security community now appears to exist, security policies are not crafted with a view toward defense against other Western European states because the possibility of armed conflicts among those states is thought to be so remote.

In spite of these changes in the international system, diplomacy will continue to operate through the same inferential logics as in past eras. One reason is that diplomacy between states and groups of states that are potential armed rivals continues today. Another is that, even if armed conflict is unlikely between certain states, these states still have many conflicting interests. As long as they lack a common sovereign to guarantee contracts, therefore, there are analogues to armed conflict that imply similar modes of communication.

Trade wars and real wars, for instance, have certain common aspects. Both generally involve costs to each side and in both cases, often, the outcome is uncertain. Neither party knows who will outlast the other, or which side will win particular battles or court cases along the way. As a result, once the sides know the outcome, each might prefer to have settled on the outcome right away rather than incurring the costs of conflict. Countries still form into coalitions and support other members of the coalition while opposing rival coalitions.

Consider how the mechanisms of private diplomatic signaling could operate in such contexts. If one state, the Signaler, makes a maximalist demand in the trade dispute, another, the Target, might refuse to negotiate on that basis. Since the Target might realize that the Signaler would be aware of the possibility of such a reaction from the Target, the Target could reason that the Signaler had been willing to give up a greater likelihood of a compromise for the chance at an even better deal. Here, the

[17] Cohen and Westerbrook (2002).

Scope of the Demand would indicate to the Target that the Signaler was highly resolved for a better deal, as in negotiations over war and peace. If the Signaler and Target are not the bitterest of rivals, then the trade dispute may result in worsened relations more generally. For instance, the Target may ally itself more closely to a coalition opposed to the Signaler. Thus, the Risk of a Breach mechanism is also likely to operate in such contexts, and particularly so when the Signaler is in a weaker position relative to the Target and therefore risks more. Since support in international bodies and guarantees of financial assistance in necessity still hold benefits, Encouragement of a Protégé is likely to embolden and convey information to Targets, especially when there are reasons to think that the Target will not easily back down. Similarly, since coalitions still have more influence than states acting alone, a Diplomatic Approach will suggest that perhaps the approaching state needs an ally for a purpose, namely, that it foresees the possibility of some form of conflict with a third party.

There is also, however, a sense in which the game theoretic presentation conceals the dependence of the findings on particular international cultures. This relates to the specific assumptions of the models, and the assumptions about possible types are particularly important. These assumptions specify exactly what the actors can be uncertain about, and this restricts the sorts of conclusions they can draw from events. Some version of such assumptions is always necessary in any theory of learning, whether the model is formalized or not. This is because there are always infinitely many possible generalizations that can be made from any finite set of data.[18] In order to draw a conclusion, the "search space" of possible conclusions must be limited.[19] This point is easiest to appreciate in reputational theories of learning. If Germany upholds its commitment to defend Austria, for instance, does this imply that Germany will uphold its commitments in the future, that it will uphold its commitments specifically to Austria, that Germany will oppose Franco-Russian coalitions, or that Germany will bid for European hegemony? Should inferences apply to the state apparatus that resulted in a particular past action, to the individual leaders involved, the form of government or some other category of agent? The range of available conclusions must be limited from the outset for inference from data to be possible.

In the models, uncertainty centers specifically on whether a state is willing to engage in conflict of some form rather than accept particular negotiated outcomes. This assumes that there is the possibility of such

---

[18] Goodman (1983).
[19] Nowak, Komarova and Niyogi (2002).

conflict, and that it is in some sense foremost in the minds of observers. In many international contexts, these assumptions appear reasonable and it is likely that a version of this uncertainty will preoccupy the minds of decision makers so long as desired goods must be divided among claimants; as long, one might say, as politics exists. Nevertheless, the details of the assumptions about type are important. The model allows an observer to conclude that a state is willing to settle, but is effectively agnostic about why they are so. And the why relates closely to what conclusions will be drawn about that state – or that leader – in the future. The implications are very different, for instance, if the leader is willing to fight out of a desire for increased power or out of a fear of the increased power of a rival. The models further assume that all parties understand a lot about how each other understands the social context. While there is uncertainty about whether actors will engage in conflict, all understand what such a conflict would imply – they know, for instance, whether a resulting conflict would be confined to a trade war or extend to military confrontation. The Risk of a Breach model from Chapter 4 allows for uncertainty about whether an adversary will prepare for conflict, but the effect of such preparations if they are taken is known to all. In effect, there is no uncertainty over whether an adversary will prepare for conflict by forming a hostile alliance, building arms, initiating a first strike or adopting policies to diminish a state's available resources. Incorporating richer type spaces into signaling models and integrating rationalist and psychological theories of learning in international politics will be fruitful areas for continued research.

These considerations imply both a generality and many subtle context dependencies to the analysis. The results are general in the sense that in contexts like the ones described, these logics are always available. The same essential logics can also be applied to a wide range of political environments, from economic to security negotiations. The results are specific because they make assumptions about the domain of actors' uncertainty that simplifies international reality. These simplifications yield insights by allowing fundamental dynamics to emerge clearly, but they will also sometimes obscure contingencies.

Another area of evolution in the international system is in the technologies of communication. This will surely influence diplomatic practice in the future as it has in the past. Over the past century and a half, technological change has led to a process of ever greater centralization of control of diplomatic signaling. When Foreign Offices adopted telegraph technologies in the nineteenth century, this meant that important questions could be debated and answered by the highest levels of government, allowing less autonomy to far-flung state representatives. Air travel and the telephone pushed this process further. More than 60 years ago, Nicolson (1954, p. 111) could already note that "a Foreign Secretary from his desk in Downing Street can telephone to six ambassadors in the course of one morning or can even descend upon them quite suddenly from the sky." This was a far cry from Stratford Canning, British Ambassador to the Ottoman Empire, who as a law unto himself exceeding his instructions played such a pivotal role in precipitating the Crimean War and the deaths of hundreds of thousands. This contrast with the past can be seen in the statements of the Earl of Malmesbury, a celebrated diplomat, who said he had "never received an instruction that was worth reading," and a US Consular Officer in Moscow in 1980, who claimed that "we don't need an ambassador in Moscow... because he has nothing to do" and quit.[20] Even former Secretary of State and National Security Advisor Henry Kissinger proclaimed that "ambassadors don't count anymore," and National Security Advisor Zbigniew Bzezinski thought much the same way.[21] The modern, centralized mode of diplomacy likely increases the importance of diplomatic processes by reducing the perception among negotiating counterparts that diplomatic representations do not correspond to the will of the true powers in a state.[22]

The continued spread of democratic practices around the globe may have the opposite effect, however. Democratic institutions, because of their transparency and because of the competition among groups for power, may increase the credibility of public statements.[23] Democratic constraints on power can also be used as leverage in bargaining because a negotiator might claim that only a favorable agreement would be accepted by other domestic actors.[24] Nevertheless, checks on executive authority may also reduce a leader's ability to communicate effectively. It is likely that the deterrent signals of British Foreign Secretary Grey before the First World War would have had more effect if the need for Cabinet approval of military action had not been understood by all. This approval was by no means assured and, in the event, seemed greatly to depend on the German decision to march through Belgium. The ways that democratic institutions enable and retard the conduct of effective foreign policy will be the subject of continuing scholarship, but we should not dismiss the view of ancient writers, such as Demosthenes, that democratic constraints can retard effective private diplomacy, which Nicolson

---

[20] Ward and Gooch (1922, p. 158), "Consular Officer Quits in Protest Over US Policy," *Washington Post*, April 12, 1980.

[21] Shaw (2006, p. 16).

[22] Sharp (1997), Cooper (1997).

[23] Fearon (1994*a*), Schultz (2001), Weeks (2008).

[24] Schelling (1980), Milner (1997).

(1954, pp. 23–24) connects to the Athenian defeat at Chaeronea "and to that barbaric night after the battle, when Philip and his generals, drunk with wine and victory, reeled out of the royal tent, hiccupping to each other the jingle 'Demosthenes, Demosthenous,' and slithering over the corpses of Athenians, piled naked under the moon."

As new technologies of violence have enabled smaller groups to bring about greater destruction, states' security strategies have taken ever more account of the dangers of terrorism. This in turn has resulted in a growing realm of interaction between states and nonstate actors. Despite frequent state protestations that they do not negotiate with the terrorists of the day so as not to encourage the terrorists of the future, such negotiations are commonplace. In the midst of the US attempt to defeat Al Qaeda in Iraq (AQI) and the Sunni insurgency in 2007, for instance, US Lieutenant General Ray Odierno surprised many when he said that fully 80 percent of the insurgent groups in Iraq appeared to be "reconcilable" and that even a "small portion" of AQI – the precursor to ISIS – was as well. Far from refusing to negotiate with terrorists, states have built counterinsurgency and counterterrorism strategies upon the premise that such talks can be successful. Often, the mechanisms of communication between these adversaries are similar to those described above, whether talks are conducted by State Department and Foreign Office bureaucracies or, as is often the case, by proximate military commanders.[25]

In many ways, therefore, the future will likely resemble the past. In crises and outside of them, among states and between states and nonstate actors, the principles of diplomatic learning are similar. Power, for a variety of reasons, will not always be associated with credibility. Convincing an adversary to make a concession through costless private diplomacy will involve forms of risk, and the most consequential negotiating risks will remain that an inferior bargain is struck, that a threatened adversary prepares for conflict in a range of ways, including forming hostile alliances, or that an emboldened Protégé must be defended against a powerful enemy. These forms of diplomatic communication will usually reduce the likelihood of conflict, and will be possible when a balance exists between opposing incentives to mislead.[26]

Ancient Rome, for all its achievements, contributed little to the development of diplomatic practice, probably in part because its

---

[25] Trager and Zagorcheva (2006), Trager and Zagorcheva (2007).

[26] Because diplomacy involves risk, the examination of past cases will be a misleading guide to the most successful diplomatic strategies. Those that appear most successful in retrospect will often be those that involved the highest prospects of failure at the time.

overwhelming power meant that it barely needed to conduct diplomacy at all. Subjugation of surrounding lands, rather than negotiation and compromise, were more common to the Roman approach to international affairs.[27] In the immediate aftermath of the Second World War and again with the demise of the Soviet Union, the United States too had a substantial preponderance of world power. But the United States never sought to put itself in the position of Rome and today it is ever less so. Thus, diplomacy between multiple centers of power will shape the international orders of the future, and state representatives will continue to play leading roles in constructing them. The allegiances, influence spheres, red lines and other shared expectations that characterize an order will continue to develop through these exchanges.

[27] Nicolson (1954, pp. 25–35).

APPENDICES

Appendix A

Proofs for Chapters 3–6

CHAPTER 3 TECHNICAL DISCUSSION AND PROOFS

Proof of Proposition 3.1: I will show that for $h_i(u_i^l)$ sufficiently low for all i, the following strategies and beliefs constitute a perfect Bayesian equilibrium. The Signaler's strategy is: for u_s^l, send m and choose $r = 0$; for u_s^m, send m and choose $r = 1$ following x_l and $r = 0$ otherwise; for u_s^h, send h and choose $r = 1$ following x_l and x_m and $r = 0$ otherwise. The Target's strategy is: for u_t^l, choose x_l following y $\forall y \neq m, h$, x_m following m, and x_h following h; for u_t^m, choose x_l following y $\forall y \neq m, h$, x_m following m, and x_l following h; for u_t^h, choose x_l following y $\forall y$. The Target's updated beliefs are: $\mu(u_s^l \mid y) = 1$, $\mu(u_s^m \mid y) = \mu(u_s^h \mid y) = 0$ $\forall y \neq m, h$; $\mu(u_s^l \mid m) = \frac{h_s(u_s^l)}{h_s(u_s^l) + h_s(u_s^m)}$, $\mu(u_s^m \mid m) = \frac{h_s(u_s^m)}{h_s(u_s^l) + h_s(u_s^m)}$, $\mu(u_s^h \mid m) = 0$; $\mu(u_s^l \mid h) = \mu(u_s^m \mid h) = 0$, and $\mu(u_s^h \mid h) = 1$. We need not specify the Signaler's updated beliefs except to say that they must accord with Bayes' rule.

Note that beliefs following signals m and h follow directly from Bayes' rule and the Signaler's strategy, and that the Target's beliefs at other information sets are unconstrained in a PBE. Also note that these beliefs imply the properties described in the proposition. Optimality of the Signaler's strategy at the nodes following the Target's action follows from a direct comparison of the payoffs.

To see that the Signaler's action at the signaling stage is optimal, first note that no Signaler-type can do better by deviating to a signal other than m or h because this guarantees the action x_l on the part of the Target. Second, note that u_s^h Signaler-types certainly cannot do better by deviating. Given the Target's strategy and beliefs and the other components of the Signaler's strategy, this leaves two conditions that must be satisfied for the Signaler's strategy to be optimal:

$$Eu_s(m \mid u_s^l) = [h_t(u_t^l) + h_t(u_t^m)]u_s^l(x_m) + [1 - h_t(u_t^l) - h_t(u_t^m)]u_s^l(x_l)$$

$$\geq Eu_s(h \mid \bar{u}_s^l) = h_t(u_t^l)u_s^l(x_h) + [1 - h_t(u_t^l)]u_s^l(x_l) \qquad (6)$$

$$Eu_s(m \mid u_s^m) = [h_t(u_t^l) + h_t(u_t^m)]u_s^m(x_m) + [1 - h_t(u_t^l) - h_t(u_t^m)]w_s$$

$$\geq Eu_s(h \mid u_s^m) = h_t(u_t^l)u_s^m(x_h) + [1 - h_t(u_t^l)]w_s. \qquad (7)$$

Both conditions hold for sufficiently low $h_t(u_t^l)$.

To see that the Target's strategy is optimal, note that x_l is clearly an optimal choice for u_t^h following any signal and that x_l is optimal for any Target type, given the Target's beliefs, following any signal other than m or h. For Target type u_t^l, following m, x_m gives utility $u_t^l(x_m)$ with certainty, so this Target type never chooses x_h following m. Thus, the Target's strategy is optimal in the information set following m if the following condition holds:

$$Eu_t(x_m \mid u_t^l, m) = u_t^l(x_m) \geq Eu_t(x_l \mid u_t^l, m)$$

$$= \frac{h_s(u_s^l)}{h_s(u_s^l) + h_s(u_s^m)} u_t^l(x_l) + \frac{h_s(u_s^m)}{h_s(u_s^l) + h_s(u_s^m)} w_t. \qquad (8)$$

Target type u_t^l's strategy is optimal following h because, given the Target's beliefs, any other choice results in war, which is a worse outcome for this type. For Target type u_t^m, its strategy following h is optimal because a different choice produces either $u_t^m(x_h) < w_t$ or w_t, which is the same as the utility that results from its equilibrium strategy. For this Target type, following m, x_h is clearly not preferred to x_m since the latter is certain to be accepted by the Signaler. Thus, the strategy ascribed to the Target is optimal for u_t^m if the following condition holds:

$$Eu_t(x_m \mid u_t^m, m) = u_t^m(x_m) \geq Eu_t(x_l \mid u_t^m, m)$$

$$= \frac{h_s(u_s^l)}{h_s(u_s^l) + h_s(u_s^m)} u_t^m(x_l) + \frac{h_s(u_s^m)}{h_s(u_s^l) + h_s(u_s^m)} w_t. \qquad (9)$$

Conditions (8) and (9) are both satisfied for sufficiently low $h_s(u_s^l)$. ■

Note that the equilibrium described in Proposition 3.1 will not be eliminated by standard perfect Bayesian equilibrium refinements. The intuitive criterion and divinity refinements do not apply to cheap talk games and the equilibrium is neologism-proof. To see that the Proposition 3.1 equilibrium is neologism-proof, note that according to the players' strategies described in the proof of the proposition, (1) u_s^h sends a unique signal and prefers to have its type revealed and thus would not want to deviate to any neologism, (2) no type other than u_s^l would prefer to deviate to the same neologism as u_s^l and thus only neologisms in which u_s^l sends a unique signal could be self-signaling but u_s^l has no incentive to deviate to such a signal, and (3) in response to type u_s^m's equilibrium signal, the Target behaves as it would if it were sure that the Sender's type were u_s^m, which means this type of Signaler has no incentive to deviate to a neologism either alone or with u_s^l. For a clear discussion of this equilibrium refinement, see Farrell (1993).

The structure of uncertainty described in Chapter 3 implies that there is a positive probability that player utilities are risk loving. This property is not necessary for signaling of the sort described in the propositions, however. To see this, note that if there is no Target type u_t^h, but the remaining two Target types satisfy the assumptions made in Chapter 3, then the assumptions are consistent with risk averse utility functions for all types of all players. In this modified game, Proposition 3.1 still holds.[1] This result is stated as Corollary 3.1. Notice, however, that because the issue space is not divisible, there is still a positive probability that no negotiated solution exists that both sides prefer to war. I shall discuss related issues further below.

Corollary 3.1: Proposition 3.1 holds in a modified game in which the u_t^h type does not exist and in which players have risk averse utilities over outcomes in X.

Lemma 3.1: No fully separating equilibria exist in the model with discrete compromise options and only two semi-separating equibiliria are possible: where u_s^l pools with u_s^m but not u_s^h, and where u_s^l pools with u_s^h but not u_s^m.

Proof: Note that in any PBE, the Signaler type u_s^l never sends a signal that neither of the other two types send. In such an equilibrium, whether the other two types pool or send unique signals, it will always be optimal, for any set of Target beliefs consistent with Bayes' rule, for Target-type u_t^l to offer more than x_l in response to the signal or signals sent by Signaler types u_s^m and u_s^h and no Target-types can offer less than x_l. Since in equilibrium all Target types must respond with x_l following a unique signal sent by u_s^l, Signaler-type u_s^l would prefer to deviate to the message assigned to one of the other Signaler types, which means that no such equilibrium exists. Thus, no fully separating equilibria exist and only the two semi-separating equilibria described in the Lemma are possible.

Proof of Proposition 3.2: The proof of Proposition 1 demonstrates that equilibria of the first type described in Lemma 3.1 have the properties

---

[1] The proof is identical to the proof of Proposition 3.1 except that $h_t(u_t^h) = 0$ and the u_t^h component of the Target's strategy is eliminated.

described in the proposition. Thus, by Lemma 3.1, we need only show that, for sufficiently low $h_t(u_t^l)$, an equilibrium does not exist in which u_s^l pools with u_s^h.

In any such equilibrium, since Bayes' rule implies that the Target believes it is facing a u_s^m type Signaler following that type's unique signal m, u_t^l and u_t^m type Targets must choose x_m following m and u_t^h must choose x_l (since other offers would be accepted and result in lower utility for this type than conflict). This implies that $Eu_s(m \mid u_s^l) = (h_t(u_t^l) + h_t(u_t^m))u_s^l(x_m) + (1 - h_t(u_t^l) + h_t(u_t^m))u_s^l(x_l)$.

Following the common signal sent by u_s^l and u_s^h, u_t^h types must choose x_l because there is a positive probability of either of the other offers being accepted, which leads to lower expected utility than conflict for this Target type. Note that no Target type offers x_m following h because an offer of x_l yields the same probability of war and is preferable if accepted. Thus, following h, u_t^m must choose x_l because a choice of x_h will be accepted in any PBE, leading to a strictly lower payoff. This implies that $Eu_s(h \mid u_s^l) \leq h_t(u_t^l)u_s^l(x_h) + (1 - h_t(u_t^l))u_s^l(x_l)$, which implies that the equilibrium condition, $Eu_s(h \mid u_s^l) \geq Eu_s(m \mid u_s^l)$, cannot hold for sufficiently low $h_t(u_t^l)$. ∎

Proof of Proposition 3.3: By Lemma 3.1, the only equilibria in which cheap talk affects the outcome are (1) those in which the u_s^l type sends the same signal as the u_s^m type, while the u_s^h type sends a different signal and (2) those in which the u_s^l type sends the same signal as the u_s^h type, while the u_s^m type sends a different signal.

Consider the first form of signaling equilibrium. In any such equilibrium, following the signal sent by the u_s^l and u_s^m types (m without loss of generality), u_t^m Target type must choose x_m because if such Target's choose x_l, then u_s^m strictly prefer to deviate from their equilibrium strategy to the signal sent by u_s^h types (h). Further, for $h_s(u_s^l)$ sufficiently low, the Target prefers x_m to x_l following m. In any PBE, u_t^h must choose x_l following m. Following h, u_t^m and u_t^h certainly cannot offer x_h given beliefs consistent with Bayes' rule. These considerations imply that the probability of war in such cases is $h_s(u_s^h)(h_t(u_t^m)+h_t(u_t^h))+h_s(u_s^m)h_t(u_t^h)$.

In a PBE of a world without communication, clearly no Target type can make an offer that it likes less than going to war because there is a positive probability that the offer will be accepted. Thus, the equilibrium probability of war is at least $h_s(u_s^h)(h_t(u_t^m)+h_t(u_t^h))+h_s(u_s^m)h_t(u_t^h)$, which is the probability of war in the PBE with communication for sufficiently low $h_s(u_s^l)$.

Now consider the second form of signaling equilibrium. In any equilibrium of this type, the Target type u_t^h must choose x_l following the signal sent by u_s^m, and then u_s^m must choose war in a PBE. Following the signal sent by u_s^l and u_s^h, Target types u_t^m and u_t^h must choose x_l (no other feasible x that is preferred by these Target types to war has a higher chance of being accepted by the Signaler). Since Signaler types u_s^l never elect to fight, these considerations imply that the probability of war in this equilibrium is equal to $h_t(u_s^m)h_t(u_t^h)+h_s(u_s^h)(h_t(u_t^h)+h_t(u_t^m))$, which equals the minimum probability of war in the game without cheap talk communication. ∎

As just discussed in Lemma 3.1 and the proof to Proposition 3.3, an alternative signaling equilibrium may exists for this model. Here, the least resolved and most resolved Signaler's send the same signal, while Signaler's that would fight unless they are offered at least x_m send a unique signal. Thus, in this case, admitting a willingness to compromise on x_m does not increase the Target's belief that the Signaler would accept x_l over war as well. Rather, the Target knows for sure following such a signal that an offer of x_m will be accepted and avoid war while an offer of only x_l will not. Sufficient conditions for the existence of such an equilibrium are given in Proposition 3.4.

Proposition 3.4: If $h_s(u_s^l)$ is sufficiently low and $h_t(u_t^l) \in \left(\frac{h_t(u_t^m)[u_s^l(x_m)-u_s^l(x_l)]}{u_s^l(x_h)-u_s^l(x_m)}, \right.$ $\left. \frac{h_t(u_t^m)[u_s^m(x_m)-w_s]}{u_s^m(x_h)-u_s^m(x_m)} \right)$, a perfect Bayesian equilibrium exists in which the signals m and h are sent with positive probability and

(1) $\mu(u_s^h \mid h) = \dfrac{h_s(u_s^h)}{h_s(u_s^l)+h_s(u_s^h)}$ & $\mu(u_s^h \mid y) = 0 \; \forall y \neq h$

(2) $\mu(u_s^m \mid m) = 1$ & $\mu(u_s^l \mid m) = 0$

(3) $\mu(u_s^l \mid y) = 1 \; \forall y \neq m, h.$

It is doubtful that equilibria of this sort closely track many situations in international politics. The reason is that in these equilibria, the least resolved Signaler's must prefer to gamble that they will get their most preferred outcome (by sending the same signal as the most resolved types) rather than achieve x_m for sure, while Signalers that are somewhat more resolved would prefer x_m for sure rather than take a similar gamble. Why should states that are willing to fight for a better deal be less willing to take such risks? There is no reason to expect this to be the case in general. In fact, it exists only when the utility functions of the player types take on unusual forms that diverge from those common addressed in the international politics literature. Corollary 3.2 shows the sorts of conditions that are required: when u_s^l and u_s^m are equivalent at x_m and x_h and the Signaler is not too likely to be the least resolved type, then an equilibrium of the type described in Proposition 3.4 exists when the likelihood that the Target is the least resolved type is in a middle range.

Corollary 3.2: If $u_s^l(x_m) = u_s^m(x_m)$ and $u_s^l(x_h) = u_s^m(x_h)$ and $h_s(u_s^l)$ is sufficiently low, then a range of values of $h_t(u_t^l)$ exists such that an equilibrium of the type described in Proposition 3.2 exists.

The proof of Proposition 3.4 follows the form of the proof of Proposition 3.1 closely and is therefore omitted.

Robustness: Divisible Issue Spaces and Risk Aversion Consider a model in which the issue space can be infinitely divided and which is identical to the one described above, except in these respects. Following the Signaler's message, the players simultaneously announce a compromise position $a_i \in X$. If the players announce different positions, the status quo position x_l remains, where x_l satisfies the conditions on x_l from the previous model. If the players announce the same position, this agreement becomes the new status quo. Following the announcements, paralleling the previous model, the Signaler decides whether or not to go to war.

The simple protocol of announcing a point of agreement is a sensible representation of bargaining if both sides must cooperate to implement or work out a compromise agreement. The result is that equilibria exist in which both sides share in a potential bargaining surplus. And the result of that is that costless signaling is possible. Many other bargaining protocols besides simply agreeing on an announcement would yield similar results. For instance, Rubinstein models and Nash Bargaining also produce outcomes where both sides share in the bargaining surplus.[2]

Thus, in this modified model, although the issue space is infinitely divisible, costless signaling is possible. As in the case of discrete options, the players will have ideas about what particular bargaining outcomes are likely under different courses of action. Whether these outcomes are exogenously given discrete choices or arrived at through bargaining does not greatly affect the signaling dynamics as long as both sides are expected to share in the bargaining surplus. As before, so long as the Target is not overly likely to be the least resolved type, informative signaling of the sort described in Proposition 3.1 is possible. This result, which is proved as Proposition 3.5, shows that the results are robust to cases where the issue space is divisible.[3]

---

[2] For an overview of such models, see Ausubel, Cramton and Deneckere (2002).

[3] Note that in the announcement portion of the bargaining, which is similar to a Nash Demand Game, there are a continuum of mutual best responses. Any announcement of

Proposition 3.5: Proposition 3.1 holds in the modified game.

As in Proposition 3.1, the signaling dynamics represented in Proposition 3.5 do not depend on risk-averse preferences of the players. An analogous result to Corollary 3.1 applies to Proposition 3.5. Thus, costless signaling can still occur if utility functions are certain to be risk averse, the good in question is divisible, and therefore a negotiated solution exists that both sides prefer to conflict. In this case, however, the bargaining must take a particular form. In any equilibrium with the properties described in Proposition 3.5, the unique signal sent by the most resolved types cannot *be certain* to lead to an agreement that the most resolved types of each player prefer to war. If it did, then less resolved types would represent themselves as highly resolved and the signaling equilibrium constructed in the proposition would cease to exist. In the Proposition 3.5 equilibrium, after the most resolved Signaler type sends a unique signal to the Target, this type presses for a favorable settlement by making an announcement that the u_t^l Target type would accept, but the u_t^m type would not. Thus, the Signaler's high demand is associated with a risk of a lesser negotiated outcome than the middle range demand. Many other models of bargaining also involve similar risks. Unlike in other models, however, non-agreement does not directly mean war. Non-agreement means only that the *status quo* outcome obtains unless the Signaler decides to go to war. Less resolved Signaler types that prefer the *status quo* to war do not risk war by representing themselves as highly resolved.

Proof of Proposition 3.5: Take the Signaler's strategy to be: for u_s^l, send m, announce $a_s = \frac{u_s^{m-1}(w_s)+u_t^{m-1}(w_t)}{2} \equiv \chi_m$ following m, $a_s = \frac{\max\{u_s^{h-1}(w_s), u_t^{m-1}(w_t)\}+u_t^{l-1}(w_t)}{2} \equiv \chi_h$ following h, $a_s = u_s^{l-1}(w_s) \equiv \chi_l$ following any signal other than $y = m, h$, where the -1 superscripts represent the inverse of the functions, and choose $r = 0$; for u_s^m, send m, announce $a_s = \chi_m$ following m, $a_s = \chi_h$ following h, $a_s = \chi_l$ following any signal other than $y = m, h$, and choose $r = 1$ iff either $a_t \neq a_s$ or $a_t < u_s^{m-1}(w_s)$; for u_s^h, send h, announce χ_h following h, $a_s = \chi_m$ following m, $a_s = \chi_l$ following any signal other than $y = m, h$, and choose $r = 1$ iff either $a_t \neq a_s$ or $a_t < u_s^{h-1}(w_s)$.

a division such that each side receives at least its reservation value is a best response for each player. Proposition 3.5 does not depend on this feature of the game. Rather, the proof demonstrates that a communication equilibrium exists when the bargaining protocol that follows the revelation of information is expected to ensure that both players share in a bargaining surplus. The logic is nearly identical to the partially divisible good case.

Take the Target's strategy to be: for u_t^l, announce $a_t = \chi_m$ following m, $a_t = \chi_h$ following h, $a_t = \chi_l$ following any signal other than $y = m, h$; for u_t^m, announce $a_t = \chi_m$ following m, $a_t = \chi_l$ following any signal other than $y = m$; for u_t^h, announce $a_t = \chi_l$ following any signal.

The Target's updated beliefs following the signal are: for all $y \neq m, h$, $\mu(u_s^l \mid y) = 1$, $\mu(u_s^m \mid y) = \mu(u_s^h \mid y) = 0$; $\mu(u_s^l \mid m) = \frac{h_s(u_s^l)}{h_s(u_s^l) + h_s(u_s^m)}$, $\mu(u_s^m \mid m) = \frac{h_s(u_s^m)}{h_s(u_s^l) + h_s(u_s^m)}$, $\mu(u_s^h \mid m) = 0$; $\mu(u_s^l \mid h) = \mu(u_s^m \mid h) = 0$, and $\mu(u_s^h \mid h) = 1$. Note that these beliefs are consistent with Bayes' rule and the Signaler's strategy. We need not specify the Signaler's updated beliefs at its final move except to say that these beliefs must also accord with Bayes' rule.

The sequential rationality of the Signaler's war choice follows directly from the Signaler's payoffs. Consider the optimality of the Signaler's strategy at information sets at the announcement stage. For type u_s^l, at the information set following m, the Signaler's strategy results in an expected utility of $(h_t(u_t^l) + h_t(u_t^m))u_s^l(\chi_m) + (1 - h_t(u_t^l) - h_t(u_t^m))u_s^l(\chi_l)$ given the players' strategies and beliefs, whereas any other announcement results in $u_s^l(\chi_l)$ for sure. Similarly, following $m \neq m, h$, matching the Target's announcement of χ_l yields the same outcome and payoff as any other announcement. Following $y = h$, the Signaler's equilibrium strategy yields an expected payoff of $h_t(u_t^l)u_s^l(\chi_h) + (1 - h_t(u_t^l))u_s^l(\chi_l)$ whereas any other announcement yields $u_s^l(\chi_l)$ for sure.

For type u_s^m, at the information set following m, the Signaler's strategy results in an expected utility of $(h_t(u_t^l) + h_t(u_t^l))u_s^m(\chi_m) + (1 - h_t(u_t^l) - h_t(u_t^l))w_s$ given the players' strategies and beliefs, whereas any other announcement results in χ_l for sure as the status quo and thus the payoff of w_s in the game because the Signaler's strategy implies that it chooses war in the next stage. Following $m \neq m, h$, matching the Target's announcement of χ_l yields χ_l as the status quo and again the war payoff in the game, which is the same result as any other announcement the Signaler might make. Following $y = h$, the action assigned by the Signaler's equilibrium strategy yields an expected payoff of $h_t(u_t^l)u_s^m(\chi_h) + (1 - h_t(u_t^l))w_s$ whereas any other announcement again yields w_s for sure.

For type u_s^h, at the information sets following $m \neq h$, the Signaler's assigned action is again optimal because doing so results in w_s, the same expected utility as any other announcement in such an information set. Following $y = h$, the Signaler's equilibrium strategy yields an expected payoff of $h_t(u_t^l)u_s^h(\chi_h) + (1 - h_t(u_t^l))w_s$ whereas any other announcement yields w_s for sure.

I now turn to the sequential rationality of the message component of the Signaler's strategy given the players' strategies and beliefs in the equilibrium. For type u_s^h, the Signaler's strategy yields an expected utility of $h_t(u_t^l)u_s^h(\chi_h) + (1 - h_t(u_t^l))w_s$ whereas any other message m yields w_s for sure. For type u_s^m, the Signaler's expected utility from m is $(h_t(u_t^l) + h_t(u_t^m))u_s^m(\chi_m) + (1 - h_t(u_t^l) - h_t(u_t^m))w_s$ whereas its expected utility from h is $h_t(u_t^l)u_s^m(\chi_h) + (1 - h_t(u_t^l))w_s$ and w_s for sure for any other message. For type u_s^l, the Signaler's strategy yields expected utility $(h_t(u_t^l) + h_t(u_t^m))u_s^l(\chi_m) + (1 - h_t(u_t^l) - h_t(u_t^m))u_s^l(\chi_l)$ whereas its utility from h is $h_t(u_t^l)u_s^l(\chi_h) + (1 - h_t(u_t^l))u_s^l(\chi_l)$ and $u_s^l(\chi_l)$ for sure for any other message. Thus, for types u_s^l and u_s^m, the Signaler's actions at these information sets are optimal for $h_t(u_t^l)$ sufficiently low.

Now consider the Target's strategy given the Target's beliefs and the Signaler's strategy. Following h, the Target's strategy is optimal for the u_t^l type because it yields an expected utility of $u_t^l(\chi_h)$ and any other announcement yields an expected utility of w_t. The Target's strategy for types u_t^m and u_t^h of announcing χ_l is optimal because these types prefer war to χ_h and any announcement other than χ_h is expected to result in war given the other components of the equilibrium. Following m, the Target's strategy for the u_t^l type yields $u_t^l(\chi_m)$ whereas any other announcement yields expected utility $h_s(u_s^l)u_t^l(\chi_l) + (1 - h_s(u_s^l))w_t$. Similarly, the Target's strategy for the u_t^m type yields $u_t^m(\chi_m)$ and any other action for this type yields $h_s(u_s^l)u_t^m(\chi_l) + (1 - h_s(u_s^l))w_t$. Thus, the Target's strategy is optimal for u_t^l and u_t^m for sufficiently low $h_s(u_s^l)$. For the u_t^h, the Target's strategy yields $h_s(u_s^l)u_t^h(\chi_l) + (1 - h_s(u_s^l))w_t > u_t^h(\chi_m)$, and any other choice at that information set yields the same or $u_t^h(\chi_m)$. Following a signal other than m or h, the Target's strategy yields expected utility $u_t^z(\chi_l) \, \forall z$ and any other choice is expected to yield the same. ∎

The Fearon Model When the Bargaining Surplus Is Shared The Fearon take-it-or-leave-it model with cheap talk, described and analyzed on pp. 410–414 of Fearon's seminal Rationalist Explanations for War article, is as follows. There are two players, State A and State B. Nature first draws a cost of war, c_B, for State B from the set $T = \{c_0, c_1, c_2, \ldots, c_n\}$, $n \gg 0$, according to a commonly known, discrete, prior distribution $h(\cdot)$, where $h(c_i) = Pr(c_B = c_i)$ and $c_i > 0$ for all $c_i \in T$.[4] State B observes c_B, but State A does not. State B then sends a cheap talk message f from a large but finite set of messages. State A then makes a demand $x \in [0, 1]$. State B observes the demand and chooses whether to fight or not. The payoffs are $(p - c_A, 1 - p - c_B)$ if State B fights and $(x, 1 - x)$ if State B does not.

---

[4] For simplicity, I do not follow Fearon in assuming that T is the support of $h(\cdot)$.

I make only two changes to the model. First, instead of a take-it-or-leave-it demand by State A, suppose that both states simultaneously announce demands x_A and x_B, respectively. If $x_A = x_B = x$, then payoffs are $(x, 1 - x)$ as in the Fearon model. If $x_A \neq x_B$, payoffs are $(p - c_A, 1 - p - c_B)$. Second, let State A also be uncertain about State B's costs of war, so that c_A is initially drawn by nature from T according to $h(\cdot)$ and is the private information of State A.

As the claim and proof below show, communication is possible in this environment. In the equilibrium constructed in the proof, sending a signal of lower resolve to fight implies a less favorable negotiated outcome, but one in which some of the bargaining surplus from avoiding war is shared with the signaler. Sending a signal of high resolve yields the potential of a better deal, but this is not achieved with certainty in the equilibrium. For the higher cost type, making a higher demand is associated with a risk of an outcome that is even worse than the guaranteed result of the low demand. In the Chapter 3 model, the risk is of a less favorable negotiated outcome; in this modified Fearon model, the risk is war.

Claim 3.1: In the modified game, semi-separating perfect Bayesian equilibria exist in which State A updates its beliefs about c_B following the cheap talk message f.

Proof: Let $h(c_i) = 0$ for all $i \neq 1, 2$. Let $c_1 > c_2$. Take the parameters to be such that $0 < p - c_1$ and $p + c_1 < 1$. Let State B's strategy be as follows. If $c_B = c_1$, send message f_1 and announce $x_B = d_l$. If $c_B = c_2$, send message f_2 and announce $x_B = d_h$. Let State A's strategy be as follows. If $c_A = c_1$, announce $x_A = d_l$ following f_1 and $x_A = d_h$ following f_2. If $c_A = c_1$, announce $x_A = d_l$ following f_1 and $x_A = d_h$ following any other message. If $c_A = c_2$, announce $x_A = d_l$ following any message. Let the players' posterior beliefs follow Bayes' rule where possible and let the players draw the conclusion that that the other player is a high cost type following out of equilibrium actions.

Define d_l, State B's lower demand announcement to be greater than the State B cost type c_1's value for war, but less than the value for war of c_2. Formally, $d_l \in (p + c_2, p + c_1)$. Define d_h, State B's higher demand announcement, to be greater than what the low cost type of State A would accept, but acceptable to a high State B cost type. Formally, $d_h \in (p - c_1, p - c_2)$. Note the symmetry of the high and low demand announcements and the fact that all demand announcements are in the bargaining range defined by the highest cost types.

If these strategies are sequentially rational, then Bayes' rule implies beliefs that satisfy the claim. Taking the other player's strategy as given and accounting for State A's updated beliefs following the message f, State A's strategy is clear sequentially rational. Following f_1, given its updated beliefs, announcing d_l yields $d_l > p - c_A$ and any other action yields $p - c_A$. Following f_2, announcing d_h yields d_h and any other action yields $p - c_A$. Since $p - c_2 > d_h > p - c_1$, the strategy is sequentially rational for each player type following f_2. For the State B cost type c_2, at each choice node, its strategy yields, in expectation, $h(c_1)(1 - d_h) + h(c_2)(1 - p - c_2)$. Since any other actions at either node yield either $1 - p - c_2$ or $1 - d_l < 1 - p - c_2$, this type's actions are sequentially rational.

Thus, it remains only to show that the actions of the c_1 State B type are sequentially rational. At each decision node, its action yields, in expectation, $1 - d_l$. If instead this type deviates to the strategy assigned to the c_2 type, its expected payoff is $h(c_1)(1 - d_h) + h(c_2)(1 - p - c_1)$. Thus, the assigned strategy yields a higher payoff for $h(c_1)$ sufficiently low. Any other strategy yields either $1 - d_l$ or $1 - p - c_1 < 1 - d_l$. ∎

CHAPTER 4 PROOFS

A strategy for the Signaler is a pair: $(m(\eta_s), r_s(\eta_s, h))$ where $h \in H \equiv M \times A_1 \times A_2$. A strategy for the Target is a triple: $(a_1(\eta_t, m), a_2(\eta_t, m), r_t(\eta_t, h))$. Let the updated beliefs of the Target following the Signaler's Stage 1 signal be $\mu_{\eta_s}(\eta_s \mid m)$. Let $p(0) = p(1) = p$ if $p(0) = p(1)$. For some particular PBE, let $q_s(a_2, m) = \Pr(r_s = 0 \mid a_1 = 1, a_2, m)$, which is induced by Φ_{η_s} and the Signaler's strategy, and $q_t(m)$ be the probability the Target's strategy satisfies $a_1 = 0, r_t = 0$ for some signal m (which can be written $\Pr(a_1 = 0 \mid m)\Pr(r_t = 0 \mid a_1 = 0, m)$) induced by Φ_{η_t} and the Target's strategy.

The following two lemmas are used in the proof of Proposition 4.1. Without loss of generality, we suppress the a_2 notation in the proofs of the following lemmas and Proposition 4.1 so that the Target's strategy is a pair, $(a_1(\eta_t, m), r_t(\eta_t, h))$, and $q_s(a_2, m)$ is instead written $q_s(m)$.

Lemma 4.1: In an influential PBE with ineffective preparations, if $q_t(m') > q_t(m'')$, $m(\eta_s) = m'$ $\forall \eta_s$ such that $p - \eta_s > s - \epsilon$.

Proof: Suppose $p - \eta_s > s - \epsilon$. The Signaler can set $r_s = 1$ and obtain its highest expected utility at any terminal node following $a_1 = 1$: $p - \eta_s$. Therefore, any equilibrium strategies must result in an outcome with this Signaler utility following $a_1 = 1$. By assumption, $s > p - \eta_s$ $\forall \eta_s$, so optimality of the Signaler's Stage 3 choice implies $r_s(\eta_s, h) = 0$ for all h such that $a_1 = 0$ when $q_t(m) > 0$ (which implies $\Pr(r_t = 0 \mid a_1 = 0, m) > 0$). Therefore, $\forall \eta_s < p - s + \epsilon$ we can write the Signaler's expected utility in an equilibrium as a function of its signal: $Eu_s(m) = q_t(m)s + (1 - q_t(m))(p - \eta_s)$, which is increasing in $q_t(m)$. ∎

Lemma 4.2: In any influential PBE with ineffective preparations, $q_s(m) > 0 \ \forall m$.

Proof: We shall use a proof by contradiction: suppose $q_s(\tilde{m}) = 0$ for $\tilde{m} \in M$. Note that in an influential equilibrium, both signals $m = 0$ and $m = 1$ must be sent with positive probability.

First, observe that

$$q_t(\tilde{m}) = 1 - \Phi_{\eta_t}(s - p) > 0. \tag{10}$$

This follows because in any PBE, the expected Target utilities following $\tilde{m}$ are: $Eu_t(a_1 = 1, r_t = 0 \mid \tilde{m}) = Eu_t(a_1 = 1, r_t = 1 \mid \tilde{m}) = Eu_t(a_1 = 0, r_t = 1 \mid \tilde{m}) = 1 - p - \eta_t$, $Eu_t(a_1 = 0, r_t = 0 \mid \tilde{m}) = 1 - s$. (The last expected utility uses that, in an influential PBE, $r_s(\eta_s, h) = 0 \ \forall h$ such that $a_1 = 0$. If $\Pr(r_t = 0 \mid a_1 = 0, m = \tilde{m}) > 0$, this follows directly. If $\Pr(r_t = 0 \mid a_1 = 0, m = \tilde{m}) = 0$, then $q_t(\tilde{m}) = 0$. For the equilibrium to be influential, we need $q_t(\check{m}) > 0$ for $\check{m} \neq \tilde{m}$. But then $m(\eta_s) = \check{m} \ \forall \eta_s < p - s + \epsilon$ by Lemma 4.1, which implies either that $q_s(\tilde{m}) \neq 0$, which contradicts our original assumption, or that $\tilde{m}$ is not sent with positive probability in which case the equilibrium is not influential.) $q_t(\tilde{m})$ is therefore the probability that $1 - s > 1 - p - \eta_t$.

Second, observe that in equilibrium,

$$q_s(\check{m}) = 1 \text{ for } \check{m} \neq \tilde{m} \tag{11}$$

and

$$q_t(\check{m}) = 1 - \Phi_{\eta_t}(s - p + \epsilon \frac{q_s(\check{m})}{1 - q_s(\check{m})}) < q_t(\tilde{m}). \tag{12}$$

To see this, note that in equilibrium,

$$r_t(\eta_t, h) = 0 \ \forall \eta_t, h \text{ such that } a_1 = 1. \tag{13}$$

Then, let $\Pr(\tilde{m})$ be the probability the Signaler sends signal $\tilde{m}$ induced by the Signaler's strategy, so that, in a PBE, $q_s(\check{m}) = \frac{1 - \Phi_{\eta_s}(p - s + \epsilon)}{1 - \Pr(\tilde{m})} > 0$. The Target's expected utilities over strategies at the node following $\check{m}$ are the same as its expected utilities following $\tilde{m}$, except: $Eu_t(a_1 = 1, r_t = 0 \mid \check{m}) = q_s(\check{m})(1 - s + \epsilon) + (1 - q_s(\check{m}))(1 - p - \eta_t) > Eu_t(a_1 = 0, r_t = 1 \mid \check{m})$. Thus, in an influential PBE, the Target's strategy following signal $\check{m}$ must satisfy the following three conditions: (1) $a_1(\eta_t, \check{m}) = 1$, $\forall \eta_t < s - p + \epsilon \frac{q_s(\check{m})}{1 - q_s(\check{m})}$, (2) $a_1(\eta_t, \check{m}) = 0$, $\forall \eta_t > s - p + \epsilon \frac{q_s(\check{m})}{1 - q_s(\check{m})}$, and (3) $r_t(\eta_t, h) = 0 \ \forall \eta_t > s - p + \epsilon \frac{q_s(\check{m})}{1 - q_s(\check{m})}$, h such that $m = \check{m}$. This implies that

$q_t(\check{m}) = 1 - \Phi_{\eta_t}(s - p + \epsilon\frac{q_s(\check{m})}{1-q_s(\check{m})}) < q_t(\tilde{m})$. Using Lemma 4.1, this implies that

$$m(\eta_s) = \tilde{m} \ \forall \eta_s \text{ such that } p - \eta_s > s - \epsilon. \tag{14}$$

Using Bayes' rule, this in turn implies (11).

Third, I show that

$$m(\eta_s) = \tilde{m} \ \forall \eta_s < p - s + \frac{\epsilon}{1 - q_t(\tilde{m})}. \tag{15}$$

Given (11), the Target's optimal strategy a the Stage 2 nodes must satisfy $a_1(\eta_t, \check{m}) = 1 \ \forall \eta_t$. Using (13), this implies that for η_s such that $p - \eta_s < s - \epsilon$, $Eu_s(\check{m} \mid \eta_s) = s - \epsilon$ and $Eu_s(\tilde{m} \mid \eta_s) \geq q_t(\tilde{m})s + (1 - q_t(\tilde{m}))(p - \eta_s)$. Using (14), this implies (15).

Finally, observe that since $q_t(\tilde{m}) > 0$, for h such that $m = \tilde{m}$,

$$r_s(\eta_s, h) = 0 \ \forall \eta_s > p - s + \epsilon. \tag{16}$$

Thus, since Φ_{η_s} is strictly increasing and $q_t(\tilde{m}) > 0$, in a PBE, Bayes' rule, (15) and (16) do not imply $q_s(\tilde{m}) = 0$, which contradicts our original assumption. ∎

Proof of Proposition 4.1: Suppose $q_t(m') > q_t(m'')$. By Lemma 4.1, in an influential equilibrium, $m(\eta_s) = m' \ \forall \eta_s < p - s + \epsilon$. We have already observed that in a PBE $r_t(\eta_t, h) = 0 \ \forall \eta_t, h$ such that $a_1 = 1$. Then, using Lemma 4.2, the Target's expected utilities at the Stage 2 nodes for strategies and beliefs consistent with a PBE are $Eu_t(a_1 = 0, r_t = 1 \mid m) = 1 - p - \eta_t < Eu_t(a_1 = 1, r_t = 0 \mid m) = q_s(m)(1-s+\epsilon) + (1-q_s(m))(1-p-\eta_t)$. Thus, in any PBE, if $r_t(\eta_t, h) = 1$ for h such that $a_1 = 0$, then $a_1(\eta_t, m) = 1 \ \forall \eta_t, m$. This implies that in a PBE, for η_s such that $p - \eta_s \leq s - \epsilon$:

$$Eu_s(m) = q_t(m)s + (1 - q_t(m))(s - \epsilon).$$

Since this is increasing in $q_t(m)$, in any PBE, $m(\eta_s) = m' \ \forall \eta_s$ such that $p - \eta_s \leq s - \epsilon$. Since m'' is not sent with positive probability in equilibrium, no PBE can be influential. ∎

Proof of Proposition 4.2: Let the Signaler's strategy be $m(\eta_s) = 1 \ \forall \eta_s < \hat{\eta}_s$ and $m(\eta_s) = 0 \ \forall \eta_s \geq \hat{\eta}_s$; $r_d(\eta_s, h) = 1$ iff $\eta_s < p(a_2) - s + \epsilon$ & h such that $a_1 = 1$. Let the stage 3 component of the Target's strategy be: for h such that $a_1 = 1$ & $a_2 = 1$, $r_t(\eta_t, h) = 1$ iff $\eta_t < s - p(1) - \epsilon + \beta_t \equiv \check{\eta}_t$; for h such that $a_1 = 1$ & $a_2 = 0$, $r_t(\eta_t, h) = 0 \ \forall \eta_t$; for h such that $a_1 = 0$, $r_t(\eta_t, h) = 1$ iff $1 - p(a_2) - \eta_t + \beta_t a_2 > 1 - s$. Let the stage 2 component of the Target's strategy be $a_1(\eta_t, 0) = 1, a_2(\eta_t, 0) = 0 \ \forall \eta_t$; $a_1(\eta_t, 1) = 1, a_2(\eta_t, 1) = 1 \ \forall \eta_t < \hat{\eta}_t$; $a_1(\eta_t, 1) = 0, a_2(\eta_t, 1) = 0 \ \forall \eta_t \geq \hat{\eta}_t$ where $\hat{\eta}_t \equiv s - p(1) - k_t + \beta_t$. Let the Target's updated beliefs

be $\mu_{\eta_s}(\eta_s \mid 1) = \frac{\Phi_{\eta_s}(\eta_s)}{\Phi_{\eta_s}(\hat{\eta}_s)}$ $\forall \eta_s \in [\underline{\eta}_s, \hat{\eta}_s)$ and 0 otherwise, and $\mu_{\eta_s}(\eta_s \mid 0) =$
$\frac{\Phi_{\eta_s}(\eta_s) - \Phi_{\eta_s}(\hat{\eta}_s)}{1 - \Phi_{\eta_s}(\hat{\eta}_s)}$ $\forall \eta_s \in [\hat{\eta}_s, \overline{\eta}_s]$ and 0 otherwise.

An equilibrium with these strategies and Target beliefs is influential when $\hat{\eta}_i \in (\underline{\eta}_i, \overline{\eta}_i)$ $\forall i$. Note that the updated beliefs of the Signaler's must also follow from Bayes' rule in the equilibrium, but that the Signaler's optimal actions in the third stage do not depend on these beliefs. The Target's beliefs above follow directly from Bayes' rule, given the Signaler's strategy. I now show that for some Φ_{η_s} and Φ_{η_t}, if $k_t \geq \epsilon$, the above strategies are optimal and that $\hat{\eta}_i \in (\underline{\eta}_i, \overline{\eta}_i)$ $\forall i$.

The optimality of the Stage 3 component of the Target's strategy follows directly from the Target's preferences over outcomes. Given the Target's strategy, the optimality of the Stage 3 component of the Signaler's strategy follows by backwards induction.

We turn now to the optimality of the Signaler's Stage 1 choice. Given the Stage 2 and 3 components of the players' strategies, since $\hat{\eta}_t \leq \check{\eta}_t$ because $k_t \geq \epsilon$, the Signaler's expected utility from threatening is:

$$Eu_s(m = 1 \mid \eta_s) = \Phi_{\eta_t}(\hat{\eta}_t)(p(1) - \eta_s) + (1 - \Phi_{\eta_t}(\hat{\eta}_t))s \qquad (17)$$

which is decreasing in η_s because our assumptions imply $\hat{\eta}_t \in (\underline{\eta}_t, \overline{\eta}_t)$. Given the Stage 2 and 3 components of the players' strategies, the Signaler's expected utility from not threatening is:

$$Eu_s(m = 0 \mid \eta_s) = \begin{cases} p(0) - \eta_s & \eta_s < \tilde{\eta}_s \\ s - \epsilon & \eta_s \geq \tilde{\eta}_s \end{cases}$$

where $\tilde{\eta}_s = p(0) - s + \epsilon > \underline{\eta}_s$.

Type $\eta_s = \underline{\eta}_s$ prefers to threaten when

$$\Phi_{\eta_t}(\hat{\eta}_t) \leq \frac{s - p(0) + \underline{\eta}_s}{s - p(1) + \underline{\eta}_s} \equiv \ell_t \in (0, 1). \qquad (18)$$

We can choose Φ_{η_t} such that condition (18) holds. For instance, let Φ_{η_t} be such that $\Phi_{\eta_t}(\hat{\eta}_t) = \ell_t$. Then,

$$Eu_s(m = 0 \mid \eta_s = \underline{\eta}_s) = Eu_s(m = 1 \mid \eta_s = \underline{\eta}_s). \qquad (19)$$

Note also that,

$$\frac{\partial Eu_s(m = 0 \mid \eta_s < \tilde{\eta}_s)}{\partial \eta_s} < \frac{\partial Eu_s(m = 1 \mid \eta_s < \tilde{\eta}_s)}{\partial \eta_s}. \qquad (20)$$

By (19) and (20), note that if $Eu_s(m = 0 \mid \hat{\eta}_s) = Eu_s(m = 1 \mid \hat{\eta}_s)$ for $\hat{\eta}_s \neq \underline{\eta}_s$ then $\hat{\eta}_s > \tilde{\eta}_s$, and in particular,

$$\hat{\eta}_s = p(1) - s + \epsilon / \Phi_{\eta_t}(\hat{\eta}_t).$$

Below, we shall choose $\bar{\eta}_s$ such that $\bar{\eta}_s > \hat{\eta}_s$. With this specification of $\hat{\eta}_s$ and Φ_{η_t}, and the expected utilities given above, we can easily check that the Signaler's Stage 1 strategy is optimal given the players' beliefs and the Stage 2 and 3 components of the players' strategies. Using (19) and (20) again, we see that $Eu_s(m = 1 \mid \eta_s) \geq Eu_s(m = 0 \mid \eta_s) \; \forall \eta_s < \hat{\eta}_s$. Since $\frac{\partial Eu_s(m=0 \mid \eta_s \geq \bar{\eta}_s)}{\partial \eta_s} = 0$ and $\Phi_{\eta_t}(\hat{\eta}_t) > 0$, $\frac{\partial Eu_s(m=1 \mid \eta_s)}{\partial \eta_s} < 0$ and $Eu_s(m = 0 \mid \eta_s) \geq Eu_s(m = 1 \mid \eta_s) \; \forall \eta_s > \hat{\eta}_s$. Thus, using the one-stage deviation property, the Signaler's strategy is optimal given the Target's strategy and the players' beliefs.

We turn now to the optimality of the Target's strategy at Stage 2 nodes. Given the Signaler's strategy and our definition of $\hat{\eta}_t$, the Target's equilibrium strategy in Stage 3 and the Target's beliefs, the Stage 2 component of the Target's strategy at the $m = 0$ node $(a_1(\eta_t, 0) = 1, a_2(\eta_t, 0) = 0) \; \forall \eta_t$, gives the Target its best outcome $(1 - s + \epsilon)$ with certainty, so the Target cannot gain by deviating.

To complete the proof, it remains only to show that the Target's strategy is optimal following $m = 1$. Recall that $\check{\eta}_t \equiv s - p(1) + \beta_t - \epsilon$, and let $\dot{\eta}_t \equiv s - p(1) + \beta_t$ and $\ddot{\eta}_t \equiv s - p(0)$. Then, given the Stage 3 component of the players' strategies and the Target's updated beliefs at $m = 1$ nodes, we can write the Target's expected utilities over its four actions at Stage 2 nodes as follows:

$$Eu_t(a_1 = 1, a_2 = 1 \mid m = 1, \eta_t)$$
$$= \begin{cases} 1 - p(1) - \eta_t - k_t + \beta_t, & \eta_t < \check{\eta}_t \\ \frac{\Phi_{\eta_s}(p(1)+\epsilon-s)}{\Phi_{\eta_s}(\hat{\eta}_s)}(1 - p(1) - \eta_t - k_t + \beta_t) & \\ \quad + (1 - \frac{\Phi_{\eta_s}(p(1)+\epsilon-s)}{\Phi_{\eta_s}(\hat{\eta}_s)})(1 - s + \epsilon - k_t), & \eta_t \geq \check{\eta}_t. \end{cases}$$

(Note that $p(1) + \epsilon - s \leq \hat{\eta}_s$.)

$$Eu_t(a_1 = 1, a_2 = 0 \mid m = 1, \eta_t) = \min(1, \frac{\Phi_{\eta_s}(p(0)+\epsilon-s)}{\Phi_{\eta_s}(\hat{\eta}_s)})(1 - p(0) - \eta_t)$$
$$+ (1 - \min(1, \frac{\Phi_{\eta_s}(p(0)+\epsilon-s)}{\Phi_{\eta_s}(\hat{\eta}_s)}))(1 - s + \epsilon).$$

(Note that $\frac{\Phi_{\eta_s}(p(0)+\epsilon-s)}{\Phi_{\eta_s}(\hat{\eta}_s)} > 0$ because $s - \epsilon < p(0) - \underline{\eta}_s$ by assumption.)

$$Eu_t(a_1 = 0, a_2 = 1 \mid m = 1, \eta_t) = \begin{cases} 1 - p(1) - \eta_t - k_t + \beta_t & \eta_t < \dot{\eta}_t \\ 1 - s - k_t & \eta_t \geq \dot{\eta}_t \end{cases}$$

$$Eu_t(a_1 = 0, a_2 = 0 \mid m = 1, \eta_t) = \begin{cases} 1 - p(0) - \eta_t & \eta_t < \ddot{\eta}_t \\ 1 - s & \eta_t \geq \ddot{\eta}_t. \end{cases}$$

Since $k_t \geq \epsilon$ and $[(1-p(1))-(1-p(0))] > k_t - \beta_t$, $\dot{\eta}_t > \check{\eta}_t \geq \hat{\eta}_t > \ddot{\eta}_t$. We first show that Target types $\eta_t < \hat{\eta}_t$ have no incentive to deviate from the proposed equilibrium. For $\eta_t < \hat{\eta}_t$, the Target has no incentive to deviate to $(a_1(\eta_t, 1) = 0, a_2(\eta_t, 1) = 1)$ because $Eu_t(a_1 = 0, a_2 = 1 \mid m = 1, \eta_t) = Eu_t(a_1 = 1, a_2 = 1 \mid m = 1, \eta_t) \; \forall \eta_t < \hat{\eta}_t$. Since $Eu_t(a_1 = 1, a_2 = 1 \mid m = 1, \eta_t) > Eu_t(a_1 = 0, a_2 = 0 \mid m = 1, \eta_t) \; \forall \eta_t < \ddot{\eta}_t$ and $Eu_t(a_1 = 1, a_2 = 1 \mid m = 1, \eta_t) \geq Eu_t(a_1 = 0, a_2 = 0 \mid m = 1, \eta_t) \; \forall \eta_t \in [\ddot{\eta}_t, \hat{\eta}_t]$, Target types $\eta_t < \hat{\eta}_t$ have no incentive to deviate to $(a_1(\eta_t, 1) = 0, a_2(\eta_t, 1) = 0)$. Further, $Eu_t(a_1 = 1, a_2 = 1 \mid m = 1, \eta_t) \geq Eu_t(a_1 = 1, a_2 = 0 \mid m = 1, \eta_t) \; \forall \eta_t \in [\underline{\eta}_t, \hat{\eta}_t)$ when

$$\frac{\Phi_{\eta_s}(p(0) + \epsilon - s)}{\Phi_{\eta_s}(\hat{\eta}_s)} \geq \frac{-s + p(1) + \epsilon + \eta_t + k_t - \beta_t}{-s + p(0) + \epsilon + \eta_t}.$$

Since the RHS is increasing in η_t, let

$$\ell_s \equiv \frac{-s + p(1) + \epsilon + \overline{\eta}_t + k_t - \beta_t}{-s + p(0) + \epsilon + \overline{\eta}_t}$$

so that, taking the other components of the players' strategies as given, $Eu_t(a_1 = 1, a_2 = 1 \mid m = 1, \eta_t) > Eu_t(a_1 = 0, a_2 = 1 \mid m = 1, \eta_t)$ $\forall \eta_t \in (\underline{\eta}_t, \hat{\eta}_t)$ if $\frac{\Phi_{\eta_s}(p(0) + \epsilon - s)}{\Phi_{\eta_s}(\hat{\eta}_s)} > \ell_s$. Below, we shall choose Φ_{η_s} so that this is true. (Note that our assumptions, in particular (2) and $(1 - p(1)) - (1 - p(0)) > k_t - \beta_t$, imply that $\ell_s \in (0, 1)$.)

We now show that all Target types $\eta_t \geq \hat{\eta}_t$ prefer the action prescribed by the Target's equilibrium strategy at Stage 2 nodes following $m = 1$ (again taking other elements of the equilibrium as given). $Eu_t(a_1 = 0, a_2 = 0 \mid m = 1, \eta_t = \hat{\eta}_t) \geq Eu_t(a_1 = 1, a_2 = 0 \mid m = 1, \eta_t = \hat{\eta}_t) \Leftrightarrow \frac{\Phi_{\eta_s}(p(0) + \epsilon - s)}{\Phi_{\eta_s}(\hat{\eta}_s)} \geq \frac{\epsilon}{p(0) - p(1) + \beta_t - k_t + \epsilon} \equiv \ddot{\ell}_s \in (0, 1)$. Since $\frac{\partial Eu_t(a_1 = 1, a_2 = 0 \mid m = 1, \eta_t)}{\partial \eta_t} < \frac{\partial Eu_t(a_1 = 0, a_2 = 0 \mid m = 1, \eta_t)}{\partial \eta_t} \; \forall \eta_t > \hat{\eta}_t$, if $\frac{\Phi_{\eta_s}(p(0) + \epsilon - s)}{\Phi_{\eta_s}(\hat{\eta}_s)} \geq \ddot{\ell}_s$, $Eu_t(a_1 = 0, a_2 = 0 \mid m = 1, \eta_t) \geq EU_t(a_1 = 1, a_2 = 0 \mid m = 1, \eta_t) \; \forall \eta_t \geq \hat{\eta}_t$. Let $\hat{\ell}_s = \max(\ell_s, \ddot{\ell}_s)$.

We can now choose Φ_{η_s} such that $\overline{\eta}_s > \hat{\eta}_s$ and $\frac{\Phi_{\eta_s}(p(0) + \epsilon - s)}{\Phi_{\eta_s}(\hat{\eta}_s)} = \hat{\ell}_s$.[5] Given such a Φ_{η_s}, $Eu_t(a_1 = 1, a_2 = 1 \mid m = 1, \eta_t)$ is at least as high as the expected utility of any other Stage 2 action $\forall \eta_t < \hat{\eta}_t$. Further, $Eu_t(a_1 = 0, a_2 = 0 \mid m = 1, \eta_t) \geq Eu_t(a_1 = 1, a_2 = 0 \mid m = 1, \eta_t) \; \forall \eta_t > \hat{\eta}_t$ since $\frac{\Phi_{\eta_s}(p(0) + \epsilon - s)}{\Phi_{\eta_s}(\hat{\eta}_s)} \geq \ddot{\ell}_s$.

Since $\ddot{\eta}_t < \hat{\eta}_t \leq \ddot{\eta}_t < \hat{\eta}_t$, and using the definition of $\hat{\eta}_t$ and the fact that $Eu_t(a_1 = 1, a_2 = 1 \mid m = 1, \eta_t)$ is decreasing in η_t, $Eu_t(a_1 = 0, a_2 = 0 \mid m = 1, \eta_t) \geq Eu_t(a_1 = 0, a_2 = 1 \mid m = 1, \eta_t) \; \forall \eta_t \geq \hat{\eta}_t$ and $Eu_t(a_1 = 0, a_2 = 0 \mid m = 1, \eta_t) \geq Eu_t(a_1 = 1, a_2 = 1 \mid m = 1, \eta_t) \; \forall \eta_t \geq \hat{\eta}_t$. Thus,

---

[5] Note that such a choice of distribution is sufficient but not necessary for the proposed equilibrium to exist. We need only that (1) there is *some possibility* that the Signaler has high enough costs that it would not be willing to make a threat in a particular context, and (2) this probability that the Signaler has high costs is not so great that the Target never takes the Signaler's threats seriously and thus never makes preparations for conflict.

no Target type can gain by deviating from its equilibrium strategy only in Stage 2. Again using the one stage deviation property, this ensures that the Target's equilibrium strategy is optimal at the Stage 2 nodes, given our specification of Φ_{η_s}. ∎

Proof of Proposition 4.3: We shall first show that the following strategies and beliefs constitute a PBE. Let the Signaler's strategy be $m(\eta_s) = 0 \ \forall \eta_s$, $r_s(\eta_s, h) = 1$ iff $\eta_s < p(a_2) - s + \epsilon$ & h such that $a_1 = 1$, and let the Stage 3 component of the Target's strategy be: for h such that $a_1 = 1$, $r_t(\eta_t, h) = 0$ iff $1 - s + \epsilon - k_t a_2 \geq 1 - p(a_2) - \eta_t - k_t a_2 + \beta_t a_2$; for h such that $a_1 = 0$, $r_t(\eta_t, h) = 1$ iff $1 - p(a_2) - \eta_t + \beta_t a_2 > 1 - s$. The Stage 3 components of the players' strategies follow directly from backwards induction. Let the Stage 2 component of the Target's strategy be $a_1(\eta_t, 0) = 1, a_2(\eta_t, 0) = 0 \ \forall \eta_t$; $a_1(\eta_t, 1) = 1, a_2(\eta_t, 1) = 1 \ \forall \eta_t \leq \tilde{\eta}_t$; $a_1(\eta_t, 1) = 0, a_2(\eta_t, 1) = 0 \ \forall \eta_t > \tilde{\eta}_t$. Since the Signaler pools on m=0, the Target does not update its beliefs following this signal. Off the equilibrium path, let the Target's beliefs be $\mu(\underline{\eta}_s \mid 1) = 1$ (and note that these beliefs are unconstrained by Bayes' rule in a PBE).

We now verify that the Stage 2 component of the Target's strategy is optimal. Given the other components of the players' strategies and beliefs, the Target's expected utilities from actions at Stage 2 nodes following $m = 1$ are: $Eu_t(a_1 = 1, a_2 = 0 \mid m = 1, \eta_t) = 1 - p(0) - \eta_t$,

$$Eu_t(a_1 = 0, a_2 = 1 \mid m = 1, \eta_t)$$
$$= \begin{cases} 1 - s - k_t & \eta_t \geq s - p(1) + \beta_t \\ 1 - p(1) - \eta_t - k_t + \beta_t & \eta_t < s - p(1) + \beta_t \end{cases}$$

$$Eu_t(a_1 = 0, a_2 = 0 \mid m = 1, \eta_t) = \begin{cases} 1 - s & \eta_t \geq s - p(0) \\ 1 - p(0) - \eta_t & \eta_t < s - p(0) \end{cases}$$

and

$$Eu_t(a_1 = 1, a_2 = 1 \mid m = 1, \eta_t)$$
$$= \begin{cases} 1 - p(1) - \eta_t - k_t + \beta_t & \eta_t < s - p(1) - \epsilon + \beta_t \\ 1 - p(1) - \eta_t - k_t + \beta_t & \eta_t \geq s - p(1) - \epsilon + \beta_t \\ & \& \ p(1) - \underline{\eta}_s > s - \epsilon \\ 1 - s + \epsilon - k_t & \eta_t \geq s - p(1) - \epsilon + \beta_t \\ & \& \ p(1) - \underline{\eta}_s \leq s - \epsilon. \end{cases} \quad (21)$$

Let case (a) be where $k_t > \epsilon$ or $p(1) - \underline{\eta}_s > s - \epsilon$, and let case (b) be where $k_t \leq \epsilon$ & $p(1) - \underline{\eta}_s \leq s - \epsilon$. Let $\tilde{\eta}_t = s - p(1) - k_t + \beta_t$ in case (a), and $\tilde{\eta}_t = \overline{\eta}_t$ in case (b). By comparing the expected utilities for each range of

Target types, we can then easily verify that the Stage 2 component of the Target's strategy following $m = 1$ is optimal given the other components of the equilibrium.

Given the players' strategies and the Target's beliefs, the Target's expected utilities from actions at Stage 2 nodes following $m = 0$ are:

$Eu_t(a_1 = 1, a_2 = 0 \mid m = 0, \eta_t) = q_s(0,0)(1 - s + \epsilon) + (1 - q_s(0,0))(1 - p(0) - \eta_t),$

$$Eu_t(a_1 = 0, a_2 = 1 \mid m = 0, \eta_t)$$
$$= \begin{cases} 1 - p(1) - \eta_t - k_t + \beta_t & \eta_t < s - p(1) + \beta_t \\ 1 - s - k_t & \eta_t \geq s - p(1) + \beta_t \end{cases}$$

$$Eu_t(a_1 = 0, a_2 = 0 \mid m = 0, \eta_t) = \begin{cases} 1 - p(0) - \eta_t & \eta_t < s - p(0) \\ 1 - s & \eta_t \geq s - p(0) \end{cases}$$

and

$$Eu_t(a_1 = 1, a_2 = 1 \mid m = 0, \eta_t)$$
$$= \begin{cases} 1 - p(1) - \eta_t - k_t + \beta_t & \eta_t < s - p(1) - \epsilon + \beta_t \\ q_s(1,0)(1 - s + \epsilon - k_t) + (1 - q_s(1,0)) \\ (1 - p(1) - \eta_t - k_t + \beta_t) & \eta_t \geq s - p(1) - \epsilon + \beta_t. \end{cases}$$
$$\tag{22}$$

Since $1 - s + \epsilon$ is the Target's most preferred outcome, we can choose Φ_{η_s} such that $q_s(0,0)$ is high, which implies that $Eu_t(a_1 = 1, a_2 = 0 \mid m = 0, \eta_s)$ is higher than the expected utility of any other second Stage option for all η_s following $m = 0$. To see this explicitly, let $a = \max(1 - p(1) - \underline{\eta}_t - k_t + \beta_t, 1 - s + \epsilon - k_t)$, which is at least as high as the highest utility that any Target type can achieve from a Stage 2 deviation. We can then calculate the $q_s(0,0)$ required to make $Eu_t(a_1 = 1, a_2 = 0 \mid m = 0, \eta_t) \geq a$ for all η_t:

$$q_s(0,0) \geq \frac{a - 1 + p(0) + \overline{\eta}_t}{-s + \epsilon + p(0) + \overline{\eta}_t} \equiv \hat{q}_s(0,0) < 1. \tag{23}$$

We can see that $\hat{q}_s(0,0) < 1$ by comparing the numerator and denominator of $\hat{q}_s(0,0)$ for all possible values of a. Thus, we can let Φ_{η_s} be such that $\Phi_{\eta_s}(p(0) - s + \epsilon) = 1 - \hat{q}_s(0,0)$, which implies that the Target has no incentive to deviate at nodes following $m = 0$ given the Target does not deviate from its equilibrium strategy in Stage 3. Thus, by the one shot deviation property, the Target's strategy is optimal. (For a development of the one shot deviation property in the context of perfect Bayesian equilibrium, see Hendon, Jacobsen and Sloth (1996).)

We now turn to the optimality of the Signaler's strategy at the Stage 1 nodes. The Target's strategy implies that for h such that $(a_1 = 0, a_2 = 0)$, we must have $r_t(\eta_t, h) = 0 \ \forall \eta_t \geq s - p(0)$. Let $\eta_s' \equiv p(1) - s + \epsilon$ and $\eta_s'' \equiv p(0) - s + \epsilon$. Then, since $\tilde{\eta}_t > s - p(0)$, given the other components of the players' strategies, we have:

$Eu_s(m = 1 \mid \eta_s) =$

$$
\begin{cases}
(1 - \Phi_{\eta_t}(\tilde{\eta}_t))s + \Phi_{\eta_t}(\tilde{\eta}_t)(p(1) - \eta_s) & k_t > \epsilon \\
(1 - \Phi_{\eta_t}(\tilde{\eta}_t))s + \Phi_{\eta_t}(\tilde{\eta}_t)(p(1) - \eta_s) & k_t \leq \epsilon \ \& \ \eta_s < \eta_s' \\
(1 - \Phi_{\eta_t}(\tilde{\eta}_t))s + (\Phi_{\eta_t}(\tilde{\eta}_t) - \Phi_{\eta_t}(s - p(1) \\
\quad - \epsilon + \beta_t))(s - \epsilon) \\
\quad + \Phi_{\eta_t}(s - p(1) - \epsilon + \beta_t)(p(1) - \eta_s) & k_t \leq \epsilon \ \& \ \eta_s \geq \eta_s'.
\end{cases} \tag{24}
$$

$$
Eu_s(m = 0 \mid \eta_s) = \begin{cases} s - \epsilon & \eta_s \geq \eta_s'' \\ p(0) - \eta_s & \eta_s < \eta_s''. \end{cases} \tag{25}
$$

Since $\eta_s'' > \eta_s'$, $Eu_s(m = 0 \mid \eta_s < \eta_s') \geq Eu_s(m = 1 \mid \eta_s < \eta_s')$ when

$$
\Phi_{\eta_t}(\tilde{\eta}_t) \geq \frac{s - p(0) + \eta_s}{s - p(1) + \eta_s}.
$$

Since the RHS is increasing in η_s, let $\gamma \equiv \frac{s - p(0) + \bar{\eta}_s}{s - p(1) + \bar{\eta}_s}$ so that $\forall \eta_s < \eta_s'$ $Eu_s(m = 0 \mid \eta_s) \geq Eu_s(m = 1 \mid \eta_s)$ if $\Phi_{\eta_t}(\tilde{\eta}_t) \geq \gamma$. $Eu_s(m = 1 \mid \eta_s' \leq \eta_s)$ is at most $(1 - \Phi_{\eta_t}(\tilde{\eta}_t))s + (\Phi_{\eta_t}(\tilde{\eta}_t) - \Phi_{\eta_t}(s - p(1) - \epsilon + \beta_t))(s - \epsilon) + \Phi_{\eta_t}(s - p(1) - \epsilon + \beta_t)(p(1) - \eta_s) < (1 - \Phi_{\eta_t}(s - p(1) - \epsilon + \beta_t))s + \Phi_{\eta_t}(s - p(1) - \epsilon + \beta_t)(p(1) - \eta_s)$. Setting this less than $Eu_s(m = 0 \mid \eta_s' \leq \eta_s < \eta_s'') = p(0) - \eta_s$ yields:

$$
\Phi_{\eta_t}(s - p(1) - \epsilon + \beta_t) \geq \frac{s - p(0) + \eta_s}{s - p(1) + \eta_s}
$$

which must hold when $\Phi_{\eta_t}(s - p(1) - \epsilon + \beta_t) \geq \gamma$. By similar reasoning, $Eu_s(m = 1 \mid \eta_s \geq \eta_s'') \leq Eu_s(m = 0 \mid \eta_s \geq \eta_s'')$ when

$$
\Phi_{\eta_t}(s - p(1) - \epsilon + \beta_t) \geq \frac{\epsilon}{s - p(1) + \eta_s}.
$$

Since the RHS is decreasing in η_s, let $\gamma' \equiv \frac{\epsilon}{s - p(1) + \eta_s''} \in (0, 1)$. Thus, we can choose Φ_{η_t} to be such that $\Phi_{\eta_t}(\min(\tilde{\eta}_t, s - p(1) - \epsilon + \beta_t)) \geq \max(\gamma, \gamma')$, which implies that, fixing the other components of the equilibrium, the Signaler has no incentive to deviate from its equilibrium strategy in Stage 1. Thus, the strategies and beliefs given above constitute a PBE for the Φ_{η_t} specified.

Finally, note that (1) this equilibrium is not influential because only one signal is sent with positive probability, and (2) there is strictly positive probability that $\eta_s \in [\underline{\eta}_s, p(0) - s + \epsilon)$ & that in case (a) $\eta_t \in (\tilde{\eta}_t, \bar{\eta}_t]$ or in case (b) $\eta_t \in [\underline{\eta}_t, \bar{\eta}_t]$. In either case (a) or case (b), if η_s & η_t are in the ranges specified here, $r = 1$, $m = 0$ and if the Signaler were to deviate to $m = 1$, no war occurs. ∎

CHAPTER 5 PROOFS

Proof of Proposition 5.1: I will show that under the conditions given in the proposition, the following strategies and beliefs constitute a perfect Bayesian equilibrium. The Third Party's strategy is: if $c_d = \underline{c}_d$, send $m = 1$ and fight; if $c_d = \bar{c}_d$, send $m = 0$ and don't fight. The Target's strategy is: following $m = 1$, accept the Protégé's offer x iff $x \leq p^a + c_t$; following any other message m, accept the protégé's offer x iff $x \leq q$. The Protégé's strategy is: following $m = 1$, demand $x = p^a + \bar{c}_t$; following any other message m, demand q; fight following accepted offers iff $x < \mu_g p^a + (1 - \mu_g)p - c_g$ and following rejected offers iff $q < \mu_g p^a + (1 - \mu_g)p - c_g$. Let $\mu_t(m, x)$ represent the Target's updated beliefs following m and x that $c_d = \underline{c}_d$. μ_t will refer to this function in the proofs. The Protégé and Target's updated beliefs are $\mu_g(1) = \mu_t(1, p^a + \bar{c}_t) = 1$, $\mu_g(m) = 0$ $\forall m \neq 1$ $\mu_t(m, x) = 0$ $\forall m \neq 1, x \neq p^a + \bar{c}_t$. We need not specify the players' updated beliefs about the Target's type following the Target's decision because player choices do not depend on these beliefs.

The optimality of the Target's strategy follows directly from its preferences and equilibrium beliefs, and the players' beliefs follow directly from Bayes' rule and the Third Party's strategy. To see that the Protégé's strategy is optimal, note that given its beliefs and the Target's strategy, following $m = 1$, the Protégé must demand either $p^a + \underline{c}_t$ or $p^a + \bar{c}_t$. Since $p^a + \underline{c}_t$ is accepted with certainty, a lesser demand yields a worse outcome for the Protégé. Any demand $x \in (p^a + \underline{c}_t, p^a + \bar{c}_t)$ incurs the same risk of conflict as $p^a + \bar{c}_t$ but yields a worse outcome if accepted. Any demand above $p^a + \bar{c}_t$ is sure to be rejected, which leads to a worse outcome than $p^a + \underline{c}_t$. Following the logic given in the text, for $p^a + \bar{c}_t < 1$, the Protégé prefers the higher demand when equation (3) holds. Call the RHS of equation (3) $\hat{h}_t$. Announcing q following $m \neq 1$ is optimal because any other strategy yields at most q given the players' strategies and beliefs. The optimality of the Protégé's war choice follows directly from its preferences and updated beliefs. The optimality of the Third Party's choice at its final choice node follows directly from its preferences. Given the player's strategies and beliefs which generate the expected utilities given in the text, the Third Party of type $c_d = \underline{c}_d$ prefers to send message $m = 1$ if equation (5) holds. Call the RHS of equation (5) $\tilde{h}_t$. Let $\bar{h}_t = \min\{\hat{h}_t, \tilde{h}_t\}$. Similarly, the Third Party of type $c_d = \bar{c}_d$ prefers to send message $m = 0$ if equation (4) holds. Call the RHS of equation (4) $\underline{h}_t$.

For sufficiently low $p < q, \underline{h}_t < 1$. Thus, for sufficiently low $\underline{c}_t$ and c_g, $\hat{h}_t > \underline{h}_t$. Similarly, for $\underline{c}_d$ sufficiently low, $\tilde{h}_t > \underline{h}_t$. Thus, for $h_t \in (\underline{h}_t, \bar{h}_t)$, the Protégé's strategy is optimal, as are the message choices of both Third Party types.   ∎

Costless Signals to Separate Audiences

I now consider a modification of the model in which the Third Party sends separate private signals to the Protégé and Target. Let the message to player i be $m_i \in M$, so that in the cheap talk stage, the Third Party chooses the messages $(m_g, m_t) \in M \times M$. In this case, the perfect Bayesian equilibrium described in Proposition 5.1 still exists. The proof is essentially identical to the proof of Proposition 5.1: the Third Party sends $(0, 0)$ instead of 0 and $(1, 1)$ instead of 1 and the other players' strategies are unchanged. While this equilibrium exists, however, it may not be a reasonable prediction about behavior in this strategic context. The reason is that the equilibrium relies on the Protégé assuming, following a signal 0 indicating a lack of support, that the Target has received the same signal. As a result, upon receiving such a signal, the Protégé declines to make a demand beyond the status quo, and the Third Party therefore has no incentive to misrepresent its level of resolve to the Target. But in a rich natural language, the Third Party might communicate to the Protégé a message similar to "I'm telling you that I'm not willing to fight, but I'll tell the Target that I am willing to fight." The Third Party would have incentive to make just such a representation, and the Protégé would have reason to believe it. In this case, the signaling equilibrium would break down because unsupported Protégés would have incentive to make the same demand they would make if they had been supported.[6]

The uninformative equilibrium is also unconvincing, however, because it implies that private statements of support have no emboldening effect on bargaining behavior. This is clearly ruled out by the case evidence discussed above. A simple way of altering the model such that private statements of support will have an emboldening effect is to conceive of the bargaining between Protégé and Target as public and therefore to add an audience cost, a, that the Protégé pays if it makes a demand $x > q$ but then accepts q without a fight. Importantly, only the Protégé, which is not signaling and has only one "type," pays the audience cost; the Protégé's audience costs do not matter to the Third Party. In this case, once again because the Third Party's private signals have an

---

[6] The communication equilibrium does not satisfy the spirit of Farrell's (1993) neologism-proof refinement. For further discussion of what constitute reasonable communication equilibria, see Matthews, Okuno-Fujiwara and Postlewaite (1991) and Farrell and Rabin (1996).

emboldening effect on its Protégé, reasonable equilibria look exactly like the equilibria described in the previous section. Proposition 5.2 shows that an equivalent equilibrium to the one described in Proposition 5.1 exists, even if the Third Party can convince the Protégé that a show of strength has been made to the Target although a private lack of support has been conveyed to the Protégé, so long as the audience cost, a, is in a middle range. $\mu_i(m_i)$ represents player i's updated belief that $c_d = \underline{c}_d$ following message m_i. The conditions for the existence of the signaling equilibrium are less strict than the conditions for signaling in Proposition 5.1 because here, following the Third Party's private signals, when the Target sees an action by the Protégé (which does not occur in equilibrium) that defies the Target's expectation of the aggressive behavior of a supported Protégé, the Target concludes that the Protégé will not be supported. In effect, the Third Party cannot have an incentive to say one thing to the Protégé and another to the Target because the latter will figure this out from the Protégé's conduct.

Proposition 5.2: For p sufficiently low, $p^a + \bar{c}_t < 1$ and h_t and a in middle ranges, a separating perfect Bayesian equilibrium exists in which $\mu_i(0) = 0$ and $\mu_i(1) = 1$ $\forall i$. Furthermore, if a message $m_g = 0^*$ exists, such that the Protégé takes actions conditional on the expectation that $c_d = \bar{c}_d$ and $m_t = 1$ is sent to the Target, $\bar{c}_d$ Third Party types have no incentive to deviate to $(0^*, 1)$, and therefore the equilibrium still exists.[7]

Proof of Proposition 5.2: Similar strategies and beliefs to those specified in Proposition 5.1 will again be shown to constitute a perfect Bayesian equilibrium. The Third Party's strategy is: if $c_d = \underline{c}_d$, send $(1, 1)$ and fight; if $c_d = \bar{c}_d$, send $(0, 0)$ and don't fight. The Target's strategy is: accept the Protégé's offer x if $x \leq q$ or $x = p^a + \bar{c}_t$, $c_t = \bar{c}_t$, and $m_t = 1$, and reject otherwise. The Protégé's strategy is: following $m_g = 1$, demand $x = p^a + \bar{c}_t$; following any other message m_g, demand q; fight following accepted offers iff $x < \mu_g p^a + (1 - \mu_g)p - c_g$ and following rejected offers iff $q - a < \mu_g p^a + (1 - \mu_g)p - c_g$. The Protégé and Target's updated beliefs following the message are $\mu_g(1) = \mu_t(1, p^a + \bar{c}_t) = 1$, $\mu_i = 0$ $\forall m_i \neq 1$, $\forall i$, $\mu_t(1, x) = 0$ $\forall x \neq p^a + \bar{c}_t$. We need not specify the players' updated beliefs about the Target's type following the Target decision because player choices do not depend on these beliefs.

The optimality of the Target's strategy follows directly from its preferences and equilibrium beliefs, and the players' beliefs are consistent with

---

[7] Note that in this equilibrium, the more resolved Third Party type sends the messages $(1, 1)$ and the less resolved type sends the messages $(0, 0)$.

Bayes' rule and the players' strategies. The optimality of the Protégé's war choice follows directly from its preferences and updated beliefs. To ensure that the Protégé cannot make a credible demand without the expectation of Third Party support, assume that audience costs a are not too large so that $q - a \geq p - c_g \Leftrightarrow a \leq q - p + c_g \equiv \bar{a}$. Given the Target's strategy, the Protégé must demand either q or $p^a + \bar{c}_t$. Following $m_g = 0$, the Protégé's utility from $x = q$ is q, whereas its utility from $x > q$ is $q - a$. Following $m_g = 1$, the Protégé's expected utility from $x = p^a + \bar{c}_t$ is $h_t(p^a - c_g) + (1 - h_t)(p^a + \bar{c}_t)$, which is strictly greater than q and strictly greater than its expected utility from some other $x > q$, which is $p^a - c_g$. Thus, the Protégé's strategy is optimal.

The optimality of the Third Party's choice at its final choice node follows directly from its preferences. Given the players' strategies and beliefs which generate the expected utilities given in the text, the Third Party of type $c_d = \underline{c}_d$ prefers to send message $(1, 1)$ over the message $(0, 0)$ if equation (5) holds. Call the RHS of equation (5) $\bar{h}_t$. Any other message yields either q or $p^a - \underline{c}_d$ in expectation, which are both strictly worse outcomes. Similarly, the Third Party of type $c_d = \bar{c}_d$ prefers to send message $(0, 0)$ to $(1, 1)$ if equation (4) holds. Call the RHS of equation (4) $\underline{h}_t$. As in Proposition 5.1, for sufficiently low $p < q$, $\underline{h}_t < 1$. $\underline{h}_t < \bar{h}_t$ because $p^a - \underline{c}_d > p$ by assumption. Thus, for $h_t \in (\underline{h}_t, \bar{h}_t)$, the Protégé's strategy is optimal, as are the message choices of both Third Party types.

Furthermore, in this equilibrium, if we assume that the Protégé optimizes under the expectation that $c_d = \bar{c}_d$ and $m_t = 1$ following 0^*, the Protégé's expected utility for $x = p^a + \bar{c}_t$ is $h_t(q - a) + (1 - h_t)(p^a + \bar{c}_t)$. This is less than or equal to q, the Protégé's utility from announcing q in the equilibrium, when

$$h_t \geq \frac{p^a + \bar{c}_t - q}{p^a + \bar{c}_t - q + a} \equiv h'_t.$$

Note that $\underline{h}_t \geq h'_t$ if $a \geq q - p$. Thus, to ensure this is the case, take $a \in [q - p, q - p + c_g]$. Thus, the Protégé's optimal action at this information set is to choose q given the players' equilibrium strategies and beliefs. This implies that the $\bar{c}_d$ type Third Party cannot gain by deviating to the messages $(0^*, 1)$. ∎

In interpreting this result, several things should be born in mind. First, the audience cost applies only to the Protégé, which is involved in a public contest with the Target, and not to the Third Party, which sends private, costless signals. The Protégé's audience cost does not figure in the Third Party's calculations. Second, the Protégé is not signaling its type; only the Third Party is. Third, the key conditions for costless signaling described in Proposition 5.1 must hold in this new setting for signaling to occur. If emboldenment does not occur as a result of the Third Party's private signal to its Protégé, signaling by the Third Party is impossible. The addition of the audience cost to the Protégé's calculations does not alter that fact. Therefore, one way of understanding this result is to say that if the models of the field appropriately describe dyadic diplomacy in public contexts, then private diplomacy can be effective through the mechanism described in triadic diplomacy. Fourth, even if the Target ignores the private signal from the Third Party, equilibria exist that are nearly identical to the equilibria described in Proposition 5.2, but in which (1) the Third Party's private signal to the Protégé allows the Protégé to infer the Third Party's type, and (2) the Target learns the Third Party's type from observing the Protégé's behavior. This result is useful in interpreting cases and is stated formally as Proposition 5.3.

Proposition 5.3: For p sufficiently low, $p^a + \bar{c}_t < 1$ and h_t and a in middle ranges, a separating perfect Bayesian equilibrium exists in which $\mu_g(0) = 0$, $\mu_g(1) = 1$, and $\mu_t(m_t, p^a + \bar{c}_t) = 1 \; \forall m_t$ and $\mu_t(m_t, x) = 0 \; \forall m_t, x \neq p^a + \bar{c}_t$. Further, in this equilibrium, following $m_g = 1$, the Protégé chooses $x = p^a + \bar{c}_t$, and following any other signal, the Protégé chooses $x = q$.

Proof of Proposition 5.3: Similar strategies and beliefs to those specified in Proposition 5.1 will again be shown to constitute a perfect Bayesian equilibrium. The Third Party's strategy is: if $c_d = \underline{c}_d$, send $(1, 0)$ and fight; if $c_d = \bar{c}_d$, send $(0, 0)$ and don't fight. The Target's strategy is: accept the Protégé's offer x if $x \leq q$ or if $x = p^a + \bar{c}_t$ and $c_t = \bar{c}_t$, and reject otherwise. The Protégé's strategy is: following $m_g = 1$, demand $x = p^a + \bar{c}_t$; following any other message m_g, demand q; fight following accepted offers iff $x < \mu_g p^a + (1 - \mu_g)p - c_g$ and following rejected offers iff $q - a < \mu_g p^a + (1 - \mu_g)p - c_g$. The Protégé and Target's updated beliefs following the message are $\mu_g(1) = \mu_t(m_t, p^a + \bar{c}_t) = 1 \; for all m_t$, $\mu_g = 0 \; \forall m_g \neq 1$, $\mu_t(m_t, x) = 0 \; \forall m_t, x \neq p^a + \bar{c}_t$. We need not specify the players' updated beliefs about the Target's type following the Target decision because player choices do not depend on these beliefs.

The optimality of the Target's strategy follows directly from its preferences and equilibrium beliefs, and the players' beliefs are consistent with Bayes' rule and the players' strategies. The optimality of the Protégé's war choice follows directly from its preferences and updated beliefs. To ensure that the Protégé cannot make a credible demand without the expectation of Third Party support, assume that audience costs a are not too large so that $q - a \geq p - c_g \Leftrightarrow a \leq q - p + c_g \equiv \bar{a}$. Given the Target's strategy, the Protégé must demand either q or $p^a + \bar{c}_t$. Following $m_g \neq 1$, the Protégé's utility from $x = q$ is q, whereas its utility from $x > q$ is $q - a$ or $x = p^a + \bar{c}_t$ is $h_t(q-a) + (1-h_t)(p^a + \bar{c}_t)$. The latter is less than or equal to q when

$$h_t \geq \frac{p^a + \bar{c}_t - q}{p^a + \bar{c}_t - q + a} \equiv h_t'.$$

Following $m_g = 1$, the Protégé's expected utility from $x = p^a + \bar{c}_t$ is $h_t(p^a - c_g) + (1-h_t)(p^a + \bar{c}_t)$, which is strictly greater than q and strictly greater than its expected utility from some other $x > q$, which is $p^a - c_g$. We shall see below that an h_t exists satisfying all conditions such that the protégé's strategy is optimal.

The optimality of the Third Party's choice at its final choice node follows directly from its preferences. Given the player's strategies and beliefs which generate the expected utilities given in the text, the Third Party of type $c_d = \underline{c}_d$ prefers to send message $(1, 0)$ over the message $(0, 0)$ if equation (5) holds. Call the RHS of equation (5) $\bar{h}_t$. Any other m_g yields q, which is a strictly worse outcome, and the choice of m_t does not influence the Third Party's expected utility. Similarly, the Third Party of type $c_d = \bar{c}_d$ prefers to send message $(0, 0)$ to $(1, 0)$ if equation (4) holds. Call the RHS of equation (4) $\underline{h}_t$. As in Proposition 5.1, for sufficiently low $p < q$, $\underline{h}_t < 1$. $\underline{h}_t < \bar{h}_t$ because $p^a - \underline{c}_d > p$ by assumption. Thus, for $h_t \in (\underline{h}_t, \bar{h}_t)$, the message choices of both Third Party types are optimal. Note that $\underline{h}_t \geq h_t'$ if $a \geq q - p$. Thus, to ensure this is the case, take $a \in [q - p, q - p + c_g]$. Thus, the Protégé's strategy implies optimal actions at each information set. ∎

When the Target May Attack the Protégé

The models discussed above assume that the Target does not have the option to force a revision of the status quo q in its favor. If the Target does have such an option, signaling by the Third Party may be impaired because revealing an unwillingness to support a high demand by a Protégé may also indicate an unwillingness to defend a Protégé against attack and therefore precipitate just such an attack. Thus, the possibility of aggression by the Target in response to pacific behavior by the Protégé can eliminate the signaling equilibrium.

Signaling is still possible, even when the Target may itself choose to attack, however. To see this, suppose that in the game described above with separate, private signals sent to the two audiences, the Target may elect to start a war against the Protégé when the Protégé elects not to start one itself. The war payoffs for the players are the same as in the case where the Protégé starts the war, and the Third Party also has the same choice to join the war or not. Proposition 5.4 gives a set of sufficiency conditions for signaling to occur in this modified game. Note in particular the condition that $\underline{c}_t$ be in a middle range. This is required to ensure that the Target would not choose to start a war over accepting the status quo when the Target learns that the Third Party will not fight with the Protégé. In particular, the Target's payoff for the status quo, $1 - q$, must be at least as large as the low cost type Target's expected utility for war, $1 - p - \underline{c}_t$. This is true so long as $\underline{c}_t$ is not too low. By contrast, if the Target is certain to attack when it knows the Third Party will not join the conflict, or even if only low Target cost of conflict types will attack, reasonable signaling equilibria do not exist.

Proposition 5.4: For p less than but sufficiently close to q, $p^a + \bar{c}_t < 1$ and h_t, a and $\underline{c}_t$ in middle ranges, a separating perfect Bayesian equilibrium exists in which $\mu_i(0) = 0$ and $\mu_i(1) = 1$ $\forall i$. Furthermore, if a message $m_g = 0^*$ exists, such that the Protégé takes actions conditional on the expectation that $c_d = \bar{c}_d$ and $m_t = 1$ is sent to the Target, $\bar{c}_d$ Third Party types have no incentive to deviate to $(0^*, 1)$, and therefore the equilibrium still exists.

Proof of Proposition 5.4: The following strategies and beliefs will be shown to constitute a perfect Bayesian equilibrium. The Third Party's strategy is: if $c_d = \underline{c}_d$, send $(1, 1)$ and fight at a conflict node; if $c_d = \bar{c}_d$, send $(0, 0)$ and don't fight. The Target's strategy is: following $m_t = 1$, accept the Protégé's offer x iff $c_t = \bar{c}_t$ and $x = p^a + \bar{c}_t$; following any other message m_t, accept the Protégé's offer x iff $x \le q$; fight following accepted offers if $1 - x < \mu_t(1 - p^a) + (1 - \mu_t)(1 - p) - c_t$ and following unaccepted offers if $1 - q < \mu_t(1 - p^a) + (1 - \mu_t)(1 - p) - c_t$. The Protégé's strategy is: following $m_g = 1$, demand $x = p^a + \bar{c}_t$ and fight if an offer is rejected and $x - a < p^a - c_g$ or if an offer is accepted and $x < p^a - c_g$, and otherwise do not fight; following any other message m_g, demand q and do not fight unless a demand $x < p - c_g$ is accepted. The Protégé and Target's updated beliefs following the message are $\mu_g(1) = \mu_t(1, p^a + \bar{c}_t) = 1$, $\mu_i = 0$ $\forall m_i \ne 1$, $\forall i$, $\mu_t(1, x) = 0$ $\forall x \ne p^a + \bar{c}_t$. We need not specify the players' updated beliefs about the Target's type following the Target decision because player choices do not depend on these beliefs.

The optimality of the Target's strategy follows directly from its preferences and equilibrium beliefs, and the players' beliefs are consistent with Bayes' rule and the players' strategies. Note that the Target's strategy implies that it will not fight if $\mu_t = 0$ when $1 - q \ge 1 - p - \underline{c}_t \Leftrightarrow \underline{c}_t \le q - p$ and this implies the Target would not fight for other values of μ_t. Since we have seen in the text that $\underline{c}_t < 1 - p^a$ for the supported Protégé's offer to risk war, take $\underline{c}_t \in (q - p, 1 - p^a)$, which range exists for q sufficiently close to p, ensuring that the Target will not choose war following equilibrium behavior by the players. The optimality of the Protégé's war choice follows directly from its preferences and updated beliefs. The Protégé's choice of q following $m_g \neq 1$ is optimal because the Protégé optimizes under the expectation that $m_t = 0$ and therefore that a demand $x > q$ will not be accepted. Following $m_g = 1$, the Protégé's choice of $p^a + \bar{c}_t$ yields a lottery over $p^a + \bar{c}_t$ and a supported war $(p^a - c_g)$, and any other choice results in a supported war with certainty, implying that the Protégé's choice of x is optimal at each information set. The optimality of the Third Party's conflict choices follow directly from its preferences.

Following the message $m_g = 0^*$, the Protégé's expected utility for a high demand is $h_t(\max\{q - a, p - c_g\}) + (1 - h_t)(p^a + \bar{c}_t)$. Assuming that $q - a \geq p - c_g$, this is less than or equal to q, the Protégé's utility from announcing q in the equilibrium, when

$$h_t \geq \frac{p^a + \bar{c}_t - q}{p^a + \bar{c}_t - q + a} \equiv h_t'.$$

To ensure that the Protégé cannot make a credible demand without the expectation of Third Party support, assume that audience costs a are not too large so that $q - a \geq p - c_g \Leftrightarrow a \leq q - p + c_g \equiv \bar{a}$. Given the player's strategies and beliefs which generate the expected utilities given in the text, the Third Party of type $c_d = \underline{c}_d$ prefers to send messages $(1, 1)$ over the messages $(0, 0)$ if equation (5) holds. Call the RHS of equation (5) $\tilde{h}_t$. Any other message yields either q or $p^a - \underline{c}_d$ in expectation, which are both strictly worse outcomes. Similarly, the Third Party of type $c_d = \bar{c}_d$ prefers to send message $(0, 0)$ to $(1, 1)$ if equation (4) holds. Call the RHS of equation (4) $\underline{h}_t$. Note that $\underline{h}_t \geq h_t'$ if $a \geq q - p$. Thus, to ensure this is the case, take $a \in [q - p, q - p + c_g]$.

Note that because $p < p^a - \underline{c}_d$ by assumption, $\underline{h}_t < \tilde{h}_t$. Thus, for $p < q$, we can set $h_t \in (\underline{h}_t, \tilde{h}_t)$, so that the message choice of both Third Party types is optimal. Furthermore, since $h_t > \underline{h}_t \geq h_t'$, if we assume that the Protégé optimizes under the expectation that $c_d = \bar{c}_d$ and $m_t = 1$ following 0^*, the protégé's optimal action at this information set is to choose q given the player's equilibrium strategies and beliefs. Thus, the $\bar{c}_d$ type Third Party cannot gain by deviating to the messages $(0^*, 1)$. ∎

CHAPTER 6 PROOFS

Without loss of generality, set $u_{s1}^1(0) = u_{1s}^1(0) = u_{21}^1(0) = 0$ and $u_{s1}^1(1) = u_{1s}^1(1) = u_{21}^1(1) = 1$. Let $\mu_1(u_{s2}^{z_{s2}} \mid m_y)$ be the Potential Ally's updated belief that the Signaler is type $u_{s2}^{z_{s2}}$ following message m_y and $\mu_2(u_{s2}^{z_{s2}} \mid x^{s1})$ be the Target's updated belief that the Signaler is type $u_{s2}^{z_{s2}}$ following the Potential Ally's choice of x^{s1}. Let p_{ij} be the probability that a coalition of i and j defeats the third state in a conflict. Let p_i^j be the probability that i defeats j when the third state does not fight. The text specifies that u_{s2}^2 is such that the Signaler prefers a war only against the Target to the *status quo*. For this to be so regardless of the particular strategies of the Potential Ally and the Target, this implies the technical assumption that $u_{s2}^2(x_q^{s2}) \leq p_s^2 u_{s2}^2(1) + (1 - p_s^2)u_{s2}^2(0) - p_{s2}$. Define the following conditions to be used below:

(C1.1) $u_{1s}^1(x^{1s}) \geq p_{12} - c_1$

(C2.1) $u_{12}^1(x_q^{12}) \geq p_{s1}u_{12}^1(1) + (1 - p_{s1})u_{12}^1(0) - c_1$

(C3.1) $p_{s1}u_{12}^1(1) + (1 - p_{s1})u_{12}^1(0) + u_{1s}^1(x^{1s}) \geq p_{12} + u_{12}^1(x_q^{12})$

(C1.2) $u_{2s}^1(x_q^{2s}) \geq p_{12}u_{2s}^1(1) + (1 - p_{12})u_{2s}^1(0) - c_2$

(C2.2) $u_{21}^1(x_q^{21}) \geq p_{s2} - c_2$

(C3.2) $p_{s2} + u_{2s}^1(x_q^{2s}) \geq p_{12}u_{2s}^1(1) + (1 - p_{12})u_{2s}^1(0) + u_{21}^1(x_q^{21})$.

Proposition 6.1 (formal): When c_s, c_1, $u_{2s}^1(1) - u_{2s}^1(x_q^{2s})$ and $u_{s2}^2(x_q^{s2}) - u_{s2}^2(0)$ are sufficiently low and x_q^{12} is sufficiently high, a perfect Bayesian equilibrium exists in which (1) $\mu_1(u_{s2}^1 \mid m_1) = \mu_1(u_{s2}^2 \mid m_2) = 1$, and (2) $\text{Pr}(S \text{ does not attack } 2 \mid \check{x}^{s1}) = \text{Pr}(S \text{ attacks } 2 \mid \hat{x}^{s1}) = 1$.

Proof of Proposition 6.1: I will show that the following strategies and beliefs constitute a perfect Bayesian equilibrium when the conditions given in the proposition are met. *Signaler's Strategy*: For type u_{s2}^1, choose m_1 in the first stage, and in the fourth stage, Attack the Potential Ally if $x^{s1} < \hat{x}^{s1}$, and otherwise do not Attack. For type u_{s2}^2, choose m_2 in the first stage, and in the fourth stage, Attack the Potential Ally if $x^{s1} < \check{x}^{s1}$, and otherwise Attack the Target. *The Potential Ally's Strategy*: Following m_1 choose $\hat{x}^{s1}$ and following any other message choose $\check{x}^{s1}$. In the fifth stage, choose Neutral if C1.1 and C2.1 hold; choose Join 2 if C1.1 and C3.1 do not hold; choose Join S if C2.1 does not hold and C3.1 holds. (Note that these conditions are an exhaustive partitioning of the parameter space.) *The Target's Strategy*: choose neutral if C1.2 and C2.2 hold; choose Join 2 if C1.2 and C3.2 do not hold; choose Join S if C2.2 does not hold and C3.2 holds. *The Potential Ally's beliefs following m*: $\mu_1(u_{s2}^1 \mid m_1) = \mu_1(u_{s2}^2 \mid m_y) = 1$, $\mu_1(u_{s2}^2 \mid m_1) = \mu_1(u_{s2}^1 \mid m_y) = 0 \,\forall y \neq 1$. *The Target's beliefs following* x^{s1}: $\mu_2(u_{s2}^1 \mid \check{x}^{s1}) = \mu_2(u_{s2}^2 \mid x^{s1}) = 1$, $\mu_1(u_{s2}^2 \mid \check{x}^{s1}) = \mu_1(1 \mid x^{s1}) = 0$ $\forall x^{s1} \neq \check{x}^{s1}$.

The players' beliefs follow directly from the players' strategies and Bayes' rule, at information sets where it can be applied. The optimality of the Potential Ally and the Target's strategies in the fifth stage follows directly from the players' preferences. Thus, we must only show the optimality of the messaging component of the Signaler's strategy and of the Potential Ally's choice of x^{s1}.

In the separating equilibrium, given the Signaler's strategy, the Potential Ally's choice of x^{s1} must either be 0 or leave the Signaler indifferent between attacking the Potential Ally and the Signaler's most preferred alternative – attacking the Target for type u_{s2}^2 and remaining neutral for type u_{s2}^1. Thus, given its beliefs following m_2, x^{s1} must be such that one of the following three equations is satisfied, or be zero if the relevant equation has no solution:

$$u_{s1}^1(x^{s1}) + p_s^2 u_{s2}^2(1) + (1 - p_s^2)u_{s2}^2(0) = p_s^1 + u_{s2}^2(x_q^{s2})$$

(when 2 remains neutral if S attacks 1)

$$u_{s1}^1(x^{s1}) + p_s^2 u_{s2}^2(1) + (1 - p_s^2)u_{s2}^2(0) = p_{s2} + u_{s2}^2(x_q^{s2}) - c_s$$

(when 2 joins S if S attacks 1)

$$u_{s1}^1(x^{s1}) + p_s^2 u_{s2}^2(1) + (1 - p_s^2)u_{s2}^2(0) = (1 - p_{12}) + u_{s2}^2(x_q^{s2})$$

(when 2 joins 1 if S attacks 1).

Note that in each case, by the technical assumption about $u_{s2}^2(x_q^{s2})$, $\check{x}^{s1} = 0$. This implies that C1.1 holds. For sufficiently high x_q^{12}, C2.1 also holds. Thus, given the conditions in the proposition, the Potential Ally's strategy implies that, following m_2, it chooses $\check{x}^{s1}$ and remains neutral if the Signaler attacks the Target.

Take $u_{2s}^1(1) - u_{2s}^1(x_q^{2s})$ to be sufficiently low that C1.2 must hold even if $c_2 = 0$. According to the Target's strategy, this implies that the Target will not attack the Signaler if the Signaler attacks the Potential Ally. Thus,

$$\hat{x}^{s1} = p_s^1 - c_s \text{ (when 2 remains neutral if S attacks 1)}$$

$$\hat{x}^{s1} = p_{s2} - c_s \text{ (when 2 joins S if S attacks 1).}$$

In either case, C1.1 does not hold at $\hat{x}^{s1}$ for sufficiently low c_s and c_1. Similarly, C3.1 does not hold for sufficiently high x_q^{12} and sufficiently low c_s. Thus, at any information set following $\hat{x}^{s1}$ where the Signaler attacks the Target, the Potential Ally will join the Target.

We can now state the condition for the Signaler of type u_{s2}^2 to prefer to send m_2 given the other components of the equilibrium:

$$u_{s1}(\check{x}^{s1}) + p_s^2(1)u_{s2}^2(1) + (1 - p_s^2)u_{s2}^2(0) - c_s \geq u_{s1}^1(\hat{x}^{s1}) + u_{s2}^2(x_q^{s2}).$$

This holds for $u_{s2}^2(x_q^{s2})$, c_s, and $u_{s2}^2(x_q^{s2}) - u_{s2}^2(0)$ sufficiently low, the conditions given in the proposition. (Note that the equilibrium implies that the Signaler is indifferent between m_2 and other signal different from m_1.) Finally, note that by the definition of $\hat{x}^{s1}$, Signalers of type u_{s2}^1 are indifferent between sending m_1 and sending another signal, which would result in a choice of x^{s1} such that the Signaler would choose to attack the Potential Ally.   ∎

Appendix B

The Inference Dataset

The database comprises inferences drawn in the *Confidential Print* of the British Government between 1855 and July, 1914 about the security-related behavior and intentions of other great powers in Europe. The other European great powers were: Austria–Hungary, France, Germany, and Russia. The inferences were drawn from letters, memoranda, dispatches, speeches, and other documents deemed important enough by the British Foreign Office to be included in its archive, known as the Confidential Print. Inferences were classified as "security-related" if they concerned relative power, decisions about the use of force, alliance politics or influence or control over territory. Inferences about economic matters were also included when these were presented as affecting security concerns.

Documents of substantive importance from these years have been included in three published documents collections. The first is the well-known *British Documents on the Origins of the War* (ed. G. P. Gooch and Harold Temperley), a 13-volume set containing many of the most important documents from the years 1898–1914. The second documents collection is the series of "blue" and "white" books (named for the distinctive color of their covers) offered to Parliament and published as *Parliamentary Papers*. The third collection of papers is the largest: *Documents on British Foreign Policy*. The editors of this documents collection have ensured that the material consists only of documents that are unavailable in the other two collections. Together, these three collections provide a comprehensive record of all substantively important documents from the *Confidential Print* over this time period.

An observation in the dataset is an inference by the British about another European power. Inferences were defined by both the ground or cause of the inference and the conclusion drawn. If multiple inference causes were listed for the same conclusion, multiple observations were coded. Similarly, if one cause resulted in two conclusions, this was coded as two observations. In the case that a single action or state of affairs resulted in inferences about the behavior of three states, that was coded as three observations. If an identical inference was drawn on multiple occasions, only the first instance was coded as an observation and the number of identical inferences was listed as a variable.

A full codebook is available on the author's website, but I shall note in general terms how certain variables were coded here. The *Inference Cause* variable categorizes the ground or cause of the inference and was much used above in Chapter 2. Inferences were categorized as caused by military change when any change in the military situation, such as mobilization of troops, increase in capabilities or victory in battle, was listed as the reason for the inference. Other categories of inference causes coded include: Public and Private Diplomacy, Alliance Status Quo, Alliance Change, Leadership Change, Public Sentiment, Domestic Politics, Intelligence, Honor or Reputation Requires, Increased Influence or Prestige, Consonant with Past Actions, and Rules of Right Conduct Dictate. The *Inference Type* variable categorizes the conclusions drawn in a number of ways including: Country More/Less Aggressive Towards Britain, Country More/Less Aggressive Towards a Third State, Country Establishing Closer Relations with a Third State, Country Likely to Build More Arms than Previously Thought, and the like. The *Private Diplomacy Mechanism* variable categorizes inferences drawn from private diplomacy (according to the *Inference Cause* variable) in terms of the stated grounds for these inference and the conditions under which the inference was drawn. Examples of these categories are: High Demands Risk Partial Concessions, Partial Concessions Suggest Low Resolve, Concessions Lessen the Probability of Conflict, the Risk of a Breach Shows Resolve, Demands Risk Hostile Actions, Support of a Protege Conveys Resolve, and Alliance Offers are Sincere. More than one *Private Diplomacy Mechanism* code could be applied to a single Inference. In the text, the proportions calculated using this variable represent fractions of the total number codings applied to all inferences. See Appendix C for the coding rules used for the *Inference Certainty* variable and the website for further particulars.

Appendix C

Demands, Offers, and Assurances Dataset

The data comprise all demands, offers, and assurances that occurred between 1900 and the start of the World War in 1914 that are noted in the British *Confidential Print*[1] and (1) were made by European great powers other than Britain to European great powers and (2) were classified as "security-related." The European great powers of the day were: Austria–Hungary, France, Germany, Great Britain, and Russia. If the British were not witness to a demand, offer, or assurance (hereafter a TOA) by another power to a third power, but the British took it for granted that a TOA had occurred, this was also coded. TOAs from a great power to a non-great power were also coded if observers took it for granted that the non-great power was so closely connected to a great power that the TOA was equally made to that great power. TOAs were classified as "security-related" if they concerned relative power, decisions about the use of force, alliance politics or influence or control over territory. TOAs about economic matters were also included when these were presented as affecting security concerns. If precisely the same TOA was made on multiple occasions, the first instance was coded as an observation and the total number of identical TOAs was listed as a variable.

A full codebook is available on the author's website, but I shall note how certain variables were coded here. TOAs were classified as demands when the proposal was known to be against the preference of the state to which the statement was made and as offers otherwise. If an inference was made as a result of a TOA, this was coded in the same observation and categorized in a number of different ways that allow for the variety of distinctions drawn in the text. The *Inference Certainty* variable was

---

[1] See Appendix B for a description of the *Confidential Print* and the documents collections used.

coded either 1, 2, or 3, based on the words used in the drawing of the inference as follows:

1 Words such as "might," "may," and "possibly." Examples of specific phrases that merited this coding include: "if a Great Power motions for disarmament, Germany might suggest that armaments be proportional to a country's population," and "If Russia were to meet Austria's wishes in this matter it might dispose her to yield on the question of Djakova."

2 Words such as "looks as if" and "likely." Examples of specific phrases that merited this coding include: "putting two and two together it looks very much as if they were trying to square us in good time," "If Austria were to make further concessions, Russia could likely be convinced not to push for more."

3 Words such as "will," "is," "would," and "wants." Examples of specific phrases that merited this coding include: "If Austria–Hungary were to occupy Belgrade, it would be considered an 'act of aggression,' which would cause Russia to respond with its own 'act of aggression'," "German diplomats are attempting to create conflict between Russia and Britain."

A TOA was coded as a *diplomatic approach* when one country offered (a) improved relations or a formal understanding, either related to a specific set of issues or more generally, (b) to relinquish a claim on a disputed good such as territory outside of a crisis, or (c) to jointly oppose aggression by a third state.

Appendix D

German Inferences Prior to World War II

The following table contains data from the multi-volume *Documents on German Foreign Policy* series published by the United States Department of State following the Second World War. The table lists every inference in these documents made by a German official that satisfies these two criteria: (1) The inference is about the intentions of other European powers in relation to Germany or Germany's allies from January of 1938 through the declaration of war in 1939. (2) The inference concerns the actions or intentions of other powers related to Czechoslovakia and Poland. Over 6,000 pages of documents were evaluated in the creation of this data.

Inference	By Whom	Written to Whom	Year	Mn	Day	Source (Series, Vol, Page)
"An unequivocal British concession regarding the Austria-Czech question in accordance with our views would clear the political atmosphere in Europe. Judging from my previous experience, however, I consider such a turn unlikely."	Ambassador in Great Britain	Adolf Hitler	1938	1	2	D, Vol 1, 166
"Weighing all factors, one comes to the conclusion that, at the present moment, France would still march if an unprovoked attack were launched against Czechoslovakia." Because of the support shown by Britain, the strong statements made publically and the interest France has in limiting German power, they will fulfill their threats though the balance of indicators is only barely on that side.	Ambassador in France	Foreign Ministry	1938	4	8	D, Vol 2, 223
France and Britain will not intervene in the Czechoslovakia question because Germany is ahead militarily and Britain's rearmament will not be finished for another two years.	Adolf Hitler	Notes	1938	4	21	D, Vol 2, 239
"I am convinced that Chamberlain, the Prime Minister, Lord Halifax, the Foreign Secretary, and a number of leading members of the Cabinet earnestly desire to in Great initiate a policy of appeasement with Germany." This inference refers to Chamberlain's policy of practical politics, which was again demonstrated at a speech on June 2.	Ambassador in Great Britain	Foreign Ministry	1938	7	5	D, Vol 2, 472
Since the current British Cabinet has been the first since WWI to make significant concessions to Germany, it is likely they will make other concessions.	Ambassador in Great Britain	Foreign Ministry	1938	7	18	D, Vol 1, 1158

Inference	By Whom	Written to Whom	Year	Mn	Day	Source (Series, Vol., Page)
Britain will "do everything possible to meet our wishes, at any rate at a price" to ensure there is peace because they do not want to go to war over "a cause that is essentially worthless."	German Charge d'Affaires in Great Britain	Foreign Ministry	1938	8	23	D, Vol 2, 605
"The British Government were prepared to demand the most far-reaching sacrifices from Czechoslovakia if only Germany would adhere to peaceful methods in settling the Czech question."	Ambassador in Great Britain	Foreign Ministry	1938	8	24	D, Vol 2, 621
The Soviet Union will not attack Germany over Czechoslovakia because the two have no common frontier.	Ambassador in the Soviet Union	Foreign Ministry	1938	8	26	D, Vol 2, 631
"It can be assumed that, in accordance with the basic trend of Chamberlain's policy, they [Britain] will accept a German expansionist policy in eastern Europe."	Ambassador in Great Britain	Foreign Ministry	1939	1	4	D, Vol 4, 367
It is unlikely there will be a peaceful settlement over Poland with Britain because Britain realizes that Germany is trying to form a hegemony which is unacceptable to her.	Adolf Hitler	Leaders of the military	1939	5	23	D, Vol 6, 576
"Even when a war is won the victor emerges with diminished strength. This is the key to an understanding of the actions of the men of less than heroic cast." Britain does not not have what it takes to fight a long war. This has been shown by the events of WWI and the actions leading up to the present moment.	Adolf Hitler	Speech to the Commanders in Chief	1939	8	14	D, Vol 7, 551

(continued)

Inference	By Whom	Written to Whom	Year	Mn	Day	Source (Series, Vol., Page)
"The men I got to know in Munich are not the kind to start a new World War."	Adolf Hitler	Speech to the Commanders in Chief	1939	8	14	D, Vol 7, 555
"All these factors argue against England and France entering the war, particularly since they are not under any compulsion. Treaties are not yet ratified."	Adolf Hitler	Speech to the Commanders in Chief	1939	8	14	D, Vol 7, 555
Poland would be more cocky if they knew that they could depend on British support no matter what.	Adolf Hitler	Speech to the Commanders in Chief	1939	8	14	D, Vol 7, 555
Britain will defend Poland because she believes it is incredibly important and her reputation, especially after all the defeats, depends on it.	Ambassador in Great Britain	Foreign Ministry	1939	8	18	D, Vol 7, 139
If Poland responds with force to German action then Britain will back Poland up, not because she is "vitally interested in the fate of Danzig, but she is vitally interested in proving that she honors her political promissory notes."	Ambassador in Great Britain	Foreign Ministry	1939	8	18	D, Vol 7, 141
If it appears that Poland would be defeated very quickly, Britain will definitely step in to defend Poland so that she will be "safeguarding her world position."	Ambassador in Great Britain	Foreign Ministry	1939	8	18	D, Vol 7, 141
Britain will defend Poland because she has had a series of diplomatic defeats and will finally stand firm on this issue.	Ambassador in Great Britain	Foreign Ministry	1939	8	18	D, Vol 7, 139
Italy may not join Germany if a general war breaks out over Poland because Poland is an issue of no importance to	State Secretary	Foreign Ministry	1939	8	20	D, Vol 7, 160

Inference	By Whom	Written to Whom	Year	Mn	Day	Source (Series, Vol, Page)
France and Britain are tied up in other areas of the world and so they are in a weakened position and won't be able to wage a war in Europe.	Adolf Hitler	Speech to the Commanders in Chief	1939	8	22	D, Vol 7, 201–202
Britain has made little military preparation and therefore is not serious about a war.	Adolf Hitler	Speech to the Commanders in Chief	1939	8	22	D, Vol 7, 203
Poland asked for a loan from Britain, but Britain refused which shows that Britain is not serious about supporting Poland in a war.	Adolf Hitler	Speech to the Commanders in Chief	1939	8	22	D, Vol 7, 203
The current propaganda war but lack of rearmament suggests that Britain is concerned about the previous times it has backed down and is trying to appear resolved but is not really serious about going to war.	Adolf Hitler	Speech to the Commanders in Chief	1939	8	22	D, Vol 7, 203
France is short of men and has done little rearmament so they are not serious about going to war.	Adolf Hitler	Speech to the Commanders in Chief	1939	8	22	D, Vol 7, 203
"Our enemies have leaders who are below the average. No personalities. No masters, no men of action."	Adolf Hitler	Speech to the Commanders in Chief	1939	8	22	D, Vol 7, 203
"Our enemies are small fry. I saw them in Munich." England and France do not have the "strength of purpose" that Hitler does and will not go to war.	Adolf Hitler	Speech to the Commanders in Chief	1939	8	22	D, Vol 7, 204

(continued)

(continued)

Inference	By Whom	Written to Whom	Year	Mn	Day	Source (Series, Vol, Page)
Hitler and Mussolini have extensive power and if either is assassinated their successor will not be as strong, so this strength of leadership will allow them to successfully win the war.	Adolf Hitler	Speech to the Commanders in Chief	1939	8	22	D, Vol 7, 201
Italy is not militarily ready for a war and may not support Germany if they go to war over Poland.	Ambassador in Italy	Secretary of State	1939	8	23	D, Vol 7, 241
Italy is convinced that Britain and France will go to war and because Italy is likely to be dragged into a war due to their location on the Mediterranean, they really do not want Germany to go to war and will not necessarily support them if they do go to war.	Ambassador in Italy	Secretary of State	1939	8	23	D, Vol 7, 242
In response to a letter from Chamberlain about negotiations, the general impression is "England 'soft' on the issue of a major war."	Colonel General Hadler	Notes	1939	8	29	D, Vol 7, 568

References

Adcock, Frank and D. J. Mosley. 1975. *Diplomacy in Ancient Greece*. London: Thames and Hudson.

Adler, Emanuel and Michael Barnett, eds. 1998. *Security Communities*. London: Cambridge University Press.

Albertini, Luigi. 1952–1957. *The Origins of the War of 1914*. London: Oxford University Press.

Alexandroff, Alan and Richard Rosecrance. 1977. "Deterrence in 1939." *World Politics* 29(3):404–424.

Allison, Graham. 1971/1999. *Essence of Decision: Explaining the Cuban Missile Crisis*. New York: Harper Collins.

Andelman, David A. 2009. *A Shattered Peace: Versailles 1919 and the Price We Pay Today*. Hoboken, NJ: John Wiley & Sons.

Ausubel, Lawrence M., Peter Cramton and Raymond J. Deneckere. 2002. "Bargaining with Incomplete Information." In *Handbook of Game Theory, Vol. 3*, eds. Robert J. Aumann and Sergiu Hart. Amsterdam: Elsevier Science B.V.

Axelrod, Robert. 1970. *Conflict of Interest: A Theory of Divergent Goals with Applications to Politics*. Chicago, IL: Markham.

Banks, Jeffrey S. 1990. "Equilibrium Behavior in Crisis Bargaining Games." *American Journal of Political Science* 34(3):599–614.

Barnhart, Joslyn N. 2015. "Status Competition and Territorial Aggresssion: Evidence from the Scramble for Africa." *Security Studies* Forthcoming.

Bayer, Resat. 2006. "Diplomatic Exchange Data Set, v2006.1." *Data Set*.

Beales, Derek. 1982. *The Risorgimento and the Unification of Italy*. London: Longman Group.

Beck, Nathan, Jonathan N. Katz and Robert Tucker. 1998. "Taking Time Seriously: Time-Series Cross-Section Analysis with a Binary Dependent Variable." *American Journal of Political Science* 42(4):1260–1288.

Bennett, D. Scott and Allan Stam. 2000. "EUGene: A Conceptual Manual (Software Version: 3.1)." *International Interactions* 26:179–204.

Benson, Brett V. 2011. "Unpacking Alliances: Deterrent and Compellent Alliances and Their Relationship with Conflict, 1816–2000." *The Journal of Politics* 73:1111–1127.

Benson, Brett V. 2012. *Constructing International Security: Alliances, Deterrence, and Moral Hazard*. Cambridge University Press.

Benson, Brett V. and Emerson M. S. Niou. 2005. "Public Opinion, Foreign Policy, and the Security Balance in the Taiwan Strait." *Security Studies* 14(2):274–289.

Berinsky, Adam J. 2009. *In Time of War: Understanding American Public Opinion from World War II to Iraq*. Chicago, IL: University of Chicago Press.

Berridge, G. R. 2004. *Diplomatic Classics: Selected Texts from Commynes to Vattel*. New York: Palgrave Macmillan.

British Foreign Office. 1914. *Great Britain and the European Crisis: Correspondence, and Statements in Parliament, Together with an Introductory Narrative of Events*. London: H.M. Stationary Office.

Bismarck, Otto Fuerst von. 1915. *Gedanken und Erinnerungen*. Berlin: J. G. Cotta'sche Buchhandlung Nachfolger.

Bogitchvich, Miloš. 1919. *Causes of the War: An Examination into the Causes of the European War, with Special Reference to Russia and Serbia*. CL van Langenhuysen.

Bogitchvich, Miloš. 1928. *Die Auswrtige Politik Serbiens 1903–1914. Band I. Geheimakten aus Serbischen Archiven*. Berlin: Brückenverlag.

Bogitchvich, Miloš. 1929. *Die Auswrtige Politik Serbiens 1903–1914. Band II. Diplomatische Geheimakten aus Russischen, Montenegrinischen und Sonstigen Archiven*. Berlin: Brückenverlag.

Bourne, Kenneth and Donald Cameron Watt. 1983. *British Documents on Foreign Affairs*. Frederick, MD: University Publications of America.

Bourne, Kenneth and Donald Cameron Watt. 1985. *British Documents on Foreign Affairs*. Frederick, MD: University Publications of America.

Bourne, Kenneth and Donald Cameron Watt. 1987. *British Documents on Foreign Affairs*. Frederick, MD: University Publications of America.

Bourne, Kenneth and Donald Cameron Watt. 1989. *British Documents on Foreign Affairs*. Frederick, MD: University Publications of America.

Bourne, Kenneth and Donald Cameron Watt. 1990. *British Documents on Foreign Affairs*. Frederick, MD: University Publications of America.

Bourne, Kenneth and Donald Cameron Watt. 1991. *British Documents on Foreign Affairs*. Frederick, MD: University Publications of America.

Bourne, Kenneth and Donald Cameron Watt. 1995. *British Documents on Foreign Affairs*. Frederick, MD: University Publications of America.

Bratman, Michael E. 1999. *Intentions, Plans, and Practical Reason*. New York: Center for the Study of Language and Inference.

Braumoeller, Bear F. 2003. "Causal Complexity and the Study of Politics." *Political Analysis* 11(3):209–233.

Braumoeller, Bear F. 2008. "Systemic Politics and the Origins of Great Power Conflict." *American Political Science Review* 102(01):77–93.

British Government Sessional Papers. n.d. *British Sessional Papers*. London: H.M. Stationary Office.

British Parliament. 1859. *British Parliamentary Papers*. London: H.M. Stationary Office.

British Parliament. 1902. *British Parliamentary Papers*. London: H.M. Stationary Office.

Brown, Michael, Sean M. Lynn-Jones and Steven E. Miller, eds. 1996. *Debating the Democratic Peace*. Cambridge: MIT Press.

Bueno De Mesquita, Bruce and David Lalman. 1988. "Empirical Support for Systemic and Dyadic Explanations of International Conflict." *World Politics* 41(1):1–20.

Bueno de Mesquita, Bruce, James D. Morrow, Randolph M. Siverson and Alastair Smith. 1999. "An Institutional Explanation of the Democratic Peace." *American Political Science Review* 93(4):791–808.

Bull, Hedley. 1977. *The Anarchical Society: A Study of Order in World Politics.* London: Macmillan Press.

Carter, David B. and Curtis S. Signorino. 2010. "Back to the Future: Modeling Time Dependence in Binary Data." *Political Analysis* 18(3):271–292.

Cecil, Algernon. 2011. The Foreign Office. In *The Cambridge History of the British Foreign Policy, 1783–1919, Vol. III*, eds. Adolphus William Ward and George Peabody Gooch. London: Cambridge University Press.

Cetinyan, Rupen. 2002. "Ethnic Bargaining in the Shadow of Third-Party Intervention." *International Organization* 56(3):645–677.

Checkel, Jeffrey T. 1998. "The Constructivist Turn in International Relations Theory." *World Politics* 50(2):324–348.

Checkel, Jeffrey T. 2001. "Why Comply? Social Learning and European Identity Change." *International Organization* 55(03):553–588.

Chen, Ying, Navin Kartik and Joel Sobel. 2008. "Selecting Cheap-Talk Equilibria." *Econometrica* 76(1):117–136.

Chiozza, Giacomo and Hein Erich Goemans. 2011. *Leaders and International Conflict.* Cambridge University Press.

Clare, Joe and Vesna Danilovic. 2010. "Multiple Audiences and Reputation Building in International Conflicts." *Journal of Conflict Resolution* 54(6): 860–882.

Clark, Christopher. 2012. *The Sleepwalkers: How Europe Went to War in 1914.* UK: Penguin.

Cohen, Raymond and Raymond Westerbrook. 2002. *Amarna Diplomacy: The Beginnings of International Relations.* New York, NY: Johns Hopkins University Press.

Colaresi, Michael P. and William R. Thompson. 2005. "Alliances, Arms Buildups and Recurrent Conflict: Testing a Steps-to-War Model." *Journal of Politics* 67(2):345–364.

Cooper, Andrew F. 1997. "Beyond Representation." *International Journal* pp. 173–178.

Copeland, Dale C. 2000. *The Origins of Major War.* Ithaca, NY: Cornell University Press.

Crawford, Timothy J. 2003. *Pivotal Deterrence: Third-Party Statecraft and the Pursuit of Peace.* Ithaca, NY: Cornell University Press.

Crawford, Vincent P. and Joel Sobel. 1982. "Strategic Information Transmission." *Econometrica* 50(6):1431–1451.

Dafoe, Allan, Jonathan Renshon and Paul Huth. 2014. "Reputation and Status as Motives for War." *Annual Review of Political Science* 17:371–393.

Danilovic, Vesna. 2002. *When the Stakes Are High.* Ann Arbor, MI: Michigan University Press.

Davis Cross, Mai'a K. 2007. *The European Diplomatic Corps: Diplomats and International Cooperation from Westphalia to Maastricht.* Basingstoke, UK: Palgrave Macmillan.

de Callières, François. 1983. *The Art of Diplomacy*. Lanham, MD: University Press of America.

Deak, Istvan. 2001. *The Lawful Revolution: Louis Kossuth and Hungarians, 1848–1849*. London: Phoenix Press.

Der Derian, James. 1987. *On Diplomacy: A Geneology of Western Estrangement*. New York, NY: Blackwell Publishers.

Die grosse Politik der europäischen Kabinette, 1871–1914: Sammlung der diplomatischen Akten des Auswärtigen Amtes. 1922. Deutsche veragsgesellschaft für politik und geschichte.

du Plessis, Armand Jean. 1961. *The Political Testament of Cardinal Richelieu: The Significant Chapters and Supporting Selections*. Madison, WI: University of Wisconsin Press.

Dugdale, E. T. S. 1930. *German Diplomatic Documents 1871–1914, Volume IV*. Methuen & Company.

Eckstein, Harry. 1975. Case Study and Theory in Political Science. In *Handbook of Political Science*, eds. Fred Greenstein and Nelson Polsby. Reading, MA: Addison Wesley.

Elliott, John Huxtable. 2002. *Imperial Spain 1469–1716*. UK: Penguin.

Fabbrini, Sergio and Raffaele Marchetti, eds. 2016. *Still a Western World? Continuity and Change in Global Order: Africa, Latin America and the 'Asian Century'*. New York, NY: Routledge.

Fang, Songying, Jesse C. Johnson and Brett Ashley Leeds. 2012. To Concede or To Resist? The Restraining Effect of Military Alliances. Technical report Working Paper.

Fanis, Maria. 2011. *Secular Morality and International Security: American and British Decisions about War*. Ann Arbor, MI: University of Michigan Press.

Farrell, Joseph. 1993. "Meaning and Credibility in Cheap-Talk Games." *Games and Economic Behavior* 5:514–531.

Farrell, Joseph and Mathew Rabin. 1996. "Cheap Talk." *The Journal of Economic Perspectives* 10(3):103–118.

Farrell, Joseph and Robert Gibbons. 1989. "Cheap Talk Can Matter in Bargaining." *Journal of Economic Theory* 48 (June 1989):221–237.

Fearon, James D. 1994a. "Domestic Political Audiences and the Escalation of International Disputes." *American Political Science Review* 88(3):577–592.

Fearon, James D. 1994b. "Signaling Versus the Balance of Power and Interests: An Empirical Test of a Crisis Bargaining Model." *Journal of Conflict Resolution* 38(2):236–269.

Fearon, James D. 1995. "Rationalist Explanations for War." *International Organization* 49(3):379–414.

Fearon, James D. 1997. "Signaling Foreign Policy Interests: Tying Hands Versus Sinking Costs." *Journal of Conflict Resolution* 41(1):68–90.

Fearon, James D. 1998. "Bargaining, Enforcement and International Cooperation." *International Organization* 52(2):269–306.

Fearon, James D. 2002. "Selection Effects and Deterrence." *International Interactions* 28(1):5–29.

Fearon, James D. and David D. Laitin. 2008. "Integrating Qualitative and Quantitative Methods." *The Oxford Handbook of Political Methodology* pp. 756–776.

Feis, Herbert. 1950. *The Road to Pearl Harbor.* Princeton, NJ: Princeton University Press.

Ferguson, Niall. 1999. *The Pity of War.* New York, NY: Basic Books.

Fey, Mark and Kristopher W. Ramsay. 2011. "Uncertainty and Incentives in Crisis Bargaining: Game-Free Analysis of International Conflict." *American Journal of Political Science* 55(1):149–169.

Filson, Darren and Suzanne Werner. 2008. "A Bargaining Model of War and Peace: Anticipating the Onset, Duration, and Outcome of War." *American Journal of Political Science* 46(4):819–837.

Finnemore, Martha and Kathryn Sikkink. 1998. "International Norm Dynamics and Political Change." *International Organization* 52 (Autumn).

Fischer, Fritz. 1967. *Germany's Aims in the First World War.* WW Norton.

Forges, Francoise. 1990. "Universal Mechanisms." *Econometrica* 58(6):1341–1364.

Forster, Robert. 1978. "Achievements of the Annales School." *The Journal of Economic History* 38(1):58–76.

Fursenko, Aleksandr A. and Timothy J. Naftali. 1999. *One Hell of a Gamble: Khrushchev, Castro, Kennedy, and the Cuban Missile Crisis, 1958–1964.* London: Pimlico.

Gaddis, John Lewis. 2006. *The Cold War: A New History.* New York, NY: Penguin.

Gartner, Scott Sigmund and Randolph M Siverson. 1996. "War Expansion and War Outcome." *Journal of Conflict Resolution* 40(1):4–15.

Gaubatz, Kurt Taylor. 1996. "Democratic States and Commitment in International Relations." *International Organization* 50(1):109–139.

Gavin, Francis J. 2004. *Gold, Dollars, and Power: The Politics of International Monetary Relations, 1958–1971.* Chapel Hill, NC: UNC Press Books.

George, Alexander L. 1991. *Forceful Persuasion: Coercive Diplomacy as an Alternative to War.* Washington, DC: United States Institute of Peace Press.

Gibler, Douglas M. 2000. "Alliances: Why Some Cause War and Why Others Cause Peace." In *What Do We Know About War*, ed. John A. Vasquez. Lanham, MD: Rowman & Littlefield.

Gibler, Douglas M. and John A. Vasquez. 1998. "Uncovering the Dangerous Alliances, 1495–1980." *International Studies Quarterly* 42(4):785–807.

Gillard, David. 1990. *British Documents on Foreign Affairs.* Frederick, MD: University Publications of America.

Gilpin, Robert. 1983. *War and Change in World Politics.* Cambridge University Press.

Goddard, Stacie E. 2006. "Uncommon Ground: Indivisible Territory and the Politics of Legitimacy." *International Organization* 60:35–68.

Goddard, Stacie E. 2009. "When Right Makes Might: How Prussia Overturned the European Balance of Power." *International Security* 33(3):110–142.

Goddard, Stacie E. 2015. "The Rhetoric of Appeasement: Hitler's Legitimation and British Foreign Policy, 1938–1939." *Security Studies* 24(1):95–130.

Goldstein, Avery. 2000. *Deterrence and Security in the 21st Century: China, Britain, France, and the Enduring Legacy of the Nuclear Revolution.* Stanford, CA: Stanford University Press.

Gooch, George Peabody and Harold Temperley. 1979. *British Documents on the Origins of the War.* London: H.M. Stationary Office.

Goodman, Nelson. 1983. *Fact, Fiction, Forecast*. Cambridge, MA: Harvard University Press.

Gottfried, Matthew S. and Robert F. Trager. 2016. "A Preference for War: How Fairness and Rhetoric Influence Leadership Incentives in Crises." *International Studies Quarterly* .

Grigoryan, Arman. 2010. "Third-Party Intervention and the Escalation of State-Minority Conflicts." *International Studies Quarterly* 54(4):1143–1174.

Guisinger, Alexandra and Alastair Smith. 2002. "Honest Threats: The Interaction of Reputation and Political Institutions in International Crises." *Journal of Conflict Resolution* 46(2):175–200.

Hall, Todd H. 2011. "We Will Not Swallow This Bitter Fruit: Theorizing a Diplomacy of Anger." *Security Studies* 20(4):521–555.

Hall, Todd H. 2015. *Emotional Diplomacy: Official Emotion on the International Stage*. Cornell University Press.

Hall, Todd and Keren Yarhi-Milo. 2012. "The Personal Touch: Leaders Impressions, Costly Signaling, and Assessments of Sincerity in International Affairs." *International Studies Quarterly* 56(3):560–573.

Hassner, Ron E. 2003. "'To Halve and to Hold': Conflicts over Sacred Space and the Problem of Indivisibility." *Security Studies* 12(4):1–33.

Healy, Brian and Arthur Stein. 1973. "The Balance of Power in International History: Theory and Reality." *Journal of Conflict Resolution* 17(1):33–61.

Helmreich, Ernst Christian. 1938. *The Diplomacy of the Balkan Wars, 1912–1913*. Cambridge, MA: Harvard University Press.

Hendon, Ebbe, Hans Jørgen Jacobsen and Brigitte Sloth. 1996. "The One Shot Deviation Principle for Sequential Rationality." *Games and Economic Behavior* 12(2):274–282.

Hill, Leonidas E., ed. 1974. *Die Weizsäcker-Papiere*. Berlin: Propylen Verlag.

Holmes, Marcus. 2013. "The Force of Face-to-Face Diplomacy: Mirror Neurons and the Problem of Intentions." *International Organization* 67(04): 829–861.

Holsti, Kalevi Jaakko. 1991. *Peace and War: Armed Conflicts and International Order, 1648–1989*. Vol. 14, Cambridge University Press.

Holsti, Ole R. 1965. "The 1914 Case." *American Political Science Review* 59(02):365–378.

Hopf, Ted. 1998. "The Promise of Constructivism in International Relations Theory." *International Security* 23(1):44–75.

Horowitz, Michael C. and Allan C. Stam. 2014. "How Prior Military Experience Influences the Future Militarized Behavior of Leaders." *International Organization* 68(03):527–559.

Horowitz, Michael C. and Matthew S. Levendusky. 2012. "The (Non-)Partisan Logic of Audience Costs." *Journal of Politics* 74(2):323–338.

Hurd, Ian. 2015. International Law and the Politics of Diplomacy. In *Diplomacy and the Making of World Politics*, ed. Ole Jacob Sending. Cambridge University Press.

Hurrell, Andrew. 2007. *On Global Order*. Oxford, UK: Oxford University Press.

Huth, Paul. 1988a. "Extended Deterrence and the Outbreak of War." *American Political Science Review* 82(2):423–443.

Huth, Paul. 1988b. *Extended Deterrernce and the Prevention of War*. New Haven: Yale University Press.

Huth, Paul and Bruce Russett. 1984. "Testing Deterrence Theory: Rigor Makes a Difference." *World Politics* 42(4):270–290.

Huth, Paul, Christopher Gelpi and Daniel S. Bennett. 1993. "The Escalation of Great Power Militarized Disputes." *American Political Science Review* 87(3):609–623.

Ignatyev, N.P. 1931. "The Memoirs of Count N. Ignatyev." *Slavonic Review* X.

Ikenberry, G. John. 2008. *After Victory: Institutions, Strategic Restraint, and the Rebuilding of Order After Major Wars*. Princeton, NJ: Princeton University Press.

Jervis, Robert. 1970. *The Logic of Images in International Relations*. New York: Columbia University Press.

Jervis, Robert. 1976. *Perception and Misperception in International Politics*. Princeton, NJ: Princeton University Press.

Jervis, Robert. 1978. "Cooperation Under the Security Dilemma." *World Politics* 30(2):167–214.

Jervis, Robert. 1997. *System Effects: Complexity in Political and Social Life*. Princeton, NJ: Princeton University Press.

Jervis, Robert. 2001. "Was the Cold War a Security Dilemma?" *Journal of Cold War Studies* 3(1):36–60.

Jervis, Robert, Richard Ned Lebow and Janice Gross Stein. 1985. *Psychology and Deterrence*. Baltimore, MD: Johns Hopkins University Press.

Kahneman, Daniel. 2011. *Thinking Fast and Slow*. New York, NY: Farrar, Straus and Giroux.

Karsten, Peter, Peter D. Howell and Artis Frances Allen. 1984. *Military Threats: A Systematic Historical Analysis of the Determinants of Success*. Westport, CT: Greenwood Press.

Katzenstein, Peter J., ed. 1996. *The Culture of National Security: Norms and Identity in World Politics*. New York, NY: Columbia University Press.

Kaufman, Robert G. 1992. "To Balance or Bandwagon? Alignment Decisions in 1930s Europe." *Security Studies* 1(3):417–447.

Kautsky, Karl. 1919. "Die deutschen Dokumente zum Kriegsausbruch. 4 Bde."

Kay, A. C., S. C. Wheeler, John A. Bargh and L. Ross. 2004. "Material Priming: The Influence of Mundane Physical Objects on Situational Construal and Competitive Behavioral Choice." *Organizational Behavior and Human Decision Processes* 95:83–96.

Kershaw, Ian. 2007. *Fateful Choices: Ten Decisions that Changed the World, 1940–1941*. New York, NY: Penguin Group.

Kertzer, Joshua D and Ryan Brutger. 2015. "Decomposing Audience Costs: Bringing the Audience Back into Audience Cost Theory." *American Journal of Political Science*. Forthcoming.

Kilgour, Mark D. and Frank C. Zagare. 1994. "Uncertainty and the Role of the Pawn in Extended Deterrence." *Synthese* 100(3):379–412.

Kim, Tongfi. 2011. "Why Alliances Entangle but Seldom Entrap States." *Security Studies* 20(3):350–377.

Kissinger, Henry. 1994. *Diplomacy*. New York: Simon and Schuster.

Krebs, Ronald R. and Patrick Thaddeus Jackson. 2007. "Twisting Tongues and Twisting Arms: The Power of Political Rhetoric." *European Journal of International Relations* 13(1):35–66.

Krieger, John F. V. 1989. *British Documents on Foreign Affairs*. Frederick, MD: University Publications of America.

Kuperman, Alan J. 2008. "The Moral Hazard of Humanitarian Intervention: Lessons from the Balkans." *International Studies Quarterly* 52(1):49–80.

Kurizaki, Shuhei. 2007. "Efficient Secrecy: Public Versus Private Threats in Crisis Diplomacy." *American Political Science Review* 101(3):543–558.

Kydd, Andrew. 1997. "Sheep in Sheep's Clothing: Why Security Seekers Do Not Fight Each Other." *Security Studies* 7(1):114–155.

Kydd, Andrew. 2003. "Which Side Are You On? Bias, Credibility, and MediationWhich Side Are You On? Bias, Credibility, and Mediation." *American Journal of Political Science* 47(4):597–611.

Kydd, Andrew. 2005. *Trust and Mistrust in International Relations*. Princeton, NJ: Princeton University Press.

Lake, David. 1992. "Powerful Pacifists: Democratic States and War." *American Political Science Review* 86(1):24–37.

Lebow, Richard Ned. 1984. "Windows of Opportunity: Do States Jump Through Them?" *International Security* 9(1):147–186.

Lebow, Richard Ned. 2010. *Forbidden Fruit: Counterfactuals and International Relations*. Princeton University Press.

Lebow, Richard Ned and Janice Gross Stein. 1989. "Rational Deterrence: I Think, Therefore I Deter." *World Politics* 41(2):208–224.

Leeds, Brett Ashley. 1999. "Domestic Political Institutions, Credible Commitments, and International Cooperation." *American Journal of Political Science* 43(4):979–1002.

Leeds, Brett Ashley. 2003. "Do Alliances Deter Aggression? The Influence of Military Alliances on the Initiation of Militarized Interstate Disputes." *American Journal of Political Science* 47(3):427–439.

Leeds, Brett Ashley, Jeffrey Ritter, Sara Mitchell and Andrew Long. 2002. "Alliance Treaty Obligations and Provisions, 1815–1944." *International Interactions* 28(3):237–260.

Leventoglu, Bahar and Ahmer Tarar. 2008. "Does Private Inforamtion Lead to Delay or War in Crisis Bargaining?" *International Studies Quarterly* 52:533–553.

Levy, Jack S. 1981. "Alliance Formation and War Behavior: An Analysis of the Great Powers, 1495–1975." *Journal of Conflict Resolution* 25(4):581–613.

Levy, Jack S. 1988. "When Do Deterrent Threats Work?" *British Journal of Political Science* 18(4):485–512.

Levy, Jack S. 1990. "Preferences, Constraints, and Choices in July 1914." *International Security* 15(3):151–186.

Levy, Jack S. 2003. Balances and Balancing: Concepts, Propositions, and Research Design. In *Realism and the Balancing of Power*, eds. Collin Elman and John A. Vasquez. Upper Saddle River, NJ: Prentice Hall.

Levy, Jack S, Michael K. McKoy, Paul Poast and Geoffrey P. R. Wallace. 2015. "Backing Out or Backing In? Commitment and Consistency in Audience Costs Theory." *American Journal of Political Science* 59(4):988–1001.

Lieber, Keir A. and Daryl G. Press. 2006. "The End of MAD? The Nuclear Dimension of US Primacy." *International Security* 30(4):7–44.

Loewenheim, Francis L. 1965. *Peace or Appeasement*. Boston, MA: Houghton Mifflin Company.

Mackie, John L. 1965. "Causes and conditions." *American Philosophical Quarterly* 2(4):245–264.

Mansfield, Edward, Helen V. Milner and B. Peter Rosendorff. 2002. "Why Democracies Cooperate More: Electoral Control and International Trade Agreements." *International Organization* 56(3):477–513.

Maoz, Zeev. 1983. "Resolve, Capabilities, and the Outcomes of Interstate Disputes, 1816–1976." *Journal of Conflict Resolution* 27(2):195–229.

Maoz, Zeev. 2000. Alliances: The Street Gangs of World Politics – their Origins, Management, and Consequences, 1816–1986. In *What Do We Know About War*, ed. John A. Vasquez. Lanham, MD: Rowman & Littlefield.

Matthews, Steven A., Mashiro Okuno-Fujiwara and Andrew Postlewaite. 1991. "Refining Cheap Talk Equilibria." *Journal of Economic Theory* 55:247–273.

May, Ernest R. and Phillip D. Zelikow. 2002. *The Kennedy Tapes: Inside the White House During the Cuban Missile Crisis*. New York, NY: WW Norton and Company, Inc.

Mearsheimer, John J. 2001. *The Tragedy of Great Power Politics*. New York: University of Chicago Press.

Mercer, Jonathan. 1996. *Reputation and International Politics*. New York: Cornell University Press.

Mercer, Jonathan. 2010. "Emotional beliefs." *International Organization* 64(01):1–31.

Miller, Steven E., Sean M. Lynn-Jones and Stephen Van Evera. 1991. *Military Strategy and the Origins of the First World War*. Princeton University Press.

Milner, Helen V. 1997. *Interests, Institutions, and Information: Domestic Politics and International Relations*. Princeton, NJ: Princeton University Press.

Mitzen, Jennifer. 2005. "Reading Habermas in Anarchy: Multilateral Diplomacy and Global Public Spheres." *American Political Science Review* 99(3):401–417.

Mitzen, Jennifer. 2006. "Ontological Security in World Politics: State Identity and the Security Dilemma." *European Journal of International Relations* 12(3):341–370.

Mo, Jongryn. 1995. "Domestic Institutions and International Bargaining: The Role of Agent Veto in Two-Level Games." *American Political Science Review* 89(4):914–936.

Monger, George. 1963. *The End of Isolation*. New York: Thomas Nelson and Sons.

Morgan, Patrick M. 1983. *Deterrence: A Conceptual Analysis*. Cambridge, UK: Cambridge University Press.

Morgenthau, Hans Joachim. 1948. *Politics Among Nations: The Struggle for Power and Peace*. New York: McGraw-Hill.

Morrow, James D. 1989. "Capabilities, Uncertainty, and Resolve: A Limited Information Model of Crisis Bargaining." *American Journal of Political Science* 33(4):941–972.

Morrow, James D. 1992. "Signaling Difficulties with Linkage in Crisis Bargaining." *International Studies Quarterly* 36:153–172.

Morrow, James D. 1994. "Alliances, Credibility, and Peacetime Costs." *Journal of Conflict Resolution* 38:270–297.

Morrow, James D. 2000. "Alliances: Why Write Them Down?" *Annual Review of Political Science* 3(1):63–83.

Mosse, W. E. 1958. *The European Powers and the German Question: 1848–71.* London: Cambridge University Press.

Nicolson, H. 1954. *The Evolution of Diplomatic Method.* London: Constable.

Nicolson, H. 1963. *Diplomacy.* London: Oxford University Press.

Nicolson, Harold. 1946. *The Congress of Vienna: A Study in Allied Unity, 1812–1822.* San Diego, CA: Harcourt Brace Jovanovich, Publishers.

Nowak, Martin A, Natalia L. Komarova and Partha Niyogi. 2002. "Computational and Evolutionary Aspects of Language." *Nature* 417(6889):611–617.

O'Hanlon, Michael. 2000. "Why China Cannot Conquer Taiwan." *International Security* 25(2):51–86.

O'Neill, Barry. 1999. *Honor, Symbols, and War.* Ann Arbor, MI: University of Michigan Press.

O'Neill, Barry. 2001. "Risk Aversion in International Relations Theory." *International Studies Quarterly* 45:617–640.

Pape, Robert A. 1996. *Bombing to Win: Air Power and Coercion in War.* Ithaca, NY: Cornell University Press.

Parker, Geoffrey. 2000. *The Grand Strategy of Philip II.* Yale University Press.

Posen, Barry R. 1984. *The Sources of Military Doctrine: France, Britain and Germany Between the World Wars.* Ithaca, NY: Cornell University Press.

Powell, Robert. 1988. "Nuclear Brinkmanship with Two-Sided Incomplete Information." *American Political Science Review* 82(1):155–178.

Powell, Robert. 1990. *Nuclear Deterrence Theory: The Problem of Credibility.* Cambridge, MA: Cambridge University Press.

Powell, Robert. 1993. "Guns, Butter and Anarchy." *American Political Science Review* 87(1):115–132.

Powell, Robert. 1996a. "Bargaining in the Shadow of Power." *Games and Economic Behavior* 15:255–289.

Powell, Robert. 1996b. "Stability and the Distribution of Power." *World Politics* 48(2):239–267.

Powell, Robert. 2002. "Bargaining While Fighting." *Paper presented at the 2002 American Political Science Association Meetings.*

Powell, Robert. 2004a. "Bargaining and Learning While Fighting." *American Journal of Political Science* 48(2):344–361.

Powell, Robert. 2004b. "The Inefficient Use of Power: Costly Conflict with Complete Information." *American Political Science Review* 98(2):231–241.

Powell, Robert. 2006. "War as a Commitment Problem." *International Organization* 60(1):169.

Press, Daryl G. 2005. *Calculating Credibility: How Leaders Assess Military Threats.* New York, NY: Cornell University Press.

Puryear, Vernon J. 1931. *England, Russia, and the Straights Question: 1844–1856.* Berkeley, CA: University of California Press.

Quackenbush, Stephen L. 2006. "Not Only Whether but Whom: Three-Party Extended Deterrence." *The Journal of Conflict Resolution* 50(4):562–583.

Ramsay, Kristopher W. 2004. "Politics at the Water's Edge: Crisis Bargaining and Electoral Competition." *Journal of Conflict Resolution* 48(4):459–486.

Ramsay, Kristopher W. 2011. "Cheap Talk Diplomacy, Voluntary Negotiations, and Variable Bargaining Power." *International Studies Quarterly* 55:1003–1023.

Rathbun, Brian C. 2014. *Diplomacy's Value: Creating Security in 1920s Europe and the Contemporary Middle East.* Cornell University Press.

Rathbun, Brian C., Joshua D. Kertzer and Mark Paradis. 2015. "Homo Diplomaticus: Mixed-Method Evidence of Variation in Strategic Rationality." *Working paper.*

Reiter, Daniel. 2009. *How Wars End.* Princeton, NJ: Princeton University Press.

Renouvin, Pierre. 1925. *Les origines immédiates de la guerre (28 juin–4 août 1914).* Alfred Costes.

Reus-Smit, Christian. 1997. "The Constitutional Structure of International Society and the Nature of Fundamental Institutions." *International Organization* 51(04):555–589.

Rich, Norman. 1965a. *Friedrich von Holstein: Politics and Diplomacy in the Era of Bismarck and Wilhelm II.* Cambridge, UK: Cambridge University Press.

Rich, Norman. 1965b. *Why the Crimean War? A Cautionary Tale.* Hanover, NH: University Press for New England.

Risse, Thomas. 2000. "Let's Argue!: Communicative Action in World Politics." *International Organization* 54(01):1–39.

Ritter, Jeffrey Munro. 2004. "Silent Partners and Other Essays on Alliance Politics." *Dissertation, Harvard University.*

Röhl, John CG. 2002. *Kaiser, Hof und Staat: Wilhelm II. und die deutsche Politik.* CH Beck.

Röhl, John CG. 2008. *"Wilhelm II: Der Weg in den Abgrund 1900–1941."* CH Beck.

Rossos, Andrew. 1981. *Russia and the Balkans: Inter-Balkan Rivalries and Russian Foreign Policy, 1908–1914.* University of Toronto Press.

Rubinstein, Ariel. 1982. "Perfect Equilibrium in a Bargaining Model." *Econometrica* 50:97–110.

Ruggie, John Gerard. 1998. "What Makes the World Hang Together? Neo-Utilitarianism and the Social Constructivist Challenge." *International Organization* 52(4):855–885.

Rupp, George Hoover. 1941. *A Wavering Friendship: Russia and Austria 1876–1878.* Cambridge, MA: Harvard University Press.

Russett, Bruce M. 1963. "The Calculus of Deterrence." *Journal of Conflict Resolution* 7:97–109.

Russett, Bruce M. 1967. "Pearl Harbor: Deterrence Theory and Decision Theory." *Journal of Peace Research* 4(2):89–106.

Saburov, Peter Alexandrovitch. 1929. *The Saburov Memoirs or Bismarck and Russia.* Cambridge, UK: Cambridge University Press.

Sartori, Anne E. 2002. "The Might of the Pen: A Reputational Theory of Communication in International Disputes." *International Organization* 56(1):121–149.

Sartori, Anne E. 2005. *Deterrence by Diplomacy.* Princeton, NJ: Princeton University Press.

Satow, Ernest Mason. 1922. *A Guide to Diplomatic Practice.* Vol. 1. Longmans, Green.

Saunders, Elizabeth N. 2015. "War and the Inner Circle: Democratic Elites and the Politics of Using Force." *Security Studies* 24(3):466–501.

Schelling, Thomas C. 1966. *Arms and Influence.* New Haven, CT: Yale University Press.

Schelling, Thomas C. 1980. *The Strategy of Conflict*. Cambridge, MA: Harvard University Press.

Schmitt, Bernadotte Everly. 1988. *The World in the Crucible, 1914–1919*. Vol. 2088. Harpercollins College Div. New York, NY.

Schorske, Carl E. 1994. Two German Ambassadors: Dirsksen and Schulenberg. In *The Diplomats: 1919–1939*, eds. Gordon A. Craig and Felix Gilbert. Princeton, NJ: Princeton University Press.

Schroeder, Paul. 1997. World War I as a Galloping Gertie. In *The Outbreak of World War I: Causes and Responsibilities*, ed. Holger H. Herwig. Boston, MA: Houghton Mifflin Company pp. 142–151.

Schroeder, Paul. 2004. *Systems, Stability, and Statecraft: Essays on the International History of Modern Europe*. Palgrave Macmillan.

Schroeder, Paul W. 1972. *Austria, Great Britain, and the Crimean War: The Destruction of the European Concert*. Ithaca, NY: Cornell University Press.

Schroeder, Paul W. 1996. *The Transformation of European Politics, 1763–1848*. Oxford University Press.

Schultz, Kenneth. 1998. "Domestic Opposition and Signaling in International Crises." *American Political Science Review* 92(4):829–844.

Schultz, Kenneth. 2001. *Democracy and Coercive Diplomacy*. Cambridge: Cambridge University Press.

Schweinitz, Hans Lothar von. 1927. *Denkwuerdigeiten des Botschafters General v. Schweinitz*. Vol. 1 Berlin: Reimar Hobbing.

Schweller, Randall L. 1994. "Bandwagoning for Profit: Bringing the Revisionist State Back In." *International Security* 19(1):72–107.

Schweller, Randall L. 2006. *Unanswered Threats: Political Constraints on the Balance of Power*. Princeton, NJ: Princeton University Press.

Sechser, Todd S. 2010. "Goliath's Curse: Coercive Threats and Asymmetric Power." *International Organization* 64(04):627–660.

Sending, Ole Jacob. 2015a. "*Diplomacy and the Making of World Politics*." Cambridge, UK: Cambridge University Press.

Sending, Ole Jacob. 2015b. "Diplomats and Humanitarians in Crisis Governance." In *Diplomacy and the Making of World Politics*, ed. Ole Jacob Sending. Cambridge University Press.

Severson, Randolph M. and Harvey Starr. 1990. "Opportunity, Willingness, and the Diffusion of War." *American Political Science Review* 84(1):47–67.

Sharp, Paul. 1997. "Who Needs Diplomats? The Problems of Diplomatic Representation." *International Journal* pp. 609–634.

Sharp, Paul. 1999. "For Diplomacy: Representation and the Study of International Relations." *International Studies Review* 1(1):33–57.

Sharp, Paul. 2009. *Diplomatic Theory of International Relations*. Vol. 111. Cambridge, UK: Cambridge University Press.

Shaw, John. 2006. *The Ambassador: Inside the Life of a Working Diplomat*. Washington, DC: Capital Books.

Shore, Zachary. 2002. *What Hitler Knew: The Battle for Information in Nazi Foreign Policy*. New York, NY: Oxford University Press.

Signorino, Curtis S. and Ahmer Tarar. 2006. "A Unified Theory and Test of Extended Immediate Deterrence." *American Journal of Political Science* 50(3):586–605.

Signorino, Curtis S. and Jeffrey M. Ritter. 1999. "Tau-B or Not Tau-B: Measuring Alliance Portfolio Similarity." *International Studies Quarterly* 43:115–144.

Siverson, Randolph M. and Michael R. Tennefoss. 1984. "Power, Alliance, and the Escalation of International Conflict, 1815–1965." *The American Political Science Review* 78(4):1057–1069.

Slantchev, Branislav. 2010a. *Military Threats: The Costs of Coercion and the Price of Peace*. New York, NY: Cambridge University Press.

Slantchev, Branislav L. 2003. "The Power to Hurt: Costly Conflict with Completely Informed States." *American Political Science Review* 47(1):123–135.

Slantchev, Branislav L. 2005. "Military Coercion in Interstate Crises." *American Political Science Review* 99(4):533–547.

Slantchev, Branislav L. 2010b. "Feigning Weakness." *International Organization* 64(3):357–388.

Smith, Alastair. 1995. "Alliance Formation and War." *International Studies Quarterly* 39(4):405–425.

Smith, Alastair. 1996. "To Intervene or Not to Intervene." *Journal of Conflict Resolution* 40(1):16–40.

Smith, Alastair. 1998a. "Extended Deterrence and Alliance Politics." *International Interactions* 24(4):315–343.

Smith, Alastair. 1998b. "International Crises and Domestic Politics." *American Political Science Review* 92(3):623–638.

Snyder, Glenn H. 1984. "The Security Dilemma in Alliance Politics." *World Politics* 36(04):461–495.

Snyder, Glenn H. 1997. *Alliance Politics*. Ithaca, NY: Cornell University Press.

Snyder, Glenn Herald and Paul Diesing. 1977. *Conflict Among Nations: Bargaining, Decision Making, and System Structure in International Crises*. Princeton, NJ: Princeton University Press.

Snyder, Jack. 1991. *Myths of Empire: Domestic Politics and International Ambition*. Ithaca, NY: Cornell University Press.

Sontag, John Philip. 1966. *Russian Diplomacy, the Balkans and Europe, 1908–1912*. Cambridge, MA: Harvard University.

Stein, Arthur A. 2000. The Justifying State: Why Anarchy Doesn't Mean No Excuses. In *Peace, Prosperity, and Politics*, ed. John Mueller. Boulder, CO: Westview Press pp. 235–255.

Stevenson, David. 1990. *British Documents on Foreign Affairs*. Frederick, MD: University Publications of America.

Stevenson, David. 1996. *Armaments and the Coming of War: Europe, 1904–1914*. Oxford University Press.

Strahan, Hew. 2005. *The First World War*. New York, NY: Penguin Books.

Talbott, Strobe. 2003. *The Russia Hand: A Memoir of Presidential Diplomacy*. New York: Random House.

Tarar, Ahmer and Bahar Leventoğlu. 2009. "Public Commitment in Crisis Bargaining." *International Studies Quarterly* 53(3):817–839.

Taylor, A. J. P. 1954. *The Struggle for Mastery in Europe, 1848–1918*. Oxford: Clarendon Press.

Thorne, Christopher. 1968. *The Approach of War 1938–39*. London: Macmillan.

Thucydides. 1989. *The Peloponnesian War*. Chicago, IL: University of Chicago Press.

Tomz, Michael. 2007. "Domestic Audience Costs in International Relations: An Experimental Approach." *International Organization* 61(4):821–840.

Tooze, Adam. 2006. *The Wages of Destruction*. New York, NY: Allen Lane.

Trachtenberg, Marc. 1990. "The Meaning of Mobilization in 1914." *International Security* pp. 120–150.

Trachtenberg, Marc. 1991. *History and Strategy*. Princeton, NJ: Princeton University Press.

Trachtenberg, Marc. 1999. *A Concstructed Peace: The Making of the European Settlement, 1945–1963*. Princeton, NJ: Princeton University Press.

Trachtenberg, Marc. 2008. "The United States and Eastern Europe in 1945: A Reassessment." *Journal of Cold War Studies* 10(4):94–132.

Trager, Robert. 2010. "Diplomatic Calculus in Anarchy: How Communication Matters." *American Political Science Review* 104(2):347–368.

Trager, Robert F. 2007. *Diplomatic Calculus in Anarchy: The Construction and Consequences of the Space of Intentions*. New York, NY: Columbia University PhD Dissertation.

Trager, Robert F. 2011. "Multi-Dimensional Diplomacy." *International Organization* 65:469–506.

Trager, Robert F. 2012. "Long-Term Consequences of Aggressive Diplomacy: European Relations after Austrian Crimean War Threats." *Security Studies* 21(2):232–265.

Trager, Robert F. 2013. "How the Scope of a Demand Conveys Resolve." *International Theory* 5(03):414–445.

Trager, Robert F. 2015. "Diplomatic Signaling among Multiple States." *The Journal of Politics* 77(3):635–647.

Trager, Robert F. and Dessislava P. Zagorcheva. 2006. "Deterring Terrorism: It Can Be Done." *International Security* 30(3):87–123.

Trager, Robert F. and Dessislava P. Zagorcheva. 2007. "Deterrence in the Age of Fanaticism and WMD." *Working Paper*.

Trager, Robert F. and Lynn Vavreck. 2011. "The Political Costs of Crisis Bargaining: Presidential Rhetoric and the Role of Party." *American Journal Political Science* 55(3):526–545.

Wagner, R. Harrison. 2004. "Bargaining, War, and Alliances." *Conflict Management and Peace Science* 21(3):215–231.

Walt, Stephen M. 1987. *The Origins of Alliances*. Ithaca, NY: Cornell University Press.

Walter, Barbara F. 2002. *Committing to Peace: The Successful Settlement of Civil Wars*. Princeton, NJ: Princeton University Press.

Waltz, Kenneth N. 1979. *Theory of International Politics*. New York: McGraw-Hill.

Waltz, Kenneth N. 2003. Evaluating Theories. In *Realism and the Balancing of Power*, eds. Collin Elman and John A. Vasquez. Upper Saddle River, NJ: Prentice Hall.

Ward, Adolphus William and George Peabody Gooch. 1922. *The Cambridge History of British Foreign Policy, 1783–1919*. Vol. 1. New York, NY: Cambridge University Press.

Watt, Donald Cameron. 1989. *How War Came: The Immediate Origins of the Second World War, 1938–1939*. London: Heinemann.

Webster, Charles Kingsley. 1963. *The Congress of Vienna*. Taylor & Francis. Abingdon, UK.

Weeks, Jessica L. 2008. "Autocratic Audience Costs: Regime Type and Signaling Resolve." *International Organization* pp. 35–64.

Weisiger, Alex and Keren Yarhi-Milo. 2015. "Revisiting Reputation: How Past Actions Matter in International Politics." *International Organization* 69(02):473–495.

Weiss, Jessica Chen. 2013. "Authoritarian Signaling, Mass Audiences, and Nationalist Protest in China." *International Organization* 67(01):1–35.

Wendt, Alexander. 1999. *Social Theory of International Politics*. Cambridge, UK: Cambridge University Press.

Werner, Suzanne. 2000. "Deterring Intervention: The Stakes of War and Third-Party Involvement." *American Journal of Political Science* 44(4):720–732.

Williams, Lawrence E. and John A. Bargh. 2008. "Experiencing Physical Warmth Promotes Interpersonal Warmth." *Science* 24(5901):606–607.

Williamson, Samuel R. 1991. *Austria–Hungary and the Origins of the First World War*. London, UK: Macmillan.

Wilson, Woodrow. 2002. "War and Peace: Presidential Messages, Addresses and Public Papers."

Wittman, Donald. 1979. "How a War Ends: A Rational Model Approach." *Journal of Conflict Resolution* 23(4):743–763.

Wong, Seanon S. 2016. "Emotions and the Communication of Intentions in Face-to-Face Diplomacy." *European Journal of International Relations* 22(1):144–167.

Woods, Kevin M. 2008. *The Mother of All Battles: Saddam Hussein's Strategic Plan for the Persian Gulf War*. Annapolis, MD: Naval Institute Press.

Xenophon. 1907. *Hellenica*. Oxford: Clarendon Press.

Yarhi-Milo, Keren. 2013a. "In the Eye of the Beholder: How Leaders and Intelligence Communities Assess the Intentions of Adversaries." *International Security* 38(1):7–51.

Yarhi-Milo, Keren. 2013b. "Tying Hands Behind Closed Doors: The Logic and Practice of Secret Reassurance." *Security Studies* 22(3):405–435.

Yarhi-Milo, Keren. 2014. *Knowing the Adversary: Leaders, Intelligence, and Assessment of Intentions in International Relations*. Princeton, NJ: Princeton University Press.

Yuen, Amy. 2009. "Target Concessions in the Shadow of Intervention." *Journal of Conflict Resolution* 53(5):745–773.

Zagare, Frank C. and Mark D. Kilgour. 2003. "Alignment Patterns, Crisis Bargaining, and Extended Deterrence." International Studies Quarterly 47(4): 587–615.

Zaller, John. 1992. *The Nature and Origins of Mass Opinion*. New York, NY: Cambridge University Press.

Zartman, William and Guy Faure. 2005. *Escalation and Negotiation in International Conflicts*. New York, NY: Cambridge University Press.

Index

Acheson, Dean, 218
Adenauer, Konrad, 2
Al Qaeda in Iraq, 224
Albania, 36, 158, 159
Alsace, 30
Amarna Letters, 5
Ancient Greece, 5
Anglo-German naval race, 23
Asia Minor, 5
Athens, 5
Audience Cost Hypothesis, 149, 160, 188, 190, 207
Audience costs, 12, 23, 105, 131, 149, 160, 164, 183, 190, 207, 249, 251, 252, 255
Austria-Hungary (Austria), 2, 23, 32, 72, 128, 142, 152, 167
  alliance relations, 1, 5, 30–33
  at the Congress of Vienna, 212
  economic relations, 32
  reasons for precipitating the World War, 166–172
  relations with Britain, 100, 143
  relations with France, 36, 37, 47, 123
  relations with Germany, 36, 76, 103, 124, 143, 145, 151, 158, 160, 166, 170
  relations with Italy, 39, 142
  relations with Russia, 1, 2, 32, 75, 78, 128, 143, 154, 155, 157, 169, 170, 174, 193, 213
  relations with Serbia, 36, 162
  relationship to Bosnia and Herzegovina, 68
  signaling, 35, 71

Austrian Emperor, 2

balance of power, 8, 15, 29, 78, 86, 101, 127, 209
Balkans, 1
  relations with Russia, 34, 155, 160, 161, 169
  relations with Turkey, 41
Balkan crises/wars, 154, 158, 170
Benson, Brett V., 106
Berchtold, Count Leopold, 166, 167, 169, 170
Bismarck, Otto von, 1, 23, 33, 71, 72, 78, 99, 100, 132, 133, 213
Bosnia, Bosnia-Herzegovina, 32, 68, 154, 170, 171
  annexation of, 154
brinkmanship, 14, 73
British *Confidential Print*, 7, 22, 23, 126, 192, 216
Buchanan, Sir George, 27, 33, 68
Bulgaria
  alliance with Serbia, 161
  First Balkan War, 158
  relations with Russia, 2, 70, 143, 154, 169
  relations with Turkey, 32
Bush, George W., 102
Bzezinski, Zbigniew, 223

Canning, Stratford, 125, 223
Castlereagh, Viscount (Robert Stewart), 213–215
Central Asia, 37

Chamberlain, Neville, 179–181, 183–186, 190
China
  nuclear weapons, 76
  relations with Taiwan, 105, 125, 126
  relations with the United States, 217, 220
Churchill, Winston, 174
Clinton, Bill, 5
Congress of Berlin, 23
Congress of Vienna, 212
constructivist, 15, 16
Cowley, Earl of (Henry Wellesley), 37, 123
Crawford, Vincent P., 49, 105
Crimean War, 5, 10, 23, 75, 125, 128, 143, 152, 213, 223
Cuba, 4, 64, 77
Cuban Missile Crisis, 2, 4, 64, 77
Czechoslavkia
  annexation of, 65
  negotiation over, 55, 116–117, 175–179, 183, 184, 190
  Sudetenland, 55, 65, 176, 178, 179

Danilovic, Vesna, 106
Danzig, 178–180
  negotiation over, 185–188
democracy, 12, 31
Der Derian, James, 15
détente, 2, 214, 217, 219
diplomacy
  definition, 16
  diplomatic approaches, 19, 35, 128, 146, 156, 158, 160–162, 168–170, 172, 183, 193, 195, 205–207
  effectiveness of signals versus effectiveness at coercing, 219
  encouragement of a protégé, 19, 103–127, 162, 163, 203–205, 217, 221
  history of, 5–6
  importance of, 208–211
  inferences outside of bargaining, 36
  private diplomacy, definition, 17
  proportion of inferences drawn, 33–39
  public diplomacy, 17–18, 25, 28, 31, 35, 36, 102, 207–208
  relationship to power, 27, 97, 101, 104, 106, 110, 115, 200–202, 219
  reputation, 9, 13, 20, 26, 35–39, 59, 65, 72, 99, 101, 107, 132, 217, 221
  risk of a breach mechanism, 18, 71–102, 133, 136, 157, 198–203, 216, 221, 222

  scope of demands mechanism, 18, 47, 70, 157, 175, 177, 183–187, 190, 196–198, 216
  study of, 10–16

East Germany, 2, 3
Egyptian Empire, 5, 220
Entente Cordial, 144, 162, 202
entrapment, 104, 115, 218
Eyre Crowe memorandum, 39, 69, 130, 133, 143, 211

Fearon, James, 9, 17, 48, 49, 53, 54, 63, 64, 66, 78, 83, 105, 106, 115, 149, 219, 237, 238
Ferdinand, Franz, 39, 159, 166, 170
First Balkan War, 155, 157, 158
First Moroccan Crisis, 100, 193, 202
Forges, Francoise, 108
Franco-Prussian War, 23, 33, 36, 76
France
  activities in Morocco, 39, 69
  activities in Vietnam, 33
  Cold War diplomacy, 132, 218
  diplomacy after the Crimean War, 128
  diplomacy before the Second World War, 131
  German evaluation of intentions of, 184
  Louis XI of, 20
  negotiations over Czechoslovakia, 116
  negotiations over Poland, 179
  Nigerian border dispute, 202
  relations with Austria-Hungary, 36
  relations with Britain, 30, 34, 35, 69, 75, 100, 130, 143, 202, 210
  relations with Germany, 24, 33, 35, 75, 100, 133, 143, 210
  relations with Italy, 34, 47
  relations with Russia, 27, 75, 78, 151
  relationship to German naval power, 209
  role in the coming of the First World War, 163
  role in the Second Italian War of Independence, 37, 123

Gates, Robert, 102
Germany (Prussia)
  alliance relations, 1, 24, 30, 34, 35, 98, 100, 133, 143, 151, 213
  and negotiations over Czechoslovakia, 55, 116, 117
  and negotiations over Morocco, 69, 100
  arming decisions, 24
  Cold War diplomacy, 132, 214, 218

decision to give up nuclear weapons, 2, 74
diplomacy before the Second World War, 130, 131, 174–191
formation of, 1, 23, 75
influence during the Great Eastern Crisis, 71, 75, 78, 100
intentions of, 33, 35, 39, 100, 128, 208–211
relations with Russia, 1
role in the coming of the First World War, 124, 151–173, 193
Great Britain
Confidential Print, 23
diplomacy before the First World War, 151
diplomacy before the Second World War, 32, 131
diplomacy during the Crimean War, 65
diplomacy following the Napoleonic Wars, 213
evaluation of German intentions, 160–166
German evaluation of intentions of, 174
guarantee to Belgium, 116
negotiations over Czechoslovakia, 116
relations with Austria-Hungary, 32, 100, 143
relations with France, 34, 35, 69, 75, 130, 144, 202
relations with Germany, 24, 34, 35, 37, 55, 98, 128, 143, 158, 161, 193, 208
relations with Japan, 128, 143
relations with Russia, 32, 37, 98, 131, 143, 144
role in the coming of the First World War, 35
Great Eastern Crisis, 1, 71, 99, 213
Great Game, 37
Grey, Sir Edward, 24, 27, 223
Guisinger, Alexandra, 9, 13

Halifax, Lord Edward Wood, 179–181, 184–187, 189
Hall, Todd, 9
Hartwig, Nicholas, 162, 163
Henderson, Sir Nevile, 180, 181
Hitler, Adolf, 41, 65, 176, 179–181, 184–190
Hittite Empire, 5
Hollweg, Bethman, 158, 160
Holmes, Marcus, 42
Hungary, 1
Hussein, Saddam, 65

Huth, Paul K., 106

Ikenberry, John, 8
Iran, 4, 18, 102, 105
Iraq, 4, 52, 53, 90, 102
Israel, 4, 75, 90, 105
Italy
relations with Austria-Hungary, 142
relations with England, 34
relations with France, 34, 143
unification, 47

Jackson, Patrick Thaddeus, 15
Japan
Pearl Harbor, 75, 128
relations with Russia, 32, 35
relations with the United States, 4, 74
Jervis, Robert, 9, 26, 37
Josef, Franz, 168, 169, 213
July Crisis, 2, 5, 152, 165, 167, 169, 171, 172
Jupiter missiles, 4

Kennedy, John F., 218
and Germany foreign policy, 214, 215
and the Cold War, 132
Berlin crisis, 3, 74, 99
Cuban Missile Crisis, xi, 4, 64
in Vienna, 2, 8
Khrushchev, Nikita, 4
Berlin crisis, 74, 99, 214
East Germany, 3
in Vienna, 2, 8
Kiderlen, Alfred, 158, 159, 165
Kiev, 6
Kissinger, Henry, 223
Kravchuk, Leonid, 6
Krebs, Ronald R., 15
Kurizaki, Shuhei, 9, 13, 51
Kuwait, 52, 53, 65
Kydd, Andrew, 9, 13

Leventoglu, Bahar, 9, 50

Machiavelli, Niccolo, 7, 17
Malmesbury, Earl of, 2, 223
Mearsheimer, John, 22, 175
effects of Russo-Japanese war, 209
Metternich, Klemens von, 213, 216
Mitzen, Jennifer, 15
Mogenthau, Hans, 9
Morocco, 68, 69, 100, 146, 202

Napoleon III, 75

Napoleonic Wars, 75, 213
Nazism, 174
Nicholson, Arthur, 161–163
Nicholson, Harold, 20
North Korea, 4, 18
Nuclear weapons
  China, 76
  Germany, 214, 223
  in Ukraine, 5, 223
  Israeli response to a nuclear Iran, 105
  Israeli response to a Nuclear Iraq, 90
  possible use during the Cold War, 3, 8,
    14, 74, 223, 224

Odierno, US Lieutenant General Ray, 224
Odysseus, 5
O'Neill, Barry, 14, 53, 56
Osirak reactor, 4, 90
Ottoman Empire, 5, 223

Palestine, 125
Peace of Paris, 23
Pearl Harbor, 4, 75
Persia, 5, 128, 144
Persian Gulf, 32
Persian Gulf War, 52–53
Piedmont-Sardinia, 47, 123
Poincare, Raymond, 154, 161
Poland
  British diplomacy and, 175, 178–183,
    188, 190
  German invasion of, 130, 189
  negotiation over Danzig, 178–180,
    185–188
popular sentiment and international
  affairs, 31, 43
Powell, Robert L., 50, 64, 77, 108
private diplomacy, *see* diplomacy
public diplomacy, *see* diplomacy
Press, Daryl, 26, 175, 190
Princip, Gavrilo, 166

Ramsay, Kristopher F., 51
Rathbun, Brian, 16
Rich, Norman, 73
Risse, Thomas, 15, 18
Ritter, Jeffrey Munro, 73
Russia
  21st century diplomacy, 102
  alliance relations, 1, 78, 98, 100, 128,
    143, 144, 154
  Cold War diplomacy, 6
  diplomacy before the Second World War,
    130, 131

  frequency of interactions with other
    powers, 193
  influence during the mid 19th century,
    174
  influence of Russo-Japanese war on, 209
  intentions of, 32, 168–171
  response to Crimean War, 143, 152
  rivalry with Britain in Asia, 37
  role in the coming of the First World
    War, 2, 27, 34, 70, 98, 133, 158, 160
  role in the Franco-Prussian war, 36, 76
  role in the Great Eastern Crisis, 71, 75,
    99
  war with Japan, 32

Sardinia, 1, 37, 47, 75, 123, 124
Sartori, Anne, 13, 20, 51
Sazonov, Sergei D., 155, 161, 162, 164,
  170
Schelling, Thomas, 13, 14, 65, 97, 113,
  116
Schroeder, Paul, 10, 11, 171
Schorske, Carl E., 131
Schultz, Kenneth A., 75, 78
Scramble for Africa, 23
Second Italian War of Independence, 37,
  123, 128
Serbia
  First Balkan War, 155
  relations with Austria, 36, 124, 151,
    154–155, 162
  relations with Russia, 70, 155, 161,
    163–164, 168, 170
Sharp, Paul, 15, 17
Slantchev, Branislav, 9, 26, 50, 73, 78
Smith, Alastair, 9, 13
Sobel, Joel, 49
South Korea, 103
Sparta, 5

Taiwan, 103, 105, 125, 126, 220
Taiwan Strait Crises, 76
Tarar, Amar, 9, 50
Taylor, A. J. P., 215
the Cold War, 2, 11, 14, 100, 103, 132,
  215, 217, 218
Thucydides, 9
Trager, Robert, 9, 13, 51
Triple Alliance, 151, 168, 171
Triple Entente, 144, 210, 211
Turkey
  alliance with Britain and France, 125
  Balkans, 41, 155
  Bosnia-Herzegovina, 32

Jupiter missiles in, 4
relations with Russia, 143, 155

Ukraine, Soviet missiles in, 5
United Nations, 4
United Soviet Socialist Republic (U.S.S.R.)
    Berlin crisis, 3
    Cuban Missile Crisis, 4, 64
    détente, 214
    fall of, 225
    Jupiter missiles, 4
    nuclear weapons, 8
    Persian Gulf War, 52
    Ukraine, 223
United States
    contemporary foreign policy, 217, 225
    Cuban Missile Crisis, 2, 64
    Kuwait (Persian Gulf War), 53, 65
    Pearl Harbor, 4, 75
    relations with Germany, 218
    relations with Japan, 74
    relations with Taiwan, 105, 125, 126
    resources during the Cold War, 74

Taiwan Strait Crises, 76
West Berlin, 3, 8

Vienna, 2, 8, 77, 165
Vietnam, 33
Vietnam War, 9

Waltz, Kenneth, 2, 12
Warsaw, 1
Wendt, Alexander, 15
West Berlin, status of, 2, 8
Wilhelm II, German Emperor, 161, 166,
    168–170
Wilson, Sir Horace, 180, 181, 185
Wilson, Woodrow, 214–215
World War One, 1, 23, 68, 70, 100, 103,
    152, 153, 166, 184, 198, 213, 214,
    216, 223
World War Two, 21, 55, 130, 174, 225,
    263

Yarhi-Milo, Karen, 9
Yeltsin, Boris, 6